PSYCHOSOMATIC SYMPTOMS

Psychosomatic Symptoms:
Psychodynamic Treatment of the Underlying Personality Disorder

Edited by

C. Philip Wilson, M.D.

AND

Ira L. Mintz, M.D.

JASON ARONSON INC.

Northvale, New Jersey
London

The editors gratefully acknowledge permission to reprint the following:

"Transference, Somatization, and Symbiotic Need," by Robert A. Savitt, M.D. Copyright © 1969, *Journal of the American Psychoanalytic Association* 17(4):1030–1054. Reprinted by permission of International Universities Press.

Earlier versions of the following chapters first appeared in the *International Journal of Psychoanalytic Psychotherapy*, Jason Aronson Inc., publisher:

"Grief and Anniversary Reactions in a Man of Sixty-two," by Cecil Mushatt, M.D., and Isidore Werby, M.D. Coyright © 1972, *International Journal of Psychoanalytic Psychotherapy* 1:83–106.

"The Role of Primal Scene and Masochism in Asthma," by Cecilia K. Karol, M.D. Copyright ©1980 *International Journal of Psychoanalytic Psychotherapy* 8:577–592.

"Parental Overstimulation in Asthma," by C. Philip Wilson, M.D. Copyright © *International Journal of Psychoanalytic Psychotherapy* 8:601–602.

Library of Congress Cataloging-in-Publication Data

Psychosomatic symptoms: psychodynamic treatment of the underlying
  personality disorder / edited by C. Philip Wilson and Ira L. Mintz.
          p.   cm.
    Includes bibliographies and index.
    ISBN 0-87668-877-6
    1. Medicine, Psychosomatic.   2. Personality disorders.
  3. Psychotherapy.   I. Wilson, C. Philip.   II. Mintz, Ira L.
    [DNLM: 1. Personality Disorders. 2. Psychoanalytic Therapy—
  Methods. 3. Psychophysiologic Disorders.   WM 90 P9753]
  RC49.P825 1989
  616.08—dc19
  DNLM/DLC
  for Library of Congress   88-19470

Manufactured in the United States of America.
Jason Aronson Inc. offers books and cassettes.
For information and catalog write to Jason Aronson Inc.,
230 Livingston Street, Northvale, NJ 07647.

To the memory of three of our teachers who were outstanding pioneers in psychosomatic medicine: George E. A. Daniels, M.D., Max Schur, M.D., and Melitta Sperling, M.D.

CONTENTS

CONTRIBUTORS

Charles C. Hogan, M.D., D. Med Sc.
Assistant Clinical Professor of Psychiatry, Albert Einstein College of Medicine; Lecturer, Columbia University College of Physicians and Surgeons; Faculty, Columbia University Center for Psychoanalytic Training and Research.

Cecilia K. Karol, M.D.
Member of the New Jersey Psychoanalytic Society; Clinical Instructor of Psychiatry, The Psychoanalytic Division, New York University Medical Center.

Ira L. Mintz, M. D.
Associate Clinical Professor of Psychiatry, New Jersey College of Medicine; Supervising Child Psychoanalyst, Columbia University Psychoanalytic Training Center; Former President of the New Jersey Psychoanalytic Society.

Cecil Mushatt, M.D.
Associate Professor of Psychiatry, Boston University School of Medicine; Senior Staff Member, Boston University Medical Center;

Senior Psychiatrist, Beth Israel Hospital, Boston; Lecturer in Psychiatry, retired, Harvard Medical School.

Charles A. Sarnoff, M.D.
Lecturer in Child Development, Columbia University College of Physicians and Surgeons; Faculty, Columbia University Psychoanalytic Center for Training and Research.

Robert Savitt, M.D.
Training and Supervising Psychoanalyst Emeritus, The Psychoanalytic Division, New York University Medical Center; Past Clinical Associate Professor of Psychiatry, Downstate Medical Center; Past President, the Psychoanalytic Association of New York.

Martin Silverman, M.D.
Clinical Professor of Psychiatry, New York University Medical Center; Chairman of the Child Analysis Committee, The Psychoanalytic Division, New York University Medical Center; Training and Supervising Psychoanalyst, Psychoanalytic Division, New York University Medical Center; Associate Editor of the *Psychoanalytic Quarterly*.

C. Philip Wilson, M.D.
Chairman of the Psychosomatic Discussion Group of the American Psychosomatic Association and the Psychoanalytic Association of New York, Inc.; Assistant Clinical Professor of Psychiatry, Columbia University College of Physicians and Surgeons; Faculty, Columbia University Center for Psychoanalytic Training and Resarch; Senior Attending Psychiatrist and Lecturer in Psychosomatics, St. Luke's Roosevelt Hospital Center; Faculty, The Psychoanalytic Institute, New York University Medical Center

PREFACE

This volume provides a blueprint for the analytic treatment of psychosomatic patients. The clinical chapters detail the psychodynamics, etiology, and technique of therapy in a wide range of cases. We explore the structure of the ego and superego and the nature of the object relations. We also provide a clinically documented explication of the psychodynamics of the various personality disorders that are masked by psychosomatic symptoms and trace their ontogenesis back to the preoedipal years, when the predisposition for the development of psychosomatic disease is first established in the context of parental psychopathology. The special difficulties encountered in treatment are detailed, particularly the technique of analysis of psychosomatic crises and special problems such as projective identification and acting out. We emphasize a technique of treatment that focuses on pregenital conflicts, part-object relations, and the central issue of the transference. Our findings closely parallel those of other analysts in their work with nonpsychosomatic patients who have severe preoedipal conflicts. We hope that we will be able to make it clear that psychoanalysis is the treatment of choice for psychosomatic patients.

The contributors to this volume have had their work greatly enriched and stimulated by their involvement in two psychosomatic research units, which are both composed of psychoanalytically trained psychiatrists specializing in the treatment of psychosomatic disorders.

The first is the Psychosomatic Discussion Group of the Psychoanalytic Association of New York, Inc. This longstanding group was led by Dr. Melitta Sperling from 1960 until her death in 1973. Since that time, the chairman has been Dr. C. Philip Wilson.

The second research unit is the Psychosomatic Discussion Group of the American Psychoanalytic Association, which has been chaired by Dr. Wilson since its inception in 1983. In these long-term research groups there has been the unique opportunity to review, study, and discuss the analyses of numerous psychosomatic cases. Thus a rich cross-fertilization has resulted from the deliberations of some fifty psychoanalysts from the major psychoanalytic centers of the United States. Particularly important has been the presentation of the psychodynamic treatment of the mother, the father, the siblings, and the spouses of these patients, which has provided an in-depth understanding of family psychopathology.

C. Philip Wilson, M.D.

Ira L. Mintz, M.D.

ACKNOWLEDGMENTS

We would like to express our appreciation to the founder of the Psychosomatic Discussion Group of the Psychoanalytic Association of New York, Inc., Dr. Melitta Sperling, for her pioneering research, teaching, and publications. We also owe a great debt to Drs. Max Schur and Otto Sperling, our teachers at the New York University Psychoanalytic Institute, and to Drs. George Daniels and Aaron Karush of the Columbia University Psychoanalytic Treatment Center.

Seminal to our research have been the contributions of the Melitta Sperling Memorial Lecturers: Drs. Norman Atkins, Lawrence Deutsch, James Herzog, Stanislav Kasl, Peter H. Knapp, Cecil Mushatt, George Pollock, Morton Reiser, Samuel Ritvo, Robert A. Savitt, and Albert Solnit.

We are indebted to the many members of the psychosomatic research groups, particularly Drs. Leonard Barkin, Stephen L. Bennett, Barton Blinder, L. Bryce Boyer, Sylvia Brody, Anna Burton, Kenneth D. Cohen, Lawrence Deutsch, Donald Dunton, Gerald Freiman, David Goldman, Eleanor Galenson, Henry Haberfeld, Charles C. Hogan, Doris M. Hunter, Mary J. Jensen, Cecilia Karol, Charles R. Keith, Edward Leader, Deborah S. Link, Charles McGann, Burness E. Moore, Muriel Gold Morris, William R. O'Brien, Mary Roberts, Howard Rudominer, Charles A. Sarnoff, Noah Shaw, Henry Schneer, Harvey J.

Schwartz, Howard L. Schwartz, Robert Schwartz, Christine Sekaer, Jacob Stump, Pietro Castel-Nuovo Tedesco, and Howard K. Welsh.

Many of the chapters and hypotheses in this volume were originally presented in the forms of lectures, electives, symposiums, and papers at the Departments of Psychiatry of St. Luke's-Roosevelt Hospital Center; the Albert Einstein College of Medicine; Saint Barnabas Medical Center; Hackensack Hospital Medical Center; the Downstate Psychoanalytic Institute; the Department of Psychiatry, State University of New York, Downstate; the Department of Psychiatry, Brookdale Hospital Center; and the Center for Psychoanalytic Training and Research of the Columbia University College of Physicians and Surgeons.

We are in debt to the staffs, students, and faculties of these institutions, especially Drs. John M. Cotton, Maurice Friend, John Frosch, Stanley Heller, Byram Karasu, Sylvan Keiser, Clarice Kestenbaum, Sandor Lorand, David M. MacDonald, Helen C. Meyers, John W. Rosenberger, Nathaniel Ross, John A. Sours, and Theodore Van Itallie.

Likewise, our work has been enriched by the many discussants of psychosomatic papers that we have given throughout the United States, particularly Drs. Norman Atkins, Stanley Friedman, Raymond Gehl, Daniel L. Goldstein, Clayton Gotwals, Norman Oberman, Frank H. Parcells, Sherwin S. Radin, Howard Schlossman, Frederick F. Shevin, and Roy M. Whitman.

Drs. Richard Galdston, Athol Hughes, and Naama Kushnir focused and clarified our psychosomatic research in their excellent book reviews of our anorexia volume.

And, finally, we want to express our gratitude to our wives for the support and work that they contributed to the preparation of this book.

C. P. W.

I. L. M.

It is as though a mechanism for abnormal instinctual discharge had been laid down organically, which could be made use of in quite different circumstances — both in the case of disturbances of cerebral activity due to severe histolytic or toxic affections, and also in the case of inadequate control over the mental economy and at times when the activity of the energy operating in the mind reaches crisis-pitch. . . . The 'epileptic reaction,' as this common element may be called, is also undoubtedly at the disposal of the neurosis whose essence it is to get rid by somatic means of amounts of excitation which it cannot deal with psychically.

Freud
Dostoevski and Parricide

The Symptom and the Underlying Personality Disorder

C. Philip Wilson, M. D.
Ira L. Mintz, M. D.

Although symptoms such as asthma or ulcerative colitis are uniformly similar, psychosomatic patients themselves vary widely. They differ in genetic makeup, psychodynamics, and type of character disorder, ranging from hysterical and obsessive-compulsive to borderline and near-psychotic. Constitutional, environmental, and emotional factors are expressed in a complex interaction for which the symptoms are the final common pathway.

For psychoanalysts it is axiomatic that symptom complexes (of which psychosomatic diseases are one of many components) are multi-determined and overdetermined. We recognize the importance of the family history and associated genetic vulnerabilities. Likewise, somatic compliance is significant. Thus, phase-specific events, such as trauma or infection, may sensitize or damage an organ system, predisposing it for the development of psychosomatic symptoms. For example, childhood respiratory infections may predispose the respiratory system for the development of asthma, or later in life a respiratory disease may precipitate an asthmatic attack.

However, it is not a question of which factor—genetic, environmental, immunologic, traumatic, infectious, or emotional conflict (neurosis) — is paramount, but whether interference in the operation of one of these factors results in the significant amelioration or long-term cessation, that is, "cure," of the psychosomatic symptom. We have found that the psychoanalytic treatment of the underlying personality disorder leads to a resolution or marked diminution of psychosomatic symptoms.

In Part I of this book, "Psychodynamic Structure," Wilson begins in Chapter 2 by focusing on the crucial importance of the analysis of the personality disorder that underlies psychosomatic symptoms. Shifting unconscious conflicts can be manifested in a single patient's life span by a variety of different psychosomatic diseases as well as other symptoms. If psychosomatic symptoms are cleared before there has been sufficient change in the underlying neurosis and object relations, they may be replaced by psychogenic equivalents: self-destructive acting out, an addictive disorder, neurotic or severe regressive (psychotic) symptom formation, or an alternate psychosomatic symptom.

Wilson reviews the metapsychology of psychosomatic disease and the depression that underlies psychosomatic symptoms. Relevant clinical material demonstrates the processes of internalization involved in the development of psychosomatic symptoms and the replacement of psychosomatic symptoms by neurotic symptoms such as perversions.

Mushatt in Chapter 3 underscores the importance of analysis in the treatment of patients with psychosomatic and somatopsychic illness. His hypotheses are derived from Felix Deutsch's studies of the development of the body image. Clinical case material is presented to show the development of the body image and the ego. Symbolic representations are laid down in the body from all phases of development, so that physical function and dysfunction may express psychic activity in every developmental phase from the primary narcissistic through to the genital level.

The body is in a continued silent dialogue with the environment and with the individual and the various parts of his personality. The nonverbal or preverbal dialogue can be decoded by the analyst. Physical symptoms in sessions signal the presence of charged repressed transference fantasies. Mushatt presents relevant clinical material illustrating his points, particularly the process of separation of self from the object and some of the difficulties these patients have with speech, an example of which is narcissistic retentiveness. The appropriateness of the use of the couch versus vis-à-vis sessions is discussed in terms of the patient's capacity to tolerate separation.

Wilson in Chapter 4 presents the results of psychodynamic research with a large number of psychosomatic families. While acknowledging exceptions, he concludes that in the great majority of families there is a characteristic psychosomatic family profile and that the predispositions for developing the personality disorders that underlie psychosomatic symptoms are established early in life by disturbances in the parent–child relationship. In most cases the psychosomatic personality disorder seems largely the result of preoedipal parent–child psychopathology rather than oedipal neurotic conflicts.

Wilson reviews medication, surgical intervention, and conjoint therapies, emphasizing that the medical and surgical treatments that may be necessary for survival have dynamic meanings, so that precipitous relief of symptoms may be dangerous to a patient's mental functioning. Adult patients, such as those with asthma or ulcerative colitis, are continued on medication until they learn in analysis that they can abort or stop the psychosomatic symptom.

A dynamic approach to history taking is presented. A method of treatment is advocated with modifications of classical analytic technique. Conjoint treatment of the parents is utilized when necessary. In most cases there is a preliminary phase of vis-à-vis treatment.

Sarnoff in Chapter 5 offers an explication of the symbolic processes involved in the production of psychosomatic phenomena. His hypothesis is that the type of symptom produced relates to the cognitive level at which the symbolizing function was operating at the stage of early trauma or fantasy to which the patient has regressed in response to current trauma. Psychosomatic disorders are characterized by tissue changes, fluid shifts, and physiological modifications. The affects and fantasies expressed reflect fixations or regression to pregenital, prephallic levels. The organs involved are usually visceral and have symbolic meanings relating to oral, respiratory, cutaneous, and anal incorporations. The symbolizing function forms the bridge between psyche and soma. Sarnoff's clinical examples document the point that failure to mature in the developmental lines associated with the development of the system consciousness or the march of objects from self to others results in a predisposition to develop psychosomatic symptomatology.

In Chapter 6, Wilson suggests that whereas oedipal conversion symptoms evidence the defense of projection, pregenitally rooted psycho-somatic symptoms can be viewed as a manifestation of a projective identification. Predisposition to the ego's defense of projective identification and the development of a psychosomatic symptom have been established by early parent–child psychopathology. Wilson presents the psychodynamics of projective identification in a patient with *status asthmaticus,* in the crisis self-starvation of a hospitalized anorexic, and in a fulminating ulcerative colitis case. The point is made that the more severe the psychosomatic symptom, the more intense is the projective identification. Regressive projective identification can result in analyzable transference psychosis. The technique of interpretation of projective identification is detailed.

In Chapter 7, Wilson's clinical material from a migraine patient shows that psychosomatic patients do not usually free-associate early in treatment and that dreams can be used to demonstrate to the patients their impulse disorder and other pregenital conflicts in the dyadic transference. Research on sand and stone symbolism is reviewed because these symbols mask crucial early and preverbal conflicts about symbiosis, separation–individuation, and sadomasochism.

In contrast to the psychoanalytic treatment of psychosomatic patients, Mushatt and Werby in Chapter 8 illustrate the effectiveness of once-a-week analytic psychotherapy in the treatment of severe headaches of eight-year duration for which no other treatment had been successful. Even in a once-a-week psychotherapy, the analyst was able to skillfully and patiently permit the gradual unfolding of a therapeutic relationship with a provocative, masochistic 62-year-old and carefully uncover and deal with the crucial conflicts in this man's life.

Of particular relevance was the return of symptoms on various anniversaries of traumatic experiences many years earlier. The repeated interpretations of these connections and the insight derived played an important role in the resolution of conflict and symptom relief.

It was remarkable that despite infrequent psychotherapy, this 62-year-old patient with definite organic disease—including two myocardial infarctions, a markedly masochistic, guilt-laden personality structure, and multiple psychosomatic symptoms—had the capacity for insight, symptom resolution, and further psychological growth. The skillful handling of the therapy was aided by a sensitive internist, who worked well with the patient and the analyst with minimal compromising of the therapeutic procedure.

Mintz and Wilson in Chapter 9 present clinical vignettes to

document the protean nature of psychosomatic symptoms. Mintz explores the psychodynamics of psychosomatic bleeding and a "fat lip," and Wilson presents a range of phenomena such as the analysis of psoriasis of the glans penis, hysterical conversion symptoms involving the zipper, the disturbance in the sense of time, the unconscious meanings of vitreous floaters, nasal mucus secretions, and the crucial initial phase of analysis of severely incapacitating urticaria. Wilson also discusses the technique of interpreting speech mannerisms that are defensively used by these patients.

Part II of this book, "The Respiratory System," focuses on asthmatic symptoms. Chapters 10 through 14 illustrate that, regardless of additional complicating genetic, immunological, and infectious aspects of the disease, the psychoanalytic treatment was successfully concluded with a subsiding of asthmatic symptoms. Some of the patients also suffered from anorexia nervosa, which was treated successfully.

Mintz in Chapter 10 illustrates both the primary and secondary roles of the asthmatic's air symbolism in a series of detailed clinical cases and highlights its theoretical, dynamic, and clinical importance. He presents four vignettes describing the unconscious ways in which air is used to symbolize conflict. It can change its form from air to steam; change its intensity from stillness to violent movement; and change its movement from passage into and out of the lung and gastrointestinal system to movement outside of the body on the skin, and then to movement projected into the environment in the form of tornados, volcanos, earthquakes, and windstorms.

Mintz further suggests that the unconscious importance of air is derived from the infant's sucking, which draws in an admixture of milk and air, both having the potential for becoming incorporated in the unconscious fantasy of the benign or ambivalently cathected early-milk-mother.

It is also hypothesized that the effects of nebulizers, allergens, respiratory infections, and exercise are multidetermined and warrant additional investigation into their symbolic meanings to the patient. The data suggest that the psychological component may play a role in the disease by incorporating the loving or ambivalently cathected introjects in the inspired air. These introjects are capable of initiating or aborting an asthmatic attack.

Mintz's clinical material, describing the importance of the unconscious meaning of air to these patients, confirms information provided by other patients. The result of this work is a new, dynamic, and theoretical construct about asthmatic disease.

In Chapter 11, Mintz discusses a patient initially viewed as having an uncertain prognosis because of clear-cut genetic factors, a markedly allergic component, and the early onset of the disease at age 18 months. When treatment began, the patient suffered from symptoms so severe, she was sometimes unable to walk up stairs and had to sleep sitting up, wrapped in a blanket. Mintz presents extensive clinical material, permitting the reader to view the gradual unfolding of the treatment situation — the techniques used to facilitate the emergence of crucial conflicts and the methods adopted to deal with them. Essential transference behavior, which included a tremendous outpouring of rage, is reported verbatim along with the specific interpretations made to deal with it. The major focus upon aggressive conflict and its analysis in the transference played a predominant role in the subsiding of this patient's severe asthmatic symptoms.

Karol in Chapter 12 describes the interrelationship of primal-scene experience, sadomasochism, and asthma. Clinical material, richly detailed in dreams, fantasy, memories, and associations, illustrates that childhood witnessing of the primal scene can play a major role in the predisposition to developing bronchial asthma. In addition, the child's misperception of the experience as attracting and stimulating, as well as violent and repelling, contributes to the development of sadomasochistic fantasy and behavior. The latter, additionally layered by subsequent life experiences and psychological sequelae, contributes further to the development of asthmatic attacks.

The uncovering of a violent sadomasochistic fantasy preceding one of the patient's asthmatic attacks dramatically and convincingly illustrates the connection between the conflict and turmoil liberated by the fantasy and its symbolic regressed resolution in a current asthmatic attack. The analysis was also able to trace the source of the first asthmatic attack at age 4, which was linked to her witnessing of parental intercourse and overdetermined by an episode of near drowning and an attack of pneumonia.

Wilson in Chapter 13 notes that his experience with the analysis of seven adult patients corroborates and confirms Karol's hypothesis about the etiologic roles of primal-scene shock and masochism in asthma. He emphasizes that although the primal scene, at both the oedipal and preoedipal levels, is important, it is only one aspect of global patterns of overstimulating parental behavior, which in the pregenital maturational phases establishes the predisposition to develop asthma and in subsequent developmental phases, particularly the oedipal and adolescent years, plays a major role in causing emotional conflict, symptom formation, disturbances in object relations, and asthma. Wilson notes that asthma is a manifestation of a pregenital conversion neurosis and that the choice of the respiratory system for symptom development is determined by specific attitudes and fantasies of the parents, usually the mother. Three illustrative cases focus particularly upon the sadomasochistic impulses and fantasies that were masked by asthmatic symptoms.

Silverman's Chapter 14 is a graphic description of a severely ill, asthmatic, and anorexic child of age 10. The early course of the analysis revealed a child so dyspnoeic, weak, and anguished, regressing further into severe symptomatology, that the analyst questioned whether she could respond to psychoanalytic treatment. The dilemma was further complicated by the patient's tearful threat, "If you send me away, I'll die." The crisis culminated in a remarkable anniversary reaction that was as dramatic and illustrative as it was poignant.

Silverman presents a detailed description of the patient's markedly provocative, demanding transference behavior during her regressed, increasingly severe, asthmatic wheezing and cathectic anorexic starving, accompanied by blatant threats to die because of the manner in which the patient felt she was being treated by the analyst. Skillful technique and dedication played a crucial role in the resolution of this extremely difficult case. Silverman illustrates that the patient, like so many other psychosomatic patients, not only suffers terribly from the illness, but unconsciously needs to starve and wheeze in the service of achieving control and mastery over her own impulses and ambivalently cathected external objects and to compensate for her inner feelings of helplessness and vulnerability.

In Part III, "The Gastrointestinal System," Hogan begins in Chapter 15 by defining, describing, and discussing the physical characteristics, the pathology, the physical complications, and the general prognosis of chronic ulcerative colitis and Crohn's disease. He notes that most clinicians are pessimistic about full recovery and that recurrences, complications, and fatalities are major problems. He reviews the history of the discovery of psychopathology and cites the work of those who have achieved long-term symptom resolution by psychoanalysis. Hogan presents clinical material from analyzed cases to demonstrate the importance of the technique of treatment, which involves first the interpretation of the masochistic meanings of the patient's symptoms and behavior in the transference. Emphasis is put on the pregenital psychopathology and the importance in many cases of the conjoint therapy or analysis of the mother and of the father. Modifications of classical technique are reviewed. Hogan emphasizes that when colitis symptoms clear or subside, there is a transitory appearance of symptom equivalents, acting out, alternate psychosomatic symptoms, depression, and phobias.

Savitt in Chapter 16 unfolds graphic clinical material from the successful treatment of a bisexual male patient, who in the course of psychoanalysis, developed a recurrence of peptic ulcer. This resomatization brought into focus a recapitulation of his inadequate, infantile, symbiotic attachment to his mother. The unresolved conflict led to a negative oedipal involvement with the father. His homosexuality expressed a need to merge with the mothering father and through him with the mother. The infantile primal hunger of this patient was expressed in an intense transference: repetitive pleas for love, an insatiable desire to suck and be sucked, the wish to eat and be eaten, and a pseudohallucinatory fantasy of the analyst's presence wherever the patient went during intervals of separation between analytic sessions. Savitt connects the patient's sensation of fusion with the analytic couch and his distorted body image during sessions to the infantile primal hunger. Pertinent psychological and a presumed genetic predisposition and a disturbed parent–child relationship were thought to be etiologic in this patient.

In the Epilogue, Wilson summarizes technique in the treatment of psychosomatic patients, emphasizing that in most cases the patient is seen vis-à-vis a focus on dyadic material in the first phase of treatment, triadic material being left until later. He explores such issues as research, the results of dynamic therapy including long-term follow-ups, and the problem of the therapist as a new object in the transference neurosis. He presents a dynamic approach to hospital and nursing care and reviews the possible prevention of the development of psychosomatic symptoms in children by treatment of the parents.

As Freud showed us, thorough psychodynamic understanding of one patient can be more valuable than limited psychological scrutiny of many patients. In the majority of cases recorded in this volume, analysis achieved a marked diminution or clearing of psychosomatic symptoms and, most importantly, a resolution of the underlying personality disorder, thereby making energy available for healthy functioning. Time and the vicissitudes of life will show us whether these patients will develop further psychosomatic symptoms.

PART I

PSYCHODYNAMIC STRUCTURE

2

Ego Functioning in Psychosomatic Disorders

C. Philip Wilson, M.D.

Psychoanalysis and analytic psychotherapy represent the most comprehensive approaches to the treatment of psychosomatic disease because they focus on the resolution of the underlying personality disorders. Precipitous relief of symptoms by medical, surgical, or other treatments may be dangerous to psychosomatic patients' mental functioning or even to their lives. If symptoms are cleared before there has been sufficient change in the underlying neurosis and the object relations, the psychosomatic ego functioning may be replaced by psychogenic equivalents (Wilson et al. 1983, Wilson 1988). These symptom equivalents, which may alternate with or replace psychosomatic symptoms, include:

1. Self-destructive acting out (Sperling 1968, Wilson et al. 1983, Schwartz 1986),

2. Another addictive disorder such as obesity, alcoholism, or drug addiction,

3. Another psychosomatic symptom formation such as stiff neck, ulcerative colitis (Sperling, in Wilson et al. 1983), migraine (Hogan, in Wilson et al. 1983), and asthma (Mintz, in Wilson et al. 1983),

4. Neurotic symptom formation, or

5. Severe regressive symptom formation (Mintz, in Wilson et al. 1983).

METAPSYCHOLOGY OF PSYCHOSOMATIC DISEASE: ECONOMIC, ADAPTIVE, STRUCTURAL, DYNAMIC, AND GENETIC FACTORS

Psychosomatic symptoms are rooted in pregenital conflicts that result in an ambivalent relation with the mother and/or the father. Unresolved preoedipal, parental organ-system conflicts impair normal parenting functioning during the early developmental stages (Wilson et al. 1983). Thus parental overconcern and overemphasis on food and eating functions play a significant role in the etiology of restrictor and bulimic anorexia nervosa, and similar parental overconcern and overcontrol of flatus, bowel movements, and bowel functions play an important role in the etiology of gastrointestinal diseases such as ulcerative colitis (Sperling 1978). In the majority of analyzed cases of asthma the primary fixations are at the anal level (Sperling 1963). However, the fantasies repressed and internalized in asthma are specific for the individual case but not for asthma in general. Oral fixations and fantasies appear in every case; for example, the asthma *de novo* case (see Chapter 13) dreamt of the analyst as hamburger meat that she was eating. In a significant number of cases, urinary fantasies and fixations predominate (Knapp 1963).

In the cases of psoriasis, anal conflicts and fantasies are basic. In patients suffering from hypertension, both oral and anal conflicts and fantasies underlie the symptom. Although oral fantasies are present, anal-phase conflicts predominate in migraine cases (Sperling 1978).

These unresolved preoedipal parental fixations contribute to the difficulty of psychosexual development. Psychosomatic symptoms and their underlying personality disorders can be considered as specific pathological outcomes of unresolved oedipal conflicts in children whose preoedipal parental relationship has predisposed them to these particular reactions under precipitating circumstances.

The genetic influences on the child's organ-system complex and the developing personality disorder are parental conflicts about the general expression of aggressive and libidinal drives and their particular organ-system manifestations. In addition, the neurotic and/or addictive parents are perfectionistic, significantly denying the impact on the developing child of their exhibitionistic toilet, bedroom, and other behavior. Other genetic influences are cultural, societal, and general medical influences.

From an economic point of view, the unremitting pressure of repressed, unsublimated aggressive and libidinal drives, conflicts, and fantasies is a central issue for these inhibited patients. Loss of control is *the* primary fear of all psychosomatic patients. Consciously, the fear is of losing control of an organ-system function, such as overeating in anorexia and soiling in ulcerative colitis. Unconsciously, there is the opposite: a wish for organ-system expression — in anorexia to give in to voraciousness, in colitis to smear, and in these and the other psychosomatic conditions a wish to indulge in all sorts of forbidden impulse gratifications.

From a structural point of view these feared drive-eruptions are held in check by the terror of retaliatory punishment from a primitive archaic superego. Ego considerations are central. In the preoedipal years the ego of the psychosomatic patient becomes split. One part develops in a pseudonormal fashion: cognitive functions, the self-observing parts of the ego, adaptation, the synthetic functions, and other ego functions appear to have retained functioning capacities, varying, of course, with the underlying personality disorder. Many psychosomatic patients are described as having been perfect in childhood, with excellent records in school. Others, like the bulimic anorexics, show more evidence of disobedience and rebelling at home and in school. In many cases conflicts have been denied, displaced, partly externalized, and projected onto habits such as thumb sucking, enuresis, encopresis, nail biting, nose picking, and hair pulling (Wilson et al. 1983). In other cases there is a concomitant displacement and projection of conflicts onto actual phobic objects or situations. School phobia is a frequent finding. Some cases have a childhood history of excellent performance at home and school with an isolated episode of antisocial rebellious behavior.

From an adaptive point of view there is a developmental denial of conflicts in these patients. Masked conflicts in separation–individuation are paramount (Mushatt 1975, 1982). Many normal adaptive conflicts have been avoided or denied. It is not unusual for such patients to say that they never learned to swim or that they can't drive a car. Many of the parents raise them in an unreal and overprotected world. The perfectionistic parents impair the ego's decision-making functions with their infantilizing intrusions into every aspect of their child's life.

Although Schur (1955) emphasizes the role of regression in object relations, we feel, along with Hogan (in Wilson et al. 1983), Sperling (1978), and Mushatt (1975, 1980, 1982), that object relations are important in all their aspects—not just in those of separation (Schmale 1958) or object loss (Engel 1962).

PSYCHOSOMATIC DEPRESSION AND ITS CAUSES

As the conflicts underlying psychosomatic symptoms are analyzed, a variety of affects emerge, particularly those of depression (Wilson 1985). The analysis of affects, particularly depressive affects, is crucial to therapeutic success. However, as these affects emerge, various psychic shifts occur that result in psychosomatic symptoms being replaced by psychogenic equivalents.

The components of psychosomatic depression are overdetermined and are caused by unresolved oedipal and preoedipal conflicts. Among the important determinants are:

1. Unhappiness because of failure to achieve the perfectionistic goals required by the archaic superego.
2. Unhappiness because of neurotic guilt inflicted by the archaic superego, which legislates against the expression of libidinal or aggressive impulses and fantasies.
3. Unhappiness because of failure to achieve mature object relations.
4. Unhappiness and anger because of a failure to actualize magical narcissistic fantasies.
5. Unhappiness at adaptive failures.
6. Unhappiness because of failure to achieve normal separation-individuation from parents or parent surrogates.

DISCUSSION OF PSYCHOSOMATIC SYMPTOM EQUIVALENTS

Because of the ineffective and inconsistent ego functioning of psychosomatic patients, abrupt changes in behavior (acting out), neurotic symptoms, or different manifestations of psychosomatic disease can be caused by changes in the level of stress or in patterns of defense, in shifting intensity of drives, and in alternating levels of ego integration and regression as well as changes in object relations (Mintz 1980, Sperling 1968, Wilson et al. 1983). At different times, for reasons that are overdetermined and multidetermined, the conflicts that compose the underlying psychosomatic personality disorder can be expressed in different illnesses. Depression, anxiety, neurosis, or other psychosomatic symptoms may precede the development of psychosomatic symptoms or may appear after psychosomatic symptoms subside.

More than thirty years ago, Gero (1953) described anorexia as a depressive equivalent, and Sperling (1959) emphasized that psychosomatic symptoms in general were depressive equivalents. Bulimia has been reported as alternating with stiff neck (Wilson et al. 1983), ulcerative colitis (Tucker 1952, Sperling 1978), migraine (Hogan, in Wilson et al. 1983), asthma (Mintz, in Wilson et al. 1983), celiac disease (Ferrara and Fontana 1966), and masturbation (Levin 1985, Wilson, 1986b,c).

Concerning the general problem of psychosomatic equivalents, I have seen psoriasis replaced by asthma (Wilson 1980), migraine by ulcerative colitis and then by migraine, obesity by hypertension, and ulcer by globus hystericus (Wilson 1981). A patient of Mintz's (1980) developed in sequence ulcerative colitis, asthma, depression, self-destructive acting out, migraine, noninfectious monoarthular arthritis of the knee, angioneurotic edema, eczema, and nasorhinitis. Hogan in Chapter 15 emphasizes that when symptoms of ulcerative colitis or Crohn's disease clear in analysis, a severe depression emerges, and that such patients develop symptom equivalents: acting out, alternate psychosomatic symptoms, phobias, and severe regressive behavior. I (1988) recently detailed the replacement of bulimic symptoms by asthma and in another patient the replacement of bulimia by a neurotic character development epitomized by "bitchy" behavior. I described the replacement in a 5-year-old boy of symptoms of enuresis by asthma. In adolescence, asthma in this patient alternated with hyperventilation and acting out (see Chapter 13).

THE "LITTLE PERSON" PHENOMENON

Volkan (1965) described an anorexic patient who had a split-off, archaic part of her ego—a "little person." He related this pathological ego structure to the "little man" phenomenon described by Kramer (1955) and Niederland (1956, 1965). In my experience all psychosomatic patients, including anorexics, have a split-off, impulsive, archaic, primitive ego. A conscious manifestation of this split-off ego is the fear-of-being-fat complex.

Susan, an impulsive, anorexic high school student, brought me a series of dreams about an innocent, wide-eyed little girl who reminded her of sentimental paintings depicting a raggedly dressed child with tears in her enormous eyes. Susan was beginning to understand that these paintings showed how she tried to come across to people and to the analyst. After these dreams were analyzed, she dreamt of a little prince whom she wanted to control. Analysis showed this little prince to be her "little person" — the archaic split-off ego. The little prince was narcissistic, omnipotent, and magical. His maleness reflected her secret wish to be a boy. For her, males were aggressive and magical, while females were innocent, passive, and masochistic. The split-off part of her ego was filled with murderous rage and hatred.

Similarly, a patient whom I treated for symptoms of a phobic neurosis, obesity, and hypertension, in the terminal phase of analysis dreamt of a revolting, evil dwarf who was jumping "all over the place." The dwarf represented the split-off, impulsive, archaic part of his personality.

THE RELATIONSHIP OF PSYCHOSOMATIC PERSONALITY DISORDERS TO ADDICTION AND CHILDHOOD HABITS

To understand and treat psychosomatic patients, we need to understand the impulse disorders, the addictive personality structure (Wurmser 1980), and the habits of childhood that are frequently the developmental forerunners of psychosomatic symptoms. I have noted the frequent occurrence of thumb sucking, nail biting, cuticle chewing and eating, head banging, hair pulling and eating, and other childhood impulse disorders such as encopresis and enuresis. In some cases there is a childhood history of excessive good behavior, but therapy uncovers isolated episodes or phases of rebelliousness. Processes of internalization are involved in psychosomatic symptom formation. Habits are frequently "given up" or mastered during adolescence. However, they may be, and frequently are, replaced by psychosomatic symptoms.

In some cases we see a chaotic ego structure when a childhood habit has continued into adolescence or adulthood and coexists with a psychosomatic symptom and addiction to tobacco, alcohol, and/or drugs. In these cases, of which the bulimic anorexics are most typical, the ego has used the same defenses in its struggle with the childhood habit and impulse disorder that it uses later in trying to cope with the psychosomatic symptom, the continued habit, and the addiction. In such cases the defenses of denial, splitting, displacement, externalization, rationalization, intellectualization, withholding, and lying are deeply ingrained in the character structure.

It is extremely important from the beginning and throughout treatment to acquaint psychosomatic patients with their impulse disorder, so that they can become aware of the split-off narcissistic aspects of their personality disorder, particularly in the dyadic transference.

INTERNALIZATION
AND SUPEREGO FORMATION

My research confirms Blum's (1985) observations that

"[T]he superego is never fully independent of the original objects throughout childhood and adolescence, and the child continues to interact with the postoedipal parents (as well as with peers). The individual, his original objects, and surroundings are all different from what they were in childhood." To my mind, the superego has a far greater legacy than "as heir to the Oedipus complex" (S. Freud 1923, pp. 48–49). In addition to the preoedipal roots of the superego, the internalization and consolidation of parental relationships, authority, attitudes, and values continue beyond the oedipal phase through preadult life. Cognitively, the child can gradually make more subtle moral discriminations and more abstract moral judgments, distinguishing his own moral code from that of parents and others. The parents are at first idealized, as are their standards and values. The child's first "morality" is conformity and blind obedience to the parents' authority and appraisal.

Initially, externalized authority and global introjections give way to
more selective, enduring identifications. A. Freud (1936) stated,
"True morality begins when the internalized criticism, now embodied
in the standard exacted by the superego, coincides with the ego's
perception of its own fault" (p. 119). [Blum 1985, p. 891]

THE HEALING OF THE SPLIT IN THE EGO
AND ITS TRANSFERENCE MANIFESTATIONS

When psychosomatic symptoms subside in analysis, the split in the ego
(Wilson et al. 1985) has been partially resolved, and abrupt processes of
externalization can occur in the context of the analysis of the archaic
superego. No matter what the age of the psychosomatic patient, a delayed
adolescent maturational process occurs in analysis. Revived archaic
superego introjects emerge, coexisting with new superego developmental
elements. In this situation, the patient can abruptly project the archaic
superego introject onto the analyst (projective identification).

On the other hand, processes of internalization can occur in analysis
with the development of psychosomatic symptoms. The appearance of
psychosomatic symptoms *de novo* in the course of analysis illustrates the
psychodynamics of psychosomatic symptom formation (see Chapter 13 in
this volume).

PSORIASIS AND ACTING OUT REPLACED
BY ASTHMA

An alcoholic patient suffering from psoriasis and obesity had partially
resolved her personality disorder, and as a result she mastered her
addiction to cigarettes and alcohol, and her psoriatic lesions cleared.
Now, in the terminal phase of her analysis, she developed symptoms of
bronchial asthma for the first time in her life. The asthmatic attacks, some
seventeen in all, responded to analysis, and the patient terminated
treatment successfully, free of asthma. The conflicts that brought her
back for more analysis many years later are detailed in Chapter 13. Here
the focus is on the replacement of acting-out behavior and psoriasis by
asthma.

The patient, a single, Italian-Catholic woman, came to analysis at age 25 with intense oral conflicts. An alcoholic who drank herself into a stupor every evening after work, she was severely depressed and suicidal. She lost one job after another. Behind a façade of helpless childlike behavior was masked an overwhelming oral greed. Denial and exhibitionism characterized her neurotic parents' behavior as she grew up. The wealthy neurotic mother's addiction to cigarettes and wine was completely denied by the family. The father, a very successful real estate executive, insisted that the family was poor and lived in a rent-controlled building in an impoverished area. A compulsive man, he exercised daily in the nude in ritualistic fashion in front of his wife, son, and daughter. These exercises, which were preceded by a large glass of water and followed by a copious urination, dated from the time of the patient's earliest memory. Her brother, $2\frac{1}{2}$ years her junior, developed severe anxiety symptoms in late adolescence.

The patient was a healthy but overactive child until her brother's birth, after which she became an intractable thumb sucker. At age 5 she had pneumonia, apparently not severe enough to require hospitalization, and during this same year had nightmares and walked in her sleep. Her school record was poor. When she was 8 years old, she had a recurrence of nightmares. Puberty and menses began at age 11 to 12, and she was popular with boys but experienced intense anxiety on dates. Following graduation from a second-rate junior college at age 20, she began drinking heavily and engaged in a series of promiscuous affairs. At this time she developed severe psoriasis, which failed to respond to years of medical treatment.

The transference neurosis was intense and stormy, with holiday periods particularly difficult. In the early years of analysis she attempted suicide several times, cut and injured herself when drunk, and repeatedly had intercourse without contraceptive precaution.

At the start of analysis people were part objects to her. For example, she acted out her transference fantasies with a series of stuffed animals, naming them for me. Instead of expressing anger with me in a session, she went home to scold and punish the toy animal. Likewise she avoided positive emotions with me by expressing love and affection for her inanimate pets. Her sadomasochistic acting out was interpreted as an attempt to frighten and coerce me, as she had succeeded in doing with her parents. With the development of an intense transference neurosis, the patient no longer had to act out her emotions, and after a period of working through, she experienced a crucial change in her relations with people, who were now becoming whole objects to her. She relinquished her fetishistic stuffed creatures and for the first time realistically considered marriage, babies, and termination of treatment. Evidence of basic alterations in her ego and superego was striking.

She could now let herself feel affection and warm, friendly feelings for people. In addition to achieving promotion in her office, she began volunteer work as a teacher of underprivileged children. Although sadomasochistic oral and anal conflicts were not fully resolved, the capacity to tolerate depressed affects was *partially* developed. As a result of these structural changes in the ego and superego, most of her symptoms cleared. Alcoholism, insomnia, and impulsive behavior were no longer present. However, although the man she was dating was a healthier object choice, it was clear that she was acting out in their relationship some fantasy that she was not bringing into the analysis. She was attracted to the man's big body (he was six feet four inches) and particularly fascinated by the size of his penis.

Two days before the first asthma attack, she reported a dream in which there was a date, December 10, when she had two engagements. Two cars were running on top of a body of water. In her associations the patient said she had been happy the night before the dream, as she had received a postcard from her lover, who wanted to marry her, and also had received a kind letter from a woman friend. The date in the dream reminded the patient of her fifth year, when her mother had a therapeutic abortion. It was apparent that pregnancy fears were disturbing the patient. The night before the dream she had quarreled with her mother, who could not stand the changes in her daughter and was jealous of her lover.

Angry with her mother and furious with me, the patient hoped to become engaged by Christmas. Her associations indicated that she was idealizing her lover, and at this point I interpreted to her her wish for a magical man and magical pregnancy, a recurrent transference and genetic theme.

The next session, she had dreamt of Los Angeles and also of her brother and a girl eavesdropping on a sexual encounter in the next room. Another part of the dream was of a boat and her aunt and uncle. In that session she talked of Los Angeles, where she had had a drunken affair. Her brother, she thought, was a homosexual, and she guessed that his wife was the aggressor sexually. It was my impression that this was true of her relation with her lover and that she was referring to fellatio, but as there had been such a cooling-off in the transference, I made no interpretation and waited. In the next session, she talked about her sinus congestion, her relationship with her father, and her feeling more affection for him. In the session that followed, she reported that the night before she had awakened from a horrible dream with an asthma attack. On the previous day she had experienced a bad sinus attack. This was unusual, since sinus was not a prominent symptom in this case. She repressed the content of the dream.

Several sessions later she reported two dreams. In the first, she dreamt of a wedding and of her aunt preparing an elaborate design of watervines; in the second, she dreamt of being in Haiti and seeing an enormous octopus come over a rooftop. The octopus was really like a gigantic jellyfish. The jellyfish reminded her of her lover's ejaculation, which aroused fears in her of being eaten up. In her sessions during this period she was not communicating well. It was clear that she was having intercourse but not talking much about it. She also was angry with me and blamed me, because after all her work in analysis, she now had asthma.

Over a two-year period the patient had seventeen asthmatic attacks, all of which responded to analytic interpretation. After the first attacks I referred her to an asthma specialist, who reported he was not impressed with allergic factors in her case. I told her we could analyze the conflicts causing her asthma and that medication was unnecessary. The unconscious determinants of her attacks varied. Pregnancy fears and anal, oral, and urethral fantasies were prominent.

As analysis progressed, the patient terminated her affair with her lover and evidenced increasingly healthy ego functioning. Within two years she fell in love with and married a young businessman, and after marriage she suffered no more asthmatic attacks. A year after marriage she terminated analysis.

Before discussing the dynamics underlying the development of the patient's asthma, I should note that she never revealed the content of the nightmare coinciding with her first asthma attack. The preceding dreams expressed primal-scene and pregnancy fears.

DISCUSSION

The patient's asthma developed in the analysis as the expression of a final wish to control and defeat me by being sick and forcing a termination of treatment. As she later admitted, she wanted to marry her lover because he looked so big and healthy, but she knew she could control him. She wanted to defeat me because I had come to stand for the end of her acting out.

In the working through of unresolved oedipal conflicts in the transference neurosis, her most regressive narcissistic drives struggled for expression. A new and strict superego forced an internalization of incorporative impulses that had formerly been externalized in her acting out. Displacement upward had already been established in the symptom of stream weeping. This weeping had expressed a wish to get sympathy and pity; however, as Greenacre (1945) points out, the tears are crocodile tears and they mask intense oral-sadistic incorporative drives. This patient wanted to devour with the eyes. The tears also variously symbolized urine, semen, and saliva. This symptom had been successfully interpreted many times in the analysis. At the time of the development of asthma, there had been marked improvement in the patient's ability to let herself cry and to tolerate affects. All her oral sadism was internalized and expressed by way of respiratory incorporation. Many times previously in analysis she had expressed wishes to kill, bite, and devour me; and at other times, to kill herself in order to placate her primitive superego.

The patient's psoriasis, which had expressed preoedipal exhibitionistic drives, cleared up before the development of the asthma, which was now the last somatic outlet for this neurotic exhibitionism. A physical illness, pneumonia, which occurred at the height of the oedipal period, provided a channel (somatic compliance) for the expression of symptoms, when oedipal conflicts were revived and worked through in analysis.

Unanalyzed transference played a crucial role in the precipitation of the asthma.[1] What took me by surprise was the precipitous superego formation. Many different conflicts were interpreted during the two years that she had asthma, but I would like to emphasize the interpretation of the overly strict superego. An example occurred at the time of her third asthmatic attack. She reported that she had been walking to work and had the thought that I (the analyst) was really trying to help her; then she

---

[1] The role that transference plays in psychosomatic disorders in general was dealt with by M. Sperling in "Transference neurosis in patients with psychosomatic disorders and transference reactions occurring during analysis," *Psychoanalytic Quarterly* 36:342–355.

suddenly got asthma. In the session I pointed out that if she admits to my doing anything for her, she feels as though she must do everything to please me; she has to be perfect, and her only recourse then is to be sick and asthmatic.

I would like to contrast the dynamics in this case with those I observed in another case. The patient, a male, had been enuretic up to age 5 years, at which time, following a tonsillectomy, the enuresis cleared but he developed severe bronchial asthma. The asthma did not subside until he left home (mother) to go to college. The development of asthma clearly represented an identification with the father, who had been asthmatic for many years. Urinary fantasies were prominent in this case. The patient always used condoms in his sexual affairs. After intercourse, which was usually effected with a partially full bladder, he would urinate into the condom, ostensibly to find out if there were any leaks in the rubber. Unconsciously, urine and ejaculation were equated, and his repressed wish was to drown, impregnate, the woman with urine. The man's asthmatic attacks were a talion punishment for this sadistic infantile wish: he was drowned for wanting to drown. In this man's case, as in the first patient's, an overly strict superego was present while the patient had asthma. Polymorphous perverse impulses emerged as analysis progressed, and acting out became a serious problem. The course of analysis was the reverse of that in the asthma *de novo* case, in that he started with the strict superego and asthma that she developed in termination.

I would like to emphasize that the occurrence of asthma in the woman was a transference manifestation and an indication of incomplete analysis. If analysis had been terminated at this time, we would have accomplished only the transformation of an overt acting-out patient into a psychosomatic. In the case of the man, who replaced severe asthma with acting out, to have stopped analysis because of the danger of liberating too much id material (possibly leading to psychopathy or even psychosis) would also have been a serious therapeutic mistake, since acting out, however intense and threatening, is a transference symptom and is analyzable.

Arlow (1955) described a single attack of asthma in an analytic patient in the terminal phase of analysis. The patient had developed other respiratory diseases at critical periods of his life; however, this was his first and only asthmatic attack. Arlow felt that basically fantasies of oral incorporation caused the asthma, and he interpreted the asthma as a transference phenomenon. As in my case, the symptom cleared and the patient terminated successfully.

Many years of experience with these and other asthmatic cases have led me to the following conclusions: the mothers in each case want their children to be sick and dependent; the basic dynamic structure is the same in asthma as in the phobias; omnipotence and magical thinking play a predominant role; one psychosomatic symptom is often exchanged for another — in the woman patient the weeping and psoriasis were replaced by asthma. There is no personality profile for the asthmatic, and the unconscious fantasies behind the asthma vary from one patient to another. The psychosomatic disease can be termed a pregenital conversion neurosis, and an overstrict superego is present with the psychosomatic symptom. Sperling (1963) found similar dynamics in her work with asthmatic children.

My experience with these and other psychosomatic problems indicates that psychoanalysis is the treatment of choice for patients with psychosomatic symptoms and that psychosomatic symptoms occurring during analysis are typical transference phenomena and can be resolved only in analysis.

MIGRAINE REPLACED
BY PREOEDIPAL FANTASIES

A psychoticlike primitive fantasy replacing a psychosomatic symptom occurred in the analysis of a woman with a phobic neurosis and migraines. The patient, a hospital psychologist, was severely criticized for a report she gave to the chief of her service. When she left the hospital, she was angry and "felt a migraine coming on." It occurred to her that she could stop the migraine if she faced her anger and the associated fantasies. She then had a fantasy that she felt replaced a migraine. In the fantasy she went back into the empty office and had a large bowel movement on the chief psychologist's chair; the chief psychologist the next day was horrified and shocked by the excrement on her chair but "did not know who perpetrated this awful deed." That the chief psychologist was an older woman who reminded the patient of her mother had emerged previously in analysis. The recapitulation of an early bowel-training struggle with the mother was evident in this material and was interpreted in the transference neurosis.

PSYCHOSOMATIC SYMPTOMS REPLACED BY PERVERSIONS

A married woman came for analysis because of depression and ulcerative colitis. She soon revealed that she was in conflict about her marriage and was having an extramarital affair with a man whom she knew was an unreliable but charming "womanizer." When she restrained herself and was faithful to her husband, she experienced her ulcerative colitis; when she acted out and had sex with her lover, she was free of colitis but felt guilty and depressed.

The patient described her lover as an anal pervert who said that he wanted to do everything with her: they should be totally free with each other. To demonstrate his freedom from inhibition, he had a bowel movement on some toilet paper in front of her and wanted her to do likewise in front of him. The patient told me it made her anxious when the man requested this perverse anal behavior. She said she knew he wanted to have anal intercourse with her but she refused his anal overtures. Then she laughed in the session and said she had been to a gastroenterologist who told her that her colitis was caused by a tight anal sphincter and produced a series of glass dilators, each a little larger than the first, with which he was going to cure her constipation and colitis. She said she experienced anxiety at the sight of dilators and she knew she was attracted to them. She then stopped going to this specialist.

The patient's mother and maternal grandmother were compulsive neurotics who were obsessed with the bowel and bowel functions. Throughout her childhood, every day at breakfast they would ask her if she had had "one." They always looked into the toilet at her bowel movements, associating their size, shape, color, and consistency with her appearance and the state of her health. She was constipated in childhood and frequently was given enemas and laxatives. In her perverse affair and in proctologic examinations, the patient was recapitulating the early anal relationship with mother and grandmother. As this material was analyzed and worked through in the transference neurosis, the patient terminated her affair, resolved her marital conflicts, and experienced a resolution of her colitis symptoms.

PSYCHOSOMATIC ASTHMA REPLACED
BY PERVERSE SEXUAL BEHAVIOR

A man suffering from asthma and a compulsive neurosis experienced a clearing of asthma with the emergence of perverse sexual behavior. Other aspects of this case, "The Warsaw Ghetto asthmatic," are discussed in Chapter 13.

As is typical of psychosomatic cases, this patient first told me that he had no sexual conflicts; however, when a positive therapeutic alliance developed and his asthma cleared, he reported that he suffered from premature ejaculation. Ostensibly to prevent the humiliation of this symptom, his wife was always on top in intercourse. However, it became clear that his sexual goal was to prolong the sexual act as long as possible. He would lie still and make his wife do all the moving. Like his father he was a "farter, and jokingly farted" at his wife, whom he had taught to fart with him, although he found her a reluctant pupil. Another of his intimate pleasures was surprise pinching. He liked any soft fleshy place for a pinch except the buttocks. On the other hand, he disliked being pinched himself. He had to exert complete control in sex; if his wife tried to initiate the act, he put her off or lost his desire. He revealed that he had never been able to say, "I love you," or "Let's make love," always referring to making out or having sex as a "quickie" or "it." His original attraction to his wife had been clouded by his conscious disgust with her strong body smell, so he demanded that she bathe before intercourse. This conscious disgust masked unconscious copraphagic pleasure in smelling her odors, particularly anal and menstrual smells. He revealed a habit of always being nude with his wife, even at mealtimes, when unexpected visits from neighbors sometimes forced him to clothe himself quickly. This pleasure he rationalized, saying that a married couple should be absolutely free with each other. However, his wife, who usually wore panties, caught a lot of colds and became averse to sexual relations. He was surprised that she became "turned on again" when he began to wear some clothes around the house.

It was clear that in his behavior with his wife this patient recapitulated aspects of his early relations with his mother. He had slept in a bed next to his mother throughout childhood. The father, a noisy, exhibitionistic man who dominated his childlike, dependent wife, slept in the next room. Nightly he left to visit his mistress. This infidelity was only weakly protested by the mother, who unconsciously focused her libidinal attentions on her only son in bed next to her.

PSYCHIATRIC DIAGNOSIS IN PSYCHOSOMATIC DISEASE

Psychosomatic symptoms occur in a variety of personality disorders, sometimes in conditions close to psychoses. However, even in the most disturbed cases there is a split in the ego, with areas of relatively intact ego functioning and some capacity for a transference relationship.

Sperling (1978) differentiated the eating disorders anorexia nervosa, bulimia, and obesity from the other psychosomatic diseases because part of the patient's conflicts are conscious and there are no demonstrable changes in an organ system. We do not agree with this distinction, because the large part of the conflicts, which are manifested as eating disorders, are unconscious, and the fact that the psyche can stop menstruation (hypothalamic amenorrhea) is to us patently psychosomatic.

The question of diagnosis has to be studied in terms of the vicissitudes of the patient's development, life situation, and analytic progress. For example, the asthma *de novo* patient would have been diagnosed initially as a borderline addictive personality. When she developed asthma, she would have been diagnosed instead as a compulsive personality. All the cases I have cited—the migraine, the colitis, and the asthmatic—would initially have been diagnosed as compulsive neurotics. Seen in terms of the vicissitudes of the analysis, however, they might have been termed acting-out characters.

SUMMARY

Reviewing the economic, adaptive, structural, dynamic, and genetic factors in the ego functioning of patients with psychosomatic symptoms, emphasis was put on the fact that precipitous relief of symptoms may be dangerous to psychosomatic patients' mental functioning or even to their lives. Symptom equivalents, which may alternate with or replace a psychosomatic symptom include:

1. Self-destructive acting out;
2. An addictive disorder such as obesity, alcoholism, or drug addiction;
3. Another psychosomatic symptom formation;
4. Neurotic symptom formation; or
5. Severe regressive symptom formation (psychosis).

The components of depression that are masked by psychosomatic symptoms were reviewed; psychosomatic equivalents, long-term follow-ups, and twin studies were explored with emphasis on the effectiveness of analysis in resolving the underlying personality disorders. The "little person" phenomenon in psychosomatic patients was shown to be related to a split-off, regressed, archaic part of the personality. The defenses of the ego that develop in connection with the habits and addictions of childhood were shown to be similar to the defenses used in coping with psychosomatic symptoms.

Illustrative clinical material was presented to document the psychodynamics involved in the replacement of acting-out behavior and psychosis by a compulsive neurosis and asthma, migraine by pregenital fantasies and conflicts; ulcerative colitis by anal perversions, and asthma by perverse sexual behavior.

REFERENCES

Arlow, J. A. (1955). Notes on oral symbolism. *Psychoanalytic Quarterly* 24:63–74.
Blum, H. (1985). Superego formation, adolescent transformation, and the adult neurosis. *Journal of the American Psychoanalytic Association* 33:887–909.
Engel, G. L. (1962). *Psychological Development in Health and Disease*. Philadelphia: W. B. Saunders.
Ferrara, A., and Fontana, V. J. (1966). Celiac disease and anorexia nervosa. *New York State Journal of Medicine* 66:1000–1009.
Fink, G., and Schneer, J. (1963). Psychiatric evaluation of adolescent asthmat-

ics. In *The Asthmatic Child: Psychosomatic Approach to Problems and Treatment,* ed. H. Schneer, pp. 205–223. New York: Harper & Row.

Freud, A. (1936). *The Ego and the Mechanisms of Defense. Writings,* 2. New York: International Universities Press.

Freud, S. (1923). The ego and the id. *Standard Edition.* 19:48–49.

_____ (1933). New introductory lectures on psychoanalysis. *Standard Edition* 22:66–67.

Gero, G. (1953). An equivalent of depression: anorexia. In *Affective Disorders: Psychoanalytic Contributions to their Study,* ed. P. Greenacre, pp. 117–189. New York: International Universities Press.

Greenacre, P. (1945). Pathological weeping. *Psychoanalytic Quarterly* 3:359–367.

Knapp, P. (1963). The asthmatic child and the psychosomatic problem of asthma: toward a general theory. In *The Asthmatic Child: Psychosomatic Approach to Problems and Treatment,* ed. H. Schneer, pp. 234–255. New York: Harper & Row.

Kramer, P. (1955). On discovering one's identity: a case report. *Psychoanalytic Study of the Child* 10:47–74.

Levin, D. (1985). Bulimia as a masturbatory equivalent. *The Jefferson Journal of Psychiatry* 3:24–35.

Mintz, I. L. (1980). Multideterminism in asthmatic disease. *International Journal of Psychoanalytic Psychotherapy* 8:593–600.

Mushatt, C. (1975). Mind–body environment: toward understanding the impact of loss on psyche and soma. *Psychoanalytic Quarterly* 44:81–106.

_____ (1980). Melitta Sperling Memorial Lecture. Presented at the Psychoanalytic Association of New York, February 25.

_____ (1982). Anorexia nervosa: a psychoanalytic commentary. *International Journal of Psychoanalytic Psychotherapy* 9:257–265.

Niederland, W. G. (1956). Clinical observations on the "little man" phenomenon. *Psychoanalytic Study of the Child* 11:381–395.

_____ (1965). Narcissistic ego impairment in parents with early physical malformations. *Psychoanalytic Study of the Child* 20:518–534.

Schmale, A. H., Jr. (1958). Relationship of separation and depression to disease. *Psychosomatic Medicine* 20:259–277.

Schur, M. (1955). Comments on the metapsychology of somatization. *Psychoanalytic Study of the Child* 10:119–164.

Sperling, M. (1959). Equivalents of depression in children. *Journal of the Hillside Hospital* 8:138–148.

_____ (1963). Psychoanalytic study of bronchial asthma in children. In *The Asthmatic Child: Psychoanalytic Approach to Problems and Treatment,* ed. H. Schneer, pp. 138–155. New York: Harper & Row.

_____ (1968). Acting-out behavior and psychosomatic symptoms: clinical and theoretical aspects. *International Journal of Psycho-Analysis* 49:250–253.

_____ ed. (1978). *Psychosomatic Disorders in Childhood.* New York: Jason Aronson.

Tucker, W. I. (1952). Lobotomy case histories: ulcerative colitis and anorexia nervosa. In *Anorexia Nervosa,* ed. J. E. Meyer and H. Feldman, pp. 51–59. Stuttgart: Georg Thieme.

Volkan, V. D. (1965). The observation of the "little man" phenomenon in a case of anorexia nervosa. *British Journal of Medical Psychology* 38:299–311.

Wilson, C. P. (1968). Psychosomatic asthma and acting out: a case of bronchial asthma that developed *de novo* in the terminal phase of analysis. *International Journal of Psycho-Analysis* 49:330–335.

_____ (1980a). The family psychological profile of anorexia nervosa patients. *Journal of the Medical Society of New Jersey* 77:341–344.

_____ (1980b). Parental overstimulation in asthma. *International Journal of Psychoanalytic Psychotherapy* 8:601–621.

_____ (1981). Sand symbolism: the primary dream representation of the Isakower phenomenon and of smoking addictions. In *Clinical Psychoanalysis,* ed. S. Orgel and B. D. Fine, pp. 45–55. New York: Jason Aronson.

_____ (1982). The fear of being fat and anorexia nervosa. *International Journal of Psychoanalytic Psychotherapy* 9:233–255.

_____ (1985). Psychodynamic and/or psychopharmacologic treatment of bulimic anorexia nervosa. In *Fear of Being Fat: The Treatment of Anorexia Nervosa, and Bulimia,* rev. ed., ed. C. P. Wilson, C. G. Hogan, and I. L. Mintz, pp. 345–362. Northvale, NJ: Jason Aronson.

_____ (1986a). The psychoanalytic psychotherapy of bulimic anorexia nervosa. In *Adolescent Psychiatry,* ed. S. Feinstein, pp. 274–314. Chicago: University of Chicago Press.

_____ (1986b). A discussion of E. Levin's paper: Bulimia as a masturbatory equivalent. *The Jefferson Journal of Psychiatry* 3:24–35 (1985) and 4:77–87 (1986).

_____ (1986c). Letter in response to J. M. Jonas's paper: The biological basis and treatment of bulimia. *The Jefferson Journal of Psychiatry* 4:78–82 and 4:83–85.

_____ (1988). Bulimic equivalents. In *Bulimia: Psychoanalytic Treatment and Theory,* ed. H. J. Schwartz, pp. 489–522. New York: International Universities Press.

Wilson, C. P., Hogan, C. G., and Mintz, I. L. (1983). *Fear of Being Fat: The Treatment of Anorexia Nervosa and Bulimia.* Rev. ed. Northvale, NJ: Jason Aronson, 1985.

Wurmser, L. (1980). Phobic core in the addictions and the paranoid process. *International Journal of Psychoanalytic Psychotherapy* 8:311–335.

3

Loss, Separation, and Psychosomatic Illness

Cecil Mushatt, M.D.

PSYCHOANALYTIC APPROACH TO PSYCHOSOMATIC ILLNESS

This chapter presents a rationale for the use of a psychoanalytic approach in treating psychosomatic and somatopsychic illness. Like Deutsch (1940, 1947, 1959), Sperling (1946, 1967, 1973), and many others, I believe that this approach can offer patients very effective help, even when one is concerned only with limited goals, such as bringing about temporary remissions. This view opposes that of Nemiah and colleagues (1976). According to their proposed theory of alexithymia, patients with psychosomatic disease cannot be treated psychoanalytically, because some inborn defect renders them incapable of fantasy life and appropriate emotional experience. In fact, however, patients with psychosomatic illness are overburdened by primitive emotions and fantasies, which their bodily language both defends against and symbolically expresses. This bodily language can be decoded.

Deutsch and Sperling contributed greatly to the understanding of the symbolic representations in physical symptoms by extending Freud's concept of conversion. They showed that conversion symptoms could be pregenital in origin and could involve not only the voluntary sensori-motor system, but also organs under control of the autonomic nervous system. They arrived at their conclusions by different routes—Deutsch, particularly through his study of the development of the body image and the manner in which symbolic representations of the outside world are laid down in the body.

In an earlier paper (1975), I explained how people's incapacity to tolerate loss or separation, actual or symbolic, precipitated and aggravated psychosomatic disease. I dealt at length with Deutsch's formulations (1940, 1953, 1959) and my own elaboration of them. Certain aspects of that paper bear summarizing here.

Disruption of personal relationships and of one's self-image can trigger the revival of reactions, psychic and somatic, from a number of levels of the developmental task of separation of self from object—the task of individuation. The more closely these reactions are derived from the earliest symbiotic level, the more likely are the physical symptoms to be indistinguishable in their meaning from psychotic responses such as melancholia, as Daniels (1940) and Sperling (1946) have pointed out. The physical symptom, when archaic in meaning, may mask a diffuse process with extensive impairment of the ego, or, in the better-integrated person, it may localize the primitive organization within the ego, leaving the rest of the ego free for higher maturation. There can be great variation, then, in the extent to which patients fulfill criteria for classical analysis, as well as in the type of transference and its manageability in analysis.

I believe that when organic change has taken place, the physical symptom is both expressive of and defensive against primitive fantasies and emotions, though it is not necessarily true that absence of organic damage precludes primitive psychic activity.

Psychosomatic cases vary considerably in the extent to which primitive sexual and aggressive elements pervade the personality and in the extent of ego defects. There are variations in the degree to which transformation of primitive instinctual forces takes place with development of defenses against them, and in the extent to which ego resources are lost or maintained in the provocative circumstances in which physical symptoms appear. There are thus variations in the degree of symbiotic attachment and in the degree of maturity or immaturity of ego functioning. Ego defects result in persistence and intensification of pregenital strivings, which in turn may aggravate the ego defects.

Deutsch (1940, 1959) believed that study of the formation of the body image could illuminate the mind–body–environment relationship. Unless the body image evolves well beyond the primitive stages where the subject and object are one, there can be no ego development, only symbiotic existence, psychosis, severe psychosomatic disease, or death. Formation of the body image depends on the process of conversion, which as defined by Deutsch, has to be distinguished from conversion as a symptom. This process makes restitution for loss, concrete or symbolic, experienced in the course of separation of self from object. According to Deutsch the beginning of objectification of the outside world is the first loss in the symbiotic state. Objectification of objects takes place in part by projection of what primordially was once considered part of one's self. The loss is undone by the symbolic restoration within the body and the psyche of representations of the outside world. Internalized symbolic representations in the body are formed through fusion of external sensory perceptions and reactive internal sensory perceptions. As part of the development of the body image, basic physiological and physical functions may be influenced permanently and even altered. The symbolic representations laid down in the body are derived from all phases of development, so that physical function and dysfunction may express psychic activity from all developmental levels from primary narcissistic through to the genital level.

The evolution of the body image is an essential protection against the threat of disintegration from separation from the earliest period of life onward. Thus the organism is a psychophysiological entity from birth — through fusion of emotional and bodily processes and external and internal sensory perceptions. In this context the term psychosomatic can be used to encompass all physical illness. It includes not only the psychosomatic in the classical, restricted sense (emotional processes triggering physical disease) but also the somatopsychic (physical processes triggering psychic reactions), as well as the operation of both phenomena simultaneously, as commonly occurs. Loss (with depression) or anticipation of loss (with anxiety) may be expressed in physical terms, and physical dysfunction may evoke a sense of loss or threat of loss of key persons. Often it is difficult to assess how much is psychosomatic and how much is somatopsychic, the psychic activity being so similar.

According to this hypothesis, physical function and dysfunction with psychological meaning can express the degree of harmony or disharmony, respectively, between the individual and himself and key external figures. Conversion symptoms, that is, physical symptoms with psychological meaning, arise in body parts when there is disharmony between the individual and internalized representations, between the individual and introjected objects symbolized in the body parts, and between the individual and key persons in the environment. Restoration of good function depends psychologically on undoing the fusion with body function of early sensory configurations arising from the environment, which in turn requires resolving the conflict between the individual and key persons in the past and present, with resolution of disharmony between symbolizations within the body and through it in the ego.

In effect, to quote Deutsch, the body is in a continual silent dialogue with the environment and with the individual and the various parts of his personality. The nonverbal or preverbal dialogue can be decoded. Often if a patient reports a physical reaction during a session and is asked to decode the associated message or statement, he can bring meaningful associations. As Deutsch (1958) and Sperling (1967) have emphasized, physical symptoms occurring during sessions, even in the case of nonpsychosomatic patients, usually signal the presence of charged repressed transference fantasies.

The process of separation of self from object and the evolution of a sense of individuality can be understood as characterized by a series of experiences involving loss of part of oneself to the outside world and reunion within the body and the ego through internalized symbolization of external objects. The successful mastery of the separation–individuation processes as described by Deutsch and by Mahler (1968) depends on a healthy emotional climate in relation to key figures in early life. Reactions to loss and separation may carry with them to a varying degree the history of adaptive reactions in the various levels of the separation-individuation process. The better integrated and thereby the better individuated the individual, the more moderate are reactions likely to be, physically and psychically, to loss and physical illness. The more severe physical and psychic reactions are seen in those who show marked impairment of the individuation process — that is, marked impairment of the ego — and who depend on a strong symbiotic relationship for survival. Deutsch pointed out that a patient's possible risk of severe relapses in the course of treatment can be predicted from one's knowledge of the complexity of pathological symbolizations within the organ system. I have been able to describe this in the case of a young man with peptic ulcer (Mushatt 1959).

BODY IMAGE AND ORGAN LANGUAGE

Some clinical material will illustrate the preceding remarks on body image, loss, separation and reunion, and the use of organs to symbolize relationships with the external environment.

A young man who sought treatment for ulcerative colitis, as I reported in some detail in an earlier paper (1975), had a mild relapse after long remission when his mother was hospitalized with a fatal illness. He said that as he sat at her bedside, he had a fantasy of caressing his mother's breasts to soothe and comfort her. Then he had a fantasy of pulling off his mother's breasts and pushing them under the skin of his own chest. At another time during his vigil she clawed at her body and called "Momma! Momma!" Later he said with much emotion, "She is my mother. I don't want her to go. I lived inside her once."

He spoke of biology classes as a student when he once "tore out an animal's insides." His professor remarked on the animal's big "duff." With great discomfort he then reported the fantasy of tearing out his mother's heart and her "duff." He had the fantasy of eating her "duff" and "I would then have one for myself." Then, to his own great surprise, he demonstrated with his hands how he would press his mother's heart into his chest. "Then I would have my mother with me." Soon he burst out crying, "Mother, come back, I want my mother!" This was an anguished cry out of childhood, recalling for him vividly the emptiness and loneliness of the house when he would come home from school, when both parents were out working until late in the evening.

He now reviewed his compulsive looking at women, attracted by the size of their bosoms. His fantasies could now be seen as the unconscious ones of a young child through which he tried to restore the presence of his absent mother by incorporating parts of her into his own image, thereby identifying with her. This material illustrates the significance of all sensory modalities, here especially vision and touch, and especially the fantasy of physical touch, in developing the body image and in establishing identifications both psychically and physically.

During further work the expression of love and longing for his mother was replaced by the breakthrough of unrelenting rage at his mother over her unavailability, expressed through the same and other destructive fantasies. Both polarities of love and hate found expression in adult life in what seemed to the patient to be an irreconcilable dilemma — an intense longing for the companionship of women and a simultaneous spiteful resentment toward them. In the course of this phase of analysis, the patient intermittently developed psychosomatic symptoms identical with those of which his mother would complain when she returned home after a long day's work.

Here we see some determinants of poor differentiation between love and hate and of fantasies expressing an inner threat of disintegration from loneliness, rage, and guilt. The afflicted individuals are highly intolerant of separation, and they have a powerful sense of the insolubility of the task of individuation and of sexual differentiation within the self. In varying degrees of intensity and pervasiveness a defensive response arises within the ego, with fixation in a narcissistic, borderline, or psychotic position, or with psychosomatic disorders.

In the more pathological cases we usually find concurrently in the nonbodily ego a marked impairment of the capacity for differentiation between concrete and symbolic images. For instance, we see the equation of eating food with oral incorporation of objects, as I described in a case of peptic ulcer with severe anorexia (1959). Patients are often afraid to identity with — or rather to maintain identification with — the therapist when identification becomes equated unconsciously with destruction of the object. The opposite also occurs: the fear of renunciation of old hostile identifications is derived from the equation of such renunciation of identification with destruction of the object. To quote one patient, "If I am not depressed like my parents, I deny their existence." That is, she would destroy them if she did not identify with them.

The other side of the fear of being destructive is the fear of being destroyed by merging with the object. A patient with ulcerative colitis said, "I am afraid of liking people. There is something destructive about it. I feel that somehow I might lose myself in the other person." Here we see the fear of merging versus the fear of totally incorporating the object. The inability unconsciously to differentiate between concrete and symbolic processes may lead to organic suicide. This occurs, for instance, when the patient unconsciously cannot distinguish between psychologically effecting separation from pathological identifications and concrete destruction of the object, or between psychological detachment from part of oneself and destruction of an organ. Patients often push for operation in the fantasy that it will free them from pathological attachments. As one patient with ulcerative colitis expressed it some weeks after colectomy, "I feel as though an evil part of me has been cut out."

The material that follows is from an earlier paper (Mushatt 1954), supplemented by an additional drawing and associations. It illustrates early body-image formation, how bowel function was used to symbolize relationships with external key figures, and how the bowel now tended to function in accordance with the dynamic relationship of the individual with his external and internal environment.

This young man developed ulcerative colitis at age $15\frac{1}{2}$ when his father became incapacitated by heart disease. The father died one year later, and on the first anniversary of his father's death the patient had to be hospitalized because of a very acute relapse. He was seen in psychotherapy. Five months later, on Memorial Day, his morbid reaction to his father's death broke through, accompanied by another acute flare-up. In reviewing his sense of guilt over his father's death, he told of a fantasy of committing the perfect murder in which the body was ground up and flushed down the toilet. Later he told of earlier fantasies of becoming an explorer and being crowned King of the Cannibals. Now he wished he could bring his father back to life. In fact, he felt that his father was with him, watching him. Sometimes he felt his father in his brain and throughout his body.

Just before Memorial Day he had been digging clams, and he had two sets of fantasies. He felt he would find a skeleton, perhaps his father's. "I would shit on it, and so give back to father something that belonged to him, and I could forget him." Then he felt that "I had to dig up the whole clam flat, dig everything out and I'd be all right. I felt I had to get my father out of me. He was sitting there in my intestine, saying I've done wrong, that I tried to steal the old lady. It's a mental picture I have of him—I felt sick and I wanted to vomit and to defecate."

Eighteen days later he said he could not describe in words what he felt but he could draw it. I gave him a pencil and paper and he produced the drawing in Figure 3.1.

The patient at first explained the drawing as follows. The left half shows his body and his fantasies about what is inside and outside his body. The figures and objects to the right and left of the body outline are in the outside world. The patient is standing in mud. Inside the body outline at the top are a shovel and basket to illustrate how he discovered

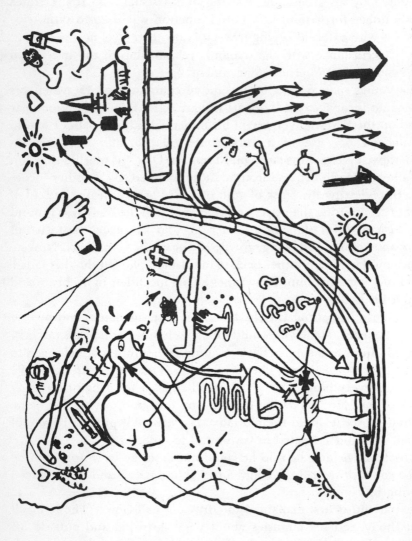

Figure 3.1. A patient's spontaneous drawing demonstrating internalization of external figures in graphic, primitive form. It also shows his fantasies of freeing himself from pathological identifications, from anger, and from guilt through expulsion via the bowel.

his fantasies while digging clams. (I could add that it could symbolize his difficulty in integrating an identification with his mother and father.) To the right is his father's corpse, the cross being the tombstone and the arrow piercing the corpse representing the murder of his father. The amorphous mass above the corpse is the goo that had to be restored to his father. From this mass an arrow leads to the representation of the patient's colon. The black cross below the colon is the Iron Cross for his victory over his father. Above the center are two heads attached to each other. The small one is the patient's and the large one is his father's. The patient felt his father's head was attached to the back of his. He had constantly to watch his father, and he was frightened. His fear is represented by beads of perspiration. Above his father's head is a box with a dagger in it, representing the patient dead in the coffin and his penis, which has been cut off. This is his punishment. His mother weeps over his fate. Her eyes and tears are shown below the handle of the shovel inside the body outline. That is, he sees through his mother's eyes, he identifies with her, and he weeps for her. Just outside the body outline at the left above are his mother's hair (the wavy lines) and his mother's heart.

Outside the body outline (which, it should be noted, is very hazy) the patient represents his idea of how his recovery will take place. All internalized objects—represented by his father's head, his father's corpse, a broken heart, two large arrows, and a number of smaller arrows—had to be expelled through his bowel. The patient said, "I should've put a penis in the shit in which I am standing. It's father's. It came out of my bowel." The lines sweeping up from below show him trying to rise up from the mud to a church, trees, and the sun. He would get well when he reached them, and then he could obtain love (the heart). The large hand is his desire for a helping hand.

The patient's drawing expresses almost a pre-ego level of development or a regression to such a level, described in terms of his body image. Internalization is expressed in graphic primitive form. Superego development is portrayed in archaic form and confirms the view of Daniels (1940) and Sperling (1946) that ulcerative colitis masks a melancholic core. He shows how intensely he is identified with his mother; he sees through her eyes and weeps her tears. His overidentification with one parent can presage danger to the patient. He shows also how he views the task of recovery—namely, freeing himself from identification with his harsh father and his depressed mother (the broken heart). These symbolic separations are expressed through riddance by the bowel. Later the patient expressed the fantasy that by removal of the bowel he could be freed from these pathological attachments and identifications.

Here we see primitive aggression and guilt, both of which are central to precipitation and perpetuation of psychosomatic symptoms. Very striking is the faintness of the patient's body outline, indicating the blurring of ego boundaries and the symbiotic character of his psychological position. This may have been enhanced by his being in his adolescence.

The whole picture may have an ominous ring, but in fact therapy turned out to be promising. A month later the patient produced another drawing in vivid colors in chalk, as shown in Figure 3.2. At this time, although his stools were still watery, his bowel was much improved and his mood was better. He described the drawing as follows:

> The figure in red is myself armless. In the center of the figure is a blue area representing my open bowels. I am looking at the box with the padlock on it. This box contains the feelings that I have expressed. The box cannot be moved. Everything is locked away in there and it cannot get out now. The thoughts are those I've had about my mother and father. I am also watching the hand reaching for the axe. The axe is to cut the chain leading from the block of granite to my bowels. The block of granite and the box on it are all in one piece. The hands are mine. The heart is love. I have to go up along the green path to reach love. My face expresses anxiety and hope. The two tufts of hair are part of my personality—a regular guy. The eye is that of Dr. Mushatt, who has wisdom, calmness, and an "everything will be okay" in it. I have two feelings about the closed lips. The power of words and soon there will be no need for me to speak because I shall be well, and soon you will not have to speak either. The purple around the lips indicates that the mouth is receding. The need for speech is becoming less. Extending from the eyes is a long arm, Dr. Mushatt's, on which there is a hand reaching for the axe. I want the doctor to take the axe and cut the chain. This will get me free of my attachment to the block and from ideas about my mother. The heart is love and understanding on my part. The arms and the hands are mine.

Earlier the patient had said that he felt his arms had been detached from him:

Figure 3.2. A patient's drawing of his self-image and the symbolic representation of his attempt to gain freedom from inner conflict and conflict with his family.

I need my arms to obtain love and to make love. There is a hook
attached to my bowel. From it runs a chain to the block of granite.
The opening in the bowel is flexible. The blue is the present condition
of my bowel, and represents water. The granite block is black. It is
the ideas I have had and it cannot be moved. It stays put. I want to
seek love. It means giving up my mother to whom I became a
husband through fantasy. Seeking love was a commitment of adultery. Not wanting to do wrong, to prove that no such thought entered
my mind, I used my bowels as a means of distraction. Being like a
baby was to be one. Prove I'm a baby who cannot do such things as
adultery and I will be safe. I want love, but when I go after it, the
chain pulls the flexible wall open and my bowels run. The eye of Dr.
Mushatt and his hand reaching for the axe is what is holding me up.
I mean that Dr. Mushatt has not succeeded in undoing the chain. If
he could cut the chain, I would be free.

The self-portrayal in this second drawing is the more common one
by a patient with psychosomatic disease, showing on the one hand a sense
of omnipotence with the desire for omnipotent control over the environment, and on the other a sense of helplessness with a demand for
omnipotence on the part of the therapist. The presenting conflict
appeared to be oedipal, but the patient came into the oedipal phase poorly
prepared, and it was failure in pregenital development that was primary.
The desire to displace the father existed not so much on a genital-sexual
level as on a more infantile level of wishing to have an exclusive
attachment to his mother. As he put it later when he decided to break off
therapy, "Your policy is to make me grow. I want to be a baby to my
mother longer." Coinciding with resolving his conflicts with his father and
grieving over him, there was marked improvement in bowel activity, but
lasting remission came only after he worked over his relationship with his
mother.

As rage and guilt were alleviated, he found it possible to identify
with me in various ways. I think this enabled him to detach himself more
from his depressed mother and his fantasy of father as a hateful parent.
At his own request, this patient terminated treatment after two years.
Intermittent contact was maintained with him. About eighteen months
afterward, he wrote to say that he had completed training in commercial
telegraphy and was about to leave for sea as a radio operator. It is
significant that his father had served in the mercantile marine as

a steamfitter. His father's life, because of his father's silent nature, had always been a mystery to the patient.

The fantasy of bodily functions controlled by internalized objects is described by Knapp and colleagues (1966) in the case of a man with severe asthma:

> I have to find a happy medium between the two extremes, between my heart racing like a motorboat and all the things happening too fast, like saliva flowing so freely and the mucus running out of my nose and water coming up and my stomach turning. And, of course, the other extreme: "I'm dying or my heart's stopping altogether, then nothing is happening at all, no air getting into my lungs." I have to find a happy medium between the two and sort of will things to happen or think them to happen. *I get my armies of people to control all body functions,* to get in the right place, which is halfway between the two extremes.

The significance of bodily secretions and excretions in expressing emotions and fantasies is illustrated by a young man who often spoke of feeling depressed. When finally asked to describe his depressive feelings, he said that he felt nauseous. Later when he could allow himself to cry, the nausea disappeared.

Another young man whom I described in detail in an earlier paper (1959) complained of a desire to vomit. In association he uncovered the fantasy of smashing the analyst with an axe and of "sleeping with women instead of murdering them." "I think of me with an axe, smashing you, the blood, and my vomiting and shitting at the same time. I am aware of my penis now, pushing it out, and ejaculating. The act of retching and throwing the axe are the same. I think of vomiting over people." On another occasion, he said, "I can't cry by myself. I am liable to throw up. . . . Instead of crying, I want to gag and to vomit."

SPEECH AND ITS PSYCHOSOMATIC COMPONENTS

The development of speech is central to the separation–individuation process. Patterns and manner of speech may have complex symbolic meaning and express multiple identifications. Affectively meaningful language can be understood as externalizing one's inner perceptions of and relationships to internalized objects. It can symbolize a loss or separation, a giving up of old identifications, as well as restitution, reunion, and incorporation of new identifications by exchange of language. Changing one's patterns and manner of speech may involve abandoning old identifications in exchange for new ones and in this sense can symbolize loss, separation, and restitution.

When there is no return or response from the environment, either verbally or nonverbally, discomfort over the loss is heightened and threatens the individual's ego integrity. A young woman who suffered from extreme anxiety for a very long time was very difficult to treat because she could not freely associate. After a few comments or associations she would say, "What do you have to say now? Say anything, anything will do. I get very angry when you don't say anything." Finally she was able to clarify the problem: "When I speak, I feel that I am losing my words, and when you don't speak, I feel very uncomfortable, because I am not receiving something in return." This problem was carried over into other aspects of her life, especially in completing her college study assignments. The insight she achieved greatly improved her work in therapy.

As Solnit (1979) pointed out, failure in the development of object relationships can affect speech and the capacity for object relationships. As an example, another young woman, whom I have described elsewhere (1975), formerly psychotic and suffering from anorexia, had great artistic talent and was studying art. She was a very silent person and suffered from a severe work block. When she completed a painting, she would obliterate it. Finally, after reporting her obliteration of a landscape painting, she said, "Those trees and fields are mine. They are part of me. If I leave them on canvas, they will no longer be mine." This was a residue of the earliest symbiotic state when the body and external world are one, and it represents the essence of narcissism.

Such narcissistic phenomena are seen often in psychosomatic patients, in whom varying degrees of failure to resolve the separation–individuation process are accompanied by varying degrees of narcissistic organization. Fears of their fantasies of voraciousness and insatiability, accompanied by fear of destructiveness and the resulting primitive guilt, can be seen in varying levels of intensity. This pattern is most clearly evident in anorexia and bulimia. Such fears are derived in part from the fear of separation and of the effect of separation on the object.

Murray (1964) gives an elegant description of narcissitic entitlement. In their narcissism, patients expect to be made omnipotent and
expect omnipotence in the therapist. More common is the opposite side
of this wish, namely the wish for infantilization and for fusion with the
therapist. The intensity of their narcissistic expectations and of the
depression, anger, and guilt that arise from failure to realize them is a
measure of the blurring of the boundaries between the self and the outside
world, a measure of the depth of symbiotic attachment.

A person's narcissistic organization may have important effects on
speech and communication. For the purpose of understanding these
effects, I shall use the term "narcissistic retentiveness" to refer to the
aspects of narcissistic entitlement defined by Murray. This retentiveness
may be considered anal in character, but its intensity, I believe, is
determined by earlier developmental failures.

Narcissistic retentiveness can be an important aspect of resistance.
Narcissistic individuals resent parting with anything of themselves. They
want a lot for very little. For instance, they want a lot of understanding
for very little meaningful communication; they want to change without
changing, without giving up anything of themselves in return for change.
Obese patients want the benefits derived from reasonable weight and
freedom from the psychological determinants of overweight without
giving up overeating or any of their body weight or their psychological
problems, or even the space they occupy through their obesity. This
attitude carries over into speech. Murray alludes to it in describing the
intellectual level and emotional remoteness at which his patient worked in
analysis.

Among these narcissistic phenomena is the magical thinking that
operates in such patients, which plays a part in the inhibition of
communication as well as in repression of affective ideation. They fear the
power of thoughts and, even more, the power of verbalization of thoughts
and feelings. Angry thoughts, and especially their verbalization, can kill.
Such patients often, after a session of emerging hostility, will phone later
just to hear the therapist's voice to make sure he is still alive.

Narcissistic retentiveness manifests itself in various other ways. In
several papers (1954, 1959, 1975) I have described the significance of
bodily secretions and excretions in expressing separation and reunion,
loss, destruction, and restitution, and this can be studied as part of the
narcissistic symbiotic problem. For instance, as Deutsch pointed out
(1958), on a primitive level, inspiration can be understood as symbolic of

taking in part of the world. Expiration can express restoration to the outside world of what had become part of oneself, and at the same time giving up to the outside world a part of oneself; that is, breathing can express union–loss–separation–reunion. The respiratory spasm of asthma can symbolize an unconscious effort to retain attachment to key objects as well as to destroy the symbolized incorporated figures. This is a much deeper level of interpretation with greater implication than Alexander's "cry for the mother."

A man with asthma, a brilliant research physicist, exhibited marked symbiotic dependency covering murderous rage and profound guilt. He feared exertion because it meant losing energy and strength and perspiration; it would wear him out. He wore the same suit day-in, day-out, for several years, never having it cleaned, because cleaning meant disposing of all his accumulated sweat. He kept postponing completion of his research projects because completion meant publication, and publication meant giving his ideas to others. For long stretches in the analysis, most hours ended up with the same theme — that is, he gave little of himself verbally or emotionally that was meaningful. This man also suffered from bladder sphincter spasm. In intercourse his suffering was twofold: not only was he afraid of losing strength from the exertion and from loss of semen, but he also experienced premature ejaculation. One aspect of the latter was that he resented his wife receiving any of his semen or having any pleasure from the act; the pleasure should be all his.

Another of my patients with premature ejaculation (1975), who came for treatment for ulcerative colitis, for a considerable time seemed inaccessible. He presented a series of associations and fantasies, each significant on the surface but expressed without emotion and leading nowhere. Finally it occurred to me that his unconscious hope was to arouse my interest and leave me excited but without understanding — without what he regarded as the ultimate pleasure for the analyst. This became clear when he finally described his perfunctory sexual foreplay; he aroused his wife and then "poof," he ejaculated and "she was left high and frustrated." Later he became enraged over his progress in analysis. "What's in analysis for me?" he asked. "All that happens is that I get in deeper and deeper and I have to keep going more. I have to think about my wife and my children and their needs and I have to work harder." Around the same time he had his first experience in several years of complete relief from premature ejaculation. He spoke in almost identical angry terms. "I got in deep, and then I had to keep going and going, and my wife wanted more and she got more pleasure."

Both of these patients show how narcissistic requirements invade and influence speech. They also show how physical symptoms and instinctual behavior can find expression in many ways in ego activities, in nonsexual interpersonal behavior, and even in the manner of association and communication in analysis and psychotherapy.

These remarks raise further questions about the sexualization of speech as part of the sexualization of the separation–individuation process. The latter may be induced by deprivation of appropriate sensory and emotional stimulation or by inappropriate excess of both in early life. As an example of the sexualization of speech, inhibition of affective speech may often unconsciously serve as an invitation to the analyst to force himself on the patient — to try, as it were, to penetrate the patient's mind. In this way the patient's speech unconsciously symbolizes an invitation to a sexual encounter. Often, if asked, patients in such a situation will be able to report a sense of sexual arousal.

A man in his fifties complaining of nausea and joint pains, for a long time had talked very circumstantially and inconsequentially, mostly about his physical symptoms. He had been showing much improvement physically. During a session he now complained that in the past I should have done more to make him talk: I should have dragged things out of him. Later in the session he told with embarrassment of a recent sexual encounter. The woman had "sucked and sucked on my penis like I had never experienced before. It was great. I didn't have to do anything myself." Then his face lit up. He said, "When I said that, I thought of my saying that you should have dragged things out of me, sucked things out of me when I wouldn't talk freely." Now, for the first time, he could discuss his sexual transference fantasies, and subsequently he became more open, spontaneous, and animated in speech. He could express both separation from me and identification with me, identifying with what he felt I expected of him. For him, speech had been invaded by the sexualization of the separation–individuation process.

In patients who speak in a droning, hesitating monotone, or in hypochondriacal or circumstantial and inconsequential terms, there frequently can be obtained a childhood history of enemas or suppositories or bitter resentment against bowel training. Their manner of speaking may reflect an unconscious demand for the therapist to try to drag meaningful thoughts and feelings out of them, expressing the symbolic expectation of enemas or suppositories accompanied by associated sexual fantasies or a hostile, narcissistic retention. It may express a reluctance to take an active initiative toward growth and a demand for a symbolic sexualized transference. For example, a man with a psychosomatic disorder had been alternately silent or talking in a very circumstantial manner or ruminating about his daydreams for self-advancement. I remarked that he showed very little interest in trying to realize his daydreams. He broke into a smile and said, "My father used to tell people to shit and get off the pot. I agree that because my father told me to do so, I would not do it. I used to sit on the toilet, reading interminably while my father shouted outside the bathroom for me to hurry up. This has been the organizing principle of my life." Little comment need be made on the effect of this principle on his speech.

Several years later this patient revealed another secret out of childhood even more significant for understanding his manner of communicating. He had been droning away, saying little of any consequence. I drew his attention to this, and to his surprise, he recalled the many occasions in childhood when his mother would try to give him suppositories. He would enjoy fighting her off. He realized that he derived great pleasure from my trying to get him to talk animatedly while he continually rebuffed me in his characteristic way. During the remainder of the session, he alternated between free, animated speech and lapses into his circumstantial droning.

Thus silence, and its equivalents such as circumstantial, affectless speech or inconsequential chattering, can be used to express hostility and to provoke the environment. As another example, a man with acute thyrotoxicosis recently brought under control, who spoke in this way, had been talking plaintively of his impotence. He had come to realize that his impotence served to provoke his wife and to express his anger toward her. For some time, too, we had been examining his manner of speaking in sessions. Now, for a change, he spoke animatedly:

> Last day you told me that I drive my wife up a wall by the way I speak
> and that I try to do that to you. You are right about my wife, but it
> would not make sense to do that to you. I have to tell you, my mother
> and father were visiting this week. I am no match for my father, but
> I can see from him where I learned to speak the way I do. My father

had been reading a book, and he wanted to tell me about it. He nearly drove me crazy the way he spoke, weighing every word and making what he had to say, which was little, seem like a long *megillah* [a long circumstantial story].

There are patients who speak with superficial animation but fail to finish their sentences, jumping from one idea to another in a way that prevents recognition of connections between the ideas. At the same time, emotional expression keeps building up. Often such patients may be found to have practiced postponement of reaching a climax during masturbation. Men may have a history of *ejaculatio retardiva,* women a history of failure to reach orgasm. In such instances, they find it difficult to reach any conclusion in understanding their associations. This may be the verbal counterpart of the narcissistic aspects of premature ejaculation in men and frigidity in women; they spill out their thoughts quickly or "leak out" their thoughts and have difficulty in providing further associations.

Compulsive masturbation, too, may find expression in the manner of speaking. A young man complained constantly in sessions, taking trivial experiences and working himself up into a state of turmoil and high indignation over them, to the point that they became virtually unanalyzable. He recognized that he derived great pleasure from the turmoil and rage. His manner of speaking gradually changed as he came to understand it as representative of his compulsive masturbation. The latter subsided, too, as he gained understanding of the motivations for it, especially uncovering the fantasy of developing a huge penis and engaging in violence and aggression. In class, this young man would experience rage at any teacher who criticized his work in any way. He felt he should be regarded as the most brilliant of students, beyond criticism. With his brilliance he could "punch out" his fellow students. His fantasy of being himself a big destructive phallus became clear to him. When the implications of this deeper fantasy were clarified, not only did his behavior in class with his fellow male and female students improve, but his manner of communicating progressed to more constructive meaningful associations and emotional expression. I have observed a similar process in a female patient.

In another woman, the fantasy of her body as a phallus affected her speech. She spoke of her upside-down anatomy, such that her mouth was the orifice of the phallus, and speaking freely was an ejaculatory function.

She was afraid to speak freely for fear of losing her conspicuous individuality and strength. When she did speak, often it was with a rush of ideas. She also described speaking as equivalent to defecating.

A woman with colitis whom I have followed on and off over many years, and who for seven and a half years had been free of colitis symptoms, had been extremely provoked by her boss. She felt she had no alternative but to resign from an excellent professional position. In describing her conference with him, she emphasized her effort to maintain her dignity and self-control. She told me, "You have made me into a lady. I don't get angry as I used to. I could have had a ball getting angry." She said she was angry at me over this, but only later did she report the extent of her anger. In that session with me she had felt like choking me, and in the conference with her boss had felt like taking a coffee pot off his desk and smashing him over the head with it. "I felt you had taken my power away, my power was my tremendous anger."

Her power lay also in her colitis symptoms. They protected her from an awareness of her murderous rage and her guilt, and they satisfied her murderous fantasies as well as her masochism. That same week she had a severe relapse requiring hospitalization. This was her first relapse in seven and a half years, except for a one-day episode of rectal bleeding the previous year, four days after her wedding anniversary. There were multiple determinants for this severe colitis attack. One was that I had asked her permission to use for a lecture material from her experience with colitis. At this time she had been doing well, and discharge from therapy had been under consideration. In discussing her acute relapse, and after alluding to my request, she said, "I said last week that I'd like to get even with you, and I wondered is there something like this. I'll show you, Dr. Mushatt. You won't be able to say that I'm cured. Now that's the stupidest thing to think." This illustrates the unrelenting anger and desire for revenge that we see in many psychosomatic patients. We see here, also, their possessiveness of emotions and fantasies — especially of symptoms. This narcissistic attitude affects speech and the level and manner of communication.

Often, speaking in an intellectual, affectless, or circumstantial manner can be construed as an effective form of silence, disguised overtly as inaccessibility and detachment, through which patients can unconsciously maintain symbiotic bonds. A graphic example was provided by the anorexic silent woman referred to earlier. She uncovered the fantasy of holding my penis tightly in her mouth as she lay on the couch. She spontaneously related this to her silence: "If I speak freely, I shall have to let go of your penis and of you." In her silence, disguised as detachment, she maintained her symbiotic bond with me. Through affective speech, she separated herself from me as well as lost something of herself to me.

Weinberger (1964) draws attention to the relationship between silence, masochism, and depression. Such silence may have angry and provocative implications. Often such patients have a great preoccupation with foul odors. Their love of foul odors goes hand in hand with the love of making a stink, figuratively and literally. This is part of their sadomasochistic behavior.

The above remarks, I hope, make clear that speech is affected by psychosomatic processes and may be altered by unconscious psychological requirements. Most of the examples I have given reflect the narcissistic aspects of the personality organization of the patients.

IDENTIFICATIONS

I believe that the stronger the symbiotic position, the stronger are the narcissistic elements, and this in part accounts for the difficulty in treating such patients. They have more ambivalence, primitive aggression, pregenital sexual problems, archaic guilt, and archaic and magical thinking. They also experience greater difficulty in making sustaining identifications that can undo the effect of older, ambivalent identifications with past key figures. The level on which identification with the therapist takes place is important. The more closely it approaches incorporation and unconscious equation with destruction of the object, the harder it is for the patient to form new, stable identifications essential for bringing about remission and cure. One must bear in mind that for such patients the line between love and hate can be very blurred. Ambivalent behavior derived from this equation of incorporation and destruction of the object often is interpreted by the therapist as reflecting profound hostility. Rejection of identification with the analyst and rejection of his interpretations and of the help they may offer, though often interpreted as expressing hostility, may, in fact, be due to the patient's unconscious concern for the therapist's welfare.

In patients with more mature egos, the higher the level at which identification takes place, the more likely they are to respond not only to psychoanalytic therapy but to medical therapy. They are able to establish a satisfying symbiotic or partially symbiotic relationship sufficient to establish remissions or to sustain remissions for lengthy periods. This helps explain the positive effect of solely medical treatment in the hands of physicians who can achieve a good transference relationship with their patients.

Knapp and colleagues (1970) studied cases of asthma and tried to process analytic material in order to predict the onset of symptoms. They used with some success a concept of "safe position" or "partial symbiotic equilibrium." If this position was threatened by strain on defenses— especially if the patient found himself unable to move forward and at the same time unable to tolerate the regressive aspects of a symbiotic attachment—physical symptoms would occur. Where symptoms go under cover, owing to positive transference, the patient has often established in fantasy an undisturbed and undisturbing, partially symbiotic position with the therapist. This situation needs to be taken into account when assessing cure or stability of remissions of physical symptoms. The establishment of a positive transference or a partially gratifying symbiotic relationship may make physical symptoms unnecessary as well as the primitive rage and guilt. This transference occurs especially when the patient has developed greater tolerance for identification with reduced primitive guilt and when the equation of identification with destruction of the object has been at least partly resolved.

Some determinant for patients' unconsciously holding onto symptoms and to disease of organs may be listed as follows:

1. Defense against awareness of primitive rage, guilt, depression, and sexual conflict.
2. Expiation and martyrdom out of guilt.
3. Secondary gain of maintaining control over key persons and arousing concern and guilt in them. Internally, this can be seen as unconsciously causing pain to the object symbolized in the organ as a form of revenge. In the latter case the symptom, as described by Sperling (1946) in cases of ulcerative colitis, often can be seen as a defense against a melancholic reaction.
4. Unconsciously maintaining the fantasy of keeping alive one who has died by reproducing his symptoms, thereby denying the loss and avoiding the pain of mourning.

5. The magical fantasy of freeing the object from disappointment and suffering by suffering oneself—out of love motivated by guilt arising from hostility. In the magical thinking that prevails, the magical fantasy of "me for you" is frequently observed.

An example here will illustrate item 5 above. A woman with colitis had spent many hours in therapy railing in anger at her mother and father and reveling in her sense of revenge for the treatment she had received in her earlier years. Her father had left the home when the patient was 4 years old. Her mother, left with two children and living in abject poverty, had become bitter, depressed, withdrawn, and probably psychotic. The patient herself had been living an isolated and unhappy life. Her colitis, long in remission, recurred in mild form at a point when she was making striking progress in her life emotionally and socially. Some time later, after years of separation, the patient went to spend a vacation with her mother, and about a week and a half after her return home, she exploded with a severe relapse that required hospitalization several weeks later, and ultimately colectomy.

She told how she had found her mother completely changed, happy, and with lots of friends. Her mother had told her she need not worry about her; rather, the patient should live her own life. "I felt an incredible rage toward my mother, but I could not express it for fear of spoiling her vacation. I wanted to tell her what a bloody asshole she had been." Later, describing her return home and the pain in her abdomen, she said, "I felt like Christ with a sword stuck in my belly. I am the absorber of all pain. When I met my mother and saw how she had changed, I felt I was out of a lifetime commitment. . . . I get angry at people who do nice things for me. I wanted them to do nice things for my mother. I've been engaged in a vendetta against the world to punish them for not helping my mother." About six months after the colectomy, she said, "I am enjoying myself. I feel it is immoral. I don't think I've said (although, indeed, she had before the operation) that I realized that I wanted to die to save my mother. When I woke up after the operation, I felt angry at the doctors. I felt they had taken away my pain and suffering." Much later she said, "I know that my suffering had nothing to do with the change in my mother's life." In this patient and through the effect on her bowel, to quote from a poem by James Joyce (1912), "Christ and Caesar were hand and glove." Magical thinking and beliefs are of great importance in sustaining physical symptoms.

RELAPSES

It is easy to understand that remissions based largely on transference responses leave the patient very vulnerable to relapses, particularly when the negative or excessively positive transference has been relatively untouched, and especially when the therapist deviates even slightly from his fantasied role.

Relapses that occur after long remissions and after substantial in-depth work are more complicated to explain. Resolution of primitive aggression and primitive guilt, either alone or combined with sexual conflict, pregenital and genital, can be a long and tedious process. These conflictual areas keep the individual vulnerable to expression, by physical symptoms, of separation and loss, actual or symbolic. A frequent example is seen when the patient is at a point of movement toward major change. This is often experienced unconsciously as a sense of loss of a part of one's self, carrying with it a fear of separation from the analyst by risking movement toward termination. There can then be a striking regressive fight against change expressed by a return of physical symptoms.

Anniversaries of severe traumatic experiences, of the loss of key persons by death, separation, or disillusionment and disappointment, are particularly to be observed as precipitants of relapses. These reactions reflect the degree to which internal separation from key persons and ambivalent identifications have not been achieved. Anniversary reactions accompanied by physical symptoms often provide further opportunity for resolution and development in the separation–individuation process. In the case of the woman who was enraged at me over the loss of her power to get angry, her relapse had a number of anniversary determinants, all converging simultaneously to evoke a massive reaction. After I drew her attention to the nature of these determinants, she recovered within a week. In over ten years since then, she has not had a relapse, and there has been marked progress in her life. This relapse could retrospectively be seen as indicating the imminence of her abandonment of her bitter resentment, primarily toward her mother, also toward her father, and toward her husband for his failure to live up to her fantasy of finding an idealized mother in him. It reflected, too, anger at me for my role in her making such significant moves in her life, thereby sustaining such narcissistic losses. She now showed a readiness to develop her life unencumbered by her reactions to earlier disappointments, to separate from me, and to give up the use of her bowel for expressive and defensive purposes and for secondary gain.

THE SIGNIFICANCE OF THE USE OF THE COUCH

As pointed out earlier, in cases where there is impairment of the capacity to differentiate between concrete and symbolic, and where narcissistic elements are strong, we can expect serious hazards not only from psychic reactions but also from somatic reactions. These reactions may occur where analysis is carried deeply too quickly, and especially when the couch is used without prior adequate preparation of the patient, although sometimes such preparation may not prevent them.

It is important to note here that using the couch, with the analyst removed from view, limits the ability of the senses and motor organs to maintain the integrity of the ego—especially the body image. The threat of destruction of the body image, induced by this sensorimotor deprivation and by the analyst's detachment, mobilizes with great intensity the processes at all levels by which individuation has taken place. Impassivity on the part of the analyst, rather than detachment, greatly aggravates the problem. The greater the opportunity for sensory perception through all sensory modalities, and for motility—either concretely or, especially, symbolically—and for response from the environment, the less the threat to the body ego and through it to the ego. The restrictions imposed by the classical analytic procedure create both a threat and a sense of loss that trigger the complex projection–introjection patterns of past and present relationships and their internal representations by which the ego and body ego have been established. This accounts in part for the intensity of the transference when the couch is used.

Vision is most important as a defense against the threat of separation, especially in individuals with impaired ego development. Such persons often require the concrete presence of key persons for the maintenance of their psychic and physical integrity, or at least the symbolic visualization of these persons made possible by the knowledge of their whereabouts and accessibility. Deprivation of visualization of the object intensifies the use of other sensory modalities, especially touch, together with arousal of oral fantasies, in an attempt to restore a sense of relatedness to objects. This in turn tends to intensify the sexualization of the transference in very infantile terms.

A man whose asthma had been relieved for a considerable time during vis-à-vis therapy had a recurrence of the asthma the moment he started to use the couch. As soon as he lay down, he complained: "I cannot see you." This led him to a great deal of clarification and understanding of his intense symbiotic dependency, and with this came relief from his asthma. Persons whose mastery over the processes of individuation has been seriously impaired, especially those in whom the fantasy of the external world as once part of themselves remains strong, often cannot tolerate well the experience of the couch in analysis, no matter how perceptive and skillful the analyst. The transference may become hard to manage, and the process of identification with the therapist is made very difficult. Such patients, as I indicated earlier, cannot tolerate an overly passive or overly detached attitude on the part of the analyst. Many psychosomatic cases fall into this category. The defense against such a threat is either severe exacerbation of physical symptoms or mobilization of primitive psychic activity, or both.

SUMMARY

This chapter by no means covers fully the issues involved in the psychoanalytic treatment of patients with psychosomatic illness, but I hope it conveys something of the complexity of cure by such treatment. Undoubtedly much of what has been said applies also to the understanding and treatment of a wide variety of psychological disturbances. One characteristic of psychosomatic cases which differentiates them from borderlines and psychotics, however, is their capacity for ready attachment and identification. This makes for quick, positive, and intense transference responses, even though the identification is often highly ambivalent and unstable and varies in its level of primitivity. This characteristic is especially important for short-term or limited goals in treatment, and even for the successful medical management by physicians.

Another major difference in psychosomatic cases is that a key form of expression, communication, and defense lies in bodily language. In addition, acuteness and exacerbation of physical symptoms often carry a different and more serious kind of threat to life, while relapses may lead to irreversible organ changes with physical disability. These aspects may affect significantly the character of countertransference, which may hamper analytic work. Negative countertransference may very easily develop as a result of idealization of the psychological approach or as a result of seduction of the therapist by analytically interesting and meaningful material. The therapist may thereby be blinded to the need to have the patient investigated medically and, if necessary, treated medically. Such countertransference plays into a patient's masochism. To quote one patient, "My illness is my wages of sin."

Even in the acute phases of physical illness, I believe that an analytic approach offers the best form of help for those who need and desire psychological help. The considerations I have outlined will determine how this approach may best be undertaken. When the goals of treatment are ambitious, "classical" analysis with the use of the couch may be the treatment of choice for some patients from the beginning and can be very effective. For other patients, the use of the couch may at first be unwise or unsafe; rather, a period of vis-à-vis psychoanalytic psychotherapy is required. This does not obviate the need for a consistent analytic attitude on the part of the therapist. In such cases, the first need is for progress in regard to the patient's capacity to tolerate separation and in the direction of some resolution and transformation of primitive rage and guilt, together with some resolution of narcissistic characteristics. After this has been accomplished, and when the patient has been able to retain an internalized image of the therapist, transition to the couch can be very constructive and rewarding.

Some patients who start with the use of the couch must later be treated in vis-à-vis therapy in order to help them master their primitive fantasies, especially transference fantasies. In some cases, one must be content with limited achievement — that is, limited to maintaining remissions and to moderate personality changes — especially if limited treatment is the wish of the patient or if danger from deep analysis can be predicted. Motivation for treatment imposed on the patient by the therapist is bound to have negative effects. My own preference is usually to start out with vis-à-vis psychoanalytic psychotherapy, and then, if desirable, to change to the use of the couch. When the goals of therapy are limited, often one must be content to deal to a large extent with derivatives of deep fantasies.

In both long-term and short-term treatment, one should proceed slowly towards one's goals. At first we may have to be content to deal with patients in terms of ego psychology and self-object differentiation and to try to translate instinctual strivings for the patient into such terms. However, I fully agree with Sperling (1946) and Wilson (1980; see Epilogue, this volume) that early interpretation should be made of primitive fantasies and instinctual strivings and also of impeding transference fantasies, negative or positive, when one senses a readiness and tolerance on the part of the patient. Even when the goals in treatment are limited, I feel that one should aim to help the patient achieve some measure of freedom from vulnerability and psychic pain. My own experience has been that even with sessions limited to once or twice a week, one can often help a patient to maintain very long-term remissions and achieve significant personality changes. Supportive treatment alone, on the other hand, tends to use techniques which reinforce and perpetuate the patient's vulnerability and give merely the illusion of freeing the patient.

REFERENCES

Daniels, G. E. (1940). Treatment of ulcerative colitis associated with hysterical depression. *Psychosomatic Medicine* 2:276-285.

Deutsch, F. (1940). *Social Service and Psychosomatic Medicine Newsletter, American Association of Psychiatric Social Workers* XI:1-9.

_____ (1947). Analysis of postural behavior. *Psychoanalytic Quarterly* 16:195-203.

_____ (1949). Thus speaks the body. Analysis of postural behavior. *Transactions of the New York Academy of Medicine* 12:58-62.

_____ (1958). Personal communication.

_____ (1959). Symbolization as a formative stage of the conversion process. In *On the Mysterious Leap from the Mind to the Body. A Workshop Study on the Theory of Conversion,* ed. F. Deutsch, pp. 75-97. New York: International Universities Press.

Joyce, James (1912). *Gas from a Burner: The Critical Writings of James Joyce,* ed. E. Mason and R. Ellmann. London: Faber, 1959. Quoted in D. Krause, *Sean O'Casey, the Man and his Work.* New York: Macmillan, 1960 and 1965.

Knapp, P. H., Mushatt, C., and Nemetz, S. J. (1966). Asthma, melancholia and death. I. Psychoanalytic considerations. *Psychosomatic Medicine* 17:114-133.

Knapp, P. H., Mushatt, C., Nemetz, S. J., Constantine, H. and Friedman, S. (1970). The context of reported asthma during psychoanalysis. *Psychosomatic Medicine* 32:167-188.

Mahler, M. S. (1968). *On Human Symbiosis and the Vicissitudes of Individuation.* Vol. I. New York: International Universities Press.

Murray, J. M. (1964). Narcissism and the ego ideal. *Journal of the American Psychoanalytic Association* 12:477-511.

Mushatt, C. (1954). Psychological aspects of non-specific ulcerative colitis. In *Recent Developments in Psychosomatic Medicine,* ed. E. D. Wittkower and R. A. Cleghorn. Philadelphia: Lippincott.

_____ (1959). Loss of sensory perception determining the choice of symptom. In *On the Mysterious Leap from the Mind to the Body. A Workshop Study on the Theory of Conversion,* ed. F. Deutsch, pp. 201–234. New York: International Universities Press.

_____ (1975). Mind–body–environment: toward understanding the impact of loss on psyche and soma. *Psychoanalytic Quarterly* 64:81–106.

Nemiah, J. C., Freyburger, H., and Sifneos, P. E. (1976). Alexithymia. A view of the psychosomatic process. In *Modern Trends in Psychosomatic Medicine,* vol. III, ed. O. Hill. London: Butterworth.

Solnit, A. L. (1979). Some applications of the theory of object constancy in childhood. Paper presented at the Joint Meeting of the Western New England Psychoanalytic Society and the Boston Psychoanalytic Society and Institute, Inc., October 20, 1979, Stockbridge, Mass.

Sperling, M. (1946). Psychoanalytic study of ulcerative colitis in children. *Psychoanalytic Quarterly* 15:302–329.

_____ (1967). Transference neurosis in patients with psychosomatic disorders. *Psychoanalytic Quarterly* 36:342–355.

_____ (1973). Conversion hysteria and conversion symptoms—a revision of classification and concepts. *Journal of the American Psychoanalytic Association* 21:745–771.

Weinberger, J. (1964). Triad of silence: silence, masochism, and depression. *International Journal of Psycho-Analysis* 45:304–308.

Wilson, C. P. (1980). The psychodynamic treatment of hospitalized anorexia nervosa patients. *Bulletin of the Psychoanalytic Association of New York* 15:5–7.

4

FAMILY PSYCHOPATHOLOGY

C. Philip Wilson, M.D.

My research and that of my colleagues (Karol 1980, Mintz 1980, Mintz and Wilson 1982, Wilson et al. 1983) has confirmed, refined, and expanded upon Sperling's finding (Sperling 1950a, 1951, 1952, 1953, 1955, 1957, 1959a,b,c, 1960a,b, 1973, 1974, 1978, 1983) that the predispositions for the development of the personality disorders, which are masked by psychosomatic disorders, are established in early childhood by a disturbance in the parent–child relationship.

In a number of psychosomatic families we have detailed (1) the psychoanalytic treatment of psychosomatic patients and the concurrent psychoanalysis of the mother, father, and siblings (Hogan et al. 1987); (2) the psychodynamic counseling of parents together or separately; (3) the psychoanalytic treatment of a parent, usually the mother; (4) the psychodynamic treatment of the mother and young child (Sperling 1978, 1983, Galenson 1987); (5) the analysis or analytic psychotherapy of the significant other and the siblings; (6) the unplanned, fortuitous development and/or clearing of psychosomatic symptoms in a significant other or a child in the course of the analysis of a psychosomatic patient or of a nonpsychosomatic neurotic patient (Wilson, Chapter 12);

(7) the supervision of professionals in the treatment of psychosomatic patients.

A psychosomatic personality disorder can be considered to be a specific pathological outcome of unresolved oedipal conflicts in patients whose childhood preoedipal relationship to the mother and/or the father prediposed them to this reaction under precipitating circumstances.

Whether oedipal or preoedipal conflicts predominate varies from one case to another and is reflected in the diagnosis. In many cases the psychosomatic personality disorder seems largely the result of preoedipal parent–child psychopathology rather than oedipal neurotic conflicts.

FAMILY PSYCHOLOGICAL PROFILE

We have investigated the family psychological profile in over four hundred psychosomatic families. There is a complex range of parental behaviors and complicated conflicts and identifications. Whatever genetic, constitutional factors there may be, they do not preclude psychoanalytic treatment. Some of our bulimic cases (Wilson 1985d) would have been diagnosed "endogenous depression"; however, they were analyzable. The parallel is with asthmatics, some of whom have a constitutional genetic predisposition. Such asthmatic patients can be successfully analyzed. After analysis they may still test positively for allergies, but they no longer experience asthmatic attacks in conflictual situations (Sperling 1978, Wilson 1968, 1980c, this volume, Chapter 12). In addition, we see anorexic families where the restrictor anorexic daughter has been unconsciously chosen for special attention by the mother, whereas the obese son has been neglected. In other families, such as that of the Gothic boy asthmatic (Wilson 1980c, and Chapter 13), the son has been unconsciously chosen, whereas the daughter has not been so controlled and is an acting-out adolescent. Of course, the same individual may develop a sequence of psychosomatic symptoms; for example, one woman came for migraine headaches that subsided in analysis but were replaced by symptoms of chronic ulcerative colitis. Nevertheless, the following parental attitudes and behaviors could be observed in the majority of families.

ACRONYM AND DESCRIPTION OF THE FAMILY PSYCHOLOGICAL PROFILE

Study of over 400 psychosomatic families revealed a parental psychological profile described by the acronym PRISES.[1] P = perfectionism, R = repression of emotions, I = infantilizing decision making for the psychosomatic-prone child, S = the organ system chosen because of unconscious parental conflicts for the development of psychosomatic symptoms, E = sexual and toilet exhibitionism whose significance is denied, S = the selection of one child for the development of psychosomatic symptoms because of unconscious parental conflicts.

Discussion of Components of the Acronym

1. **Perfectionism.** Most of the parents evidenced perfectionism. They emphasized good behavior and social conformity in their children. Many were physicians, educators, business leaders, religious leaders—pillars of society. Parental overconscientiousness was reflected in the exemplary childhood and adolescent developmental performance of the psychosomatic-prone child.

2. **Repression of emotions.** Repression of emotions was found in every family group; it was caused by the parents' hypermorality. Some parents kept such strict control over their emotions that they never quarreled in front of their children. Aggressive behavior in the children was not permitted, and aggression in general was denied. (For example, one father's military service for which he was decorated was disdained by the family.) Most families laughed at the father's assertive behavior and saw him as the "spoiler" in the sexual relationship; the mother was seen as a superior moral figure. The father's authority was diminished further by his busy schedule, which left him little time for his children. The fathers were frequently workaholics, who, however, hid their business and

---

[1]This profile is modeled on the one I described in over 100 families of anorexia nervosa patients (Wilson 1980a, 1980b, 1982, 1986a, Wilson et al. 1983). That profile was PRIDES: P = perfectionism, R = repression of emotions, I = infantilizing decision making for the anorexia-prone child, D = parental over-concern with dieting and fears of being fat, E = sexual and toilet exhibitionism, S = selection of one child for the development of anorexia nervosa.

professional success from their children. Although he might be president of a large corporation, the father would downplay and minimize his business successes and would himself defer to the mother as the superior moral authority.

3.   **Infantilizing decision making.** The parents' overconscientious perfectionism in these families resulted in infantilizing decision making and overcontrol of the children. In some of the families, fun for fun's sake was not allowed. Everything had to have a noble purpose; the major parental home activity might be intellectual discussion and scholarly reading. It was no surprise that the psychosomatic-prone children hated their long hours of compulsory study. (For example, the Gothic boy asthmatic's punishment for disobedience was to have mathematics read to him by his parents.) In therapy these patients find it difficult to become independent and mature and to rid themselves of the humiliating feeling that they are puppets whose strings are being pulled by Mother and Father. This conflict with the parents appears in the transference as a childlike inability to make decisions, accompanied by attempts to get the analyst to make decisions for them.

4.   **Organ-system choice.** The child's organ system has been selected for the development of psychosomatic symptoms because of repressed unconscious pregenital conflicts and fantasies of the parents, particularly the mother (M. Sperling, 1950a,b, 1951, 1952, 1953, 1955, 1957, 1959c, 1960a,b, 1970, 1973, 1974, 1978). These were, in ulcerative colitis, unconscious anal-phase conflicts and fantasies; in anorexia nervosa, fears of being fat and dieting; in asthma, conflicts and fantasies involving the lungs, air, and breathing; in headaches and migraine, conflicts and fantasies involving the head; in skin diseases, specific dermatologic oedipal and preoedipal conflicts and fantasies.

5.   **Exhibitionistic parental sexual and toilet behavior.** Exhibitionistic parental sexual and toilet behavior, whose significance was completely denied, was found in every family. Doors in these homes were not locked, and bedroom and toilet doors often were left open, facilitating the curious child's viewing of sexual relations and toilet functions. The children frequently witnessed parental sexual intercourse. Such experiences, coupled with parental hypermorality and prudishness, caused an inhibition in normal sexual development. One asthmatic boy slept

between his parents in their king-size bed until the age of 18, when a psychologist friend of the family told them that this sleeping arrangement was damaging the son's normal development. When the boy began sleeping in another room, his asthmatic attacks subsided but were replaced by acting-out behavior. The unconscious pregenital anal conflicts of an ulcerative colitis patient's mother and grandmother were expressed in their daily discussion of and examination of the daughter's bowel movements; the size, consistency, and color of the fecal product were connected by them with the patient's appearance and the state of her health.

6. **Unconscious selection of the child.** In these families there was an emotional selection of one child by the parents for the development of psychosomatic symptoms. This child was treated differently than the other children. Such a choice may result from (a) the carry-over of an unresolved emotional conflict from the parents' childhood; e.g., the infant may represent a hated parent or brother or sister (M. Sperling 1973); (b) an intense need to control the child, so that the child is treated almost as a part of the body of one parent (c) the psychological situation and emotional state of the parent(s) at the time of the child's birth; for example, the child may be infantilized because he or she is the last baby, or maybe over-cathected by a parent who has suffered a recent loss. An asthmatic patient, for example, had been the child of old age, born when his mother was 42 and his father 70. The last of four children, he was babied by his mother, in whose bedroom he slept until age 12, when he "broke the slats of his bed." One cause of his asthmatic wheezing was his identification with his elderly father, a semi-invalid suffering from chronic bronchitis and emphysema who slept in the room next to the mother.

Another example was the mother of an anorexic girl, who revealed in her analysis that she treated her anorexic second daughter "Y" very differently than her healthy older sister "S." "S" had been born in the United States very early in the marriage, when the relationship to the husband was healthy, and the mother gave "S" autonomy and independence. "Y," the anorexic daughter, had been born in the Far East, where the family had been sent on business. In the company compound where they lived in luxurious style, the mother deduced from his behavior an unpleasant aspect of her husband's history. When he had been out in the Far East traveling alone on business over the years, he had had casual sexual relationships with several company wives. Depressed and unhappy at his infidelity, she was contemplating divorce when "Y" was born. The mother decided to stay in the marriage and masochistically kept her unhappiness to herself. However, in an attempt to relieve her depression, she took "Y" as a love object and devoted herself totally to "Y" to the exclusion of her husband and others.

EXCEPTIONS TO THE FAMILY PSYCHOLOGICAL PROFILE

Hogan (1983a), in discussing anorexia nervosa, confirmed the difference in character structure of the restrictor and the bulimic anorexic but questioned the relevance of the family psychological profile in the eating disorders. He noted a restrictor anorexic who grew up with alcoholic parents. Sperling (1983) detailed the analysis of a restrictor anorexic whose mother was psychotic. I have also seen exceptions to this profile. One restrictor anorexic came from a family where the father, mother, and siblings were all obese. Another restrictor's family included a father who was an alcoholic gambler. I realize that the number of cases we have seen is limited and the complexities of early development are multiple. Moreover, in some families one child may be a restrictor, another bulimic. Nevertheless, in the great majority of cases the family psychological profile is applicable. In many adolescent cases, conjoint or individual therapy of the psychosomatic parents that focuses on aspects of the family psychological profile is essential for therapeutic success.

It remains for future research, particularly more analyses of the parents of these "exceptions" to determine whether the etiologic factor has been the parents' unconscious selection of a particular child to develop the predisposition for psychosomatic symptoms, or whether the "exception" evidences differences in genetic, constitutional endowment and/or differences in preverbal and early verbal psychological development.

Shengold (1978) defines "soul murder" as a person's "dramatic designation for a certain category of traumatic experiences, those instances of repetitive and chronic overstimulation alternating with emotional deprivation that are deliberately brought about by another individual" (p. 533). In discussing Shengold's work on this problem, I noted (1978b) that psychosomatic symptoms often mask "soul murder." I cited an anorexic patient's parents who forbade any expression of aggression. A routine discipline at mealtimes was face slapping. While Shengold traces the cause of "soul murder" in his patients to actual experiences of torture, seduction, and rape, in our studies of psychosomatic patients we have found only a few cases of aggressive and sexual physical abuse (incest and rape). Most often we found that somatization was caused by the repetitive impact of the parental attitudes and behavior that we describe in the psychological profile. There has been overparenting rather than under-parenting.

However, the hypermorality of the psychosomatic parents can lead to traumatic physical punishment under the guise of moral discipline. For example, the father of an adolescent boy with ulcerative colitis cried in my office, saying that he caused the son's colitis because he beat his son when he misbehaved, just the way his father had beaten him. While this was a psychodynamic oversimplification by the father, the beatings of the son were an important aspect of the father's total infantilizing control of his child. The degree of "soul murder" in a given case can limit the potential for analytic results. In such cases it is most important to persuade the parents to do conjoint therapy.

ALTERNATING PSYCHOSOMATIC SYMPTOMS IN THE SAME PATIENT

Alternating psychosomatic symptoms are an aspect of psychogenic equivalents, which are discussed in Chapter 2. Very complicated processes are involved in cases where a patient develops two different psychosomatic symptoms (Sperling 1978, 1983, 1985d, Wilson 1988b). In one case, the structure of the patient's psychosomatic personality disorder was established by typical parental perfectionism, repression of emotions, infantilizing decision making for the child, parental toilet and sexual exhibitionism, and the selection of this child for the development of psychosomatic symptoms because of unconscious conflicts of the parents, in this case because this was the last, the youngest, child. However, the choice of the organ system for the development of the first psychosomatic symptom, ulcerative colitis, was determined by the patient's identification with his father, whose obsessive–compulsive neurosis was manifested at home, particularly by his frequent and noisy passing of gas (farting). This anal behavior was unconsciously encouraged by the mother, who in response to her husband's farting would weakly remonstrate but then giggle or laugh. Any such behavior by the son, however, was strictly forbidden.

The symptoms of anorexia nervosa (restrictor fat phobia) that appeared when the ulcerative colitis symptoms cleared were determined largely by the patient's identification with his mother's fears of being fat and her preoccupation with dieting (i.e., with mother's fear-of-being-fat complex).

In two other cases asthma replaced bulimic anorexia nervosa. An important psychodynamic cause of the asthma was the internalization of aggressive and libidinal impulses and fantasies that had formerly been acted out in the starving, gorging, and vomiting.

CONSULTATION TECHNIQUE
IN PSYCHOANALYTIC CASES

It is important to understand the motivation, the source, and the method of referral for psychosomatic patients. Although some patients come because they are aware of emotional conflict, others are referred by their physicians because medical or surgical treatment has not effected a symptom cure. The source of referral is important: unless the internist (adult patients) or pediatrician (children) understands an analytic approach, a split transference between the medical and psychoanalytic specialists can block treatment.

Because most psychosomatic patients utilize extreme denial and are ambivalent about treatment, whoever pressures or brings the patient to consultation should be regarded as an auxiliary ego. In many cases, with adults as well as children, the parents bring the patient for consultation. These parents are usually highly motivated, well-meaning people who will do everything they can for their sick child. It is healthy for a child to grow up in a home where there are rules, limits, and a parental example of impulse control, responsibility, and ethical behavior; however, in their *over*conscientiousness the parents of psychosomatic patients overcontrol their children. The adolescent child and frequently the adult psychosomatic patient who evidences conflicts in separation–individuation is in a situation of realistic and neurotic dependence on the family, so that changes in the parents' behavior and attitudes can be crucial for therapeutic success. Parents may try to terminate treatment when the first strivings toward independence emerge, which may first be manifested by rebelliousness and acting out. Other adult psychosomatic patients may have transferred separation–individuation conflicts to the boy friend, girl friend, or spouse, so that the cooperation, understanding, and in some cases the therapy of the parent surrogate may be necessary.

With respect to their understanding that psychosomatic symptoms are emotionally caused, patients fall into three groups. One group have no idea that their symptoms have any connection with emotional conflict. The second group have some understanding that stress plays a part in the precipitating symptoms. The third, relatively small group are psychologically sophisticated and understand that conflicts cause or precipitate symptoms. The therapist should inform the patient that his or her symptoms are emotionally caused and acquaint the patient with the therapist's experience in the treatment of psychosomatic disorders. The fact that other patients have been cured of their symptoms by psychodynamic treatment should be emphasized. The analyst should proceed from a position of authority, thereby permitting the development of the intense pregenital relationship in which the therapist is a new and different object, besides being a transference object. Neither trial analysis nor having the patient consult a number of different analysts is advisable with these regressed ambivalent patients.

THE PROBLEM OF MEDICATION, SURGICAL INTERVENTION, AND CONJOINT THERAPIES

Most patients with psychosomatic symptoms have received many years of treatment with a variety of therapies, particularly medications, with at best a symptomatic improvement. They have been promised cures that were not forthcoming, and they are apt to be mistrustful of the analyst, a mistrust which should be interpreted early in therapy. Relative to this problem is an article by Bruch (1974) on the perils of behavior modification in the treatment of anorexia nervosa and my recent research (Wilson 1988a,b). With the patient's permission (or with the family's permission with children and adolescents), the analyst should discuss the case with other professionals who are treating the patient. In a psychosomatic crisis, the patient's life must be saved with whatever treatment is available. However, in such regressive cases there is a potential for an intense transference relationship, and psychological interpretation may be life-saving. Hogan and I explore this issue in depth in Chapters 2, 6, 13, and 15.[2]

The depression, anxiety, and phobias that underly psychosomatic symptoms are caused by multiple preoedipal and oedipal conflicts. A crucial goal of therapy is to strengthen the psychosomatic patient's ego so that they can face and tolerate both realistic and neurotic depression. Psychosomatic patients are obsessed with fantasies of remaining young forever and being free of any conflict, realistic, or neurotic. They do not want to grow up (Wilson et al. 1983). They deny the conflicts they manifest, like their dependency on their parents or parent surrogates. They vehemently deny the masochistic nature of their symptoms and their character structure. The aim of psychodynamic treatment is to analyze their defenses against experiencing painful emotions, particularly depressed feelings. It is an advance in therapy when they become depressed and cry. To relieve depression by medication prevents the analysis of this most important aspect of their neurosis.

Moreover, depending on their character structure, psychosomatic patients may act out feelings of resentment against authority figures (the analyst, medical specialists, nursing staff, parents, etc.) by not taking prescribed medication, or overdosing with the drug (Wilson 1985d).

Because of unresolved oral conflicts, psychosomatic patients believe in magical solutions to problems and are intolerant of delay, and are ambivalent about such a lengthy learning process as analytic therapy. The temporary removal of symptoms can result in premature termination of treatment.

The crucial therapeutic force is the transference neurosis. Patients must reexperience in the transference the dyadic relationship with the mother and understand depression and rage at not being able to control the therapist as they did the mother. Likewise, later in therapy, the triadic Oedipus complex emerges and can be analyzed in the transference neurosis. If the patient is on medication, the transference loses its intensity and the therapist's interpretations become diluted and intellectual.

---

[2]Patients with chronic psychosomatic symptoms, such as ulcerative colitis or asthma, usually continue on medication until analysis reveals to them the unconscious causes of their symptoms and motivates them to go off medication.

In those situations where the use of medication is necessary, that is, medical crisis, or when patients cannot be motivated for psychotherapy, in treatment stalemates, or where cost and therapist availability are problems, the use of drugs, surgery, or other treatments may be a trade-off with potentially disadvantageous consequences. Therapeutic stalemates can occur in chronic cases where there has been a long-term resistance to insight and change in analytic therapy.

While medical and/or surgical treatment in intractable cases may be necessary, we have found that, even in severely regressed states, knowledgeable interpretations have resolved the impasses. Before resorting to medication or surgery, one is well advised to try consultation and/or supervision. In cases seen in consultation and supervision, therapeutic impasses have been resolved by a deeper psychodynamic understanding, a review of the countertransference conflicts of the therapist, and an exploration of the often subtle treatment sabotage on the part of the parents, who frequently are unable to accept self-assertive behavior by the enmeshed patient. It must be kept in mind that medical or surgical treatment may ameliorate or clear a psychosomatic symptom (as in ulcerative colitis), but it cannot change the underlying impulsive, masochistic personality disorder. Postsurgical psychotherapy or analysis usually is of limited value because symptom relief vitiates the motivation for treatment.

With adolescents and children, it may be appropriate and possible to stop medications and other treatments relatively soon with the cooperation of the parents and other specialists. With adult patients, it is often necessary to form a therapeutic alliance before approaching the problem of weaning the patient from medication and other treatments. Some patients may continue medication for a long time until in analysis their ego's capacity to tolerate symptoms has matured. Asthmatics, for example, are often addicted to inhalers and medications (Mintz, Chapter 10 this volume). The transference, genetic, and symbolic meanings of different modalities of treatment have to be carefully explored and interpreted. For example, an asthmatic patient (the Warsaw Ghetto asthmatic, Chapter 13) long after his symptoms had cleared, took an inhaler with him like a fetish. Without it he felt anxious. It symbolized his mother and the analyst. One of its meanings was that the inhaler nozzle in his nostrils symbolized the nipple in his mouth. Likewise, ulcerative colitis patients are consciously anxious if there is not an available toilet nearby. Even though analysis may resolve ulcerative colitis symptoms, real progress has not been achieved unless this toilet anxiety has been resolved.

Another frequent symptom of psychosomatic patients is insomnia. They are often psychologically addicted to hypnotic drugs, an addiction which requires careful and thorough analysis. In the interview with the parents, the therapist should assess their capacity for psychological understanding. This will help the therapist decide whether they need psychotherapy concurrently with the patient. No matter what psychopathology the parents may exhibit, they should be asked to do psychotherapy themselves *only* for the sake of their sick child; otherwise, because they are perfectionistic and deny conflicts, they may become angry, refuse therapy, and obstruct treatment. Parents of adolescent patients should be forewarned that the child may soon become hostile and critical of the therapist and want to stop; the parents then will have to back up treatment. The therapist should take emergency calls from anxious parents and quiet their anxieties by interpretation. In some cases the therapist needs to explain carefully how and why his or her treatment differs from the patient's previous therapies.

TAKING A PSYCHOSOMATIC HISTORY

When taking a history in order to understand psychosomatic patients and their parents, questions about the nature and the development of the conscience (superego) are important. Questions about the family's religion, ethical and moral values, rules, regulations, and attitudes about social issues reveal cogent information. The therapist should try to find out about how rules and regulations were enforced. Enforcement in these families ranges from the subtle and terrifying threat of a total loss of approval and love to explosive physical punishment, such as slapping on the face and mouth or other beatings. For example, an asthmatic patient revealed in analysis her hatred of her father, who used to beat her severely for misbehavior and whose nickname for her was the equivalent of "little dog." Bear in mind that the psychological and physical discipline and punishment inflicted by psychosomatic parents is due to their perfectionism and hypermorality. Except for the parents of the obese, psychosomatic parents do not usually neglect their children; on the contrary, they overcontrol them.

Although the ego structure, diagnosis, and motivation for treatment vary from one case to another, all psychosomatic patients are very guilty people who tend to deny conflict and control emotions. They may withhold information and minimize their problems. The therapist should be aware that patients may not be giving straight answers about their object relations, their symptoms, and their sexual life but should not pressure them too much with further questions. They must be allowed to tell their story as it is. It may be only after months or even years of therapy that they will level with themselves and the therapist about their conflicts. Amnesia for childhood events is frequent in these patients.

Sometimes the psychosomatic patient may be silent and negativistic. The best approach is to interpret the need to control emotions and deny conflict. The therapist may decide, based on a knowledge of the patient's history, to detail the patient's problems to him. It is not wise to accept a patient who has severe psychosomatic symptoms for therapy shortly before vacation, because there is a serious risk that he may express his unconscious anger at the therapist by an exacerbation of symptoms. Adolescent psychosomatic patients should be told that they will be informed of any communications or conversations with the parents.

SITUATIONS INVOLVING
SEPARATION–INDIVIDUATION

In taking a history from the patient and the parents, the therapist should focus on situations that involve separation–individuation (Mahler 1972, Mahler and Furer 1968, Mahler et al. 1970). The first major separation is birth. Breast-feeding and weaning should be asked about in detail. Because of their overconscientiousness, many psychosomatic mothers have trouble dividing up their time. One anorexic mother worked as secretary to her general practitioner husband and could not relax for breast-feeding. The daughter was bottle-fed, and the mother's feedings were compulsive and pressured. In the daughter's later anorexic behavior, she took revenge on her parents by keeping them at the table endlessly watching her cut up food that she did not eat.

Bladder and bowel control, walking, and talking all involve separation–individuation. The birth and death of siblings and relatives, particularly the death of grandparents, involve profound separation conflicts. One asthmatic recalled in her analysis that her parents, when she was age 4, had denied her grandmother's death. She was not taken to her beloved grandmother's funeral but was told that "grandmother went to sleep."

The first school experience is also very important. Frequently there is a history of school phobia — in nursery school, kindergarten, or first grade. Any geographical moves of the family provoke separation–individuation conflicts. Because of the immaturity of their ego, psychosomatic-prone children usually do not adjust well to new schools and new friends. Each school graduation involves conflict. Frequently psychosomatic patients do well in high school but procrastinate on the major maturation step of graduating from college. It is important to inquire about all situations that involve separation from the family, such as sleep-overs, camp, and college. Could the patient handle things on his own, or did he telephone home often? Also, how did the parents handle the separation? Daily phone calls to and from the psychosomatic child away at college are common in the psychosomatic family.

The first love affair can provide very useful information; the nature of all the patient's object relations is important. Frequently psychosomatic patients will tell you that one or the other of their parents is their best friend and they are not close to their peers. Another conflict is illness in either the patient or his parents. Later in life the loss of a mate or a parent may be significant in precipitating an anxiety, which then may manifest itself in psychosomatic symptoms.

METHOD OF TREATMENT

The technique advocated is intensive psychotherapy or analysis of the psychosomatic patient with concurrent psychotherapy of parents, if necessary. For adolescent patients, a different therapist should treat the parents. If the same therapist treats both the parents and the adolescent patient, the adolescent patient will distrust the therapist, who becomes identified too closely with the judging parents. In some cases the mother, father, or both need intensive therapy to change their unhealthy relationship with the child. Where the patient refuses or resists treatment, preliminary therapy of the parents can often lead to a healthy motivation.

The technique of psychotherapy differs from one case to another.

Modified classical or traditional psychoanalytic treatment methods are often used. For example, in certain cases, even though the patient may be seen three or four times a week, the couch may not be used until late in therapy. If the only practical arrangement is psychotherapy, much can be accomplished in two sessions a week, although three sessions are better. It is useful therapeutically for patients who can do so to pay some part of the fee themselves.

SUMMARY

Psychoanalytic research with over four hundred psychosomatic families revealed a parental psychological profile that appears to be etiologic in establishing a personality disorder in the children that later manifests itself in psychosomatic symptoms. An acronym for this profile is PRISES. P = perfectionism. R = repression of emotions. I = infantilizing decision making for the psychosomatic-prone child. S = the choice of an organ system for the development of psychosomatic symptoms, which is determined by specific parental conflicts and fantasies. E = sexual and toilet exhibitionism whose significance is denied. S = the unconscious selection of a child for the development of psychosomatic symptoms because of unconscious parental conflicts. The technique of taking a psychosomatic history and the problem of medication and/or surgery were reviewed.

Exceptions to the family profile were cited and their possible causes reviewed. The psychodynamics of alternating psychosomatic symptoms in a patient were detailed. Consultation technique was presented with emphasis on the complications of a split transference with the medical specialist, and the importance of gaining the parents' or parental surrogates' cooperation and understanding so that the analyst can essentially be in charge of the treatment. Parents must agree to conjoint therapy or analysis, if necessary. The problems of medication, surgical intervention, and conjoint therapies were reviewed.

The technique of taking a psychosomatic history was detailed with emphasis on a careful exploration of the discipline in psychosomatic families, which, in some cases, may result in character pathology like that of "soul murder." Questions about situations involving separation-individuation when psychosomatic symptoms most often appear are particularly important. The method of treatment was briefly summarized.

REFERENCES

Bruch, H. (1974). Perils of behavior modification in the treatment of anorexia nervosa. *Journal of the American Medical Association* 230:1409–1422.

Freiman, G. V. (1983). Psychoanalysis: the case of Carol. In *Fear of Being Fat: The Treatment of Anorexia Nervosa and Bulimia,* rev. ed., ed. C. P. Wilson, C. C. Hogan, and I. L. Mintz, pp. 255–262. Northvale, NJ: Jason Aronson, 1985.

Freud, S. (1900). The interpretation of dreams. *Standard Edition* 2:557–560.

Galenson, E. (1987). Psychodynamic treatment of the mothers of anorexia infants. Personal communication, December 1, 1987.

Hogan, C. C. (1983a). Object relations. In *Fear of Being Fat: The Treatment of Anorexia Nervosa and Bulimia,* rev. ed., ed. C. P. Wilson, C. C. Hogan, and I. L. Mintz, pp. 129–149. Northvale, NJ: Jason Aronson, 1985.

―――― (1983b). Psychodynamics. In *Fear of Being Fat: The Treatment of Anorexia Nervosa and Bulimia,* rev. ed., ed. C. P. Wilson, C. C. Hogan, and I. L. Mintz, pp. 115–128. Northvale, NJ: Jason Aronson, 1985.

―――― (1983c). Technical problems in psychoanalytic treatment. In *Fear of Being Fat: The Treatment of Anorexia Nervosa and Bulimia,* rev. ed., ed. C. P. Wilson, C. C. Hogan, and I. L. Mintz, pp. 197–215. Northvale, NJ: Jason Aronson, 1985.

―――― (1983d). Transference. In *Fear of Being Fat: The Treatment of Anorexia Nervosa and Bulimia,* rev. ed., ed. C. P. Wilson, C. C. Hogan, and I. L. Mintz, pp. 153–168. Northvale, NJ: Jason Aronson, 1985.

Hogan, C. C., Mintz, I. L., and Wilson, C. P. (1987). The psychoanalytic treatment of the mother, father, and bulimic anorexic child. Psychosomatic Discussion Group of the American Psychoanalytic Association, C. P. Wilson and H. L. Rudominer, Chairmen, December 16, 1987.

Karol, C. (1980). The role of primal scene and masochism in asthma. *International Journal of Psychoanalytic Psychotherapy* 8:577–592.

Mahler, M. S. (1972). On the first three subphases of the separation–individuation process. *International Journal of Psycho-Analysis* 53:333–338.

Mahler, M. S., and Furer, M. (1968). *On Human Symbiosis and the Vicissitudes of Individuation.* New York: International Universities Press.

Mahler, M. S., Pine, F., and Bergman, A. (1970). The mother's reaction to her toddler's drive for individuation. In *Parenthood: Its Psychology and Psychopathology,* ed. E. J. Anthony and T. Benedek. Boston: Little, Brown.

Mintz, I. L. (1983a). An analytic approach to hospital and nursing care. In *Fear of Being Fat: The Treatment of Anorexia Nervosa and Bulimia,* rev. ed., ed. C. P. Wilson, C. C. Hogan, and I. L. Mintz, pp. 315–324. Northvale, NJ: Jason Aronson, 1985.

_____ (1983b). Anorexia nervosa and bulimia in males. In *Fear of Being Fat: The Treatment of Anorexia Nervosa and Bulimia*, rev. ed., ed. C. P. Wilson, C. C. Hogan, and I. L. Mintz, pp. 263–303. Northvale, NJ: Jason Aronson, 1985.

_____ (1983c). Psychoanalytic description: the clinical picture of anorexia nervosa and bulimia. In *Fear of Being Fat: The Treatment of Anorexia Nervosa and Bulimia*, rev. ed., ed. C. P. Wilson, C. C. Hogan, and I. L. Mintz, pp. 83–113. Northvale, NJ: Jason Aronson, 1985.

_____ (1983d). Psychoanalytic therapy of severe anorexia: the case of Jeanette. In *Fear of Being Fat: The Treatment of Anorexia Nervosa and Bulimia*, rev. ed., ed. C. P. Wilson, C. C. Hogan, and I. L. Mintz, pp. 217–244. Northvale, NJ: Jason Aronson, 1985.

_____ (1983e). The relationship between self-starvation and amenorrhea. In *Fear of Being Fat: The Treatment of Anorexia Nervosa and Bulimia*, rev. ed., ed. C. P. Wilson, C. C. Hogan, and I. L. Mintz, pp. 335–344. Northvale, NJ: Jason Aronson, 1985.

Sarnoff, C. A. (1983). Derivatives of latency. In *Fear of Being Fat: The Treatment of Anorexia Nervosa and Bulimia*, rev. ed., ed. C. P. Wilson, C. C. Hogan, and I. L. Mintz, pp. 327–334. Northvale, NJ: Jason Aronson, 1985.

Shengold, L. L. (1978). The problem of the soul murder. *Bulletin of the Psychoanalytic Association of New York* 23(1):8–10.

_____ (1979). Child abuse and deprivation: soul murder. *Journal of the American Psychoanalytic Association* 27:533–560.

Sperling, M. (1950a). Children's interpretation and reaction to the unconscious of their mothers. *International Journal of Psycho-Analysis* 31:1–6.

_____ (1950b). A contribution to the psychodynamics of depression in women. *Samiksa* 4:86–101.

_____ (1951). The neurotic child and his mother. *American Journal of Orthopsychiatry* 21:351–364.

_____ (1952). Psychotherapeutic techniques in psychosomatic medicine. *Specialized Techniques in Psychotherapy*, ed. G. Bychowski and J. Despert, pp. 279–301. New York: Basic Books.

_____ (1953). Food allergies and conversion hysteria. *Psychoanalytic Quarterly* 22:525–538.

_____ (1955). Psychosis and psychosomatic illness. *International Journal of Psycho-Analysis* 36:320–327.

_____ (1957). The psychoanalytic treatment of ulcerative colitis. *International Journal of Psycho-Analysis* 38:341–349.

_____ (1959a). Current concepts of ulcerative disease of the gastrointestinal tract. *New York State Journal of Medicine* 59:3800–3806.

_____ (1959b). Equivalents of depression in children. *Journal of Hillside Hospital* 8:138–148.

_____ (1959c). Psychiatric aspects of ulcerative colitis. *New York State Journal of Medicine* 59:3801–3806.

_____ (1960a). The psychoanalytic treatment of a case of chronic regional ileitis. *International Journal of Psycho-Analysis* 41:612–618.

_____ (1960b). Symposium on disturbances of the digestive tract II: Unconscious phantasy life and object-relationships in ulcerative colitis. *International Journal of Psycho-Analysis* 41:450–455.

_____ (1970). The clinical effects of parental neurosis on the child. In *Parenthood,* ed. E. Anthony and T. Benedek, pp. 539–569 Boston: Little, Brown.

_____ (1973). Conversion hysteria and conversion symptoms: a revision of classification and concepts. *Journal of the American Psychoanalytic Association* 21:772–787.

_____ (1974). *The Major Neuroses and Behavior Disorders in Children.* New York: Jason Aronson.

_____ (1978). Anorexia nervosa (part 4). In *Psychosomatic Disorders in Childhood,* ed. O. Sperling, pp. 129–173. New York: Jason Aronson.

_____ (1983). A reevaluation of classification, concepts, and treatment. In *Fear of Being Fat: The Treatment of Anorexia Nervosa and Bulimia,* rev. ed., ed. C. P. Wilson, C. C. Hogan, and I. L. Mintz, pp. 51–82. Northvale, NJ: Jason Aronson, 1985.

Sperling, O. (1978). The concept of psychosomatic disease. In *Psychosomatic Disorders in Childhood,* ed. O. Sperling, pp. 3–10. New York: Jason Aronson.

Welsh, H. D. (1983). Psychoanalytic therapy: the case of Martin. In *Fear of Being Fat: The Treatment of Anorexia Nervosa and Bulimia,* rev. ed., ed. C. P. Wilson, C. C. Hogan, and I. L. Mintz, pp. 305–314. Northvale, NJ: Jason Aronson, 1985.

Wilson, C. P. (1968). Psychosomatic asthma and acting out: a case of bronchial asthma that developed *de novo* in the terminal phase of analysis. *International Journal of Psycho-Analysis* 49:330–335.

_____ (1970). Theoretical and clinical considerations in the early phase of treatment of patients suffering from severe psychosomatic symptoms. *Bulletin of the Philadelphia Association of Psychoanalysis* 20:71–74.

_____ (1971). On the limits of the effectiveness of psychoanalysis: early ego and somatic disturbances. *Journal of the American Psychoanalytic Association* 19:552–564.

_____ (1973). The psychoanalytic treatment of hospitalized anorexia nervosa patients. Paper presented at the meeting of the Psychoanalytic Association of New York, November 19.

_____ (1974). The psychoanalysis of an adolescent anorexic girl. Discussion group on "Late adolescence." S. Ritvo, Chairman. Meeting of the American Psychoanalytic Association, December 12.

_____ (1977). Group discussion on "The parent–child relationship in anorexia nervosa." Regional Psychoanalytic Meeting, Grossinger's Hotel, October 20.

_____ (1978a). The psychoanalytic treatment of hospitalized anorexia nervosa patients. Panel discussion "Anorexia nervosa." *Bulletin of the Psychoanalytic Association of New York* 15:5–7.

_____ (1978b). Discussion of Shengold's paper, The problem of the soul murder. *Bulletin of the Psychoanalytic Association of New York* 23(1):9.

_____ (1980a). The family psychological profile of anorexia nervosa patients. *Journal of the Medical Society of New Jersey* 77:341–344.

_____ (1980b). On the fear of being fat in female psychology and anorexia nervosa. *Bulletin of the Psychoanalytic Association of New York* 17:8–9.

_____ (1980c). Parental overstimulation asthma. *International Journal of Psychoanalytic Psychotherapy* 8:601–621.

_____ (1980d). The psychodynamic treatment of a hospitalized anorexic patient. Discussion group on "Psychoanalytic considerations in patients with organic disease or major physical handicaps." P. Castelnuovo-Tedesco, Chairman. Meeting of the American Psychoanalytic Association, December 18.

_____ (1982). The fear of being fat and anorexia nervosa. *International Journal of Psychoanalytic Psychotherapy* 9:233–255.

_____ (1983a). The fear of being fat in female psychology. In *Fear of Being Fat: The Treatment of Anorexia Nervosa and Bulimia,* rev. ed., ed. C. P. Wilson, C. C. Hogan, and I. L. Mintz, pp. 9–27. Northvale, NJ: Jason Aronson, 1985.

_____ (1983b). The family psychological profile and its therapeutic implications. In *Fear of Being Fat: The Treatment of Anorexia Nervosa and Bulimia,* rev. ed., ed. C. P. Wilson, C. C. Hogan, and I. L. Mintz, pp. 29–47. Northvale, NJ: Jason Aronson, 1985.

_____ (1983c). Contrasts in the analysis of bulimic and abstaining anorexics. In *The Fear of Being Fat: The Treatment of Anorexia Nervosa and Bulimia,* rev. ed., ed. C. P. Wilson, C. C. Hogan, and I. L. Mintz, pp. 169–193. Northvale, NJ: Jason Aronson, 1985.

_____ (1983d). Dream interpretation. In *Fear of Being Fat: The Treatment of Anorexia Nervosa and Bulimia,* rev. ed., ed. C. P. Wilson, C. C. Hogan, and I. L. Mintz, pp. 245–254. Northvale, NJ: Jason Aronson, 1985.

_____ (1983e). Fat phobia as a diagnostic term to replace a medical misnomer: anorexia nervosa. Meeting of the American Academy of Child Psychiatry, October, San Francisco, California. Tapes 96 and 97 by Instant Replay, 760 S. 23rd St., Arlington, VA 22202.

_____ (1985a). Obesity: personality structure and psychoanalytic treatment.

Panel on "Compulsive eating: obesity and related phenomena." P. Castelnuovo-Tedesco, Chairman. Winter Meeting of the American Psychoanalytic Association, December 21, 1985, New York. Tapes obtainable from Teach Em, Inc., Pluribus Press, Inc., 160 East Illinois St., Chicago, IL: 60611.

_____ (1985b). The psychoanalytic treatment of anorexia nervosa and bulimia. Panel on "Anorexia nervosa and bulimia." P. Castelnuovo-Tedesco, Chairman. Spring Meeting of the American Psychoanalytic Association, Denver, May 19. Tapes obtainable from Teach Em, Inc., Pluribus Press, Inc., 160 East Illinois St., Chicago, IL 60611.

_____ (1985c). The treatment of bulimic depression. Paper presented at Grand Rounds, Department of Psychiatry, St. Luke's–Roosevelt Hospital Center, New York, March 6.

_____ (1985d). Psychodynamic and/or psychopharmacologic treatment of bulimic anorexia nervosa. In *Fear of Being Fat: The Treatment of Anorexia Nervosa and Bulimia,* rev. ed., ed. C. P. Wilson, C. C. Hogan, and I. L. Mintz, pp. 345–362. Northvale, NJ: Jason Aronson.

_____ (1986a). The psychoanalytic psychotherapy of bulimic anorexia nervosa. In *Adolescent Psychiatry,* ed. S. Feinstein, pp. 274–314. Chicago: University of Chicago Press.

_____ (1986b). A discussion of F. Levin's paper, Bulimia as a masturbatory equivalent. *The Jefferson Journal of Psychiatry* 3:24–35 (1985) and 4:77–84 (1986).

_____ (1986c). Letter in response to J. M. Jonas's paper, The biological basis and treatment of bulimia. *The Jefferson Journal of Psychiatry* 4:78–82 and 4:83–85.

_____ (1988a). Psychoanalytic treatment of anorexia nervosa and bulimia. In *The Eating Disorders,* ed. B. J. Blinder, B. F. Chaitin, and R. Goldstein. Jamaica, NY: S. P. Medical and Scientific Books.

_____ (1988b). Bulimic equivalents. In *Bulimia: Psychoanalytic Theory and Treatment,* ed. H. Schwartz, pp. 475–503. New York: International Universities Press.

Wilson, C. P., Hogan, C. G., and Mintz, I. L. (1983). *Fear of Being Fat: The Treatment of Anorexia Nervosa and Bulimia.* Rev. ed. Northvale, NJ: Jason Aronson, 1985.

_____ (1987). Discussion group of the American Psychoanalytic Association. Chairmen, C. P. Wilson and H. L. Rudominer. New York, December 16, 1987.

Wilson, C. P., and Mintz, I. L. (1982). Abstaining and bulimic anorexia: two sides of the same coin. *Primary Care* 9:459–472.

5

EARLY PSYCHIC STRESS AND PSYCHOSOMATIC DISEASE

Charles A. Sarnoff, M.D.

SYMBOLIC PROCESSES IN PSYCHOSOMATIC SYMPTOMS

The idea of a source of psychosomatic symptomatology in recent trauma is not new. Simpson (1972) reveals to us that as early as the time of the New Kingdom in ancient Egypt, there was acceptance of the idea that emotions could produce physical illness. The following poem illustrates this well.

> Seven days have passed, and I've not
> seen my lady love;
> a sickness has shot through me.
> I have become sluggish,
> I have forgotten my own body.
>
> If the best surgeons come to me,
> my heart will not be comforted with
> their remedies.

> And the prescription sellers, there's no
> help through them;
> my sickness will not be cut out.

> Telling me "she's come" is what will
> bring me back to life.

In spite of this long history of psychosomatic awareness, psychoso-maticians cannot yet agree on the mechanism that translates emotions into bodily changes. Descriptive phrases such as "the magical leap" fail as explanations. This chapter will explain the symbolic processes involved in the production of psychosomatic phenomena. The basic idea is that the type of symptom produced relates to the cognitive level at which the symbolizing function was operating at the stage of early trauma or fantasy to which the patient has regressed in response to current trauma.

THE MEANING OF "PSYCHOSOMATIC"

The term or category *psychosomatic* refers to a cluster of symptoms deemed to be alike on the basis of a single characteristic, namely, they are physical symptoms having psychological roots. It covers a protean group of psychic phenomena having in common the use of the soma to express a memory that serves for the mastery of a past or recent trauma. Because a single word has been deemed adequate to represent a multifaceted concept, a difficulty has occurred in that the concept itself has come to be considered unitary. It would be better if one were to set aside this unitary concept in favor of recognizing the multiplicity of intrinsic clinical characteristics that make up the easily differentiated states, or subcate-gories, grouped under the general term *psychosomatic*. The key to doing so is to understand the intrinsic nature of each state.

The intrinsic explanatory and differentiating characteristics of the subcategories are a variety of complex mental events that are enacted by the symbolizing function. Different levels of regression are accompanied by different types of symbolization. Different types of symbolization produce different types of symptoms.

Like blind men feeling an elephant, today's investigators disagree on the nature of psychosomatic symptoms and the therapeutic approaches indicated, since each handles a different part of the beast. What they need are theoretical-clinical tools for the accurate differentiation and description of the symbolic characteristics found in "psychological somatic" symptoms.

EARLY ATTEMPTS AT A DYNAMIC EXPLANATION

Sarnoff (1957) attempted a differentiation into "somatic preoccupations, somatic anxiety equivalents, hysterical conversion symptoms, and true psychosomatic illnesses" (p. 79). This seemingly useful nosology does not provide sufficiently subtle differentiations for psychoanalytic investigators, since it does not include the various possibilities introduced by the developmental topographic dimension. As Reiser (1966) has stated, "Consideration of the topographic dimension of altered level of consciousness may aid in understanding these reactions" (p. 571).

Theories of psychosomatic disease usually attempt to formulate dynamics for this group of varied units as a single whole. This results in the exclusion of alternatives. Dynamics derived from a few cases of a single entity may be generalized to apply to the total psychological somatic complex of symptoms.

For instance, it has been proposed that psychosomatic conditions are really *somatopsychic,* since patients have been observed to develop anxiety in relation to their physical symptoms and then perpetuate them. Within this theoretical framework, treatment of all psychosomatic symptoms requires that one deal with the anxiety that is secondary to the symptom. Renaming the entire group of conditions to conform to the findings of a single subunit, however, does not change the intrinsic differentiated nature of the symbolizing function that is at work in forming the individual and quite different entities that make up the psychosomatic group.

An example of such a generalization of a parochial observation is found in the work of Schur (1955), who extended his findings in skin lesions to somatization in general. He postulated a " 'psychosomatic' phase of development" (p. 126) to which one regresses when "the ego loses the capacity of secondary process thinking . . . uses unneutralized energy and desomatization fails" (p. 126). "There seems to be a parallel between the prevalence of primary process thinking, the failure of neutralization, and the resomatization of reactions" (p. 133). "In the condition leading to the first eruption or the recurrence of an eruption after a prolonged interval, we can see a regression to the precursors of thought, affect, instinctual drives and defensive action—expressed exclusively on the somatic level" (p. 143).

Within Schur's theoretical context, treatment results from

> anything counteracting . . . regressive reactions which accompany
> affects and instinctual drives. . . . As the analysis proceeds in the
> uncovering of unconscious conflicts, the predominance of primary-
> process thinking recedes and simultaneously patients who used to
> think, feel, and act with their skin, learn to use normal channels of
> expression (pp. 160–161).

It should be noted that Schur's concepts of regression to a thought precursor, utilizing the patient's own skin as an expression of conflict, is very much in keeping with one of the mechanisms described in the present paper.

Schur's concept cannot be generalized to all conditions called psychosomatic, since he considered only one possible point at which regression would stop. There are many possible stopping points on the paradigmatic developmental lines that provide the genetic patterns for the regressions that produce somatic symptoms of psychic origin. (See below; the phases of direct representation and concrete symbols can relate to Schur's theory.) Such simplification of the dynamics of the psychosomatic concept excludes alternative possibilities. An example is Schur's explanation that "awareness of danger" with reactive regression to a psychosomatic phase is the dynamic of psychosomatic disorders (p. 125). Although his hypothesis is undoubtedly correct for some skin lesions, two important alternatives suggested by Freud are to be considered in creating a general theory to explain ills designated psychosomatic.

THE ORIGIN OF THE SYMBOLS USED DURING PSYCHOSOMATIC SYMPTOM FORMATION

Freud (1939) suggested that psychological symptoms can be produced when the repressed finds its way to consciousness "if at any time in recent experience impressions or experiences occur which resemble the repressed so closely that they are able to awaken it. . . . [W]hat has hitherto been repressed [does not] enter consciousness smoothly and unaltered, it must put up with distortions. . ." (p. 95).

The first alternative is that danger has content in the form of core fantasies specific for each person. These core fantasies may contribute to the formation of some illnesses designated as psychosomatic. The second alternative is that the distortion of the core fantasy may occur through one of a multitude of symbolic forms. One possibility is that, as Schur suggests, regressive symbolization will proceed to a point where primitive somatic expression takes place. However, symbolization of core fantasies through somatic channels may also occur at a higher level of sophistication, including psychoanalytic symbols representing content or affect.

By way of illustration of such alternatives, we may quote M. Sperling (1968), who tells us that "the psychosomatic patient . . . act[s] out . . . impulses, wishes and fantasies internally in a variety of somatic symptoms (p. 252)." In essence, then, a psychosomatic symptom can represent a symbolic acting out of a fantasy, with the organs of the body serving as the protagonists in a world encompassed by the body's boundaries.

The stages through which the system consciousness passes during its ontogenesis (see Sarnoff 1976, Appendix A) may, in part, provide the basis for the intrinsic characteristics of symbol formation to be used in the differentiation of conditions called psychosomatic.

Psychosomatic symptoms are based upon symbolizations using cognitive skills derived from multiple genetic roots. They represent the result of regressions along both the ontogenesis of the system consciousness and the march of psychic representations of self from the body ego to reality objects. Thus are formed parallel developmental lines during the ontogenesis of the symbols that are the basis for psychosomatic disorders. Each psychosomatic symptom should be understood according to the stage of regression reached along both of the developmental lines that produce it.

THE ONTOGENESIS OF THE SYSTEM CONSCIOUSNESS

The system consciousness develops during the first twenty-six months of life. This ontogenesis contributes to the development of both primary process and secondary process thinking.

The system consciousness has three stages.

■ **The primal system consciousness** dominates during the first fourteen months of life. It consists of "a sense organ for perceptions alone" (Freud 1900, p. 600).

■ **The abstract system consciousness** dominates during the period encompassing fifteen to twenty-six months. It consists of the ability to be aware of organized memories of visual and verbal percepts. Reflective awareness is possible. Thought processes developed from this ability can attract consciousness. Abstract relationships between objects that can generate affects attract consciousness and provide for the ability to sustain anxiety and discomfort.

■ **The mature system consciousness** begins at twenty-six months. It is a concomitant of the maturational development of the mechanism of repression. The content of consciousness excludes thoughts and associations that have a potential for producing high levels of anxiety. At this stage in the ontogenesis of consciousness, psychoanalytic symbols are produced that support repression.

THE SOMATIC MARCH OF SYMBOLS

Awareness gradually expands about the self and beyond the self. Each new awareness is accompanied by a tendency to appreciate the new thing or experience in terms of that which was already known. At first there is discomfort. Then there are body products or parts that can be linked to discomfort. Then there are people who are understood in terms of the internal experiences. Through these links symbolic prototypes can be developed, and later symbols can be formed.[1]

This phenomenon was richly described in the early psychoanalytic literature, although at no one place in its entirety. A full picture can be gathered from a combination of extracts. Ferenczi (1912) stated that "bodily organs (principally the genital ones) can be represented not only by objects of the outer world, but also by other organs of the body. In all probability, this is even the more primary kind of symbol creation" (p.

---

[1]Sand and stone symbols are examples of protosymbols (Chapter 7).

275). Ferenczi here presents the outline of a developmental series. In symbolization, first bodily organs (i.e., genital ones) are represented by other organs of the body, then later these bodily organs are represented by the outer world. Klein (1930) describes a phase in childhood during-which aggression felt toward the mother creates anxiety: "Since the child wishes to destroy the organs, penis, vagaina, breasts that stand for the objects, he conceives a dread for the latter. This anxiety contributes to make him equate these organs in question with other things . . . which form the basis of . . . symbolism" (p. 24).

Jones (1916) takes the developmental line a step further when he says that "all symbols represent ideas of the self and the immediate blood relatives" (p. 102). "The self comprises the whole body or any separate part of it" (p. 103).

Using these historical references as a base, we can now outline the march of objects used during the ontogenesis of symbols. It should be noted that this provides us with the second paradigmatic line for the understanding of manifestations of symbol formation, including those with regressive characteristics.

1. The first step in the line of march is that primitive part of self—*felt need*—an urge for discharge without an object. Perceptual cathexes alerted by these needs cathect the self. A presymbolic self–self stage of object relations exists at this point. The self–self stage is seen clinically in infantile autism and in malignant depression.

2. The second step is manifested in the articulation and discharge of the felt need through an undifferentiated object consisting of the primitive self-world continuum. This stage could be called the self–self-world stage.

3. The third step is the focusing of this activity on those organs of the body whose sensory representations in the growing memory systems of the child provide them with psychic representation. (It should be noted that the vast majority of psychosomatic symptoms involve organs which have psychic representations, functions that can be felt, and positions at the interface of the body and the outside world. Psychosomatic ills of the ligament of Treitz or the space of Retzias rarely appear.) The somatic memory traces established during this phase provide the templates that affect later psychophysiological responses during regression that produce psychological somatic manifestations. Mahler (1969) has described some of the pathogenetic phenomena that occur in early childhood (the

symbiotic phase) that participate in this setting of the stage for later somatic psychopathology. She says, "Whenever organismic distress occurs, the mothering partner is called upon as the major contributor to the maintenance of the infant's homeostasis. Otherwise, neurobiologic patterning processes are thrown out of kilter, and somatic memory traces are set at this time" (p. 13). This is a phase which prepares the way for the fourth step.

4. The fourth step is the utilization of these psychic representations of body organs or affects (organized, recognizable separations) as objects to substitute symbolically for other organs or affects, in the gratification, or defense against the gratification, of needs. This can be called the self–organ/affect stage.

5. The fifth step is the shift to the use of elements (loved ones) in the object world, once differentiation has occurred, as symbolic representations of the organ. This can be called the self–outside stage.

6. The sixth step is the substitution of displaced objects as symbols of the loved objects. This can be called the later self–object stage and does not concern us here. It is important in phobia formation.

Regression along this developmental line was postulated by Ferenczi (1912) when he stated, "The symbolic identification of external objects with bodily organs makes it possible to find again . . . *all the wished for objects of the world in the individual's body*" (p. 275).

SPECIFIC CLINICAL ENTITIES

Table 5.1 (p. 95) illustrates the disparate nature of the regressions accomplished in the production of somatic symptoms of psychological origin. Up to this point, we have traced the two developmental lines. They are represented in the vertical and horizontal projections. The clinical conditions with which we are about to deal are examples of the products of regressions of the symbolizing function of the ego, characterized by varying degrees of weakness in repression of content and affect and varying degrees of inward turning as a result of regression during the search for mastery through a substitute object.

Somatopsychic Disorders

Somatopsychic disorders (see Step 2, Table 5.1) are products of the awareness of organ change. These are clinical responses to the presence of physical discomfort derived from pathology that is of somatic origin. These discomforts are interpreted secondarily to be life threatening or potentially castrative. Freud (1914) summed up the libido distribution in this state when he quoted the line, "Concentrated is his soul in his jaw tooth's aching hole" (p. 39). In the production of this psychic state, interpretation of what is real, seen at the level of self–organ awareness, is elaborated into the context of a preexisting fear fantasy. A typical case history follows:

Mr. T. E. was a 38-year-old, married architect. He developed severe head-aches, oppressive feelings in his chest, pain in his chest, and an awareness of his heartbeat. A similar condition was reported in six of his wife's co-workers. All seven were seen by an internist, who diagnosed the condition as pericar-ditis on the basis of electrocardiographic changes reflecting subpericardial myositis. The intensity of the symptomatology caused great anxiety in Mr. E., who became convinced that he would die during one of the attacks.

When seen psychiatrically, it was noted that he had a history of repeated neurotic depressive reactions whenever a family member became ill and an unresolved symbiotic attachment to his mother.

(We have limited this case presentation to what is essential to our needs: the subject's development of anxiety in response to his perception of physical illness in himself.)

Somatic Anxiety Equivalents

Somatic anxiety equivalents (see Step 1, Table 5.1) are examples of affect expressed in hyperreactivity of normal physiology. They are clinically characterized by the presence of strong somatic responses in which one aspect of the total physiological anxiety reaction is predominant. There is a direct somatic expression of affect. The following was observed by the author:

There is a waterside farm situated fifty miles up river from Iquitos on the Peruvian Amazon. There, small wild monkeys with large eyes are tied to the house poles. They are kept thus as a ready source of fresh meat. When approached, they screech and defecate. Thus is revealed the nature of their terror.

The specific response—hyperventilation, diarrhea, tachycardia, trembling—may be consistent for a given individual, and familial patterns are not unknown. A typical case history follows:

Mr. A. E. C. was a 23-year-old medical student faced with a difficult examination, upon the outcome of which his future in medicine hinged. Upon entering the building in which he was to take the examination, he developed abdominal cramps and diarrhea. He was able to take the examination successfully.

The direct expression of affect through somatic channels may be a manifestation of more complex levels of development. The description provided here requires only a quite primitive personality organization, including the direct representation of affect characteristic of the primal system consciousness; there is no requirement of self–organ differentiation. At its most primitive, this is a self–self manifestation.

Somatic Anxiety Equivalents Used for Secondary Gain

Awareness of the connection between the anxiety state and the anxiety equivalent symptom (see Step 5, Table 5.1) produces a psychological state related to the perceptual organization of the abstract system consciousness. The groundwork is laid for the establishment of an anxiety equivalent as a means of communicating one's discomfort to others. It may become a symbolic linkage upon which a true psychoanalytic symbol can later be developed. A level of regression at which the self–organ/affect step predominates and the abstract system consciousness is functional can produce somatic anxiety equivalents for seconary gain. This can occur when this awareness is used to communicate the affect to another (see Table 5.1, Step 3). The following case illustrates this:

Master J. J. was a boy who lived in a serene home with an understanding mother, a quiet father, and a 9-year-old sister. At age 4 the boy had had an episode of diarrhea, accompanied by fever and abdominal cramps. One day, when he was 5, the father and the children returned home late for dinner. The mother grew angry and shouted. The child grabbed his stomach and began to complain of pain. He could not communicate his fears directly. When the father tried to comfort him, the child turned toward the mother. The child was expressing his anxiety through a symptom known to attract the mother's compassion. He was relating to an "outside object," though it appeared that he had regressed to the cathexis of a part of himself. The nature of his condition can be summed up by the fact that the symptom cleared when he was finally able to verbalize his concern in the words, "Are we a happy family again?" The symptom, an anxiety equivalent, was used as a communication reflecting a level of self–outside object relations.

Hypochondriasis

Hypochondriasis (see Step 3, Table 5.1) refers to the use of physical symptoms to deflect one's attention cathexes from external stress. It is clinically characterized by the presence of marked concern with bodily organs and functions in the absence of comparable severity in physical symptomatology. No psychoanalytic symbolization is present, although there often has been a difficulty with object relationships or even a true phobia at the self–object level. From these the individual has regressed to the comfort of complaining about a hypochondriacal symptom that withdraws him from mature object relations and the situation in which the manifest phobia is grounded. This condition is supported by a cognitive constellation including regression to a prepsychoanalytic symbol, self–object orientation.

Mr. E. R. was a 46-year-old, childless, former storekeeper who lived with his wife and sister. When he came for treatment, he was unemployed, although he had an excellent past work history.

The cause of his referral was an incapacitating heart condition manifested in difficult breathing, a pressing feeling on the chest, pain, and fear of death. No objective findings were detected by an internist. He was sent for psychiatric evaluation and treatment. During the treatment hours, the patient's attention was noted to be directed toward his heart whenever his life situation was discussed. The heart symptoms cleared up after he was able to work through recent traumatic events. He was a small man, who had been robbed, trussed up, and left unattended for hours in the back of his store. He developed a fear of going into the street which he could not explain.

The analysis of the phobia revealed an unconscious fantasy of seeing two people fighting, one of whom would leave the fight to come over to strike him. This fantasy he could relate to childhood fears of his father, who often threatened him during fights with his mother.

Organ Changes of Psychological Origin without Psychoanalytic Symbolization

Organ changes expressing conflict, anxiety, and affect in the absence of psychoanalytic symbolization (see Step 4, Table 5.1) are manifested in syncretic anxiety equivalents, direct somatizations (Schur 1955), infantile eczema, and nocturnal anxiety episodes at age 22 months. This condition is supported by a cognitive constellation including regression to a prepsychoanalytic symbol, self–organ orientation. It is clinically characterized by the presence of physical discomforts associated with signs of specific physical changes either in the form of tissue damage, muscular contractions, autonomic changes, or shifts of fluids within the body.

Spitz (1965) provides a clinical example. He described a population at high risk for infantile eczema. Characteristically, this condition appeared during the second half of the first year of life and tended to disappear between the twelfth and fifteenth month. The lesions consisted of weeping and exfoliation favoring skin folds, localized on the flexor side (axillary, inguinal, popliteal, etc.). The children were found to differ from unaffected youngsters in their cutaneous reflexes, evidence of an increased readiness of response of the skin (an innate factor), and in that the incidence of eight months' anxiety was markedly below (15 percent vs. 85 percent) the incidence in the control group.

Spitz related this symptom to a disturbance in object relations, which in turn was related to characteristics of the mothers. They were found to have "unusually large amounts of unconscious repressed hostility . . ." (p. 229), and "they did not like to touch their children" (p. 230). In effect, the children were systematically deprived of cutaneous contact. Unable to use normal means of locomotion because of their age and unable to find normal gratifications of their *felt need* for object relations from the mother, "It is as if the children cathected the cutaneous covering . . . with increased libidinal quanta" (p. 240). Spitz hypothesizes that the child provides himself with the cutaneous stimulation that is not forthcoming from the environment.

TABLE 5.1. Fixation Levels of Regression along the Ferenczi Developmental Line and the Line of the System Consciousness

March of Objects	COGNITIVE PERCEPTUAL ORGANIZATION OF CONSCIOUSNESS		
	Primal System	Abstract System	Mature System
	Phase during which psychoanalytic content symbols are not available		Phase of psychoanalytic symbolization of content and affect
	Direct Representation	Concrete Symbols	
Self–Self Steps 1 and 2*	1. Affect expressed in hyperreactivity of normal physiology—somatic anxiety equivalent		
Self–Organ Self–Affect	2. Awareness of organ changes—somatopsychic disorders		6. Organs used as psychoanalytic symbols to express affect-laden fantasy content Pregenital phase: Psychosomatic (pregenital conversion), e.g., ulcerative colitis
Steps 3 and 4	3. Use of physical symptoms to draw attention from external stress—hypochondriasis 4. Organ changes expressing anxiety and affect Infantile Eczema Pavlov's Dog	Anxiety episode at 22 months	Genital phase: Conversion hysteria, Hysterical paralysis
Self–Outside Step 5		5. Affect expressed in hyperreactivity of normal physiology— somatic anxiety equivalent for secondary gains and communication	Phobias

*See text

This extract provides clinical proof of the existence of somatic signs of psychological origin during the developmental period when the primal system consciousness holds sway. Spitz points to the self–outside potentials of the psyche of the child, but demonstrates a failure to achieve this level and an expression of the self–organ phase manifested in the eczema.

A supporting phenomenon is described by Spitz (1965) from the work of Pavlov. In the establishment of a conditioned reflex, dogs were required to differentiate between stimuli applied within a given perimeter of the dog's thigh. The points were brought closer and closer together, "thus forcing the dog to perform an increasingly difficult task" (p. 235). Most of the dogs in the experiment "developed an 'experimental neurosis'. " Some dogs "when discrimination became impossible . . . developed eczema in the perimeter of the electrical stimulation." This example, in a subhominid species, of biological capability for the development of somatic signs as the result of psychological inputs is pertinent to our work. The existence of self–organ cathexes in the context of a primal system consciousness is within the realm of possibility for the animal psyche (see above—differentiation of man and beast). It is also within the realm of the psychic states to which an adult may regress. The self–organ cathectic organization for the expression of drives, which in turn is based upon the self–organ perceptual organization (i.e., state of development of psychic representations of organs as possible objects— see Step 4) can seek expression of drives through each of the stages of organization of the perceptual system's consciousness.

A person can regress to the combined self–organ/primal system consciousness and develop skin lesions such as Schur described, or the person can regress to the point where a fantasy is expressed accompanied by anxiety and somatic symptoms with awareness of the affects and conflicts expressed in the symptoms. Crying and paroxysmal tachycardia are examples of this. Sarnoff (1970), Sperling (1952), and Wulff (1928) described cases in which anxiety, somatic symptoms, and sleep disturbances characterized the nonpsychotic psychopathology of early childhood, prior to the development of the capacity for repression of the link between the symbol and what is symbolized.

Sarnoff (1970) and Sperling (1952), writing on the development of phobias, reported that a move to the phase of psychoanalytic symbols and self–outside cathexes accompanied the disappearance of somatization.

Organs Used as Psychoanalytic Symbols to Express Affect and Fantasy

Symptomatology based upon psychoanalytic symbol formation can represent affects (anxiety, guilt, hostility) as well as fantasy contents (see Step 6, Table 5.1). Both can be displaced onto countercathectic substitutes. The symbolic linkages from which the psychoanalytic symbols—which serve as countercathexes—are formed, are derived from two sources, external and internal. Symbols using external referents are the classical psychoanalytic ones, such as those found in hysteria, delusions, obsessions, and phobias. Symbols using internal referents are not always easily recognized as symbols, although at times one hears them referred to as protosymbols. When a part of the body can function as a symbol of another organ, or of a repressed affect, or of the pain of an unresolvable or unrealizable relationship with an object in reality, or an attempt to resolve it, then a psychosomatic disorder requiring the use of psychoanalysis is present.

Manifest contents serve to represent latent contents. Affects and organs serve to represent latent affects. The relationship between the latent affects or fantasy contents, and those organs, affects, and contents in which they are manifested symbolically, disappears from conscious awareness. When this representation can be accomplished solely through the use of self-to-outside cathexes, with new symbolic objects substituted for the primary content of the fantasy, neurotic symptoms (i.e., phobias) result. A large displacement masks meaning and diminishes the affective valence of the latent content to the point that the quality that attracts consciousness is lost. Thus the latent content is repressed. When, rather than outside objects, the body and bodily feelings are used to symbolize latent content, the affects remain strong, and affects as symbols of other affects such as depression or anger become a means of expression of drives.

Attention cathexes directed toward body organs can be used as psychoanalytic affect symbols for latent affects. For instance, fluid extravasations (i.e., urticaria) can be used to express, unknown to the patient, unconscious hostility and weeping.

A psychoanalytic affect symbol is formed from the displacement of cathexes from one affect to another affect, an organ, or an external object. These objects usually have a strong affective component (fire, shadow, etc.). When such a symbol succeeds, the latent affect is masked. There is decathexis of the original affect. The strength of the decathexis varies with the amount of displacement of attention cathexes from the latent to the manifest affect. In this situation what happens to the original fantasy content? It goes into repression.

How does affective psychoanalytic symbolization support repression of the original fantasy content, making it latent? The original fantasy content gained the quality that attracted consciousness from the disturbing affects associated with it. These fantasies have a high valence for such affects. When the original associated affects are represented in psychoanalytic symbols in the form of organs or other affects, and are in this way themselves repressed, their high affective valence is in effect neutralized. The quality that attracts consciousness is lost, and the original fantasy contents slip out of consciousness. They are recathected when the associated affects are recathected.

Greenacre (1965) describes the displacement of affects as follows: "Tears may come rather tardily and even then be displaced either as to the object or situation which elicits them or appear as edematous effusions in the should be weeper's own body" (p. 213).

Miss K. L., a 19-year-old single college girl, was referred for treatment by a gynecology resident from the hospital to which she had been admitted for a third episode of high fever accompanying a septic instrument-induced abortion. The resident considered her repeated pregnancies to be suicidal gestures. Once in treatment, the patient explained that her episodes of sexual activity occurred during periods of hazy awareness (dissociation states), during which she was not fully in control of her behavior. These states began while on dates and were related to feelings of attraction to her date, which were contrary to her moral code. Because of her state of altered awareness and confusion, she neither instituted nor insisted upon birth-control measures. Analysis of the symptom revealed an unconscious desire to "have a little boy with her father." The boys with whom she conceived represented both her father and the "little boy." During one of her sessions, when she was speaking of what the abortions meant to her, a fantasy occurred to her that she could not put into words. She fell silent. A look of dismay came across her face. "Dr. Sarnoff, look," she said, pointing to the volar aspect of her right forearm. A giant hive, raised, blanched, was there. "What thought did you have just as you became silent before the hive appeared?" I asked. "I thought of you as a man, I wanted to get inside your belly and rip your guts out," she replied. As she spoke, the hive disappeared.

Greenacre (1965), commenting on tears and urticaria, said:

The whole consideration of tears in weeping presents many inter-esting facets. . . . [It] is a situation in which the nucleus of a primitive physical defensive activity is later used in a much more complicated way and assumes the role of a quasi-psychic defense. There are questions also regarding the relationship of tears and tearfulness to disturbances of other fluid discharges in the body such as . . . the periodic appearance of fluid in body tissues in response to psychological as well as to physiological initiations, as in urticaria . . . [these are examples of] the body's use of fluid in psychosomatic defenses. [p. 218]

Conditions in which organs are used to express affects and fantasy contents are exemplified by psychosomatic disorders (in this chapter, I limit the use of this term to pregenital, protosymbolic symptoms, usually associated with incorporation) and hysterical conversion symptoms.

Psychosomatic disorders are characterized by tissue changes, fluid shifts, and physiological modifications. The affects and fantasies ex-pressed reflect fixations or regressions to pregenital (prephallic) levels. Thus the organs involved are usually visceral and have symbolic mean-ings relating to oral, respiratory, cutaneous, and anal incorporations.

Hysterical conversion symptoms are characterized primarily by modifications in function and sensation. The affects and fantasies expressed reflect fixations or regressions to phallic and oedipal levels, although the object relations expressed may have oral components. The organs involved are usually parts of the perceptual apparatus, the genitals, and the somatic motor apparatus. They usually have symbolic meanings relating to phallic genital and oedipal strivings, identifications, and the inhibition of aggressive urges. Occasionally visceral phenomena, such as stigmata, are seen, but these are rare. What is required to produce these psychic states is regression to the self–organ/affect (Steps 2 and 3 on Table 5.1) cathectic system. The aim is to establish psychic representations to be used as object for the discharge of drives in the presence of a functioning mature system consciousness.

In psychosomatic disorders affective symbolizations are manifested in the symbolization of self–affect cathexes and the symbolization of latent fantasy content by the use of bodily organs. Among psychosomatic disorders are included asthma, mucous colitis, regional ileitis, ulcerative colitis, and peptic ulcer.

Sperling, who did major work in the field of the therapy of psychosomatic disorders, pointed out the psychosomatic patient's tendency to develop acting-out behavior or phobias when somatization is analyzed and the person begins to use outside objects to deal with his conflicts. For this reason, the fantasies which form the basis for the somatic symptoms must be analyzed and their relationship to the symptoms worked through. Although it is true that interpretation of defenses and work on reality testing will help to resolve the fixations in development along the lines of the ontogenesis of the system consciousness and the march of objects, such work will only hand the conflict and fantasy on to the new personality, which will transmute it into new symptoms or characterological pathology.

The traumas most often associated with fixation points in the developmental lines of consciousness and the march of objects are inadequate attention and object loss. In the latter case the choice of symptom reevokes the somatic experience of the lost one. In other words, the symptom provides for the patient a recreation of the early cognitive awareness through which the lost one was primarily perceived and remembered — not through images, visual or verbal, but through sensory experience such as odor or abdominal pain.

The case history presented below is a typical one.

Psychosomatic disorder—mucous colitis: Mr. J. L., a 30-year-old, single, advanced graduate student, came to treatment for repeated depressive episodes associated with the loss of girlfriends whom he considered potential wives. The depressions did not interfere with his work but were accompanied by weight loss up to twenty pounds. At times he attempted to communicate with his lost loves. These attempts were accompanied by sudden cramps in the left side and by severe rectal fullness such that he had to seek a toilet immediately or risk soiling himself. This latter contingency never did occur but was a constant threat. He produced diarrhea in which the scybala was lost in the massive outflow of fluid. This cramping sometimes lasted for days, accompanied by pruritis ani. Episodes could be traced back to age 8 to 10. Sometimes they were associated not with calls to lost loves but with periods of working with handsome men who looked younger than their actual age, and with situations in which people in a position to praise him lavished their praise on others, ignoring his own achievements.

One particularly acute episode that occurred during the analysis was analyzed intensely and became the basis for his working through this condition. He succeeded to the extent that now, eight years after the analysis of the condition, he is symptom free.

He had met a young woman with whom he fell in love. An intense sexual affair, including frequent cohabitation in his apartment, provided three months of bliss. During the next three months his lover gradually lost her mastery over sadistic urges that she had been consciously controlling. At times, she would obsess for days before screaming at him that she thought he was dirty. Also she introduced situations that led him to obsess that she was seeing other men. Her behavior severely jeopardized the future of the relationship. It would have been terminated through a period of slow, sticky disentanglement, as had been his pattern in the past, except that she had become pregnant. He felt it his responsibility to remain with her until she could obtain an abortion. This resolve was strengthened by fear that she might carry out a threat to report him to his employers, who required high moral standards for the work he performed. In the face of all this danger, he experienced no diarrhea until a need arose to terminate the relationship quickly: he met another girl. He took her out in the afternoon and would have stayed with her through the evening, if he had not made a dinner appointment to discuss the abortion with the pregnant girl. As the march of cramps moved across his abdomen, he recalled my question, "What were your thoughts and feelings at the time of the cramps?"

He found that the cramps stopped when he recalled that he had just entertained, and then banished from consciousness, a wish to murder the pregnant girl. His cramps were equated with cramps during the abortion. The dejecta were associated to the baby, the murdered girl, that which had happened to his image of himself, and tears that were not overtly possible for him at these times. It is striking that during sustained episodes of cramping, he had quiescent periods during which he described the feelings in his abdomen as "crying."

Associations brought into consciousness repeated painful enemas in early childhood at the hands of his mother. He also recalled a maid whose departure during the third year of his life he experienced as a major trauma.

This case illustrates the use of the function of a body organ for the affective symbolization of strong affects involved in a reality situation. It should be noted that the presence in consciousness of the affects and the symptoms alternated and did not occur simultaneously. The hostile, murderous affect was symbolized by the colitis symptoms. Fantasy content also was symbolized by the organ symptoms. To what extent the fantasy determined the symptom and to what extent this was secondary symbolization interpretation is unclear. Certainly once the patient makes such an interpretation, a symbolic linkage has been established upon which later psychoanalytic symbol formations can be based, reinforcing the use of the symptom as an expression of the latent fantasy.

Hysterical conversion symptom: Mr. A. J., a 27-year-old former pilot, had been commended for bravery and physical courage. He came to analysis because of premature ejaculations, occasional retarded ejaculations, occasional impotence, anaesthesia of the distal two-thirds of his penis, and difficulty in meeting and talking to girls.

During the analysis it became clear that he had severe castration anxiety. He had visual fantasies of a penis with a cord tied tightly at its base. The penis turned blue and fell off. A similar fantasy involved vaginismus, resulting in amputation of the penis for gangrene. In another fantasy he saw a rocket flying down toward the mouth of a cave at an angle of about 20 degrees; as the rocket approached the cave, it became flaccid and couldn't get there.

The analysis of these fantasies as the root of his anaesthesia resulted in the slow resolution of that condition. The impairments of sexual function can be seen as inhibitions that symbolized his castration fears. Note that there was a symbolization of his aggression in the projection of it onto the cave and the vaginismus fantasies. Affective symbolization was the present, but the content symbolization predominated.

SUMMARY

Early trauma produces distortions in the ego. This phenomenon is addressed in this chapter in terms of the developmental lines that are the basis for the establishment of a strong symbolizing function. The symbolizing function forms the bridge between the psyche and the soma. In the earliest years of life, affects and organs can be represented symbolically through dysfunctions in other body organs. After sufficient differentiation has occurred, organs and bodily functions can symbolize external objects and situations. Failure to mature in the developmental lines associated with the development of the system consciousness, or with the march of objects from self to other, results in a predisposition to develop psychosomatic symptomatology.

REFERENCES

Ferenczi, S. (1912). Symbolism. In *The Selected Papers of Sandor Ferenczi,* vol. 1, pp. 253–281 New York: Basic Books, 1950.

Freud, S. (1900). The interpretation of dreams. *Standard Edition* 4, 5.

_____ (1914). On narcissism. *Standard Edition* 14.

_____ (1939). Moses and monotheism. *Standard Edition* 23.

Greenacre, P. (1965). On the development and function of tears. *Psychoanalytic Study of the Child* 20:209–219.

Jones, E. (1916). The theory of symbolism. In *Papers on Psychoanalysis,* 5th ed., pp. 87–144. London: Bailliere, Tindall, & Cox, 1948.

Klein, M. (1930). The importance of symbol formation in ego development. *International Journal of Psycho-Analysis* 12:24–39.

Mahler, M. (1969). *On Human Symbiosis and the Vicissitudes of Individuation.* New York: International Universities Press.

Reiser, M. (1966). Toward an integrated psychoanalytic physiological theory of psychosomatic disorders. In *Psychoanalysis — A General Psychology,* ed. R. M. Lowenstein, L. M. Newman, M. Schur, and A. J. Solnit, pp. 570–582. New York: International Universities Press, 1966.

Sarnoff, C. A. (1957). *Medical Aspects of Flying Motivation.* San Antonio: U.S. Air Force.

_____ (1970). Symbols and symptoms. *Psychoanalytic Quarterly* 39:550–562.

_____ (1976). *Latency.* New York: Jason Aronson.

Schur, M. (1955). Comments on the metapsychology of somatization. *Psychoanalytic Study of the Child* 10:119–164.

Simpson, W. K. (1972). *The Literature of Ancient Egypt.* New Haven: Yale University Press.

Sperling, M. (1952). Animal phobias in a two year old child. *Psychoanalytic Study of the Child* 7:115–125.

_____ (1968). Acting out behavior and psychosomatic symptoms. *International Journal of Psycho-Analysis* 49:250–253.

Spitz, R. (1965). *The First Year of Life.* New York: International Universities Press.

Wulff, M. (1928). A phobia in a child of eighteen months. *International Journal of Psycho-Analysis* 9:354–359.

6

PROJECTIVE IDENTIFICATION

C. Philip Wilson, M.D.

PROJECTION AND OEDIPAL CONVERSION SYMPTOMS

Psychosomatic symptoms rooted in oedipal-phase conflicts use projection as a defense. Patients usually project aspects of their strict superego onto objects. An example occurred in the following case:

A 38-year-old businessman came to analysis for symptoms of premature ejaculation, anxiety, and low back pain. These symptoms dated back to his marriage ten years earlier. He had now agreed to a separation and divorce from his wife.

In the first weeks of analysis, he decided that he would ask his wife to rejoin him and to stop the divorce proceedings. He found that he suffered from premature ejaculation during intercourse with other women, and he was very guilty about being separated from his only child, a boy of age 4. The patient's father, an irresponsible salesman, had deserted his family when the patient was 8 years old. When the patient found himself doing the same to his son, he became more and more guilty.

The wife and son rejected the patient, and analysis proceeded with the assistance of a strong positive transference, the patient feeling that he had found in me a new and magical father. After six months the patient had been free for several months of headaches and backaches. Now instead of getting headaches he got angry – in the transference with me, and in reality with his wife and others. The patient's mother had always complained of headaches and backaches, and in this case these symptoms represented an oedipal-phase identification with the mother. The cathexis of this homosexual identification was decreased by the strengthening of his masculine identification, represented by the positive transference identification with me in the analysis.

Further evidence of the oedipal root of this man's symptoms was a repetitive nightmare dating from the oedipal period in which he was being chased across an open lot by ghosts (the oedipal parents). From the first, I interpreted the headaches in the context of repressed anger; the backaches, in terms of masochistic behavior: oh, my aching back!

Of course, at this early stage of analysis his identification with his mother could not be shown to him, nor was it clear what specific unconscious fantasies were repressed in his psychosomatic symptoms. Such material emerges later in analysis, during the working through of the transference neurosis, when there is a transitory return of symptoms.

This material clearly confirms Sperling's (1978) observation that psychogenic headaches are often rooted in oedipal-phase conflicts, unlike migraine headaches, which are genetically caused by preoedipal conflicts.

In this case, as is routine with oedipal conversion symptoms, the defense of projection of superego criticism onto objects, including the analyst, was interpreted repeatedly, which led to a clearing of the patient's headaches. Another such case that involves "zipper conflicts," is described in Chapter 9. Of course, psychosomatic patients utilize both projection and projective identification as defenses.

PROJECTION, PROJECTIVE IDENTIFICATION, AND PSYCHOSOMATIC DISEASE

The mind–body problem, the process of somatization, the puzzle of psychosomatic disease etiology – these can be resolved by viewing psychosomatic symptoms as somatic manifestations of projections and projective identifications.

The focus in this section is on projective identification in patients with severe psychosomatic symptoms. My hypothesis is that (1) such psychosomatic symptoms are manifestations of projective identifications; (2) the predisposition to the ego's defense of projective identification and the development of severe psychosomatic symptoms are caused by an early disturbance in the parent–child relationship.

PROJECTIVE IDENTIFICATION, TRANSFERENCE, PSYCHOSIS, AND PSYCHOSOMATIC ILLNESS

Psychosomatic patients routinely use the defense of projective identification (Bion 1956, Boyer and Giovacchini 1980, Carpinacci et al. 1963, Carter and Rinsley 1977, Cesio, 1963, 1973, Giovacchini 1975, Grinberg, 1972, 1976, 1979, Hughes 1984, Kernberg 1976, M. Klein 1955, Ogden 1978, Perestrello 1963, D. Rosenfeld and E. Mordo 1973, H. A. Rosenfeld 1952, Searles, 1965). As Hogan (1983a) and (Wilson et al. 1983) recently demonstrated, psychosomatic patients project unacceptable aspects of the personality—impulses, self-images, superego introjects—onto other people, particularly the analyst, with a resulting identification based on these projected self-elements. These patients attempt to control objects, including the analyst, by unconsciously inducing the object to experience the conflicts that developed in the patient as a child in the parental relationship. In some cases the patient may even unconsciously induce psychosomatic symptoms in the therapist. Prolonged use of projective identification by some patients results in the appearance of transference psychosis (Sperling 1955, Wilson 1971). I will detail here the psychodynamics of projective identification in states of severe regression, such as those seen in (1) *status asthmaticus,* (2) the crisis self-starvation of restrictor anorexics, (3) the life-threatening crises of the bleeding ulcerative colitis patient.

Projective Identification in Psychosomatic Suicide

It is a central thesis of this chapter that the more severe the psychosomatic symptom, the more intense will be the use of projective identification.

Case 1: Status asthmaticus

In the second year of analysis, a compulsive male asthmatic called me on the phone during the summer vacation break.[1] I had received a prior call from the patient's internist, who told me that the patient had been hospitalized for *status asthmaticus*. All I could hear on the phone was wheezing. I made the interpretation that he was choking me to death inside himself in rage at my leaving him. The patient's wheezing lessened, and he began to give details of his illness. The hospital physician later called to say the patient was much improved and the next day he was discharged. The rest of the vacation he had no serious asthma nor did he call me again.

In analysis in the fall, he said that in his asthma attack he would not cooperate; he fought using the respirator and other treatment; he wanted to die. When he had been able to get me and his internist on the phone, he felt he had control of us, and following my phone interpretation he became aware of a fantasy directed at me. He fantasied he was an Arab terrorist who hijacked an Israeli airplane. In his fantasy, because his demands for money and power were not met, he killed all the families on the plane by blowing it up. These families, he realized, represented me and my wife and children. Following his awareness of these fantasies and their transference meaning, he relaxed and cooperated in the therapy of his status asthmaticus, of which this was his only attack.

Why was this admittedly inexact interpretation effective? As with other psychosomatic patients, the rise and fall of asthmatic attacks in reaction to the transference had been interpreted. This patient's asthma had developed at age 3, when he was first separated from his mother because she was hospitalized for an elective abortion. His murderous rage at his mother and the baby *in utero* were internalized and repressed in his asthma. This phase of childhood was recapitulated in the transference neurosis, and when he developed the *status asthmaticus* he felt in the transference that I was as impossible to reach as his mother had been as a child. When he was able to reach me and when I accepted his murderous aggression by my interpretation, I convinced him in the transference that I was not the original mother whom he conceived to be hypermoral and disapproving of aggression. There eventually was an amelioration of the projective identification of his archaic punitive superego onto me and everyone else. Of course, this was one of a long series of interpretations that focused on this patient's masochism, and the result was a cumulative one.

---

[1]Other aspects of this case are discussed in Chapter 13.

However, such a patient in this situation without effective interpretation may carry out psychosomatic suicide. What I particularly want to emphasize is that the patient's wheezing *status asthmaticus* on the phone is an expression of a life-threatening global projective identification. We can call it a transference psychosis.

Case 2: Ulcerative Colitis

A 23-year-old single man suffering from ulcerative colitis was referred to me for an emergency consultation by the family physician, because immediate surgery had been advised. The physician knew of my work and had informed him of my experience.

He presented a history that is typical of such patients. The younger of two children, he was the favorite of his parents. His mother had done everything for him as a child and he had been spoiled and doted upon. He had been a good child and did everything with his parents. Too much togetherness prevailed in the family. He was inhibited in terms of male competition and athletics and was late in dating girls. In his personal habits he was messy.

The father was a brilliant, passive-aggressive man who was also catered to and spoiled by the mother. He was an agreeable person who never lost his temper; he suffered from intense headaches and had a habit of farting at home, which was tolerated with little comment by the mother. He was a successful businessman but avoided situations of conflict, changing jobs when his bosses asked too much of him or were too critical.

The patient's ulcerative colitis developed during his senior year at college, when he was faced with graduation and a job decision. His symptoms had lessened when he took a bank job in the city.

In my initial consultations I concluded that the patient was suitable for analysis, but his surgeon had warned him that there was danger of perforation and that immediate surgery was indicated. I told the patient that his symptoms were emotionally caused. I informed him that other patients with ulcerative colitis had resolved the symptoms and their conflicts in analysis. I then asked whether he would approve of my talking with his surgeon about having another surgical consultation. The patient agreed. The consulting surgeon said there was not an immediate risk of perforation, and we began analysis four times a week, using the couch.

This patient responded quickly to interpretations of his masochism. Within two weeks his acute colitis attacks subsided. There was no recurrence of ulcerative colitis crisis in the ensuing four years of analysis, which resulted in a clearing of his colitis and a shift from part- to whole-object relations and a resolution of his masochistic personality disorder.

The dramatic amelioration of symptoms in the psychosomatic crisis occurs in this and other cases, because the patient's intense, global projective identification is thwarted by the analytic confrontation. To the patient, to be operated on means unconsciously that his colitis, which represents his rage and anger, will be cut out. The surgical procedure will carry out the dictates of his archaic superego.

An illustration of these psychodynamics occurred in a case reported to me by one of my colleagues. A 42-year-old man who lived at home was hospitalized for increasingly severe ulcerative colitis, which did not respond to steroid treatment. A psychiatric consultation was advised, but the patient refused it. After a colostomy the colitis cleared, but the patient on the medical ward verbalized murderous rage toward his mother. Before a psychiatric consultation could be accomplished, the patient killed himself. Surgery in this case did not act as a punishment by the superego. It removed the symptoms that masked the patient's parental hatred. His suicide expressed the self-punishment that formerly had been carried out by the colitis.

With a confrontational psychoanalytic consultation the patient develops a powerful pregenital dyadic transference, in which the analyst is a new and different object who will promote health and accept the expression of aggressive and libidinal drive manifestations (Sperling 1967, Wilson 1971). Influenced by this transference, the patient's acute symptoms can lessen before analytic working through and insight have occurred.

Case 3: Crisis Self-Starvation of Restrictor Anorexics

The mortality rate in anorexia nervosa is from 1 to 10 percent (Asbeck et al. 1972, Crisp 1979, Sours 1968). Many of these cases are restrictor anorexics who starve themselves to death. In the case material that follows, drawn from our anorexia volume (Wilson et al. 1983), I detail psychoanalytic technique in training a life-threatening restrictor anorexic crisis.

The patient was a 25-year-old single woman who was seen in consultation in the hospital. She was under combined psychiatric and medical treatment that included thorazine and nutritional supplements. The history revealed that the anorexia of four months duration had developed after Frances terminated an affair, during which she had not used any contraceptives. She manifested symptoms of insomnia, fasting, amenorrhea, and difficulties in concentration while working. She had gone for office psychotherapy for three months prior to hospitalization. She had liked the psychiatrist, but symptomatically she had gone downhill. She had developed suicidal fears of killing herself with a razor and had refused to eat anything but a little ice cream. When seen on the ward, she was being tube-fed per the nasal passage. The parents were seen together in consultation and, at the analyst's request, wrote up their observations on their daughter.

Patient's History. Frances was the second of two girls. Following a normal pregnancy, the mother had been unable to nurse Frances because of a fever of unknown origin. Frances was described as a "good baby," but at age 2 she developed hair pulling, which continued until age 3. A psychiatric consultation at that time yielded no specific therapeutic recommendations.

At first, Frances was a good eater, but then she became difficult, forcing the mother to devise games to feed her. She was phobic about new situations, such as getting haircuts, meeting strangers, entering stores, and taking train rides. Fire engines and ambulance sirens frightened her.

She showed an early musical talent. A school phobia appeared when she started kindergarten. Her mother stayed in school with her until she adjusted. At age 5, Frances reacted to the birth of a sister by hiding and crying. Analysis revealed that she had had no preparation for the birth. From that time on, she had a fear of hospitals. She was an excellent student. The mother described her as "a complex, fearful, but basically cheerful child."

In the latency years she showed strong tomboy wishes, rejected frilly feminine clothes, and insisted on boys' clothes. She played all contact sports, including touch football, and was extremely competitive with boys. From age 3 to 9 she had a good friend, an effeminate boy three years her senior, who played endlessly with her, inventing games, dressing up, and making believe. In later years the boy was used as a babysitter.

Although Frances was a conscientious older sister, she actually was jealous and envious of her younger sibling until her college years. Throughout childhood she was not a big eater. During her college years she was 30 pounds underweight.

In high school Frances had few friends and was not close to any of her teachers, nor did she have any dates or crushes on boys. She had no memory of masturbation. She was very conscientious about her studies, getting up at 4:30 A.M. to review her homework. She excelled in sports and enjoyed music and art. She chose a women's college to avoid problems of dating. Scholastically, she did well and went on to graduate school, where she began to date.

Her first serious affair led to intercourse but was marred by intense arguments, because she refused to use any contraceptives. During the affair she began to develop symptoms of anxiety, insomnia, hyperactivity, and anorexia nervosa. These symptoms worsened until her roommate forced her to seek treatment. She was in supportive therapy for three months before being hospitalized. In the hospital, she did not want to see members of her family and would take no advice from them. The family sought the consultation.

The father was a compulsive professional man who said that he "could not stand children." The mother was also compulsive. She had enjoyed many interests prior to marriage—for example, biking, music, skiing—but had "given them up" for the sake of her husband. She was a strict disciplinarian at home. When deeply provoked, she would slap the children on the face.

Psychodynamic Hospital Treatment. When first seen in the hospital, Frances was walking around the locked ward pushing an intravenous apparatus. With typical anorexic denial of conflict, she did not reply to questions. The analyst introduced himself, informing her that her parents had asked him to see her because he was an anorexia specialist. She made no reply and tried not to look at him. He told her that the problem in his work with her would be for them to find out why she felt forced to starve herself to death. She again made no reply.

The next day, when the analyst came in to see her, she thrust her arm at him, saying angrily, "Look what those interns did to me!" The intravenous needle had come out and her arm was black-and-blue and swollen from repeated attempts to reinsert it. The analyst talked with the nurse and residents, who said that Frances had fought off their attempts to reinsert the needle. The analyst interpreted to the patient that her conscience was so strict that she could not admit to anger, that she fought with the residents but had to deny it. She burst out, "The nurses and interns are fascists!" The analyst made the interpretation that he knew the staff members were concerned with her health; that anyone who tried to control her made her angry, but her conscience did not permit anger. Her associations were to childhood; she had a "funny" memory that at age 8 she had cut her sister with some scissors. The analyst asked her if she could remember her sister's reactions or what had caused the incident. Frances could not recall anything more. The analyst interpreted to her that her conscience was so strict that she could not remember her mother's anger or her own, just as she disapproved of her own and the interns' aggression.

The analyst had a conference with the attending physician and informed him that Frances was developing a positive therapeutic relation. He asked the physician if he could delay on hyperalimentation, which was being considered because Frances's weight was near half normal. He said he could wait for a week. Then the analyst met with the hospital staff and explained that he wanted all attempts to encourage Frances to eat stopped, because he wanted to make Frances responsible for her eating.

The next session, the analyst told Frances that as soon as she put on enough weight, she could leave the hospital and come to his office for analytic therapy. He explained that behind her anorexic symptoms she had conflicts about men, marriage, pregnancy, and childbirth. She made no reply, but talked about her boyfriend who was coming to the hospital to see her; she did not want to see him, as he upset her. The analyst interpreted to her that her way of dealing with conflict was to avoid it. Food upset her, so she didn't eat; her boyfriend bothered her, so she avoided him; the analyst told her things that angered her, so she ignored him. Frances said she would see her boyfriend, but he had pushed her too hard to get married. The analyst pointed out that she had begun dieting when she was dating him because she was afraid of getting pregnant. Frances said that she had avoided reading about pregnancy in adolescence, that she used to think that pregnancy came from kissing.

Frances began to eat and gain weight. She called the analyst at his office to ask permission to leave the hospital to do special exercises. The analyst interpreted to her that she was denying how ill she had made herself. The next day the nurses told him she was fasting and losing weight again. She reported a dream of being given the intravenous feeding again, but would not associate to it. Interpretations were made that she was angry with the analyst for not letting her do anything she wanted, that she hoped to defeat him by being fed intravenously again.

The next session she said she had had a fight with her boyfriend, that he was too demanding. The analyst interpreted to her that she wanted to control her boyfriend and her analyst totally. She reported dreams of skiing and of having her periods again. She began to eat and put on more weight. The foregoing emergency phase of therapy lasted three weeks; in the subsequent three weeks of hospital therapy, she evidenced a developing positive transference. The content of her sessions largely involved her conflicts with her boyfriend and her work, and the analyst continued to interpret her wishes to deny conflict and anger with him because of his confronting her with her neurosis. She stopped fasting; intravenous feeding became unnecessary, and she put on enough weight so that she could be discharged for office analytic treatment. In her subsequent analysis, she was able to resolve her anorexic symptoms and her underlying personality disorder.

DISCUSSION

Frances had received joint psychiatric and medical treatment, which had resulted in a splitting of the transference, an intensified anger at being controlled, and subsequent self-starvation and resistance to medical treatment. When the analyst was able to stop the forced medical treatment, the transference became concentrated on him. In this process, the analyst carefully studied his countertransference and counterreactions to Frances's negativistic behavior. He realized that if she resisted further, his treatment would be interrupted to save her life, as her weight had dropped to near half normal. Instead of worrying about Frances's dying, which was the affective state she wanted to induce in him, the analyst interpreted her masochism and suicidal impulses.

In discussing the problem of how far the analyst should go in interpreting intense denial, A. Freud (1968) refers to Bond's treatment of an anorexic girl. He countered her fantastic denial of self-destruction (extreme emaciation) by telling her that she would die. With Frances, as with other anorexics, the effects of the self-starvation did not impair her ego functioning. On the contrary, often when patients' masochistic impulses are most intense and the results of their behavior most pathological and self-destructive, the split-off, silent, rational part of the ego is ready for a confrontation, and the potential for a positive transference is heightened. Alcoholics Anonymous (personal communication 1979) believes that some addicts have to experience "the gutter" before they will face what they are doing to themselves and battle their addiction. The psychological situation is similar to that seen in patients who have made a serious attempt at suicide. The analytic consultant brings out to patients, in the context of their life history and personal psychodynamics, that the problem is to find out in therapy why they want to kill themselves. Frequently, with such an approach, suicidal patients can be released from the hospital for analysis with no recurrence of serious suicidal behavior. In the case of Frances, she evidenced a positive transference throughout her analysis and did not resume any life-threatening fasting.

PROJECTIVE IDENTIFICATION AND SELF-OBSERVING FUNCTION OF THE EGO

The more severe the psychosomatic symptoms, the more primitive is the level of regression. In this situation the defense of denial and splitting occurs with intense projective identification, which can lead, if prolonged, to the appearance of a transference psychosis. As Hogan, Mintz, and I demonstrated in anorexics, psychosomatic patients project unacceptable aspects of the personality—impulses, self-images, superego introjects—onto other people, particularly the analyst, with a resulting identification based on these projected self-elements. Their extreme psychoticlike denial of conflict is caused by primitive projective identification onto others of archaic, destructive superego introjects.

From one point of view I would agree with Hogan (1983b) and Giovacchini (1975) that the object-relationship qualities of the transference can be viewed as a hierarchical continuum and that this continuum of regressive positions is consistent with the views of Arlow and Brenner (1964). The analyst has to be aware of the patient's degree of regression and the particular level of development of the self and object representational projections (Blum 1977, Boyer 1979, Boyer and Giovacchini 1967, 1980, Giovacchini 1975, Kernberg 1975, 1976). I do not agree with Porder (1986), who emphasizes identification with the aggressor while rejecting projective identification. Certainly, identification with the aggressor is important, but with severe psychosomatic symptoms the regression is to preverbal and early verbal stages, at which level projective identification occurs as a defense.

From another point of view, however, transference psychosis can be differentiated from regressive transference in psychosomatic patients as well as in other patients with severe preoedipal psychopathology. In the life-threatening regressive state of the *status asthmaticus,* Case 1, the bleeding ulcerative colitis, Case 2, and the dangerous self-starvation of the restrictor anorexic, Case 3, it is my hypothesis that the total dominance of the archaic primitive superego represents a psychotic state. The self-observing functions of the ego are close to a nonfunctional level in regard to intrapsychic processes. The patients felt that they should die, and in the *status asthmaticus* and the restrictor self-starvation they fought any life-saving efforts.

The key to the interpretation of the silences and projective identification that occur in psychosomatic patients is the persistent interpretation of derivatives of the archaic primitive superego and the projection of such introjects onto the analyst. For example, Frances (Case 3) would fix on the tone of my voice to prove to herself that I was harsh and critical. She would repress or distort the content of what I said or take it out of context. Careful recapitulation of what had been said was sometimes necessary.

Another difficult resistance with such patients is that they split off fantasies and thoughts about the analyst, which they withhold. The patient revealed in the session that she carried on a secret dialogue with me. Another of my patients avoided negative transference feelings by purchasing stuffed animals, which she named for me. She would then get angry with and scold the stuffed animals, instead of verbalizing these feelings in sessions.

This conscious withholding of material in sessions can provoke counterreactions and countertransference in the analyst, such as feelings of being teased, drowsiness, or a sense that something is not being said or that the patient is trying to hypocritically comply.

To return to the clinical material: The analyst has to use construction, reconstruction, and active intervention with such patients. I asked the patient whether she felt nauseous when she sat up in the session, because I felt that she was recapitulating a childhood phase of anorexia in the transference. With such patients one can expect that they may sit up, or even jump up, and/or leave a session. As I have described elsewhere (Wilson et al. 1983), the analyst should not react with any manifestation of a desire to control the patient, as the parents have done.

An example of intense (psychotic) projective identification was the case of Joshua, a chronic anorexic 60-year-old rabbi, who denied conflicts and was silent for a week. Each day he would wait in the therapy room of the hospital, pull out the therapist's chair, give him a pad and pencil, and politely listen while the therapist constructed aspects of his life from the voluminous case record to show him his masochism. For example, his wife had left him, and his synagogue had ousted him, because he was too moral. On the seventh day, in response to this line of interpretation, he started scratching his forearm, to which the therapist called attention, making the interpretation that he made Joshua angry, but that Joshua took out this anger on himself by scratching. For the first time, his attitude of polite listening changed to one of excited interest, and he told the therapist a dream about a man who had burned himself to death. His associations were to a famous religious leader who had been burned to death as a martyr. After this communication, for a time he flooded sessions with dreams in which he succeeded in situations where he had failed in real life. Psychotherapy effected a resolution of Joshua's anorexic symptoms and improved functioning in his personal life and work. This type of case could be used by certain clinicians (Nemiah 1976) to demonstrate alexithymia. Indeed, this man had been diagnosed as schizophrenic and had been given drug and electroshock treatment—to no avail. His dreams demonstrated typical magical undoing, a pregenital defense of anorexic patients.

In certain other cases the transference psychosis can be prolonged. For example, a 40-year-old, unmarried interior decorator came to analysis with symptoms of ulcerative proctitis. When the unconscious anal conflicts that were masked by and expressed in her symptoms were analyzed, the ulcerative proctitis symptoms cleared, but the patient developed a transference psychosis that lasted four months. She had the repeated paranoid conviction that certain black men were following her in the street with the intent of mugging her. She was convinced that her lover, a business executive, was having an affair with his young secretary, although his faithful, loving behavior with the patient belied her suspicions. Analysis of these paranoid ideas led back to dyadic anal-phase sadomasochistic conflicts and fantasies and triadic oedipal themes. However, throughout her analysis she maintained a basic positive transference, although at times, of course, paranoid transference material had to be worked through.

COUNTERTRANSFERENCE

An overview of countertransference can be found in articles by Glover (1955), Orr (1954), Reich (1960), and Langs (1975a,b). A book on countertransference (Epstein and Feiner 1979) offers articles that are most pertinent to the problems encountered in the therapy of psychosomatic patients. Particularly relevant is Boyer's chapter on countertransference with severely regressed patients (1979), in which he details his inner experiences as analyst in selected difficult treatment situations (transference psychoses) and describes how he utilized an understanding of his reactions, fantasies, and emotions to resolve such impasses. Thomä (1967) notes the countertransference conflicts aroused in the analyst by a prolonged negative transference in an anorexic patient. He also describes a typical countertransference response to anorexics, where the therapist becomes the overindulgent, infinitely loving mother.

My experience with patients with severe characterological, psychotic, and borderline disorders correlates with and confirms Boyer's emphasis on the important role of projective identification by the patient and counteridentification by the analyst in the treatment of these difficult patients. Moreover, a remarkably consistent psychological profile of the family is evident. The understanding of this profile is crucial for the analyst's comprehension of the provocative acting out, which is actually reenactment behavior that symbolically informs the analyst of past activities, events, and relationships (Boyer 1979, Ekstein 1976, Robertiello 1976). Crucial for the analysis of these patients is the analyst's understanding of their nonverbal expressive behavior (Bruch 1978, Mushatt 1980, Sperling 1967, Wilson 1971, 1980). The symptoms of psychosomatic disease are a form of nonverbal behavior, and the task of the analysis is to make the patients aware on a verbal level of the conflicts that are masked by their symptoms.

Countertransference Problems

Sperling (1967) discusses and illustrates countertransference problems in patients with psychosomatic disorders. She warns that the analyst has to withstand patients' perpetual testing, be aware of nuances and changes in transference feelings, and—most important—preserve the analytic role and avoid falling in with patients' wishes to turn the analyst into the image of the omnipotent mother. She notes further that these patients can pick up almost imperceptible nuances in the tone of voice, facial expression, movements, and even feelings of the analyst. Annoyance or irritation on the part of the analyst is taken to mean rejection and intensifies the need for control of the object (analyst) and situation (analysis) at any cost (exacerbation or return of illness). Worry or anxiety on the part of the analyst is taken as an expression of love—the kind of love patients have received from their mother, which means a reward (anxiety, worry) for being sick. Like the mother, the analyst is worried and expresses love toward the patients when they are sick. Sperling emphasizes that skillful handling of the transference, with correct, well-timed interpretations, is crucial. A last point is that the transference cannot be split with another medical specialist; rather, the analyst must be basically in charge of treatment.

The case reports presented in this chapter document Sperling's main points about countertransference and explore certain points that she does not touch on, such as the fantasies that these patients provoke in the analyst and the problem of gaining a full therapeutic alliance with adult patients who start treatment under the domination of a medical specialist.

The cases support Sperling's statement that the patient tries to turn the analyst into the image of the omnipotent mother. However Sperling's observation seems to be a global oversimplification of a series of projective identifications that alternately try to turn the analyst into the complete source of pleasure (the breast-food-all-giving mother) and into the critical, punishing mother who demands perfection. Sperling's brief comments are on countertransference in the analysis of psychosomatic cases in general.

The countertransference reactions we shall look at next, while they are attributed to anorexics, apply to psychosomatic patients in general.

Bruch (1978), a Sullivanian interpersonal relations therapist, emphasizes that the therapist must not be intimidated by the anorexic's manipulative behavior and thereby replay the role of the intimidated parent. Bruch gives examples of how she used the anger that anorexics stirred up in her for interpretative purposes. One such technique was to interrupt the patient in a loud, angry voice in order to be listened to. Another was to withdraw to a defensive position and point out that the anorexic was a voluntary patient and could see someone else.

Selvini Palazzoli (1978) notes that few patients are better than anorexics at driving the analyst into a corner and provoking countertransference reactions. Mintz (1983) emphasizes the negative results of being overanxious and phoning a patient, and of giving approval when the anorexic patient starts to eat more.

Hogan (1983a,b) notes that drowsiness and educative or coercive tactics are common countertransference reactions to anorexics. Boyer (1979) and McLaughlin (1979) review countertransference reactions of drowsiness or sleep in the analyst. The core fantasy in sleep-inducing associations and behavior involves fusion with the analyst as the mother in the transference. One chronically late analysand, who was finally gaining some insight into her omnipotent resistance, suddenly devalued analysis and the analyst and threatened to see an astrologist. The analyst had a countertransference reaction of drowsiness, which the patient noted. His drowsiness was a sort of rebound phenomenon: if the patient was going to dismiss the analyst and his ideas, then he would dismiss her, too. The affect of drowsiness reflected the symbiotic fusion fantasies of the patient.

With respect to coercion, Hogan notes that the therapist of one patient threatened to discontinue treatment if she repeated her initial act of shoplifting. In response, the patient repeated and expanded her shoplifting adventures without ever informing the therapist again. She enjoyed typical anorexic "glee" at "getting away with it." Treatment was obviously useless, as she replicated her relation with her mother.

Flarsheim (1975) has written about the therapist's collusion with the patient's wish for suicide. One suicidal anorexic patient provoked hostility in him and he then wished she would cease to exist (commit suicide). Flarsheim told the patient some aspects of his countertransference hostility and felt that this revelation improved the therapeutic relationship and contributed to the patient's improvement, although the patient had to be hospitalized. Flarsheim emphasizes that when anorexics give up their food addiction, they become addicted to the analyst in the transference. He also stresses that anorexic symptoms defend against suicidal impulses.

Another countertransference problem arises from female patients' rationalization of their penis envy, conflicts with men, and accusation that the analyst is antifeminist. Many adolescent anorexics state that Freud was antifeminist, that penis envy is a discarded notion, and so on. The analyst has to be very careful about countertransference in this potentially provocative situation. He must keep in mind that this attitude is defensive and that underneath, these patients are frightened. They have been repeatedly exposed to the oedipal and preoedipal primal scene and to extremely exhibitionistic parental, sexual, and toilet behavior, whose significance has been completely denied. The major defense of the unconsciously terrified anorexic female is to control the objects and situations that provoke anxiety. All these patients lie about their sexual behavior, as well as about other matters.

In the countertransference and counterreactions, analysts experience (1) resentment that their authority and professional training and knowledge are being challenged, (2) resentment that Freud's and their positions are distorted, and (3) above all, the feeling that patients are trying to pick a fight. One effective therapeutic technique is to analyze the patient's defensive rationalization. For example, analysts may point out that Freud never made up his mind about female psychology—that he changed his mind often, said different things at different times, and is widely misquoted. They may tell patients that they are in favor of women's rights and realize that women have been discriminated against; they may emphasize that little boys envy women; and so on, depending on each patient's character structure, history, or defenses.

Another important countertransference problem occurs when a patient's symptoms have cleared, the underlying neurosis is being analyzed, and suddenly the patient devalues the male analyst and expresses a wish for a female analyst. This wish expresses the desire to find in the analyst the early omnipotent breast-mother whom they can control. The resistance occurs when they have not effected a basic change in the quality of their object relations and have not worked through their symbiotic attachment to the parents. Analysts' counterreactions of resentment and anger can be intense. They may wish to get rid of patients in retaliation. With adolescent patients, the wish for a change to a woman analyst may be promoted by the parents, who unconsciously do not want their daughter to mature. This transference conflict requires careful and thorough interpretation. Women analysts encounter the same resistance when they refuse to be the symbiotic mother in the transference; patients will express the wish for a different, often a male, analyst.

A common characterologic defense of anorexic gorger-vomiters is an ego attitude of bitter cynicism and sarcasm. They respond to interpretations with, "So what?" "I've heard that before." "You and your psychoanalytic crap." These defenses occur following a phase of positive transference and therapeutic progress. The analyst should pursue the interpretation of these patients' strict superego, which disapproves of the anger at the analyst and demands an iron control over it. Unhappiness, depression, hopelessness, loneliness, frustration, guilt, and suicidal ideas are masked by this defense of the ego. Cynicism and sarcasm reflect an extreme ego ideal of perfection that these patients demand of themselves and of other people. Understanding this aspect of the anorexic's character structure enables analysts to resolve their intense counterreactions and countertransference.

Finally, analysts should not be deceived by the appearance of healthy functioning in anorexics whose symptoms are gone but whose underlying conflicts are still unresolved. If such patients are allowed to go away to college before they are ready, dangerous suicidal behavior and the return of intense symptoms can be expected.

Other Problems

Patients seldom develop serious psychosomatic symptoms during sessions. This is evidence of the power of the pregenital transference and the fact that the analyst is a new and different object besides being a transference object. If symptoms do occur, analysts should examine their countertransference carefully. In the treatment of patients with gastrointestinal symptoms (regional ileitis, ulcerative colitis, spastic colitis), analysts should interpret not only the patient's wish to turn objects (mother, analyst) into feces and destroy them but also, at a later stage, the destructive turning of objects into flatus. Here, unanalyzed anal-phase conflicts of the analyst can cause countertransference problems.

Likewise, difficult countertransference problems arise in therapists who themselves suffer from psychosomatic symptoms or who have any chronic organic illness. If a patient develops an acute exacerbation of a psychosomatic symptom—for example, has to be hospitalized for *status asthmaticus,* severe ulcerative colitis, or acute anorexic starvation—the analyst may decide to see the patient in the hospital, but such hospital sessions should be analytic, not supportive. In these situations the therapist should carefully scrutinize himself for possible countertransference factors.

Psychosomatic patients by the process of projective identification can induce psychosomatic symptoms in the therapist, such as borborigmae (the therapist's gut crackles). Analysts have to analyze such phenomena in themselves in the context of fantasies and emotions, libidinal and aggressive, that have been provoked by the patient. Cohler (1975) reported how an anorexic patient succeeded in repeating her undifferentiated, fused relationship with her mother with her female therapist. She was verbally abusive to the therapist and attempted "to bind her therapist to her by not differentiating between their personalities" (p. 403). The therapist felt "confused and completely smothered and overwhelmed by the patient." The therapist, expressing the ultimate in a projective identification by the patient, lost her appetite, became anorexic and amenorrheic, and fantasied that she was pregnant with the patient, "who would live forever within her body" (p. 404). The therapist became increasingly afraid of merging with the patient, and the patient became increasingly disturbed.

PROJECTIVE IDENTIFICATION
IN COLLOQUIAL LANGUAGE

In a paper entitled "Head Shrinker Fantasies or Who Is Shrinking Whom?" (1975), I detailed the psychodynamics of the term *head shrinker* as applied to psychiatrists and psychoanalysts. The term appears to have come into general colloquial use since its appearance in the musical, *West*

Side Story, in the late 1950s. I now realize that its use denotes a general use of projective identification by the public.

The public clings to the term head shrinker for complex emotional reasons. Psychoanalysis shows that patients fear that the therapist will deprive them of their secret pleasures and fantasies and, moreover, will indulge in and enjoy the pleasures stolen from the patients. Thus the "shrink" represents the castrating parents and other authority figures of childhood. "Headshrinker" has an opposite unconscious meaning—"head swelling"—and indeed patients hope to develop magical brain power from therapy so that they can become omnipotent. Comparable primitive fantasies underlie patients' magical expectations of doctors in general.

When an analytic patient repeatedly uses a particular phrase, we call it a mannerism of speech. Mannerisms of speech and gesture in everyday life have been explored in a fascinating book by Sandor Feldman (1959). Also relevant are Oberndorf's (1918) paper on "People Who Do Not Like Their Names," Stekel's (1911) work on the obligation of names in which he discusses the hidden relation between names and professions, and Abraham's (1911) paper on "The Determining Power of Names." Feldman himself points out some further uses of first names and pet names, emphasizing that they are used by people to show closeness or superiority, as with a child, or to express familiarity and equality. Some years ago I (1968a) analyzed in detail a mannerism of speech, "The Boyfriend, the Girlfriend" (see Chapter 9 of this volume). An English analyst, Ella Freeman Sharpe, in a communication (1946), "A Note on the Magic of Names," pointed out the impact on the unconscious of words we use consciously. Characterologic rigidity, which is often manifested by a patient's language, was emphasized by Fenichel (1945) and W. Reich (1949).

Anthropologic research (*Encyclopedia Brittanica* 1985) reveals that headhunting has been worldwide; it dates at least to the Stone Age and perhaps to paleolithic times. It has been associated with (1) ideas of the head as the seat of the soul, (2) ideas of conveying to the cannibalistic eater the soul matter of the eaten; and (3) phallic and fertility cults. Headhunting continued into the last century in parts of the world. The American Indian's scalping of a victim is a derivative of headhunting.

The true head shrinkers were the Jivaro Indians of the Montana region of Ecuador. They were split into many tribes who used to fight each other. A victorious Jivaro beheaded his victim and packed the skull with hot sand, thus shrinking it to the size of a small monkey's head, while preserving the features intact as a vivid caricature. The heads of certain animals were treated similarly and were considered trophies. The young women of the tribes enthusiastically promoted headhunting, probably because men successful at it seemed virile and fearless, but possibly, they also unconsciously wanted to headhunt.

The head has complex symbolic significance. In mythology and in the fantasies of children, birth can occur in the head. A creative idea or product is spoken of as a brainchild. In reality, what magic we have is located in the head. The head is the highest part of the body. Males have bigger heads than females, adults than children. Size means power to primitive tribes, to children, and to the unconscious. Intellectuals are eggheads — meaning people who give birth in the head.

Certain patients, those suffering from impulse disorders and psychosomatic patients, repeatedly use the term head shrinker or shrink for their therapist. These patients in one way or another are prone to acting out their impulses, or they would like to act out but are restrained by their conscience, which they often project onto someone else — wife, parent, husband, or doctor. The "shrink" represents both the preoedipal and oedipal parents, who are seen as magical and omnipotent.

Patients with impulse disorders are prone to use the term *head shrinker,* using the mechanism of displacement from below (the below being the area of the genitals and the excretory organs) to the head. In their habits — thumb sucking, nose picking, smoking, drinking, drug addiction, and eating — they repetitiously use the organs of the head in place of the forbidden down-below organs. In their egos we find extensive use of the defenses of denial, rationalization, projection, and belief in magic.

These addictive patients are narcissistic and fear that the therapist will "shrink" their narcissism. An illustrative anecdote concerns a young woman who has been analyzed and meets a nice young man who wants to marry her. Her suitor, however, has one condition: that she buy her dreams back from her analyst. Her analyst tells her he does not have them any more, because they are all used up. The doctor, it is implied, enjoyed the dreams he took from the patient. And, indeed, in therapy we find that writers fear the analyst will steal their plots to write his own books, stockbrokers that he will appropriate special knowledge, and so on.

Typical of certain patients who habitually called me their "shrink" was a hypermasculine man, heavily addicted to alcohol and cigarettes, who came to analysis for symptoms of depression. He billed himself as a

Casanova and had had sex with numerous women, many of whom had fallen in love with him. Some he had impregnated, always arranging it so that they felt completely responsible.

His early childhood development was relatively normal until age 6, when his father died suddenly. The little boy did not mourn his father, covering his loss by a pathological identification: after seeing the movie *Frankenstein,* he tied wires to his head and acted out the role of the Frankenstein monster who could find no one to love him. When he began analysis, he reported a dream of me: I was a hydrocephalic physician-monster, sitting in my analytic chair with filthy water oozing from my swollen head. His associations were to doctors who victimized and enslaved their patients, and to doctors who had diseased brains. These sadistic fantasies were projections of what the patient wished to do and had done. He felt guilt and fear in coming for treatment, and the dream told him: "It is the doctor who has a diseased brain, not myself."

Another Casanova came to analysis, also for depressions caused by an inability to love. In his early years he had been seduced by a perverse nursemaid who taught him to masturbate her. Such a seduction in the oedipal years (ages 4 to 6) usually results in a sadomasochistic sexual development. It effects a type of castration, in that the little boy gets erections, but before puberty he cannot ejaculate. In this case the patient developed sadomasochistic relations with women, particularly repeating a pattern of getting women to fall in love with him and then frustrating them. He was quite frank in discussing his ability to manipulate women. In treatment he referred to me as his shrink, and from the first session voiced his suspicions of me: I did all the things he was guilty of— particularly that I seduced female patients, who had to pay me in the bargain.

A most graphic head-shrinker dream was reported by a married woman who consulted me about problems she was having with her son. As a young woman she had come for the analysis of an impulse disorder and migraine headaches. When I asked her if she still had migraines, she said no, but that the night before the consultation she felt as if she were going to get a headache but had a dream instead. In the dream she was holding my skull in her left hand; with the index finger of her right hand she reached in through the eye socket and ran it all around the inside of the skull, scooping its contents out.

Repressed fantasies and anger result in headaches and migraines, as this patient well knew. She had been furious with me because after all her analysis she was having problems with her son. The dream condensed many conflicts, the central one at the time being her wish to kill me and to magically incorporate (scoop out) my brain. If she could magically steal my head and brain, she would not need to come for the consultation or do more therapy.

Anorexic patients often deny the serious nature of their illness and frequently don't come for treatment themselves. They are hypermoral people whose self-starvation is a form of asceticism. They have used the defense of projective identification all their lives. A typical example was a high school student, who when first seen, was on the verge of hospitalization, having brought her weight down from 140 to 74 pounds. Typically, she was dragged to treatment by her parents against her will. As treatment progressed and she became aware of her hypermorality, she started to eat and put on weight; a glint appeared in her eye and she began to slyly refer to me as her "shrink." She referred to medical specialists who examined her as "perverts" for liking the human body, which she regarded as disgusting. Her feelings were similar in some ways to those of the public in the eighteenth and nineteenth centuries who violently opposed medical research with cadavers and organized riots against the evil doctors and their disciples, the medical students.

As this girl developed a more positive relationship with me, she began to refer to my "shrinking patients" and then burst into hysterical laughter. She was projecting onto me her fantasies of magically controlling and dominating people. As you might expect, she saw men as brutal people who sadistically used women for their own pleasure. In her mind men hurt and mutilated women, whose fate it was to be mistreated. Actually this girl had been spoiled by her mother, who had been unable to say no to her. It was she who wanted to dominate and control people. When the daughter got out of hand, the father disciplined her; he was the childhood "shrink." Primal-scene memories were recovered in the analysis which revealed that the patient viewed intercourse as a sadistic attack on the female. The male phallus was seen as a dangerous magical weapon with which Father could mutilate Mother. Females, she fantasied, had once had penises but had been deprived of them for being bad; that is, females had been "shrunk." This patient had witch-doctor dreams that reflected these sadomasochistic conflicts. For many sessions she unfolded fantasies and dreams about the activities of shrinks.

Such patients can be extremely provocative, and they seize on any aspect of the physician–patient relation to substantiate their fantasies. She sexualized physical examinations by her family doctor, whom she often provoked into losing his temper. Similar provocative behavior had occurred with her father for many years.

One of the hardest things to understand is that such a patient fights to keep her feeling that she is morally superior to everyone else, particularly to her doctors. It took many sessions for her to understand that it was she who wanted to shrink people.

Psychosomatic patients and other patients with impulse disorders, those addicted to drugs, tobacco, and alcohol, will tend to be hostile to the psychiatrist and the analyst and refer to him as the shrink. These patients also are ambivalent to their medical doctor and often devalue him in various ways, preferring to call him by his first name or by a nickname such as "Doc." These patients tend to seek medical and psychiatric help only when they have gotten themselves into serious trouble. As soon as they feel better, they want to stop therapy. Where a medical regime is advised, they don't follow it for long. If their doctor is too critical or demanding, they try to find a physician whom they can control. With such patients it is particularly unwise to deviate much from a formal doctor–patient relationship.

It is not just psychiatrists who are the target of omnipotent fantasies, but the medical profession in general. Recent medical discoveries that achieve seemingly miraculous results, such as organ implants, unconsciously arouse a multitude of magical expectations. Our goal in medicine is to keep everyone healthy and happy forever, to prevent disease and human misery — a patently impossible expectation. Patients were disappointed in Freud's office, as they expected palatial furnishings of a man who knew the secrets of the mind. The general medical man is ambivalently loved and hated. Probably the projection of unconscious omnipotent fantasies plays a significant role in the great increase in malpractice suits and awards.

In conclusion, we must be aware that we cannot have it both ways: we are admired, respected, and loved for our knowledge and power to heal; antithetically, we are envied, devalued, and hated for not being able to make everyone's most secret narcissistic fantasies come true. Projective identification creates this problem.

SUMMARY

Clinical case material was presented to demonstrate projective identification in psychosomatic patients. The more severe the psychosomatic symptoms, the more intense is the projective identification. Regressive projective identification can result in analyzable transference psychosis. The analyst for such patients, besides being a transference object, is a new and different object.

The patients' masochism and the impact of their archaic punitive superego and its introjects must be interpreted from the beginning of analysis. Also requiring repeated interpretation are their use of projection and projective identification. Their impulse disorder should be interpreted early. Also, as they come to understand the strict nature of their superego, conflicts about the expression of aggression can be interpreted. However, we must bear in mind that intense projective identification will develop nevertheless as an aspect of the transference neurosis. The colloquial use of the term head shrinker for psychiatrists and psychoanalysts was shown to be a projective identification. All of the analyst's skill will be tested in this situation. If this phase can be worked through, the most gratifying analytic results can be achieved, including symptom resolution and characterologic change.

REFERENCES

Abraham, K. (1911). On the determining power of names. In *Clinical Papers and Essays on Psychoanalysis,* pp. 31–32. New York: Basic Books, 1955.

Arlow, J., and Brenner, C. (1964). *Psychoanalytic Concepts and the Structural Theory.* New York: International Universities Press.

Asbeck, F., Hirschmann, W. D., Deck, K., and Castrup, H. J. (1972). Lethal course of anorexia nervosa: alcohol and laxative abuse in a female patient. *Internist* (Berlin) 13:63–65.

Bion, W. R. (1956). Development of schizophrenic thought. *International Journal of Psycho-Analysis* 37:344–346.

Blum, H. P. (1977). The prototype of preoedipal reconstruction. *Journal of the American Psychoanalytic Association,* 25:757–785.

Boyer, L. B. (1979). Countertransference with several regressed patients. In *Countertransference: The Therapist's Contribution to the Therapeutic Situation,* ed. L. Epstein and A. H. Feiner, pp. 347–374. New York: Jason Aronson.

Boyer, L. B., and Giovacchini, P. L. (1967). *Psychoanalytic Treatment of Schizophrenic, Borderline, and Characterological Disorders.* New York: Jason Aronson.

——— (1980). *Psychoanalytic Treatment of Schizophrenic, Borderline, and Characterological Disorders.* 2d rev. ed. New York: Jason Aronson.

Bruch, H. (1978). The tyranny of fear. In *The Human Dimension in Psychoanalytic Practice,* ed. K. Frank, pp. 83–98. New York: Grune & Stratton.

Carpinacci, J. A., Lieberman, D., and Schlossberg, N. (1963). Perturbanciónes de la communicación y neurosis de contratransferencia. *Revista de Psicoanalisis* 20:63–69.

Carter, L., and Rinsley, D. B. (1977). Vicissitudes of "empathy" in a borderline patient. *International Review of Psycho-Analysis* 4:317–326.

Cesio, F. R. (1963). La communicación extraverbal en psichoanalisis: transferencia, contratransferencia, e interpretación. *Revista de Psicoanalisis* 20:124–127.

———— (1973). Los fundamentos de la contratransferencia: el yo ideal y las identificaciónes directas. *Revista de Psicoanalisis* 30:5–16.

Cohler, B. J. (1975). The residential treatment of anorexia nervosa. In *Tactics and Techniques in Psychoanalytic Therapy*, vol. 2, ed. P. L. Giovacchini, A. Flarsheim, and L. B. Boyer, pp. 385–412. New York: Jason Aronson.

Crisp, A. H. (1979). Early recognition and prevention of anorexia nervosa. *Developmental Medicine and Child Neurology* 21:393–395.

Encyclopedia Brittanica (1985), vol. 5, p. 778.

Ekstein, R. (1976). General treatment philosophy of acting out. In *Acting Out*, 2d ed., ed. L. E. Abt and S. L. Weissman, pp. 162–171. New York: Jason Aronson.

Epstein, L., and Feiner, A. H., eds. (1979). *Countertransference: The Therapist's Contribution to the Therapeutic Situation*. New York: Jason Aronson.

Feldman, S. (1959). *Mannerisms of Speech and Gestures in Everyday Life*. New York: International Universities Press.

Fenichel, O. (1945). Psychoanalytic technique and therapy in character disorders. In *The Psychoanalytic Theory of the Neuroses*, p. 539. New York: W. W. Norton.

Flarsheim, A. (1975). The therapist's collusion with the patient's wish for suicide. In *Tactics and Techniques in Psychoanalytic Therapy*, vol. 2, ed. P. I. Giovacchini, A. Flarsheim, and L. B. Boyer, pp. 155–195. New York: Jason Aronson.

Freud, A. (1968). *Indications for Child Analysis and Other Papers*, 1945–1956. Vol. 4 of *The Writings of Anna Freud*. New York: International Universities Press.

Freud, S. (1933). Femininity. In *New Introductory Lectures. Standard Edition* 22.

Giovacchini, P. L. (1975). Various aspects of the analytic process. In *Tactics and Techniques in Psychoanalytic Therapy*, vol. 2, ed. P. L. Giovacchini, A. Flarsheim, and L. B. Boyer, pp. 5–94. New York: Jason Aronson.

Glover, E. (1955). *The Technique of Psycho-Analysis*. New York: International Universities Press.

Grinberg, L., ed. (1972). *Practicas Psicoanaliticas Comparadas en las Psicosis*. Buenos Aires: Editorial Paidos.

———— (1976). *Teoria de la Identificación*. Buenos Aires: Editorial Paidos.

———— (1979). Countertransference and projective counteridentifications. *Contemporary Psychoanalysis* 15:226–247.

Hogan, C. C. (1983a). Technical problems. In *Fear of Being Fat: The Treatment of Anorexia Nervosa and Bulimia,* rev. ed., ed. C. P. Wilson, C. C. Hogan, and I. L. Mintz, pp. 197–216. Northvale, NJ: Jason Aronson, 1985.

–––––– (1983b). Transference. In *Fear of Being Fat: The Treatment of Anorexia Nervosa and Bulimia,* rev. ed., ed. C. P. Wilson, C. C. Hogan, and I. L. Mintz, pp. 153–168. Northvale, NJ: Jason Aronson, 1985.

Hughes, A. (1984). Book Review, *Fear of Being Fat: The Treatment of Anorexia Nervosa and Bulimia,* ed. C. P. Wilson, C. C. Hogan, and I. L. Mintz. New York: Jason Aronson. *International Journal of Psycho-Analysis* 64(4):499.

Kernberg, O. F. (1975). *Borderline Conditions and Pathological Narcissism.* New York: Jason Aronson.

–––––– (1976). *Object-Relations Theory and Clinical Psychoanalysis.* New York: Jason Aronson.

Klein, M. (1955). On identification. In *New Directions in Psychoanalysis,* ed. M. Klein, P. Heimann, and R. Money-Kyrle, pp. 309–345. London: Tavistock.

Langs, R. (1975a). The patient's unconscious perception of the therapist's errors. In *Tactics and Techniques in Psychoanalytic Therapy,* vol. 2, ed. P. I. Giovacchini, A. Flarsheim, and L. B. Boyer, pp. 239–250. New York: Jason Aronson.

–––––– (1975b). Therapeutic misalliances. *International Journal of Psychoanalytic Psychotherapy* 4:77–105.

Laurents, A., Bernstein, L., and Sondheim, S. (1957). *West Side Story.* New York: Dell, 1965.

McLaughlin, J. T. (1979). The sleepy analyst: some observations on states of consciousness in the analyst at work. *Journal of the American Psychoanalytic Association* 23:363–382.

Mintz, I. L. (1983). The clinical picture of anorexia nervosa and bulimia. In *Fear of Being Fat: The Treatment of Anorexia Nervosa and Bulimia,* rev. ed., ed. C. P. Wilson, C. C. Hogan, and I. L. Mintz, pp. 83–114. Northvale, NJ: Jason Aronson, 1985.

Mushatt, C. (1980). Melitta Sperling Memorial Lecture. Presented at the Psychoanalytic Association of New York, February 25.

Nemiah, J. C. (1976). Alexithymia: a view of the psychosomatic process. In *Modern Trends in Psychosomatic Medicine,* vol. 3, ed. O. W. Hill, pp. 430–439. New York: Appleton-Century-Crofts.

Oberndorf, C. P. (1918). Reaction to personal names. *International Journal of Psycho-Analysis* 1:223–230, 1920.

Ogden, T. H. (1978). A developmental view of identifications resulting from maternal impingements. *International Journal of Psychoanalytic Psychotherapy* 7:486–506.

Orr, D. (1954). Transference and countertransference. *Journal of the American Psychoanalytic Association* 2:621–670.

Perestrello, M. (1963). Um caso de intensa identificaçäco projetiva. *Journal Brasileiro de Psiquiatria* 12:425–441.

Porder, M. (1986). Identification with the aggressor. Paper given at the meeting of the American Psychoanalytic Association, December 20, 1986, New York.

Reich, A. (1960). Further remarks on counter-transference. *International Journal of Psycho-Analysis* 41:389–395.

Reich, W. (1949). Character analysis and character resistance. In *Character Analysis,* pp. 39–113. New York: Orgone Institute.

Robertiello, R. D. (1976). "Acting out" or "working through." In *Acting Out,* 2nd ed., ed. L. E. Abt and S. L. Weissman, pp. 40–47. New York: Jason Aronson

Rosenfeld, D., and Mordo, E. (1973). Fusión, confusión, simbiosis e identificación. *Revista de Psicoanalisis* 30:413–423.

Rosenfeld, H. A. (1952). Notes on the psycho-analysis of the superego conflict of an acute schizophrenic patient. *International Journal of Psycho-Analysis* 33:111–131.

Searles, H. F. (1965). *Collected Papers on Schizophrenia and Related Subjects.* New York: International Universities Press.

Selvini Palazzoli, M. (1961). Emancipation as magic means for the removal of anguish in anorexia mentalis. *Acta Psychotherapica* 9:37–45.

———— (1978). *Self-Starvation: From Individual to Family Therapy in the Treatment of Anorexia Nervosa.* New York: Jason Aronson.

Sharpe, E. F. (1946). A note on the magic of names. *International Journal of Psycho-Analysis* 27:152.

Sours, J. A. (1968). Clinical studies in the anorexia syndrome. *New York State Journal of Medicine* 68:1363–1365.

———— (1980). *Starving to Death in a Sea of Objects: The Anorexia Nervosa Syndrome.* New York: Jason Aronson.

Sperling, M. (1955). Psychosis and psychosomatic illness. *International Journal of Psycho-Analysis* 36:320–327.

———— (1967). Transference neurosis in patients with psychosomatic disorders. *Psychoanalytic Quarterly* 36:342–355.

———— (1978). *Psychosomatic Disorders in Childhood.* Ed. O. Sperling. New York: Jason Aronson.

Stekel, W. (1911). Die Verpflichtung des Names (The obligation of names). *Zeitschrift für Psychotherapie und Medizinis Psychologie* 3:110–114.

Thomä, H. (1967). *Anorexia Nervosa.* Trans. G. Brydone. New York: International Universities Press.

Wilson, C. P. (1967). Stone as a symbol of teeth. *Psychoanalytic Quarterly* 36:418–425.

———— (1968a). The boyfriend—the girlfriend—the detailed psychoanalytic investigation of a mannerism of speech. *Bulletin of the New Jersey Psychoana-*

lytic Society 1:10–14. Abstracted by C. Karol in *Psychoanalytic Quarterly* 38:519, 1969.

———— (1968b). Psychosomatic asthma and acting out: a case of bronchial asthma that developed *de novo* in the terminal phase of analysis. *International Journal of Psycho-Analysis* 49:330–335.

———— (1971). On the limits of the effectiveness of psychoanalysis: early ego and somatic disturbances. *Journal of the American Psychoanalytic Association* 19:552–564.

———— (1975). Head-shrinker fantasies: who is shrinking whom? Annual Meeting of the Medical Society of New Jersey, Cherry Hill, NJ, June 1, 1975.

———— (1980). Parental overstimulation in asthma. *International Journal of Psycho-analytic Psychotherapy* 8:601–621.

———— (1981). Sand symbolism: the primary dream representation of the Isakower phenomenon and of smoking addictions. In *Clinical Psychoanalysis,* ed. S. Orgel and B. D. Fine, pp. 45–55. New York: Jason Aronson.

———— (1988). Bulimic equivalents. In *Bulimia: Psychoanalytic Theory and Treatment,* ed. H. Schwartz, pp. 475–503. Madison, CT: International Universities Press.

Wilson, C. P., Hogan, C. C., and Mintz, I. L., eds. (1983). *Fear of Being Fat: The Treatment of Anorexia Nervosa and Bulimia.* Rev. ed. Northvale, NJ: Jason Aronson, 1985.

7

DREAM INTERPRETATION

C. Philip Wilson, M.D.

My colleagues and I have documented the effective analytic treatment of forty-four restrictor and bulimic anorexics. We detail a technique of dream interpretation that is applicable to psychosomatic patients in general. (1) Psychosomatic patients do not usually free-associate in the first phase of their treatment. (2) Although some cases with more ego strength can be approached with oedipal interpretations, in most cases the analyst interprets early material in terms of the current situation and the dyadic transference relation to the analyst, leaving oedipal and genetic material until later.

ALEXITHYMIA

None of the contributors to this volume agree with Nemiah's (1976) concept of alexithymia — that a hereditary constitutional defect in psychosomatic patients results in a failure of the ego's capacity to fantasize and dream. They feel that when psychosomatic patients don't report fantasies and dreams, it is a sign of intense resistance that can be analyzed.

Generally, those who are hysterical neurotics readily report dreams and fantasies, whereas the compulsive cases resist doing so. Sperling (1974) reports the nightmare dreams of a 2-year-old anorexic girl who screamed in her sleep, "The fish are eating my fingers, the cats and dogs are biting me," noting that the interpretation of the projection of her oral sadistic impulses onto the fish and animals "brought to the fore her jealousy of her baby brother" (p. 176). This case report of Sperling's is important because it demonstrates the core psychopathology of anorexics. This little girl had animal phobias and anorexia. At such an early age, anorexia is a phobiclike defense against oral incorporative conflicts. It is also significant because it demonstrates the etiologic role of dreams and fantasies in psychosomatic symptom formation.

As I have detailed in my discussion of projective identification in psychosomatic disease (Chapter 7), the extreme psychoticlike denial of conflicts, fantasies, and dreams in many psyschosomatic patients is caused by the primitive projective identification onto others of archaic destructive superego introjects. Such patients may not be cooperative in therapy, yet approaches can be devised even for extreme cases. Mintz, in a paper on self-destructive behavior in anorexia and bulimia (1988), discusses analytic technique with a restrictor anorexic who was silent for many months of treatment.

CLINICAL MATERIAL

Dreams of psychosomatic patients are presented here to demonstrate a particular technique of interpretation. The shaping of this technique is determined by multiple factors such as the transference and the quality of object relationships. A crucial consideration is the split in the ego and the extent to which this split is comprehended by the self-observing functions of the patient's ego. The first phase of analysis involves making the healthier part of the patient's ego aware of the split-off, primitive-impulse-dominated part of the ego and its modes of functioning.

Typical defenses are:

1. Denial and splitting.

2. Belief in magic.

3. Feelings of omnipotence.

4. Demand that things and people be all perfect — the alternative is to be worthless.

5. Need to control.

6. Displacement, projection, and projective identification.

7. Masochistic perfectionism that defends against conflicts, particularly those around aggression.

8. Pathological ego ideal of beautiful peace and love.

9. Fantasied perfect, conflict-free mother–child symbiosis.

10. Projective Identification.

Of course, these defenses overlap and commingle.

EARLY INTERPRETATION OF THE IMPULSE DISORDER

A special technique is called for in the treatment of psychosomatic patients. The analyst must demonstrate to patients their need for immediate gratification (their impulse disorder, that is, their primary narcissism) early in treatment (Sperling 1967, 1978, Wilson et al. 1983). Thus the patient is shown that psychosomatic symptoms mask split-off impulses and fantasies.

A migraine patient in the third week of her analysis reported a dream where she was sleeping in an apartment and a French maid was at the door. In the dream the patient was screaming. Her associations were that in early childhood she had temper tantrums when she couldn't get what she wanted, that she was angry at the cost of analysis, and that she'd like to use the money to get a bigger apartment and a maid. In my interpretation I pointed out that the patient wanted me to mother her, to be a "French maid to wait on her," as her previous therapist had done when he accepted a low fee and let her cancel sessions at short notice without being charged for them. The patient confirmed the interpretation, saying that although she had no respect for her previous therapist, his fee was no problem and she was angry at being charged if she canceled an appointment.

After this session the patient dreamt that she had no sensation in her right leg below the knee. She had no associations to the dream. I asked her what she thought she'd like to do with the paralyzed part of her leg, and the patient said she guessed that she'd like to kick me. As she mentioned this hostile wish, the patient said that she had a pain in the left side of her chest. She remembered that she had developed hypochondriacal chest pains after her father's death by a heart attack. I interpreted to her that she wished I'd die of a heart attack like father, but she got a heart attack herself as a talion punishment. The patient then stated that she had been angry at me after my interpretation of the French maid dream and had fantasies of killing herself. She thought, however, that I would not care and would replace her with another patient. She went on to say that she resented my not offering her sympathy for her migraines when I told her they were emotionally caused and could be resolved by analysis.

THE UNCONSCIOUS MEANING OF BILATERAL AND UNILATERAL (CROCODILE) TEARS

A patient in analysis reported incidental symptoms of tearing from her right eye during the analytic hour. She suffered from a repression of affect and had always been jealous of women who cried easily. Her family situation showed an unusual degree of deprivation of tender, affectionate love from either the mother or father. As the analysis progressed, bilateral silent "crocodile" tearing occurred, then silent tearing from the left eye. Subsequently, with the release and working through of deeply repressed unconscious conflicts, crying and depression occurred with appropriate affects, and the silent tearing decreased in frequency.

As often occurs once my attention had focused on the symptom, I became aware of its occurrence in other analytic patients. I have studied it so far in two female and two male patients.

Greenacre (1945), in her paper on pathological weeping, stated that "stream weeping" was a substitute for male urination, the penis envy appearing in periodic aggressive demands for the male organ accompanied by fantasies of its possession. These dynamics were confirmed in my patients when bilateral tearing occurred. Also confirmed were her findings of extreme body–phallus identification and the crucial role played in the genesis of these symptoms by the birth of a younger sibling at around age 2.

Greenacre's discussion involves primarily bilateral tearing. She reports an episode of unilateral tearing and comments on the exhibitionism involved, but in personal communication (1945) she told me she has seen the unilateral tearing in other patients, both men and women, and she felt it was caused by different traumatic episodes in early childhood. She did not suggest more specific dynamics of the unilateral tearing.

Greenacre describes the displacement up to the eyes of the female's wish to urinate like a man. From my material I conclude that the major unconscious cause of unilateral tearing is a unilateral partial incorporation of the penis. This overlies the deeper and genetically earlier visual incorporation of the maternal breast. The single trickle of tears unconsciously represents urine, semen, and milk. The eye represents the phallus and the breast. The lachrymal system is utilized as a channel for the repressed wish to urinate like a man, to ejaculate like a man, and to produce breast milk like Mother. The solitary, tearing eye is also utilized repeatedly as a silent exhibition of a crippled organ, the vagina, to arouse sympathy and pity from the observer. Antithetically it symbolizes the breast-nipple and mother milk, expressing the patient's unconscious wish to be the breast-mother and nurse the object-baby with maternal love—breast milk.

A 25-year-old unmarried office worker came for analysis complaining of difficulty in her relations with men and of being overweight. She also suffered from severe psoriasis. Conflicts centering on orality were predominant in her history.

The following dream and associations illustrated a crucial turning point in the analysis and involved interpretation of the unilateral tearing. The evening of the dream the patient left her hour angry with the analyst because instead of getting sympathy, she was asked to interrupt her drinking.[1] She returned home and had a glass of wine. This made her feel guilty, as for the previous week she had for the first time in seven years managed not to drink. She ate, felt depressed, and burst into tears. Crying and sobbing, she felt no one loved her. No one had sent her a Valentine—the father, the analyst, or any man. She wished she had a different brain, and she had vague suicidal ideas. (It may be mentioned that in the first years of analysis, she made a serious attempt at suicide, and the masochistic acting out was severe.) To master her depression she called a passive man with whom she had had a sadomasochistic affair. She expressed some hostility to him and he hung up on her.

---

[1] This was a projective identification. It was she who was trying to master her oral habits.

Feeling bitter, lonely, and angry, she went to bed and had the following dream:

> It was raining and I was looking at a house that was in a tropical country. Inside were beautiful plants and a bird of paradise and flowers. There were arches, yet the house was simple. A large man, who was married to another woman, was interested in me but he said, "You are only 5'6"." I said, "That is big enough." Then I was going to the analysis with the first man I was ever interested in.

The patient teared silently from the right eye during most of the hour. The house reminded her of her grandmother's home. Her grandmother was not like her frugal mother but spent money and had expensive things. The man she thought was the analyst. She felt angry and unloved in a subdued way during the session. "Big enough" reminded her of childhood fears of her vagina's not being large enough for the paternal phallus. The tropical country and house with the bird of paradise in it clearly involved wishes for a beautiful organ, a penis, and the rain represented the wish for male urination. Interpretations were made that the crying of one eye represented on the one hand the wish to get sympathy, and on the other the wish to urinate like a man. At this point the patient remembered that she had been awakened three times the night before by a need to urinate. Nocturnal frequency was infrequent—however, several times while drunk this patient was enuretic. The displacement to the eye of intense penis envy was interpreted. The patient confirmed the interpretations by recalling a story her father used to tell that involved the obvious superiority of the penis as a urinating organ.

Thus the direct urinary wish was gratified at night. It reappeared in a repressed displaced form with the silent stream of tears from the right eye during our session. Shortly after this, the patient, while examining the uncircumcised penis of a man with whom she was having an affair, had the return to consciousness of the long-repressed memory of the appearance of the paternal phallus. She now realized that her father's penis was circumcised. After this, her intake of alcohol decreased greatly. She had the release of more affect—first bilateral silent tearing and then sobbing during the analytic hour. She became much more relaxed and friendly with men and found, much to her surprise, that she had more requests for dates than she could accept. It should be emphasized that the interpretations made in this hour had been made in various ways many times before, and the different meanings of silent tearing had been repeatedly interpreted.

The dreams of a second unmarried woman patient in her fourth year of treatment are reported because they graphically portray the unilateral partial incorporation of a (breast) phallus. These dreams occurred after a session when the patient recovered a deeply repressed memory of seeing her father's penis when he came out of the bathroom. She recalled that the penis was at the level of her eye and thought that she must have been about three years of age. The following are three dreams which occurred Friday, Saturday, and Sunday of the weekend.

Dream 1. A crazy man is pursuing me with an erection. I knew if I aroused him he'd kill me. I ran out of the house and hid under a bush.

Dream 2. (After intercourse with her lover when the patient, as usual, was frigid) I was walking across a narrow plank over some water; I fell in and a man pulled me out. I had a thing in my right eye, but it was attached to my eye; it was a ball. They (men like doctors) could not pull it off. When they squeezed it, it went back in. It was filled with blood. (The patient thought that the ball was like tears of blood and that the analyst was the man who pulled her out of the water.)

Dream 3. Mother and I went to see a man in an office who had a baby. He was kissing me, I was embarrassed. Mother picked up the baby and put it to her breast. I thought, that is too much. (The patient thought of the analyst previously asking her if she didn't want a baby to suck on her breast.)

The scope of this chapter does not permit going into all the multiple derivatives of these dreams. In connection with the second dream the "bloody tears" attached to the patient's eye reminded her of the penis, which is engorged with blood when erect. There is a graphic depiction of a visual incorporation of the breast–phallus (testicles) in these dreams. During the hour the patient had bilateral silent tearing and complained that her eyes hurt. This patient had occasional unilateral tears, sometimes with bilateral tearing that was predominantly from the right eye. Her eyes at other times would become red and inflamed. Her history had many similarities to that of the previous case. She had urinary symptoms, a young brother was born when she was two years of age, and there was extensive use of denial in the family, coupled with much exhibitionism.

In conclusion, it would appear that there may be a gradation in pathological tearing and weeping. The unilateral "crocodile" tearing masks the most primitive oral sadism, the untearing eye remaining open for offensive and defensive purposes. This would be true of the first patient, who must have been too terrified to have both eyes closed in the situation with her father. Here the unilateral tearing represented a partial blinding of the eye by the superego, but at the same time, the patient retained the scoptophilic use of the other eye. The bilateral stream tearing may involve more superego prohibition and a greater degree of expression of some unhappy feelings. Then there would be a progression in stages to normal crying. It may be more precise to call the unilateral tearing truly "crocodilism," in that one eye does not tear at all. It is looking for the (breast) phallus to incorporate and to protect against being incorporated.

DREAM SYMBOLISM OF THE ORAL PHASE

Stone and sand symbolism masks conflicts and processes described by Lewin (1961) in his concept of the oral triad. Oral incorporative conflicts, the wish to eat and to be eaten, are represented by stone symbols, and fusion conflicts, the wish to sleep and to die, are represented by sand symbols. L. Reiser's (1987) idea of Lewin's oral triad as a template to understand bulimic symptoms actually is applicable to the symptoms of all psychosomatic patients.

Sand Symbolism

The analysis of sand symbols in the dreams of psychosomatic patients is of great importance. Spitz (1955) emphasized that infants feel thirst, but not hunger, in the hallucinatory state. I have noted that sand can be used as a pregenital symbol in which repressed oral and anal conflicts are regressively represented. Sand and quicksand can symbolize the clinging mother who does not relinquish the symbiotic tie (Glauber 1955, 1965, Wilson 1981). Sand symbolizes oral-phase thirst and/or the formless stool of the infant (diarrhea). Antithetically, it depicts asceticism — the ability to do without mother's milk, to control impulse gratification. Sand representations in dreams can symbolize aspects of the conflicts and processes involved in separation–individuation (Mushatt 1975, 1980), which in psychosomatic patients is a central problem, because of their unresolved symbiotic attachment to their parents.

A young man with obesity and hypertension described feeling as though he were "moving through mush" when he was preoccupied with conflicts in relation to his impulses and to time (Wilson 1981). He suffered from a severe impulse disorder and symptoms of anxiety hysteria, insomnia, phobias of bridges, fears of new situations, and fears of blindness. An only child, he had been spoiled by his doting mother and received little help in growing up from his narcissistic father, who avoided parental roles, insisting, for example, that his son call him by his first name. The impulse disorder was manifested by nail biting and cuticle chewing that dated from age 2; masturbation with sadomasochistic fantasies in childhood, adolescence, and adulthood; obesity that began in adolescence and increased while away at college; and, in late adolescence, addiction to cigarettes and alcohol.

He dreamt: "I am in a yacht race on the ocean; we are jammed on a sandbank; huge waves crash on the boat; it is frightening." The night before, the patient managed to curb his craving for alcohol by limiting himself to two cocktails instead of drinking all evening. His first association to sand was of being caught in the undertow as a child swimmer and having to be pulled out. Then he reported unpleasant memories of mother washing the sand off his body at the beach when he was 3 years old. Another memory was of digging a tremendous pit in the sand at the beach; when it caved in on him, his angry father had to dig him out.

Being stuck on a sandbar and destroyed by waves (id impulses) in his dream represents the struggle to free himself from his father at the risk of being overwhelmed by pregenital wishes. The associations all involved danger and being saved by his parents (the analyst). Being suffocated by sand on the beach symbolized passive and active anal conflicts; the sand was symbolic of feces, especially diarrhea (sand in his pants). As with other patients, sand also symbolized insomnia and the dry, thirsty mouth.

Sand symbolism dreams are usually amenable to analysis only in the terminal phases of treatment. The meanings of sand symbols — thirst and a dry mouth, diarrhea, conflicts with time, and its antithetical meaning of asceticism (impulse control) — should be interpreted in the context of the clinical material. Often the therapist has to ask these patients whether they have a dry mouth and, also, to focus on this symptom, since they usually feel a dry mouth is normal, unless it is intense and prolonged xerosthomia.

Stone Symbolism[2]

Thirty years of research have led me to conclude that basically stone symbolizes teeth and that it masks conflicts about oral sadistic (cannibal-istic) incorporation of the breast (mother). Stone is the most plastic of all dream symbols. Important preoedipal and oedipal meanings of stone are the teeth and the breast, feces, penis, testicles, and pregnancy. Stone can symbolize the reliable mother (Glauber 1965, Wilson 1967, 1971, 1972, 1981) and other objects with whom the child develops basic trust and object constancy.

I have reached the conclusion that stone is the most important primitive symbol because it has qualities of hardness, persistence in time and space, and tactile definiteness which makes it most readily available for organized kinesthetic visual and tactile projection by the primitive ego. Other researchers in dream symbols (Boyer 1974, Bychowski 1972, Niederland 1972, Sarnoff 1968, 1972) are in agreement with this hypothesis. In contrast, sand is inconstant in space, time, shape, consistency, and color, thus requiring further ego maturation and more developed functioning for its symbolization. Therefore, although the *drive aspect* of sand symbolism is more primitive ontogenetically and philoge-netically (sucking at the breast) than the drive aspect of stone symbolism (cannibalistic incorporation of the breast), the symbolism of sand is not used by the ego until the second year, at the earliest. The recovered memories of my patients date from the second to the fourth year. Moreover, there is little resistance to the interpretation of sand symbol-ism, whereas the interpretation of stone symbolism elicits strong and persistent resistance. Parenthetically, similar observations have been made about other pregenital symbols, such as water (Niederland 1956, 1957) and fire (Arlow 1955).

Stone has primitive antithetical meanings; on the one hand it symbolizes oral sadism (the cannibalistic incorporation of the object, the breast), and on the other hand it symbolizes the reliable mother and, by extension, basic trust and object constancy. Stone symbolism is impor-

---

[2]Stone symbols are termed protosymbols to differentiate them from the symbols detailed by Sarnoff (Chapter 5) that are dated at a later developmental stage.

tant in the analysis of psychosomatic patients, who have profound conflicts with aggression and object relations and who are ambivalent.

Several years later, the foregoing hypertensive "moving through mush" patient reported material that reflected the progress he had made in the development of capacities for impulse control (and more mature object relations). After a weekend when he wanted to act out masochistically by having an affair with a woman whom he knew to be neurotic and perverse, he reported a nightmare.

He dreamt: "To prevent a flood from drowning my wife and me, I put a big stone in an opening on a wall. I start to cross a bridge but I fall off into quicksand." His associations included a fight with his landlord, who said he made too much noise playing his stereo, and his wish to get rid of his wife, whose criticism enraged him. He said: "Maybe she'll die of cancer like my mother." This dream expressed the patient's struggle to establish impulse control. He had begun to interrupt his acting out, to control his addictions to cigarettes and alcohol; his habits of nail biting and cuticle chewing were becoming ego alien. The stone indicates an emerging wish to develop controls, to be consistent, firm, and reliable; the quicksand and the flood depict his fear of being overwhelmed by oral and anal impulses. The stone, quicksand, and water also reflect castration and pregnancy fears. In this patient a resolution of the pathological ego state was effected. In addition, he developed an organized sense of time as the deep-seated impulse disorder yielded to analysis.

IMPULSE-DISORDER DREAMS

The dreams of the "moving through mush" patient illustrate a general finding in psychosomatic patients. Anxiety dreams of storms, flood, earthquakes, threatening waves, fire, and other disasters reflect, aside from their individual dynamic and genetic meaning, their fears of being overwhelmed by their impulses. Such dreams early in analysis should be interpreted in the immediate context, with specific individual psychodynamics left until a later phase.

The technique of dream interpretation is further documented in several chapters of this volume (Chapters 2, 4, 6, 9) and in the chapter on dream interpretation in our anorexic volume (Wilson et al. 1983).

SUMMARY

Dreams of a migraine patient were presented to show that psychosomatic patients do not usually free associate early in analysis and that dreams are utilized to demonstrate to the patient their impulse disorder and other pregenital conflicts in the dyadic transference.

Additional case material was presented to demonstrate the technique of interpretation and psychodynamics of (1) pathological crying and (2) stone and sand representations, which are the universal symbols of Lewin's oral triad. Oral incorporative conflicts — the wish to eat and be eaten — are represented by stone and fusion conflicts — the wish to sleep and to die by sand.

REFERENCES

Arlow, J. A. (1955). Notes on oral symbolism. *Psychoanalytic Quarterly* 34:63–74.

Boyer, L. (1974). Personal communication. Letter, June 16, 1974.

Bychowski, G. (1972). Discussion of C. Wilson's stone paper. Presented to the New Jersey Psychoanalytic Society, January 13.

Glauber, I. (1965). Personal communication about stone symbolism and quicksand as they relate to his paper, "On the meaning of agoraphobia." *Journal of the American Psychoanalytic Association* 3:701–709 (1955).

Greenacre, P. (1945). Psychological weeping. *Psychoanalytic Quarterly* 14(1): 62–75.

Lewin, B. (1961). *The Psychoanalysis of Elation.* New York: Psychoanalytic Quarterly, Inc.

Mintz, I. L. (1988). Self-destructive behavior in anorexia nervosa and bulimia. In *Bulimia: Psychoanalytic Treatment and Theory*, ed. H. J. Schwartz, pp. 127–171. New York: International Universities Press.

Mushatt, C. (1975). Mind–body environment: toward understanding the impact of loss on psyche and soma. *Psychoanalytic Quarterly* 44:81–106.

———— (1980). Melitta Sperling Memorial Lecture. Presented at the Psychoanalytic Association of New York, February 25.

Nemiah, J. C. (1976). Alexithymia: a view of the psychosomatic process. In *Modern Trends in Psychosomatic Medicine*, vol. 3, ed. O. W. Hill, pp. 403–409, New York: Appleton-Century-Crofts.

Niederland, W. G. (1956). River symbolism, Part 1. *The Psychoanalytic Quarterly* 25:469–504.

_____ (1957). River symbolism, Part 2. *The Psychoanalytic Quarterly* 26:50–75.

_____ (1972). Discussion of C. P. Wilson's paper, "Further reflections on stone as the earliest ontogenetic and philogenetic symbol." Presented to the New Jersey Psychoanalytic Society, January 13.

Reiser, L. (1987). The oral triad in bulimia. Paper presented at meeting of the American Psychoanalytic Association, December 18, New York.

Sarnoff, C. (1968). Personal communication. Letter, October 23, 1968.

_____ (1972). Personal communication. Letter, February 14, 1972, discussing protosymbols.

Sperling, M. (1967). Transference neurosis in patients with psychosomatic disorders. *Psychoanalytic Quarterly* 36:342–355.

_____ (1974). *The Major Neuroses and Behavior Disorders in Children.* New York: Jason Aronson.

_____ (1978). *Psychosomatic Disorders in Childhood.* Ed. O. Sperling. New York: Jason Aronson.

Spitz, R. (1955). The primal cavity: a contribution to the genesis of perception and its role for psychoanalytic theory. *Psychoanalytic Study of the Child* 10:215–239.

Wilson, C. P. (1967). Stone as a symbol of teeth. *Psychoanalytic Quarterly* 36:418–425.

_____ (1968). Psychosomatic asthma and acting out: a case of asthma that developed *de novo* in the terminal phase of analysis. *International Journal of Psycho-Analysis* 49:330–335.

_____ (1971). Panel report: On the limits of the effectiveness of psychoanalysis: early ego and somatic disturbances. *Journal of the American Psychoanalytic Association* 19:552–564.

_____ (1972). Further reflections on the stone as the earliest symbol. Paper presented to the New Jersey Psychoanalytic Society, January 13.

_____ (1980a). Parental overstimulation in asthma. *International Journal of Psychoanalytic Psychotherapy* 8:601–621.

_____ (1980b). On the fear of being fat in female psychology and anorexia nervosa patients. *Bulletin of the Psychoanalytic Association of New York* 17:8–9.

_____ (1981). Sand symbolism: the primary dream representation of the Isakower phenomenon and of smoking addictions. In *Clinical Psychoanalysis,* ed. S. Orgel and B. D. Fine, pp. 45–55. New York: Jason Aronson.

_____ (1986). The psychoanalytic psychotherapy of bulimic anorexia nervosa. In *Adolescent Psychiatry,* ed. S. Feinstein, pp. 274–314. Chicago: University of Chicago Press.

Wilson, C. P., Hogan, C. C., and Mintz, I. L. (1983). *Fear of Being Fat: The Treatment of Anorexia Nervosa and Bulimia.* Rev. ed. Northvale, NJ: Jason Aronson, 1985.

8

GRIEF AND ANNIVERSARY REACTIONS

Cecil Mushatt, M.D.
Isidore Werby, M.D.

Depression from bereavement and unresolved grief and from anniversary reactions can play an important part in triggering not only psychiatric symptoms but also physical illness, even when, in the latter, organic factors are involved. This point of view is supported by an extensive literature, of which the following references represent only a small sampling: Abraham (1924), Berliner (1938), Bressler (1956), Hilgard (1953), Knapp and colleagues (1966), Mushatt (1954, 1959, 1965), Lindemann (1945), and Pollock (1970). This is a psychological study of a special instance of headache in a man who was seen in psychoanalytic psychotherapy from 1960 to 1965, once a week in the first year and subsequently once or twice a month. The patient had been under the regular medical care of Isidore Werby since 1956. Both physicians maintained frequent contact with each other throughout; their joint work was crucial to the treatment of this patient.

Our hope is to show how the meaning and function of this man's particular physical symptoms can be understood in these terms as well as to demonstrate the kinds of conflicts that lead to pathological grief reactions and the manner in which resolution and mastery take place. We shall show how, at the late age of this man, partial liberation from severe emotional trauma sustained in much earlier years could be achieved by psychotherapy, combined with psychologically oriented medical care, to permit a considerable measure of equanimity in older years. We hope also to demonstrate how, through the resolution of relevant emotional conflicts, the burden on the cardiovascular and pulmonary systems, already impaired from chronic organic disease, could be reduced significantly so as to facilitate more effective response to medication.

THE PATIENT

Mr. D. at one time held a part-time position in a community organization, and later, until his retirement in 1965, he served as an engineer for a company which provided consultation services in regard to the maintenance of public institutions. When he was first seen in psychiatric consultation in December 1960, he had an eight-year history of incapacitating left-sided headaches which had been recurring with little respite since they had begun suddenly in June 1952 when he was 54 years old. There had been no prior similar history and no family history of headache. Mr. D. had seen a number of physicians, and various therapeutic procedures had been tried unsuccessfully, including the injection of the sphenopalatine ganglion and two surgical operations (namely, division of the temporal and supraorbital arteries and, later, undercutting of nerves in the scalp).

In some way, Mr. D. discovered that a combination of ergotamine tartrate and caffeine (cafergot) was the one medicational arrangement that gave relief with any certainty, but its use was contraindicated because he had hypertension. He antagonized his physicians by his irascible and insistent demands for the drug. Mr. D. managed to obtain supplies of the drug and used it of his own accord, often in anticipation of a recurrence of the headaches. Dr. Werby had the unenviable task of tolerating this self-medication until Mr. D. could be weaned of it. Mr. D.'s blood pressure ranged from 160 to 190 systolic and 100 to 110 diastolic. It was never clear to what extent the elevation of blood pressure was caused or aggravated by the self-prescribed use of cafergot.

The nerve resection in the scalp was done late in 1955. Postoperatively it was discovered that the superior oblique muscle of the left eye had been damaged accidentally during the operation, resulting in severe diplopia. Mr. D. refused to undergo an operation for repair of the damage. In an attempt to compensate for the double vision, he developed severe torticollis, which was only partially relieved by the use of powerful lenses.

Because of his double vision, Mr. D. could not drive his car, and he became wholly dependent on his wife for car transportation. He used his resentment of this dependence to justify his very hostile behavior toward her. In the course of therapy it became clear that Mr. D. knew that the use of an eye patch over the affected eye could help him to counteract the double vision, but he would not use one. Thus the eye damage and the torticollis became significant psychologically, requiring explanation beyond the obvious physical basis for them.

COURSE OF TREATMENT

On November 5, 1960, Mr. D. was admitted to the hospital because of a myocardial infarction; he was then 62. In the hospital he developed severe headaches. He demanded cafergot; when this was refused, he became enraged and depressed and was reported to have spoken of suicide. At this point Dr. Werby requested psychiatric consultation. When seen by Dr. Mushatt, Mr. D. had already become calmer and was getting relief from Darvon. When first interviewed, Mr. D. was outwardly a cantankerous man with a "chip on the shoulder"; as he described himself later: "I can be very ugly." He said that he did not want to see a psychiatrist, but in spite of this he began to give a history of his headaches. He reported that they had come on suddenly in June 1952. There were two types of headaches: a mild frontal one, easily relieved by aspirin, and a severe one, located chiefly in his left eye and to some extent in the back of his head. "It felt as though somebody was pushing my eye in, as if a blowtorch was being held against it." The description of the headache was striking. Since their onset, the headaches had recurred with incapacitating frequency, lasting from one to eighteen hours. Because of their severity, in 1954 Mr. D gave up his community post.

Mr. D. next described his experiences in the treatment of his headaches, launching into a long tirade against all his doctors prior to his present physician and describing very clearly how he had antagonized them and provoked rejection. He was also angry at himself for taking cafergot against his doctors' orders. He felt convinced that it had caused his heart attack. He also mentioned that the operation in which the eye muscle was damaged occurred when he was admitted to the hospital because of his headaches around Thanksgiving of November 1955. He saw Dr. Werby for the first time in October 1956 because of acute renal colic on the left side. Attention is drawn here to the dates and to the frequency of physical symptoms related to his left side. Mr. D. said he had "persisted in treatment with Dr. Werby because Dr. Werby has been very honest. Dr. Werby said he did not know why I had the headaches, but he has never given up trying to find out." Mr. D. felt that he had given Dr. Werby more trouble than any of his other doctors, and he "could not understand how Dr. Werby could have tolerated me for so long."

Gradually in the first psychological interview a brief but significant family history was obtained. Mr. D. had married when he was 26 and his wife was 22. They had had no children. His mother died from pneumonia and asthma after one week's acute illness at the age of 75 in February 1939. She had had asthma all her life. His father died from a heart attack in January 1941 at the age of 79. Earlier his father had had a stroke affecting his speech. His parents' symptoms, as will be seen, are very significant.

Mr. D. was the youngest of three sons. His next older brother, Tom, was then 67. When Mr. D. was 22, his eldest brother, Mike, died at the age of 28 on October 2, 1920, from electrocution while engaged in installing an electrical transformer for a power company. Mr. D. and his father had been on their way to help Mike, but had stopped at a drugstore for a drink near the installation site. A man rushed into the store to announce that Mike had been electrocuted. Mr. D. recalled seeing his brother at the site of the accident: "It was horrible. He lived for eighteen hours. His left foot was burned off. His left eye was burned as well as the left side of his face." Mr. D. had been very attached to Mike. He would never forget the accident nor how Mike looked. He said that he could easily imagine what Mike had experienced. At this point he had little realization of how vividly he could do so.

From this session it appeared probable that the headaches were initimately related to his brother and the freak accident, but it did not seem advisable yet to explore beyond these meager factual details. If this assumption were correct, it was curious that a reaction of this nature and proportion should first occur thirty-two years after the brother's death and should persist then in 1960, eight years later.

Three days after this first interview, Mr. D. was feeling better, but he was adamant in his refusal to see a psychiatrist. This attitude was respected, but he was told that he could contact the psychiatrist if at any time he felt that this would be of help to him.

Five months later, in May 1961, Mr. D. felt the need for help. In the meantime, the headaches had recurred and in April Mr. D. had developed a left Bell's facial palsy, from which he quickly recovered. He finally told his physician that the headaches started most often during the night when he would awaken angry from a dream. This information provided the opportunity for a meaningful basis for another psychiatric referral. In his first interview following his second referral, Mr. D. began by talking of the recurrence of his headaches after discharge from the hospital. Then he talked at length about his sense of guilt and unworthiness with regard to his job. "If people knew my background, they would find me uneducated and incapable of handling my job." He had, in fact, tried to convince his superior that he should not hold his responsible position "when I have Ivy League graduates working under me." In actual fact he was a very able man in his field.

Dr. Mushatt remarked on Mr. D.'s efforts to get people to reject him. This led to Mr. D.'s telling that he was seldom free of headaches and that they came on most frequently at night between one and three o'clock when he awakened angry from dreams. The dreams concerned mostly his family. His most recent dream had been one in which he was with his father and brother Mike. In it Mr. D. was angry that he had not been told about something that had to do with the power company for which Mike had worked. In association, he spoke briefly about the circumstances of his brother's death. Mr. D. and his father at that time had worked together in a moving business. They were to move a transformer into position at a site for the power company, and Mike was to install it. The patient and his father had informed Mike that they would be delayed by another job, but, as was revealed much later, Mike had become impatient and had started the preparatory work before their arrival. The scene, Mr. D. said, was still vivid to him, and he wondered why it should be so now, forty years later. Dr. Mushatt told him that it would be worthwhile to look into this very question. Very reluctantly, Mr. D. agreed to one session per week for psychological exploration. This reluctance was prognostic of his capacity for maintaining himself in a continual state of turmoil and of his masochistic self-denial of adequate opportunity to obtain relief from his symptoms.

In a patient with such a propensity for severe bodily reactions, psychotherapy presented a difficult problem. Whenever there are severe psychosomatic symptoms, it can be assumed that there has been marked disharmony in key present and past relationships. In this man, markedly hostile and guilt-laden key relationships were suggested from the manner in which he related to his doctors. In addition, the danger of somatic response in exploratory therapy and the prognosis without therapy can be predicted from the pathological nature of relationships and from the extent to which these, in their primitive representations, are symbolized in organ systems (Deutsch 1954, Knapp et al. 1966, Mushatt 1965). In this instance, if psychological components were important in producing the intractability of the headaches, relief from the pressure of primitive rage, guilt, depression, and pathological identifications — all of which together characterize pathological grief reactions — was essential. Yet undue pressure to uncover and resolve such feelings could provoke symptoms defensively. In such instances, one must proceed at first with circumspection, allowing the patient to set his own pace and carefully limiting the exploration of his inner life to what is readily accessible and tolerable. As a viable relationship of trust is established, the patient acquires the capacity to tolerate and master his primitive fantasy life and emotional arousal, thereby facilitating more effective exploration and relief.

Two sessions later Mr. D. reported being free of headaches for one week, the longest period of freedom for some time. He again recalled Mike's death and told how, as he rushed to the scene of the accident from the drugstore, he had almost stepped on Mike as he lay on the ground. The thought of this still horrified him. Then he castigated himself over a report because it was long overdue. In actuality, because of factors entirely beyond his control, he could not have finished the report. Nevertheless, he felt it should have been completed. Later in the interview he spoke of his father's violent temper outbursts and his father's intolerance of mistakes, even when made through ignorance. His father had always felt that he, the patient, should have known better. Thus, Mr. D. tormented himself with guilt, as his father had done to him. He obviously felt that, no matter what the circumstances, he should be able to arrange things differently. The self-torment over Mike was obvious.

In the same session, Mr. D. gave an account of himself that added another dimension to his sense of guilt. He told of a happy though brief period after Mike's death when he enjoyed a very intimate friendship with a much older man and his wife, Mr. and Mrs. K., and, through them, with two other men a little older than himself. He worked for Mr. K. and virtually lived in his home. His life with Mr. and Mrs. K. and the other two men clearly represented a restoration of the intactness of his own family in idealized form. (It is of importance, from the point of view of working through grief, to note that at this stage Mr. D. idealized both his mother and father in their relationship to him.) To Mr. D.'s chagrin, Mr. K. died suddenly when he was about to launch Mr. D. on a business career. Shortly afterward, one of the other two men, with whom the patient had set up a partnership in a construction business, died unexpectedly. Friends made fun of Mr. D., saying he was a jinx. Anyone he worked with died. He protested that he did not believe in such talk; but, as if to confirm his belief in his guilt in this respect and his need for punishment, he went on to give an account of how much he had suffered and of how he had allowed his business to deteriorate in order to fulfill his obligations to the public in the part-time post he once held. Up to this point Mr. D. maintained a very guarded attitude toward the psychiatrist and could not openly acknowledge any feeling of dependence on him.

By the middle of June 1961, Mr. D. had been free of headaches for four weeks and was sleeping restfully. Characteristically, as a magical protection against losing his sense of well-being, he reviewed how much he had suffered through the headaches and the double vision. Then in one session, with great embarrassment, he confessed that he had been afraid that the psychiatrist's purpose was to prove that he was "off his rocker" and to send him to a mental hospital. After this, he became much more communicative. He reported that, in fact, he had long been afraid that he would have a breakdown, especially when he had been active in community affairs and his work had required long hours with little time for sleep, home, or his business. Even now he felt he had to go all the way to help people. At the end of this session in June, Dr. Mushatt told Mr. D. of his impending vacation in August, whereupon Mr. D. asked how much longer he would have to come for these sessions. To reassure him, Dr. Mushatt replied that he had been giving some thought to this, as Mr. D. had been doing so well. But he quickly regretted this reply, realizing that Mr. D. had been confronted with a double threat—the therapist's vacation and the implied threat of discharge. The effect of the threat of separation soon became apparent. Six days later Mr. D. returned depressed, with recurrence of headaches. He said he was depressed over the condition of mental hospitals that he had inspected. He had also inspected jails and was angry at how well prisoners were treated. "The maximum security jail is like a hotel. I have eaten there myself. The prisoners have done something which they shouldn't have done." Mr. D. was for capital punishment (that is, for electrocution), and he was angry that the law was not being enforced. He told how, nevertheless, he had helped men get released from jail. He had helped hundreds of people and had never received any thanks. He bore everybody's troubles. (Thus, on a deep level he was expressing his rage and destructive fantasies toward Dr. Mushatt, his parents, and his brothers; his feelings about the fate that he could expect as a result; and his feeling that Mike had received his just deserts.)

Dr. Mushatt commented that for years Mr. D. had felt that he must bear everyone's troubles, but that he himself deserved only to be kicked around. Only last week, in his own way, he had asked if he were going to be gotten rid of. At this he burst out laughing, saying that he did not agree. "I know I am going to be coming here for a long time," he said, expressing his first acknowledgment of his clinging need for the therapist.

Mr. D.'s headaches recurred with intensity almost every day in the next few weeks. He continued to talk depressively, and in one session, after reporting a headache, which lasted only one hour, he asked: "Can you imagine what it is like to go through thirty times that? It's like going through hell. The Man up above will tell me when I've had enough. It's been like hell on earth for me. I've got to be good not to go to hell." (In effect, instantaneous death by electrocution was too good for him!) When asked what had happened in his life to make him feel condemned to go through hell on earth, Mr. D. replied with an account of a series of accidents over a period of six years with injuries particularly to the left side of his body. In one accident in the early fall, scaffolding had collapsed and he had broken his left ankle and the ribs on his left side. In this accident he also had fallen into a hole dug for the cesspool of the house — a striking symbol of his fate in life! In another accident, again scaffolding had collapsed. He had just exchanged places on a platform with a fellow worker, but had forgotten his spirit level; when he reached down to receive it, the platform collapsed. It will soon be seen how closely this mishap resembled his brother's.

Dr. Mushatt repeatedly expressed the opinion that Mr. D. was blue because of his impending vacation, but Mr. D. rejected any such idea. Nevertheless, by the end of July (1961), he was in a much better mood and the headaches had become slight. On the night before his last session prior to Dr. Mushatt's vacation, however, Mr. D. awakened with a severe headache. The next day he spoke about the busy conferences at the office that arose from the fact that the heads of various departments were leaving for vacation in August. He did not mention Dr. Mushatt's vacation and finally had to be reminded of its imminence. He dismissed any preoccupation with the vacation: "I'd be selfish if I were to ask you to stay. In fact, you'd be crazy to stay just because I have a headache" — an acknowledgment of his unconscious wish for the psychiatrist not to leave.

In September 1961 Mr. D. reported that he had been free of headaches since his last session in July. He felt fine. He had been told that his blood pressure was normal. He was planning a vacation after his annual report was done. He had not taken a vacation for many years for fear that he might be in need of sick leave. His mother had told him, "Never look forward to the future; look what happened to Mike." His belief in superstition and magic was a powerful force in him; through it, he could deny himself relaxation from tension.

For the next seventeen months, Mr. D. was entirely free of headaches; however, significant material arose in the psychotherapeutic sessions during this period. In October 1961, in the week of the anniversary of Mike's death, he went to wakes for friends who had just died. The patient had a predilection for attending wakes, and usually headaches were the outcome, though not so on this occasion. Memories of Mike and the family were now evoked. With much hesitancy, he said, "I'm ashamed to say it, but I felt I was an unwanted child. I had to take my father's, my mother's, and my brothers' crap ever since I was born." He told how in his late teens his father had made him give up a good job to return home to work for him for a pittance. His father had not asked the other brothers. Much later, after Mr. D. had married, his wife went to work to help him support his mother and father in their retirement. After Mr. D. and his wife had been their sole source of support for thirteen years, his parents came to visit one day and his mother said they had drawn up wills and had left their house to his brother Tom. Tom, who had always been his mother's favorite, had never helped in the support of his parents. Mr. D.'s only feeling about this was hurt for his wife, who had never complained. The impact on him of this announcement by the mother did not become clear until later.

In March 1962 Mr. D. expressed fear of bragging about how well he felt; something might happen to bring on his headaches. He had thought he would never be free of them. Dr. Mushatt commented that Mr. D. still spoke as if he had been damned for life. In reply, Mr. D. told of a problem that he had been having for about six weeks — that is, since January. He had found himself unable to tolerate women. He had been getting mad at them lately. He complained that in the street, as he walked in the snow, women stepped out from doorways and almost knocked him down. Women pushed him on the subway cars. Sometimes he felt so angry that he could strike them with his fist. His wife was a contrast to these women, and again Mr. D. spoke of how she had helped to support his parents. He returned to his mother and the will, and with great discomfort said, "It's disrespectful to my mother to say that it made me angry. It knocked me off my feet." Dr. Mushatt could not resist the comment, "Like the women in the past six weeks." It is of interest that in this session Mr. D. mentioned the anniversary of his mother's death, as he recalled it at this point, on January 20. Around that time the past January, he had had a brief episode of unexplained acute dyspnea (his mother had died of asthma and pneumonia). With emotion he again spoke of how he had felt unwanted and of how badly he had been treated. When he went to work for his father, he said, "That was the beginning of the shit-end of the stick. The end of it was when they both died."

Mr. D. little realized at this point how the fantasy of liberation and revenge through the deaths of his mother and father and brother had come to plague him. It forced him to try to revive them and keep them alive within himself symbolically in order to suffer for them, while at the same time symbolically he kept them suffering through his own suffering. His hurt and bitter fantasies, with the ensuing guilt, bound him pathologically to all members of his family. This he demonstrated repeatedly by somatic dramatizations and a self-sacrificing, masochistic life. The more he did for others, the more it evoked his own disappointments. Rage, revenge, expiation, sadness, and restitution were reenacted simultaneously through physical symptoms.

During 1962 the anger and guilt seemed to ease. In October 1962, however, Mr. D. had another acute coronary thrombosis, calling Dr. Werby only after two days of typical pain. His greeting to Dr. Mushatt in the hospital was, "Well, Doc, I guess one year of peace is all I can have. Thank God for that."

In the hospital the opportunity arose to ask Mr. D. if he had any idea why he should feel so guilty toward Mike forty-two years after the accident and why he should still find it necessary to keep reliving the accident in his mind. Mr. D. replied that he could not believe that Mike would want to come back to haunt him. This time, when he reviewed his memories of the accident, he was able to say that the delayed arrival of his father and himself at the site had had nothing to do with the accident — an indication of significant easing of guilt toward Mike. It was then that Mr. D. filled in important details of the accident. Mike had been on a platform drilling into a post in preparation for the installation of the transformer. The drill was too short, and he called down for another. He crouched down to receive it, and then, as he straightened up, the back of his head touched electrified bolts. As he related this, Mr. D. raised his head, straightened his back, hunched his shoulders, and conspicuously tightened the muscles of his neck. These actions seemed to clarify a previously unexplained episode in December 1961 when Dr. Werby answered an emergency call from Mr. D., who thought he was having a heart attack. Dr. Werby found that Mr. D. was having severe spasms of his neck and shoulder muscles, with some difficulty in breathing as a result. Of significance, also, was the patient's accident during which the scaffolding broke as he reached down for his forgotten spirit level. Mr. D. made a good recovery from the coronary thrombosis.

On December 30, 1962, Mr. D. tried to reach Dr. Mushatt, who was then out of town. The next day he was contacted. After seventeen months of remission, the severe headaches had returned. Because it was unusual for Mr. D. to call, Dr. Mushatt thought he should see him as soon as possible. The city was in the midst of a severe cold storm, so the session took place in Mr. D.'s home. The patient reported that the headaches had started there on Christmas Eve when he had had fourteen visitors, among them Mike's son Mike, his wife, and children. At first it seemed that this might have had some bearing on the headaches, but it soon turned out that the actual visitors were less relevant than the absentees. Mr. D. exploded as he exclaimed that one person had not come. It was "that other fellow," meaning his brother Tom. He talked again of the property left to Tom and of how he felt that Tom had abandoned him over the years. He wished that Mike were alive, so that he could tell him what had happened. "Mike would lay Tom out in lavender. In fact, he'd lay us both out."

The headaches recurred into March 1963. In January Mr. D. recalled more clearly the onset of his headaches in June 1952. They had started suddenly when he was attending an executive meeting. The chairman of this meeting was a man with whom he had had a violent fight about six years earlier. Mr. D. at that time had refused to support this man and his colleagues in their plans. The man had threatened him, saying that, if he ever came with any request before a committee over which he presided, he would give him nothing but ice water. Mr. D. then had grabbed the man and threatened to kill him. (It is of more than passing interest that, as the patient related the first attack of headaches, he said that an ice bag, which the doctor had put on his head, had made his headache much worse!) In a session several days later, in March 1963, Mr. D. said that his headaches prevented him from thinking about anything else. When asked what came to mind when for a moment he stopped thinking of his headaches, he thought of his mother and of her death in the month of January. (Later he checked family records and found that his mother had died in February and his father in January.) He repeated the feeling of being unwanted and told of arguments between his mother and father which had indicated to him that, at the time he was conceived, his mother had not wanted any more children. She had never changed her mind about him in this respect. After his birth his mother would not have anything to do with his father sexually, and they slept in separate rooms. Later his father began drinking. Mr. D. felt responsible for this separation of his mother and father and for his father's drinking, which he felt had been caused by this separation.

During one session in March 1963, Mr. D. developed a severe headache. He had just told of how, a week prior to his mother's death, he had bought a truck to start a construction business. With the expense of the funeral, he went broke. Two years later, when his father died, he had just built his first house. Again he went broke because of funeral expenses for his father. When Dr. Mushatt said that his mother's and father's deaths must have affected him deeply, especially as they had occurred at a time when he was in a position to show how worthwhile he was, he announced almost immediately that a headache was coming on. It is worth noting that he had finished the previous session with a story of how he had once helped a colleague obtain a position, but later this man had refused to support him in a very important project. "I was so angry, I could have kicked his balls off. That would have put him in hospital and me in jail." The theme of this material and the defensive shift of anger away from his parents and brothers are clear. Dr. Mushatt's remarks served to give further impetus to the pressure for emergence of anger and guilt toward them, and the patient reacted with symptoms.

From this session in March 1963 until October 1964, Mr. D. was entirely free of headaches. In March 1963, however, he developed acute angioneurotic edema, which responded quickly to antihistamines. In telling of this bout and of the quick relief by medication, Mr. D. commented: "That's the end of my organ recitals." This spontaneous acknowledgment of his awareness of body language was striking in a man quite unsophisticated in psychological concepts. From the associations which followed, it seemed that the optimism expressed in this remark would be short-lived. Mr. D. talked at length about his religious training and how it was impossible to be perfect; every day one committed a mortal sin. But "all that is asked of you is to confess—and, if you have stolen, to pay back—and you are absolved. I believe you should always pay, no matter what." When the angioneurotic edema recurred later, he described the difficulty in speaking and swallowing arising from it as a punishment.

In August 1963 (during Dr. Mushatt's vacation), Mr. D. had a severe recurrence of angioneurotic edema with massive swelling of his uvula and tongue, which responded only slowly to medical treatment. He could scarcely swallow; he would lose his voice when speaking, and his speech was muffled. In addition, some dyspnea appeared. During one session in mid-September, he said he thought that the trouble would last "not less than six weeks. That's till this week." Then he guessed it would take a week longer. That would have been approximately September 25, and Dr. Mushatt asked if perhaps it would take two weeks more. Mr. D. replied, "You mean the second of October—Mike?" He then filled in the scene of Mike in the hospital with his face bandaged and Mike moaning in pain. He was sure that Mike had had difficulty in breathing. When the undertaker brought him home, Mike's head was placed on its side on account of the burnt left eye and left side of his face. Mr. D. tilted his head to the left. When asked whether with his head, his voice, and his tongue he were giving a picture of what Mike went through, he said he was disturbed that he could not figure out which way Mike lay, whether his head was to the right or to the left. In a subsequent session he announced: "I got a message from Mike—I mean Mike's son Mike. He said everything is all right." "A message from Mike" reminded Mr. D. that many times he had wished he could have died instead of Mike. He said it was possible—though he did not know for certain—that, by taking on Mike's symptoms, he could have freed Mike of them in heaven. He felt that Mike was looking down from heaven and saw what he had done for him and his family. The intensity of guilt over Mike was now subsiding. The sense of grief and pain over Mike's suffering and death was implicit in this account of Mike in the hospital. One element in the determination of the angioneurotic edema may have been that it represented a form of "internal" weeping as a defense against the greater pain of overt expression of grief. This is a frequent psychological component of angioneurotic edema. It should be added here that the dyspnea was due to emphysema and not to cardiac failure.

At the end of October (1963), Mr. D. had an acute exacerbation of swelling of his uvula and of dyspnea. He angrily recalled a man he had met recently at a wedding (a change from a wake!). This man had once sought an important position, and Mr. D.'s wife had worked hard to help him in his efforts. Later in the spring of 1950 or 1952, this man had spread malicious rumors about Mr. D. When Mr. D. confronted him in public, a vicious quarrel ensued. The symbolic theme of this anecdote was clear, and it could be seen that we were getting closer to events around the date of onset of the headaches in June 1952.

About a week later, in November (1963), Mr. D. was severely dyspneic. There was now to be seen a significant shift in his predominant preoccupation — away from his brother to his parents. He was convinced he had asthma. Then, for the first time, he gave a detailed account of his mother's severe asthma attacks over the years and of his terror in childhood that she would die in one of her attacks. He recalled his mother's "panting for breath and pulling big strands of mucus out of her mouth." As he recounted this, his breathing became quiet, although subjectively he still felt distress. Then he related a visit by a female cousin from the west coast several weeks prior to this session in November 1963. During his childhood this woman had lived in his home to help his mother with the family. Sometime between 1950 and 1952, this woman's daughter had come to live with Mr. D. and his wife because she had asthma and tuberculosis and needed special care, which her mother could not provide. The girl turned out to be very self-centered and demanding; Mr. D. had great difficulty tolerating her. Finally, after she had had a frighteningly severe attack of asthma, Mr. D. insisted that the girl return home. He still felt guilty about this. (This account reflected his ambivalence toward his mother, his deep concern for her and wish to help her, together with his wish to see her dead and gone — all largely because of the terror induced in him by her asthma and, as he described later, because of the resentment caused by her tyrannical behavior toward him.) A week after this session, Mr. D.'s breathing was much improved, and Dr. Werby reported that the swelling of the uvula had receded considerably. Interestingly, during this period of severe dyspnea, Mr. D. described his guilt over masturbation in his early teens and over what he called his delinquent behavior in school around puberty. He felt guilty toward his mother over both. "Had she known some of the things I did, she would have knocked my block off." His misbehavior in school had troubled his mother very much. His realization now that his behavior had, in part, been an expression of his anxiety and concern over his mother's ill health gave him a considerable sense of relief.

The visit of the cousin and the encounter with his former associate who had maligned him, by their special meaning, had triggered his recent symptoms of dyspnea and swelling of the uvula. Mr. D. had begun to unravel events, extrafamilial and intrafamilial, which had occurred around the time of onset of his original symptoms. These must have overtaxed his tenuous defenses at the time by relentlessly mobilizing the whole history of his provocative life with his parents and brothers. His symptoms not only expressed a delayed reaction to his brother's death but unconsciously served as a mode of expression for his delayed reactions to the deaths of his mother and father. The latter reactions were now being sorted out from their condensation in the reenactment of the brother's symptoms.

From November 1963 to October 1964 Mr. D. was free of symptoms, including headaches, except for some dyspnea. In October 1964 the headaches recurred repeatedly for about one month. At that time Mr. D. spoke of plans to retire on a good pension. He was afraid he would not survive to do so. He related his mother's difficulties in breathing and his father's thick speech after his stroke. On one occasion he spoke of his mother in the present tense. He was asked whether, as with Mike, he felt he could keep his mother (and father) free of discomfort by having her symptoms. He replied: "If it keeps her free, then I can take what I've got." He went on to say that he had never cried over his mother's and father's deaths, but as a youngster he had often cried when he was frightened by his mother's asthma. When telling of this, his breathing became labored. He said that he felt choked up in the chest, and he spoke of all he had done for his mother and father. He had reported earlier that he had cried over Mike from the time of his death until his burial, but not since then. He wondered aloud why his reaction to the deaths of Mike, his mother, and his father had appeared so late, and he asked: "Why did they wait so long?" By the end of the session his breathing was much improved.

By November 1964 a great deal had apparently been achieved. The symbolic entanglement of emotional processes and physical function had been loosened, with significant resolution of conflict between the patient and past and present key persons in his life and with corresponding changes in his attitude toward himself. Six months later he continued to have dyspnea from emphysema. In February 1965 he underwent an operation for empyema of the gall bladder. He retired and moved out of the city. In March 1968 he developed a dissecting aneurysm of the aorta, which was treated medically with success. His blood pressure was maintained within normal limits by medication and he did not take ergotamine tartrate.

After his retirement in June 1965, Mr. D. was not seen by the psychiatrist until September 1969, when he came for follow-up at the latter's request. Except for slight tremor of his hands and some dyspnea, he looked surprisingly fit and was in a buoyant mood. A somewhat detailed account of this session may be of interest. Mr. D. began by saying that he had just come from a check-up by his physician (Dr. Werby). He complained about his physician's wanting him to stop smoking his pipe. He had been a heavy cigarette smoker but had stopped after his first coronary attack. The cardiologist had given him permission to smoke a pipe or cigar. "My pipe is the one thing in life that I enjoy, and I don't plan to give it up. Anyway, I like to fight with Dr. Werby. Dr. Werby thinks the smoking caused the emphysema." Bronchitis was also regarded as the cause of the emphysema. "I have had bronchitis ever since I was a kid." (Was the bronchitis a link to his mother's asthma through identification?) He recognized that he had difficulty breathing, but "I keep up the land around my house. I spend about five hours a day mowing the grass, and in two or three days I do the three acres!" Mr. D. went on to say that smoking would not kill him. "I've died many times, and I'm still alive." He then told of how in March of the previous year he had developed a dissecting aneurysm. The nurse would not let him get up to go to the bathroom. During one night he did get up in spite of her, but he knocked over things when he tried to climb back over the foot of the bed because the sides of the bed were up. After that, "they tied me down." He stretched out his arms, saying: "I survived that, too."

Dr. Mushatt remarked that often Mr. D. had indicated that he would have to be crucified before he could have some peace. He had been through enough and had paid enough for what he did not need to pay. Whereupon, in almost an aside, Mr. D. mentioned the fact that, at the urging of his physician, he had consulted an ophthalmologist, Dr. Sumner Liebman. After much consideration, Dr. Liebman had performed an operation in June 1969 on both eyes to correct for the loss of function of the eye muscle damaged fourteen years earlier. Mr. D. now had no double vision whatever. (This was later confirmed by Dr. Liebman.) Mr. D. suffered now from only slight residual torticollis. For the first time since 1955, he had begun to drive his car. "It's made an awful change." Then he laughed, ". . . an awful good change. I'm not so ugly anymore. I'm better humored."

He then reviewed his long contact with his physician. He had first contacted Dr. Werby in October 1962 through a friend, after Mr. D. had moved into an unfamiliar neighborhood. He had developed acute abdominal pain (renal colic). That day had been a public holiday, but, in spite of that, "Dr. Werby came within fifteen minutes, and he returned later in the day as he had said he would. It was then that I decided to tell Dr. Werby about my headaches, and he promised to try to help me with them. God sent me to Dr. Werby and, through him, to you and to Dr. Liebman." (This last statement indicated a marked change in Mr. D. to a sense of peace with his conscience.) He then commented that his wife was waiting for him and that he would like to take leave of Dr. Mushatt. He apologized for not coming to see him sooner when he had been in the neighborhood. He thanked him for his interest and departed.

For a man who had been so deeply hurt, who had suffered so much, and who had paid so dearly for fantasied transgressions, the success of the eye operation in June 1969 was indeed an appropriate, though belated, celebration of the anniversary of the onset of his headaches in June 1952. It was also an appropriate celebration of a considerable measure of liberation from guilt and depression and from pathological bonds and identifications with all members of his family. The liberation is by no means complete. The permanent pulmonary damage, with the dyspnea, acts as a constant reminder of the inescapable bond through guilt with his mother, father, and brother. But with this sacrifice of his bodily integrity, as it were, he finally has been able to find a significant measure of freedom from his lifelong battle against melancholic depression. Finally, too, his wife has been emancipated from enslavement as a target for hostility displaced from his mother and unconsciously expressed in many ways, especially by the demands made on her as a result of not only the headaches but his double vision.[1]

---

[1] He remained entirely free of headaches until the time of his death in June 1976 at age 77.

DISCUSSION

The material of this case has been presented in a narrative form that focuses primarily on clarification of the meaning and function of this man's symptoms. The directness with which the material has been described undoubtedly will give a false impression of the therapeutic technique and process. The specific material was brought out relatively circuitously, as in any psychoanalytic psychotherapy, but the degree to which the patient himself unconsciously focused on the material, both directly and symbolically, was striking. Many sessions were spent drawing out the patient on his work, activities, and current relationships, often in a way which helped the patient to portray himself to himself in a more favorable light — in a maneuver described by Deutsch (1939). This was one approach to helping him deal with his low self-esteem, with the melancholic aspects of his makeup, and with his guilt. His primitive belief in magic and superstition were examined with him at length. This again helped to resolve guilt, fear of punishment, and his proclivity toward self-punishment and self-induced rejection by the environment.

The capacity for change in a man of this age, even with such difficult emotional problems, is very striking. Not only the complete freedom from headaches (maintained now for close to eight years) but also the seeking and success of the reparative eye operation (fourteen years after the original damage and four years after termination of psychotherapy) are impressive illustrations of the definite, though slowly progressive, growth which is possible even at a later age, when psychological maturational processes are set in motion through release from pathological identifications.

Very early in therapy, the possibilities for such change had been predicted unconsciously by the patient in various ways. Two of these will be discussed.

First, Mr. D. described significant personality growth during the period of intimate friendship in his youth with Mr. and Mrs. K., when in effect he became a member of an appreciative family. This suggested that, if a good working relationship would be established, therapeutic progress would be possible.

In the transference relationship, both authors no doubt served the symbolic function of idealized parents, with the general physician as key figure. It is unlikely that psychotherapy could have influenced this patient without his special relationship to his general physician. At the same time, the devotion and patience of his general physician alone were insufficient to undo the intractable symptoms. In his physician Mr. D. found a figure of authority who from the beginning demonstrated that the patient could trust his interest in helping him. He found a person who could bear with Mr. D.'s hostile behavior, which in other instances had provoked rejection; a person who could tolerate the continual testing of his concern for the patient; and a person who could withstand the sense of inadequacy and guilt, which the negative behavior of patients in regard to treatment recommendation often induces in physicians. The general physician's personal interest and manner of expression of concern for the patient cast him more in an idealized maternal role, which was unthreatening to the patient. The psychiatrist fulfilled more of an idealized paternal role.

Second, in a maneuver to raise his self-esteem and to improve his mood, Mr. D. was encouraged very early in therapy to speak at length about his special interests and skills over the years. With obvious pleasure he told how, as a builder, his overriding interest and satisfaction lay, not in new construction, but in the restoration of houses which were in states of serious disrepair. In context, this material was interpreted as symbolic of his inner conviction of the potentialities for change in his attitude toward himself and his own body, if he were given appropriate opportunity.

It is clear to the authors that there are important gaps in the information obtained to provide clear substantiation of the part played by psychological components in the production of the patient's symptoms. As an example, there is a striking absence of information relevant to Mr. D.'s relationship with his wife. Although he would quickly describe his own unreasonableness toward his wife and extol her for her great tolerance, Mr. D. would not permit any detailed study of his life with his wife that could have clarified his current relationships, as well as his past relationship with his mother, and their possible effect on the provocation of symptoms. His general physician, in discussions with his wife alone, became aware of the full extent of Mr. D.'s hostile and demanding behavior toward his wife, who was a target for resentment displaced from the mother. The hostility, in part, served the purpose of trying to provoke punishment through rejection. It is possible that his wife's unwavering tolerance, while sustaining him, may have intensified Mr. D.'s need for physical symptoms to assuage his guilt. Failure to obtain definitive information was partly determined by the relative infrequency of sessions, but mostly by the priority which therapeutic necessity had over scientific curiosity. Highly charged areas were explored only to the extent to which the patient could spontaneously tolerate them. As can be seen, except for brief reference to masturbation and hints of teen-age sexual exploits, there was no study of his sexual life and its significance for him.

Finally, a few remarks are pertinent on the theoretical framework in which the patient's material was interpreted. The authors were influenced by the work of Felix Deutsch (1959), who extended Freud's concept of conversion (1953). Deutsch's views may be summarized as follows. From the beginning of life, bodily processes become fused and amalgamated with emotional processes through symbolization. This occurs through fusion of sensory perception of stimuli from the environment with the sensory perceptions of the internal responses to these stimuli. This fusion is a process that is part of and essential to normal as well as pathological psychological development. Bodily functions and activities, through their symbolic representations, become a bodily language expressing the individual's relationship to himself and his environment. The overdetermination of symbolizations in any one part of the body depends on the nature of developmental experiences. Physical dysfunction with emotional significance essentially symbolizes disruption of relationships or disharmony between the individual and past and present significant persons in his environment. This, in turn, becomes a representation of disharmony between the individual and himself in the various parts of his personality. Good physical function, from a psychological viewpoint, can be considered to depend on resolution of conflict between the individual and key persons in his past and present life. The resolution of such conflict has the effect of loosening the entanglement of emotional processes and physical functions.

Thus, by resolution of conflict in relation to his brother and also significantly in relation to his mother and father, the patient's headaches were relieved permanently. It was not until significant work in relation to the mother and father had been accomplished that the headaches disappeared. The burden on the pulmonary and cardiovascular systems, already taxed by organic changes, was reduced by some measure of resolution of conflict in relation to the mother and father as well as the brother. In regard to the emotional conflicts that bore on the pulmonary and cardiovascular systems, it could be that the emotional components were somatopsychic rather than psychosomatic—that is, evoked by the developing organic disease. The symptoms arising from organic disease evoked recollections of both the mother and father. From the point of view of therapy, the argument as to whether clinical phenomena are psychosomatic or somatopsychic tends to become irrelevant if one utilizes Deutsch's concept of the mind–body–environment relationship. Loss or disharmony in human relationships (with depression) or anticipation of loss or disruption of relationships (with anxiety) may be expressed in physical terms. Disturbance of physical function may evoke a sense of loss or threat of it in relation to key figures in the environment. The latter somatopsychic reaction may, in turn, further burden the organ dysfunction, by the organ's becoming the pathway for expression of emotional conflict by the process of somatic compliance.

We believe the dead brother to be, to a large extent, a displacement figure for both parents, primarily the mother, because of the following considerations. Normally, grief invariably mobilizes the whole history of one's life with the person who has died. When positive experiences greatly outweigh the negative, the process of mourning and of grief, with detachment from preoccupation with the loss, can usually be achieved in a relatively limited time. When hurt, bitterness, and guilt with excessive ambivalence predominate, defensive maneuvers are called into play to keep such reactions out of awareness. The effect is to block or to delay the normal process of grieving, often resulting in abnormal grief reactions (Freud 1953). Pathological grief reactions are usually sustained by the quality and intensity of hostility and guilt, which, in turn, reinforce the sense of sadness. Mastery and resolution of the ambivalence lead to undoing of the morbid reactions. In this case, the pathological reactions are seen in the unconscious effort to undo the sense of loss, hostility, and guilt by incorporation and identification, at various stages of their illnesses, with the persons who had died. Organ systems became identified with the organ systems of the lost persons. The pathological nature of Mr. D.'s grief reactions can be seen to have been determined by the lifelong family climate of excessive hurt, terror, resentment, guilt, and deprivation of early gratifying relationships. In Mr. D.'s case, the dead brother was largely idealized, and little sustained resentment and sense of guilt were externalized. When resentment toward the brother appeared, it was usually only obliquely by implication. The strongest expression of resentment appeared in the account of the father's forcing the patient to give up his job to return home to work for him, while the other brothers remained free of such demands. Most of the emotions revealed toward the dead brother were depressive and related to longing for him and missing him. As already pointed out, lasting relief from the headaches was achieved only after the patient's working through of his sense of deprivation of rewarding parental dependence relationships, his bitter resentment and guilt toward his mother (and secondarily toward his father), as well as his childhood concerns over his mother in her ill health.

It could be that the symbolic condensation in the headaches of reactions to all members of the patient's family originally was facilitated by a number of factors: (1) The elements common to the symptoms of the mother, father, and brother—namely, the difficulty in breathing and speaking—provided a link. (2) Both the brother and father had been "struck" in the head—the brother by electrical shock, and the father by a stroke. (3) As already reported, in childhood the patient constantly feared that his mother "would knock his block off" for his guilt-ridden activities. (4) From his account of his early years, it is likely that the patient sustained physical beatings at the hands of his father, possibly directed at his head. This last factor is reminiscent of Engel's observations, on some cases of atypical facial neuralgia (1951). Thus, in a sense, the headaches were best suited unconsciously to dramatize somatically the lifelong ambivalence, hostility, guilt, as well as sadness and depression, in relation to all members of his family. It would undoubtedly have been easier emotionally for the patient to focus on the brother, on the surface, than on the parents.

REFERENCES

Abraham, K. (1924). A short study of the development of the libido viewed in the light of mental disorders. In *Selected Papers of Karl Abraham, M.D.*, pp. 418–464. London: Hogarth, 1942.

Berliner, B. (1938). The psychogenesis of a fatal organic disease. *Psychoanalytic Quarterly* 7:368–379.

Bressler, B. (1956). Ulcerative colitis as an anniversary symptom. *Psychoanalytic Review* 43:381–387.

Deutsch, F. (1939). Production of somatic disease by emotional disturbance. *Proceedings of the Association of Research in Nervous and Mental Diseases* 19:271.

_____ (1954). Personal communication.

_____ (1959). Symbolization as a formative stage of the conversion process. In *On the Mysterious Leap from the Mind to the Body*, ed. Felix Deutsch, pp. 75–97. New York: International Universities Press.

Engel, G. L. (1951). Primary atypical facial neuralgia: an hysterical conversion symptom. *Psychosomatic Medicine* 13:375-396.

Freud, S. (1917). Mourning and melancholia. *Standard Edition* 14:243-258.

––––– (1953). Fragment of an analysis of a case of hysteria. *Standard Edition* 7:31-122.

Hilgard, J. R. (1953). Anniversary reactions in parents precipitated by children. *Psychiatry* 16:73-80.

Knapp, P. H., Mushatt, C., and Nemetz, S. J. (1966). Asthma, melancholia and death, I. Psychoanalytic considerations. *Psychosomatic Medicine* 28:114-133.

Lindemann, E. (1945). Psychiatric aspects of the conservative treatment of ulcerative colitis. *Archives of Neurology and Psychiatry* 53:322.

Mushatt, C. (1954). Psychological aspects of non-specific ulcerative colitis. In *Recent Developments in Psychosomatic Medicine,* ed. E. D. Wittkower and R. A. Cleghorn, pp. 345-363. Philadelphia: Lippincott.

––––– (1959). Loss of sensory perception determining choice of symptom. In *On the Mysterious Leap from the Mind to the Body,* ed. Felix Deutsch, pp. 201-204. New York: International Universities Press.

––––– (1965). Discussion of "Transference neurosis in patients with psychosomatic disease" by M. Sperling. American Psychoanalytic Association Annual Meeting, April.

Pollock, G. H. (1970). Anniversary reactions, trauma and mourning. *Psychoanalytic Quarterly* 39:347-371.

9

Varieties
of Somatization

Ira L. Mintz, M.D.
C. Philip Wilson, M.D.

This chapter contains a series of vignettes on somatization. Here, serious symptoms such as psychosomatic bleeding and incapacitating urticaria are presented as well as phenomena, such as a "fat lip" and shoulder pain. The resolution of such lesser somatizations is important, but usually is not reported in the literature.

PSYCHOLOGICAL COMPONENTS IN
PSYCHOSOMATIC BLEEDING
Ira L. Mintz, M.D.

The effective use of steroids, hormones, and antibiotics in the treatment of psychosomatic disease has tended to obscure psychological factors that are significant in bleeding. Four clinical vignettes will be presented to illustrate this hypothesis.

Case 1

A 22-year-old nurse suffering from severe ulcerative colitis for seven years had been in analytic psychotherapy thrice-weekly for three years. Prior to treatment she suffered from general malaise, cramps, mucus, diarrhea, and bleeding. She originally experienced up to thirty-five stools a day. Treatment was complicated by the severity of the disease, its duration, and her mistrust of and antipathy toward physicians. The anger resulted from a long-standing relationship with her previous physician, who had proctoscoped her weekly for long periods of time.

Although the treatment was difficult and filled with frequent crises, the patient improved markedly. She had put on weight, looked healthier, and had less bleeding, cramps, and diarrhea. At this time, she suffered from two loose stools a day. Blood was usually present in the stool in small amounts. In view of the considerable improvement, one might anticipate total clearing of residual symptoms, but this did not occur. Final clearing of symptoms is usually a difficult and protracted experience. As long as any vestiges of symptoms remain, they provide a repository for conflict and for regression. This was pointed out repeatedly to the patient, and she consciously tried hard to stop the bleeding.

One day she reported that she was five weeks overdue with her period. Before this she had been regular. I encouraged her to associate to the overdue period. This resulted in a series of childhood memories about bleeding, bodily injury, and loss of control. She spoke about having skinned knees and fearing the sight of blood. She remembered wondering where her menstrual blood came from and whether *it* would ever stop. Initially, she wondered whether she was bleeding or whether the blood came from a bowel movement. It all seemed to come from the same hole. I suggested that, unconsciously, she might still have the same fantasy—that it all came from the same hole. In her strong attempt to stop the rectal bleeding, thinking in the back of her mind that it all came from the same hole, she stopped her menstrual bleeding. She thought about the possibility of that fantasy for a few moments and allowed that it might be so. Shortly thereafter, the session ended and she left.

In the next session she reported that her period started fifteen minutes after she left the office, while she was on the bus.

DISCUSSION

In this case the bleeding was in response to the presence of an unconscious infantile cloacal fantasy in which the anatomical and physiological functioning of the gastrointestinal and urogenital systems were fused, with inability to separate and differentiate their functions. As a consequence, the patient's vigorous attempt to stop the bowel bleeding resulted in her interfering with menstrual flow. The amenorrhea did not appear to be primarily related to destructive drives, separation or sexual anxiety, or transference phenomena. It arose out of an attempt to stop the rectal bleeding and to work constructively in treatment.

Case 2

The patient, a 14-year-old girl, was in five-times-a-week analysis for severe ulcerative colitis. Profuse bleeding was one of her major symptoms. She came from a psychosomatic family; two older sisters had anorexia, a younger sister had asthma, and her mother had migraine and eczema.

The analysis was stormy from the beginning. Although she was quite ill, bled markedly, and suffered from considerable cramping, she insisted (with the tacit approval of her internist) that her illness was totally organic and that she had no problems. As a consequence, she felt resentful when pressured by her parents to enter treatment. After two years of analysis with one hospitalization, she slowly began to improve.

From the very beginning, I was aware that the severe bleeding presented a threat to her life and that she could self-destructively use it in an attempt to achieve a regressive unconscious solution to a number of her conflicts. I suspected that it included her need to discharge infantile sadistic aggression, as well as an attempt to control me by threatening to die. The first period of her treatment was so stormy and chaotic, that I felt that those transference interpretations were premature and would not be effective. I contented myself with careful self-appraisal of my attitudes and feelings in response to her behavior toward me; I did not wish to unwittingly communicate undue concern and anxiety over her behavior. I felt that if she unconsciously perceived that she could control me by creating anxiety in me by bleeding, her infantile sadistic impulses would be gratified and she would continue to bleed, unmindful of the deleterious consequences to herself.

In the fourth year, she experienced occasional episodes of cramps and diarrhea. However, small amounts of bleeding persisted most of the time. I was puzzled by the continued bleeding in spite of all interpretations and decided to discuss the problem with a colleague. After a number of discussions, I realized that her bleeding might be in response to countertransference reactions that I had not recognized. Over the years my initial sensitivity to her possible attempt to control me by bleeding might have been eroded by my preoccupation with her endless outpouring of aggression, her withholding of information, her manipulations, and other issues in the analysis. Considering that possibility, I awaited the next session. The patient walked in, sat down, looked at me, and asked, "What's the matter with you? You look different." She had immediately sensed a difference in my attitude and responded to it. When I asked her what she meant, she added, "There's something different about you . . . you don't seem as interested and concerned. . . . You seem aloof." My absent anxiety was instantly recognized and described as aloofness and lack of concern. Interpretations of her attempts at controlling me by bleeding were made repeatedly, and in five to six months the bleeding stopped.

DISCUSSION

In contrast to the first clinical case, this patient's analysis was extremely difficult and illustrates a different conflict. She viewed any attempt at working together as submitting to being controlled. Her infantile, unconscious, unresolved omnipotence, dependency, and sadistic aggressive drives resulted in a need to control the external object. Her aim was to avoid perceiving herself as being controlled as well as to avoid giving in to unconscious wishes to be controlled. When she could not achieve omnipotent control over the external object, she regressed into needs for control over parts and functions of her own body, especially the colon and bleeding.

This intense conflict, present from the first sessions in the analysis when for weeks she refused to talk, continued throughout a seven-year treatment. She continually arrived late in order to control when the session began, and she introduced endless pretexts to prolong and control the session ending time by the introduction of dreams, crises, and questioning. During the sessions, when she attempted to avoid, deny, and repress distressing conflict, with abdominal cramps occurring as a consequence, she did not mention the development of these symptoms. When I deduced them from her pained expression, she attempted to deny their presence. Her persistent bleeding was another attempt at controlling me by threatening me with her increased infirmity and death. The need in the transference to attempt to achieve infantile sadistic gratification through attempts to frustrate me and to make me anxious as well as control me was most evident in the persistence of the bleeding. It served both infantile aggressive drive satisfaction and her attempts at infantile ego mastery over the object. The patient's almost uncanny immediate response to my nonverbal attitude was an indication of her exquisite pathological perceptiveness.

Case 3

The patient, a 27-year-old married lawyer with no children, suffered from ulcerative colitis of three-years duration. After a few months of twice-a-week psychotherapy it became clear that he suffered from severe feelings of inadequacy, low self-esteem, fears of responsibility, and major problems in psychosexual identity, and aggressive conflict. Overcontrolled and infantilized by his mother, he harbored deep resentment toward women. His ulcerative colitis began two months after his mother's death.

After two years of psychotherapy, problems with his wife became increasingly evident. Despite his having a good job and working very hard, he worried excessively about financial security, and his attitude created conflict between them. The conflict worsened with his wife's increasing demands to have a child and stop working. Her working provided him a buffer to his pessimistic financial preoccupations, and he persisted in his attempts to justify the postponing of her pregnancy. Her wishes meanwhile became more strident.

One morning at 6:00 A.M. the patient left a frantic message that he was bleeding to death. I phoned back and made a 7:00 A.M. appointment. The patient arrived weak, ashen, and terrified, complaining that he could hardly climb the stairs to my office. He told me he had experienced seven episodes of profuse, bright red bleeding all night, with the blood filling the toilet bowl.

Encouraged to reflect upon what could have upset him so badly that he bled, he finally spoke about a big fight between him and his wife on the preceding evening. As usual, it related to her demands to become pregnant. This time, however, she became increasingly adamant. He volunteered that he began to feel completely trapped.

Since he had spoken on previous occasions about his feelings of resentment when the pregnancy was broached, it was not difficult to get him to recognize that the bleeding represented his feeling "bloody mad" at her for attempting to coerce him when he did not feel ready. This interpretation served two functions: It dealt with the bleeding as an aggressive discharge, and it was ego supportive in that he could see it as manly anger rather than as passively feminine. As the discussion proceeded, he began to improve. By the end of the session he said that he felt much better and stronger and that he did not think that he would bleed further. He was correct.

DISCUSSION

This patient's bleeding symbolized his "bloody angry" outburst toward his wife for attempting to coerce him into becoming a father—with all the responsibilities he felt that entailed—before he felt ready and in spite of his repeated requests to her to postpone conception. Although his primary unconscious response was an aggressive one directed toward his wife, it was also secondarily directed toward himself for his feelings of intense inadequacy and insecurity, which required that he act so defensively and (in his own mind) so reprehensibly. If he were very ill, his wife would be forced to postpone becoming pregnant.

Additional determinants in the choice of rectal bleeding as the symbolic vehicle for the expression of aggression are tied to his unconscious feminine identification and to his conflict over conception or misconception. Momentary identifications with his wife's wish to be pregnant set off his own unconscious feminine identifications, symbolized by bleeding like a woman through the unconscious cloacal urogenital-bowel opening. Beyond that, however, his resentment over feeling controlled by his wife and his attempt to wrest control from her in regressed symbolic fashion resulted in the profuse bleeding, symbolizing his unconscious wish for her to abort. The patient's unconscious hatred toward his wife, expressed regressively through the vehicle of sexual identification and miscarriage, served both as a discharge of the aggression and as an attempt to exercise ego mastery over his conflict.

His ability to understand the depth of his resentment towards his wife, and his partial unconscious solution of it, was enough to permit him to stop the bleeding. I made no attempt at that time to point out or deal with his unconscious feminine identification and the additional symbolic meaning of the bleeding. I felt that his ego was already heavily burdened with his anxiety over the hemorrhaging and that it would not be wise to introduce additional problems prior to the resolution of this crisis. I also felt that his recognition of the intensity of his aggression would be sufficient to stop the bleeding.

Case 4

The patient, a 15-year-old girl, was in analysis for symptoms of depression, insecurity, anxiety, and social withdrawal. During the second year of analysis her anxieties became focused upon her physical appearance. She became markedly preoccupied with how she looked and exaggerated the effects of minute skin blemishes and other presumed physical defects. At the same time, her depression increased. Also, it became increasingly clear that her personality structure was similar to that of an anorexic and both her parents had characteristics similar to those reported in the parents of anorexic patients

It was not entirely surprising, subsequently, when a typical anorexic picture began to unfold. What was somewhat atypical, however, was that after a few months of dieting in order to lose weight, she had gained five pounds. In that setting she became amenorrheic. This episode illustrates the fallacy of attributing anorexic amenorrhea exclusively to weight loss rather than considering additional psychic determinants.

During the next eight months the patient became increasingly aware of her conflicts over control, aggression, sexuality, separation, and an ambivalent feminine identity. She then became increasingly assertive and aggressive in the transference.

In one session, feeling increasingly frustrated with herself for not progressing more rapidly, she also attacked me for not helping her sufficiently. She felt more comfortable now with her feelings of aggression and with her ability to express them toward me. She screamed at me angrily and berated me.

In the next session, somewhat abashed, yet appearing both pleased and insightful, she reported that her period had returned. She recognized its return as a sign of progress, related to her angry outburst. She agreed that the release of pent-up feelings by yelling without dire consequence was then followed by the release of menstrual bleeding. Holding back from one body opening was associated with retaining the contents of another.

DISCUSSION

Four cases of psychosomatic components of bleeding were presented: two with severe ulcerative colitis and two involving menstrual bleeding. In the two cases of colitis, although other factors were relevant, the bowel bleeding was directly related to conflicts over aggression. In the case of the male patient with colitis and major hemorrhaging, ambivalent conflict over masculine identity was a considerable factor, but the overriding conflict was over aggression. This was evident in his ability to control the bleeding after discussing his anger toward his wife.

The woman with colitis who became amenorrheic also had a problem over her sexual identity. When the amenorrhea developed, however, it seemed to be related to an unconscious confusion over urogenital-bowel functioning. Holding back on bleeding from the bowel resulted in retaining menstrual flow. Retention of contents from one body orifice (bowel) was followed by retention from another (uterus). In similar fashion with the other patient, the outpouring of aggression from the mouth initiated menstrual flow from the uterus.

These four vignettes illustrate that psychological factors should be considered when evaluating psychosomatic episodes of bleeding. They make up a part of a complex picture of features that contribute to the ultimate phenomena observed.

ON THE PSYCHOGENESIS OF A FAT LIP
Ira L. Mintz, M.D.

The patient, a 39-year-old lawyer, was referred by her gynecologist for symptoms of anxiety and depression. The overt source of the symptoms became readily apparent in the first interview. With much agitation the patient related that her best friend was suing her, because her little dog had bitten her friend's upper lip. The lip swelled, became discolored, and was hanging loose.

While the dog had been sitting on her friend's lap, her friend leaned toward the dog and made kissing sounds to it. At that moment the dog bit her upper lip. Her friend became hysterical and was rushed to the hospital. Initially, the friend reported that plastic surgery was necessary, that she was going to sue the patient, and that she should kill her dog. The patient was incredulous that her friend would treat her so badly. They had been best friends since childhood. After both had married, the two couples were inseparable for years. The husbands were partners in a large retail business, and this event with the dog had put a terrible strain upon their working relationship.

As the patient talked further, it became increasingly clear that she was very masochistic and that for years her friend taken advantage of her. Her friend would admire a dress, ask to borrow it, and not return it. This became so prevalent a pattern that the patient often would volunteer to lend the clothing before she was asked. The friend did not reciprocate, however, and the patient made no attempt to get back the clothing.

On their frequent vacations, her friend often managed to get the patient and her husband to pay for an inordinate share of their dining bills and other vacation expenses. The patient invariably asked her friend to all of her own family functions and treated her as a member of her own family. This hospitality was not reciprocated, however, and the patient and her husband were rarely invited to dinners at the friend's home. While the patient did not protest, she did find it inexplicable, especially since the two husbands worked so closely together. She also volunteered with some embarrassment, and the first trace of annoyance, that she sent her two children to summer camp where the friend's children went, although her girls disliked that camp.

The process of describing an endless series of increasingly humiliating experiences seemed to crystallize into expanding levels of resentment, so that by the end of the first consultation, the patient had become visibly annoyed with her friend's treatment of her.

During psychotherapeutic sessions, the patient's emerging aggression toward her friend alternated with bouts of moderately severe anxiety, depression, crying, and marked feelings of insecurity, inadequacy, and intense self-condemnation.

In one session the patient described her fear and agitation that her dog would bite her husband or her mother, although the veterinarian had assured her that the dog was not dangerous. She then associated to her relationship with her mother. She described her as domineering, controlling, and impossible. No matter what the patient did, she could not satisfy her mother, and she felt endlessly criticized. Because her father died when she was young, she had always been overly attached to her mother and constantly sought her approval. Her older brother was always the mother's favorite child and could do no wrong. While he was an alcoholic with an irregular work record, he was never criticized. As the patient increasingly described her mother's poor treatment of her, it appeared to parallel her relationship with her supposed best friend, who seemed to think more of the patient's husband than of her. She revealed her longstanding inadequacy as a wife and as a woman, adding that the practice of law provided her with her major satisfactions in life. She appeared overly insecure in her role as mother to her two young children.

In another session she described how her ex-friend used to fight, argue, and humiliate her, when they were alone as well as in social situations. As the anger welled to the surface, she acknowledged for the first time how resentful she felt, and how she should have asserted herself. At the end of the session she volunteered that she felt less depressed.

In the third month of treatment she revealed that, intermittently during her life, she had had asthma as well as spastic colitis. While she continued to demonstrate her severe self-punishing conscience with endless self-criticisms, her anger toward her ex-friend, Alma, and toward her husband and mother continued to mount. She realized that she felt exploited by all three and that she had accepted it, feeling that she had no rights. She recognized that when she was ready to explode, she would get an attack of asthma. Interpretations were directed primarily toward her punishing superego and how it contributed to her poor self-image. The patient continued to report experiences that had taken place with Alma, her mother, and her husband, voicing increasing anger. As she became increasingly assertive, she mentioned the subsiding of tension headaches that she had not previously mentioned.

Additional resentment became apparent when she reported she was very fearful that the plane her mother was taking to California would crash and she'd die.

Almost a year after she had been in treatment, she related the following episode. While talking to a friend who also knew her ex-friend, Alma, she had been describing how thoughtless, inconsiderate, and exploitative Alma had been. Just as she was describing how her dog had bitten Alma, her friend suddenly interjected, "Your upper lip is getting all swollen." At that moment, the patient experienced a swelling of the entire upper lip. She was startled by its suddenness and intensity. As she attempted to explore this incident in the session, she associated to some of the demanding clients in her practice. She was anxious and insecure in confronting them with their unreasonable behavior. When she did confront them in a very passive and tentative fashion, she developed a sudden swelling under the right eye. She would then find an excuse to leave the office, and while walking away, would admit to herself how angry she was with the client. At that point, the swelling would rapidly disappear. She volunteered that it had happened a dozen times in the past ten years, and always under the right eye. She was unable to consider why she developed a swelling under her eye when angry with the client. I suggested that a person's eye might swell after it was punched and that she unconsciously did to her eye what she had the impulse to do to someone else's. Resentful at the interpretation, she replied, "If you aren't careful, I'll get the swelling again."

I interpreted the transference threat to develop eye symptoms as her signal to me to go slower or she would get "sick." I also told her it expressed a need to punish herself for the guilt that she felt over her angry impulse to punch me in the eye. I could then point out the repressed aggression toward her clients who provoked her and the anger that she felt toward Alma, which was reactivated by her discussion of Alma's behavior with her friend. Her own "fat lip" represented guilt over the hidden urge to give Alma the same fat lip that her dog had produced. After some thought the patient agreed. She acknowledged that in the past she did have the urge to choke her friend to stop her from saying outrageous things and also did want to hit her.

DISCUSSION

The development of isolated areas of hives or swelling is not unusual. One 14-year-old girl with symptoms of asthma and migraine got maneuvered into the bedroom by her boyfriend. Anxiously sitting on the bed, she suddenly developed a large swelling of the upper lip just as they were about to begin kissing. The swelling so disconcerted the boyfriend that he suggested they go downstairs. Another woman of 20, who suffered from anorexia and subclinical asthma, would develop hives on her neck and upper chest during sessions. They occurred when she was discussing subjects that filled her with tension and anxiety. As the session progressed, and when she felt more able to deal with conflict, the hives subsided. Both these patients, as well as the case described above, suffered from other psychosomatic symptoms, so that the tendency to use a part of one's own body to express conflict was already established.

PSORIASIS OF THE GLANS PENIS AS AN EXPRESSION OF AN UNCONSCIOUS FANTASY OF A FECAL PHALLUS
C. Philip Wilson, M.D.

A 30-year-old unmarried teacher came to analysis for symptoms of a severe compulsive neurosis dating from early childhood. In the first session the patient reported that a month before beginning treatment, he had developed psoriasis of the glans penis for the first time.

Analytic treatment revealed that the etiologic unconscious fantasy causing the psoriasis was the wish for a fecal phallus. The patient's preferred method of intercourse was to have his girlfriend on top. In this position he could enjoy a number of fantasies. (1) His erect penis was a fecal stick, a bowel movement of his that his girlfriend was relieving him of. In this fantasy her vagina equaled an anus, but also a toilet. His ejaculation represented a defecation. (2) His erection represented the female's fecal phallus, and in the ejaculation she was having a bowel movement on him. (3) The female on top gratified homosexual fantasies that he was the woman and she the man.

Most important in the use of this position was the patient's projecting all the responsibility and initiative for the sexual act onto the girlfriend, in obedience to his strict superego, which forbade sexuality.

This patient never attempted anal intercourse, although such wishes appeared in the analysis. He and his girlfriend did indulge in anal masturbation; however, he preferred to be completely passive and to have her masturbate him, perform fellatio on him, or get on top of him in intercourse. Infrequently and reluctantly he would masturbate her or perform cunnilingus upon her.

During the first year and a half of analysis, the patient made many slips of the tongue, calling his girlfriend "mother." The transference neurosis was pregenital in nature, with a multitude of homosexual fantasies and drives being expressed: to be smelled and entered anally by me (mother); conversely, to smell and enter me; to have bowel movements on me and for me to do it on him. This patient had been grossly overstimulated by the mother, having often shared the bed and room with his parents. The element of thigmotactic fusion with his girlfriend (mother), which was expressed in the patient's sexual perversion and in his psoriasis, was most striking.

The development of psoriasis of the glans penis prior to entering analysis was the result of a structural conflict, in which the ego was exposed to the threat of punishment and guilt from a harsh superego. The psoriasis served as a punishment that prevented intercourse. The skin disease expressed exhibitionistic and passive homosexual wishes. These wishes were gratified in his examination by a dermatologist, who interdicted intercourse and prescribed ointments. The psoriasis was an attempt to show everyone his dirty fecal penis under the guise of a physical illness for which he could not be blamed. It also was an oedipal-phase castration to prevent intercourse.

As Sperling (1967) and I (1968) have described in the treatment of other psychosomatic cases, the analysis of the pregenital aspects of the transference neurosis was crucial in the resolution of the psoriasis. The patient gave up his sexual perversion and assumed the normal male position in intercourse.

Corresponding and gratifying structural changes were effected in his ego and superego, with the result that there was a marked improvement in his object relations and in his capacity to work. The clearing of the psoriasis was concurrent with his decision to face his neurosis and the unconscious anal-phase fixations that caused his illness.

DISCUSSION

I have focused here only on the psychodynamics related to the psycho-somatic symptom. Space limitations preclude detailing the anal-phase genetic material that emerged in the analysis or its relation to the development of psoriasis in adult life. I found anal-phase fixations and fantasies to be etiologic in another patient with psychosomatic psoriasis. After the psoriasis cleared, he developed asthma. A history of somatic compliance, that is, a childhood skin disease or a childhood injury of the glans penis, was not recovered in the analysis. A most significant finding in this case was that the patient had no memory of masturbation, nor were memories of masturbation recovered in analysis. Thus, the development of the psoriasis expressed a wish to be masturbated (examined) by a physician, analyst–dermatologist–mother.

The analysis of the first patient revealed a masochistic symptom that appeared when the psoriasis of the glans penis cleared up. The patient reported a series of almost-serious auto accidents during the first year of treatment. He bumped into cars in front of him and was also bumped into from behind in heavy traffic by other cars. The patient was angry with me and blamed the accidents, as he had the psoriasis, on analysis.

Careful analytic scrutiny of the accidents failed to uncover significant psychodynamics until the end of the year. The patient then revealed that in his compulsive haste, he never had enough time to stop and wipe the dirt and winter slush from the front and rear windows of his car. In his compulsive wish to save every penny, he used a small foreign car that had a poor windshield wiper and no rear defroster. These conditions allowed him to unconsciously arrange "accidents," which resulted in his being deprived of the use of his car (castrated) for long periods of time and of his money for expensive repair bills. Similar psychodynamics could be observed in the etiology of the psoriasis and of the "accidents." Underlying both symptoms, and etiologic to both, was the patient's crucial unconscious fantasy of a fecal penis. The passive and active homosexual fantasies expressed in bumping into cars in front with his dirty car (fecal penis) and have his dirty car (anus) bumped into from behind (anal entry by a fecal penis), were similar to those expressed in the multiple pregenital, sadomasochistic fantasies that caused his psoriasis. As these sadomasochistic fantasies appeared and were analyzed in the transference neurosis with the recovery of significant anal-phase conflicts, both symptoms cleared up. Oedipal-phase castration, carried out by both symptoms and the masochistic self-punishing action of an archaic superego, could be seen in the symptoms.

REFERENCES

Sperling, M. (1967). Transference neurosis in patients with psychosomatic disorders. *Psychoanalytic Quarterly* 36:3.
Wilson, C. Philip (1968). Psychosomatic asthma and acting out. *International Journal of Psycho-Analysis* 49:330–335.

VITREOUS FLOATERS: THEIR UNCONSCIOUS MEANING
C. Philip Wilson, M.D.

A 30-year-old male patient came for therapy with symptoms of a phobic neurosis, hypertension, and obesity. In the terminal phase of the analysis of his predominantly oral symptoms, he reported "The idea of spring is depressing— there is a high incidence of suicide in Scandinavia. I did well on my exams but then had anxiety and started smoking again."

The smoking was interpreted as an attempt to avoid reality (exams) and to regain the peace of the nipple and the breast milk. The patient responded: "The spots do not bother me as much at dusk, but they still do bother me. After the final exam, talking with C., they did not bother me. They are vitreous floaters." He was referring to a new symptom of white spots dancing in front of his eyes, which made him anxious. The ophthalmologist had told him they were vitreous floaters caused by infectious disease or emotional strain, but in themselves, were harmless.

Clinical material revealed that every time the patient regressed from an oedipal to a passive oral position—failing to do work he should do, watching too much TV, smoking or drinking—the floaters bothered him. When he was active and asserted himself on the job or with people, he was "aware" of the spots but not disturbed by them.

The basic meaning of this symptom came out some months later. "I was terribly sleepy after the last hour." Interpretation was made of his wanting me to be Mother and the breast. He said: "I used to steal small sums of money from father's bureau; recently, I returned some money I owe him. The vitreous floaters—why should they give me terror? When they first came, I looked up, saw all these spots, and was terrified that they'd obscure my vision and I'd go blind."

The interpretation was made that this terror hid a wish to be a blind, nursing infant. The patient confirmed the interpretation by saying that when drunk, he'd lose his vision, get "blind" drunk, and that this was suicidal.

DISCUSSION

The basic unconscious wish that makes use of the vitreous floaters is to be a blind nursing infant. The white spots represent milk to the unconscious. The interpretation of these dynamics resulted in a resolution of the patient's phobic reaction to the vitreous floaters. This change occurred, of course, in conjunction with many other interpretations, which turned the passive to the active, and with the resultant working through of the oral regression.

PSYCHODYNAMIC CONFLICTS INVOLVING THE ZIPPER: THE SIGNIFICANCE OF A RIGHT-SIDED CONVERSION SYMPTOM IN A LEFT-HANDED MAN
C. Philip Wilson, M.D.

A 40-year-old male patient was in analysis for marital conflicts. He reported the sudden development of pain in the right shoulder several hours before his treatment session and wondered whether it could be emotionally caused, as had been the case with his headaches. Thinking back, he recalled that the pain occurred when he had sexual thoughts about a pretty woman at a restaurant. "But," asked the patient, who was beginning to become aware of the unconscious and of the superego, "why the pain in the right shoulder when I am left-handed?" He answered his rhetorical question with surprise: "You know, I never realized it before, but I use my right hand to unzip my fly in order to take out my penis. I must've been guilty about wanting to have sex with that girl. All flies in men's pants are designed for right-handed men. It is extremely awkward to reach over and unzip or zip the zipper with the left hand."

The pain in the right shoulder, the patient concluded, was a punishment for his wish to use his right hand for sexual pleasure. There were transference and genetic aspects of this shoulder pain, and it masked aggressive as well as libidinal drives and fantasies. When these conflicts were worked through, the pain cleared up.

DISCUSSION

A sampling of two left-handed males revealed that they, too, without being aware of it, used the right hand to zip their flies. The question of whether their unawareness was caused by guilt about forbidden fantasies similar to those of my patient was beyond the scope of my sampling technique.

Whether men's pants manufacturers make all pants with right-sided zippers because of a conscious block about the unconscious significance of the zipper or because of a wish to save money is another puzzle beyond the range of this discussion.

Another question warranting investigation is whether women's slacks are all manufactured with right-handed zippers. Do left-handed women use the right hand to zip their flies, and can parallel psychodynamics cause them to experience similar painful right-sided conversion symptoms?

CHANGES IN THE SENSE OF TIME
IN THE ANALYSIS OF AN IMPULSE DISORDER
MASKED BY PSYCHOSOMATIC SYMPTOMS
C. Philip Wilson, M.D.

A profound distortion of the sense of time was displayed by a young man who suffered from a severe impulse disorder. His symptoms included obesity and hypertension, phobias, hypochondriacal fears, addiction to alcohol and cigarettes, nail biting, and flesh picking and tearing. At a point in his analysis when profound structural changes and improvements in ego and superego had been effected, the patient became aware that he still drained off his polymorphous perverse, sadomasochistic impulses in his "habit" of chewing and picking at the flesh adjacent to the cuticles of his fingers until bleeding occurred. In his struggle to master this habit, he reported the following dreams:

1. My mother was cured of cancer and gave me a hug. She reached for my penis and brushed the pubic hair.

2. Your wife, who is confused with my mother, is propped up in bed with pillows. I am aware of lots of children who, apparently, are yours. One of them has an intravenous feeding. I storm out in a rage, saying, what is the point of this?

3. I dreamt that I dreamed that I had a nosebleed and then I really woke up to find I did not have a nosebleed.

4. I looked at my watch and realized that I had lost a day. I thought I was going a little crazy, like an amnesia. It was as if a guy hit me and I was knocked out for 24 hours.

The patient's associations were to Negro prostitutes and to a play, *The Virgin and the Gypsy*. He recalled erotic fantasies about his mother, who got tuberculosis and spent a year in bed when he was 12 years old. He further associated to his oedipal rivalry with his father and me in the transference, which confronted him with castration fear. He responded to the fear by a feminine identification, which was expressed by nosebleeds that he induced in childhood by nose picking. These nosebleeds for him expressed a wish to menstruate in rivalry with his mother for his father's love. These associations, of course, are but a small sampling of what emerged in the analysis. I select them here in order to focus on the patient's sense of time.

One dream wish is to lose time. He achieves this in his flesh chewing and picking, by which he denies his mother's death. (She had in reality died of cancer when he was 24.) The flesh of his finger represents for him the maternal breast at which he was eternally sucking, biting, and chewing. He would occasionally bite off bits of his flesh and chew and swallow them. He said that he had it made, because the flesh of his fingers always regrew. In the transference he did not want to give up the analyst–mother by finally analyzing his sadomasochistic habit.

DISCUSSION

This patient's sense of time prior to analysis had been profoundly impaired. A college dropout, he lived on impulse with no ambition, that is, no plans for time future. Discrimination of time past from time present was constantly blurred by his addiction and his nail biting and finger chewing. With these habits he also denied castration fear and any acceptance of his own or other people's death. At the point in analysis when he dreamt of losing time, he was now finally facing reality, competing, and tolerating affects such as fear, anxiety, anger, and love, which he had been avoiding in his addictions and habits. After working through this material, the patient developed an organized sense of time as his deep-seated impulse disorder yielded to analysis.

THE ARCHAIC SUPEREGO'S ROLE
IN PSYCHOSOMATIC SYMPTOMS
C. Philip Wilson, M.D.

A psychosomatic symptom of nasal mucus secretion was depicted in the manifest content of a patient's dream: "My nostrils were wadded with cotton." Analysis revealed that the psychodynamic function served by the mucus secretion was to defend against copraphagic impulses, as the nasal secretion stopped up the nose, cutting off the sense of smell.

The patient, a 35-year-old businessman in analysis for a severe compulsive neurosis, dreamt as follows: "Sam was me. My nostrils were wadded with cotton. I was in a closed room. There were flies and insects and an instrument for icing."

He produced the following associations:

This dream was preceded by phone calls all last night, from my grandmother and from my mother. My mother keeps confusing me with her brother David. I am thinking of wanting to be a big success. I have a ringing in my ears. I also had a ringing in my ears after Betty, a house guest of my wife whom I don't like, left for Europe. I am called a brilliant financier, but I have fears of brain injury. How will I take care of my family if I get sick? I was thinking of how would I pay your bill. Sam to me is a man who has real dignity. He is an honest member of the government, but all he gets paid is $17,000 a year. If he wanted to go into private business, he would make much more. My nose being stuffed up makes me think of bloody things — of getting beaten up in childhood by another boy. We were always fighting. The other boys always were tougher. My nose has never stuffed up before. My wife is the one who has sinus, but yesterday before the dream (after the hour, when the patient knew the bill was due for his last month's analysis) my nose stopped. The icing in the dream made me think of a cake icing from my childhood that my grandmother used to squeeze out of a sack and that my wife used to make cakes. It makes me mad — my mother confusing me with her brother. I never liked him. He is too interested in money. The flies remind me of screened doors that may have holes in them — flies can get through.

DISCUSSION

This patient was working through the anal-phase meanings of money and "all or nothing" conflicts: Either he would be totally clean — idealistic, not working for money — or he would be totally greedy and dirty like his image of his uncle.

ELEPHANT SYMBOLISM
C. Philip Wilson, M.D.

Popular belief has it that alcoholics hallucinate pink elephants. To my knowledge, clinical verification of this dictum has not been offered in the analytic literature. From a patient in analysis I was able to obtain information on the symbolism of elephants in dreams.

The patient sought analysis for a severe, oral character disorder. He was obese, addicted to food, wine, alcohol, cigars, money, and his wife, whom he forced to behave, as much as possible, like a mother to him and whose nickname for him was the equivalent of "baby." A brilliant and successful businessman, he was in constant struggle with his impulses. In business he had repeatedly and "naively" become involved with patently dishonest men, who offered the lure of vast financial profits by shady business operations. His pleasure in the appurtenances of wealth was childlike and feminine in nature; money, jewels, and possessions were reassurances against castration fear and separation anxiety. At a stage in analysis when he had faced and worked through many of his conflicts and evidenced basic and characterologic and symptomatic improvements, he reported the following dream:

> There was a large elephant wearing paratrooper boots in a parade. He fell over, nearly crushing somebody. To the left was a Moscow-like building with a marquee which had side panels to protect the people from the rain.

The elephant in the dream reminded him of a slick, sleek businessman he had met the previous night. This man was bald, overweight, wore glasses, and shifted constantly from one foot to the other, like a restless elephant. The man smoked and chewed on a pipe endlessly, just as elephants are always eating if they can. This man and his friends had tried unsuccessfully to talk the patient into a dishonest business deal. The Russian part of the dream reminded him of a Russian man he had met who proudly gave him a picture of his son, with the comment that he had nothing else to give as a gift. This gift had touched the patient and his wife deeply. Then the patient recalled more of the dream, telling me that there was also a baby elephant in the dream walking beside the big one.

More associations led to his pleasure and pride in his beautiful children, a boy three years old and a girl of two, who were both healthy, fat toddlers. In further associations the patient talked of another business situation of a corrupt nature, which he wanted to get involved with and tried to rationalize by saying, "Who am I to judge these men? After all, they are not really breaking the law." He then commented that he had gone home to bed at a reasonable time, but that these men had stayed up all night, working on their business deal and that if a person's drive to make money gets out of hand, it can kill him.

The patient's father, who had conflicts similar to his own, had died of a coronary at age 50. The previous night the patient had become angry with his mother in a childish way, yelling that she shouldn't always bring his children gifts and candy and that he wanted them to like her for herself—not just for the gifts. The mother, who was also obese, vain, greedy, and exhibitionistic, yelled back at him that he hadn't been spoiled when he was young. The patient made no reply. He still was afraid of his mother, wanted an inheritance from her, and felt he might lose it if he told her that he certainly had been spoiled in every conceivable fashion. This overindulgence had included food, money, and presents of all kinds. An extreme example of this neurotic parental behavior was the patient's eighth birthday, when he had asked for a toy dump truck. When the expected day arrived, he received five of them, one from each significant relative – mother, father, maternal, and paternal grandparents, etc.

DISCUSSION

In this patient the symbolism of the elephant represents the phallic mother and at a later stage the preoedipal father. That the elephant symbolizes a breast-penis is patent. The emphasis in this symbol, however, would fall on the breast. It was a gigantic overpowering breast-symbol representation of the patient's basic conflict with his oral impulses, which were never really under control. He sweated constantly, was always on a diet, and mentally had no peace of mind, as he was always preoccupied with more and more money-making schemes and deals. Although he was successful and respected in the business world, his wife, whose strict conscience he secretly admired, repeatedly told him that he was no good because everything he did was for money.

The basic conflict reflected in the elephant dream is the patient's guilt with his own son, his fear that his elephantine greed might hurt his family. The elephant shifting from one foot to another aptly describes the state of this patient's ego, which was constantly beset by ungratified oral impulses. "The cunning, bold businessman" actually referred to the patient himself, as well as to the analyst, whom the patient had repeatedly tried to devalue because he treated patients for money. The elephant symbol reflects an identification with the mother.

CONCLUSION

It is my impression from thirty years' clinical experience in the analysis of orally fixated patients that elephant dreams would not be uniquely found in alcoholics. However, I have found the significance of such dreams and their symbolism in other patients similar to that so graphically depicted in this case. I feel that similar psychodynamics and symbolic meanings would be found in the hallucinated pink elephants of advanced alcoholics who do not come for analysis. A recurrent terror of this patient was of becoming "a bum."

This man was ambivalent about being a businessman and making money. He was obsessed with fantasies and wishes to be a millionaire, but on the other hand he admired only selfless people like his friend Sam, who worked for the government. The elephant dream indicated that processes of internalization were occurring in the analysis in the patient's development of a healthier superego structure.

THE CRUCIAL EARLY PHASE OF ANALYSIS OF SEVERE PSYCHOSOMATIC CASES AND THE ANALYSIS OF MANNERISMS OF SPEECH
C. Philip Wilson, M.D.

Unless analytic intervention is immediate and effective, experience shows that patients referred with severe psychosomatic symptoms usually stop analysis. The reason is that a working therapeutic alliance has not been achieved and the patient's symptoms worsen. The case then returns to the internist or other specialist.

Over the past thirty years my colleagues and I have successfully analyzed many patients with severe psychosomatic symptoms, and we have analyzed many psychosomatic symptoms that have developed *de novo* in the course of analysis. We have emphasized in presentations of psychosomatic case material the crucial importance of the initial phase of analysis (Sperling 1961, 1963, 1964, 1968, 1978).

Our research confirms and expands upon the analytic technique, effective therapeutic results, and psychodynamics that Sperling has described. Common findings in each patient are: the mothers in each case wanted their children to be sick and dependent; the basic dynamic structure is the same as in the phobias; omnipotence and magical thinking play a predominant role; one psychosomatic symptom is often exchanged for another; there is no personality profile but there is a family psychological profile; specific unconscious fantasies cause the psychosomatic symptoms, varying from one patient to another; the psychosomatic disease can be termed a pregenital conversion neurosis; and an overly strict superego is present with the psychosomatic symptom.

We have detailed a definite hierarchical analytic approach to the analysis of severe psychosomatic cases. From the first it is important that the referral be made by a physician who is confident that the psychosomatic symptom can be analyzed. The treating analyst requires experience in the field, since he needs authority in order to cope with the patient's relatives and the medical specialists who usually see these cases at the start. Analysts undertaking the treatment of these patients should get supervision by experienced people.

We begin by interpreting the masochistic meaning of the symptom and, in doing so, acquaint the patient with the severity of his superego. The superego in the psychosomatic does not permit the ego to be aware of aggressive or libidinal drive derivatives. This is in marked contrast to suicidal patients, who often are aware of self-destructive and homicidal impulses and fantasies. Instead of feeling guilt, as does the neurotic suicidal case, the psychosomatic experiences pain and limitation of function, which are acceptable punishments to his superego. As one internist told me: "To have a psychosomatic symptom is honorable; to be a neurotic is shameful."

Aggressive drive components must be interpreted first, with libidinal material left until later. As will be shown in my case material, if the analyst is enticed into a premature oedipal-phase libidinal interpretation, the patient often responds with an acute exacerbation of the psychosomatic symptom, which may dangerously impair the therapeutic alliance.

Our approach is not to deny constitutional factors but to devalue their importance. Likewise, we devalue the use of drugs, aiming to show the patients that since they themselves bring on the symptom, they can abort it, thereby eliminating the need for drugs.

Each occurrence of the psychosomatic symptom is analyzed to demonstrate to the patient the precipitating-day residue and, as the material emerges, the childhood conflicts that have been repressed into the symptom.

The pregenital nature of the transference in psychosomatic patients has been described by Sperling (1967, 1978), Atkins (1968), and this author (1968). This primitive aspect must be interpreted from the beginning, and the pregenital nature of the patient's object relations gradually made clear. The analyst should make no attempt to gratify the dependency demands of these patients, as is done in so-called anaclitic therapy (Margolin 1959). Where this is done, dangerous acting out and possible psychosis may ensue.

Any intense transference to the medical specialist must be dealt with or a split transference results, with analysis being sabotaged. The secondary gains derived from the symptom—to be taken care of as a helpless child, to not be blamed, and to have no demands made—are repeatedly revealed to the patient in the context of the price he pays for the symptom in lowered self-esteem, impairment of mature ego function, and healthy object relations.

When the acute psychosomatic symptom subsides, psychosomatic equivalents, including acting out, may immediately become a problem, which in turn must be dealt with in all their structural, genetic, and dynamic aspects (Atkins 1968, Sperling 1968, 1978, Wilson 1968, Wilson et al. 1983).

The case material that follows demonstrates the importance of early analytic intervention in a psychosomatic case:

A 35-year-old married woman, Mary, came to analysis with a severe case of "giant hives" and urticaria of two years duration. Three months before consultation, she had become "accidentally" pregnant, and she was trying to convince her husband, who was also her business partner, that she should have an abortion because they already had two children. Diagnostically, the picture was that of anxiety hysteria, with claustrophobia in elevators and other closed spaces. She was addicted to a hypnotic drug and drank heavily to relieve anxiety. She and her husband had frequent fights and she was contemplating divorce, wanting to go live with her father, who was a psychopath.

Severe latent homosexual conflicts as well as an unresolved father fixation soon became evident, but the urgent problem was the urticaria, which threatened her capacity to work. She had been to a host of dermatologists and allergists and found that only cortisone relieved her hives. She said, however, that when she was given cortisone she experienced such anxiety that she preferred the skin symptoms to the drug. This finding is frequent in psychosomatic cases, where if a drug suddenly clears the psychosomatic symptom, the patient is faced with her underlying neurosis or psychosis.

Initial sessions revealed that the hives had developed when she and her husband had their first major separation. He developed, for the first time in his life, bronchial asthma. Asthma, allergic skin reactions, and pruritis are a well-known syndrome in children. This couple had a psychosomatic syndrome à deux: she the urticaria and pruritis, he the asthma. Although subsequent analysis revealed that a number of conflicts were causing the skin symptoms, in the first sessions I pointed out to the patient that she was responsible for her pregnancy. She had not used her diaphragm correctly, being drunk at the time of intercourse. A particular role of being a helpless little girl, which I will discuss later, was interpreted to her, and much anger with me came up in the transference. The genetic roots of this rage, penis envy, were exposed to her in her relation to her father and particularly in relation to the fact that she wanted men to be maternal figures for her. The severe hives cleared at this time, the third week of analysis. A good therapeutic alliance was established, and she decided to have her baby, who turned out to be a beautiful little girl. Her skin symptoms cleared completely in the third year of analysis, and at the same time her husband's asthma attacks ceased.

The difficult problem of the splitting of the transference between the analyst and medical specialist was highlighted by a woman whose colits was replaced by perversions (Chapter 2). She came for analysis because, as she put it, she was castrating her son. She was indeed castrating her son, but after some weeks of analysis, she revealed that she was having an extramarital affair with an anal pervert and also that she had colitis, which did not respond to medical treatment. Although she did not go along with her lover's perversions, after she terminated her affair, she had an exacerbation of colitis, which resulted in many proctologic examinations. When I interpreted to her that she was acting out anal perversions in these examinations and that she wanted the colitis, she became angry with me. She then confirmed the interpretation by laughingly telling me about a specialist who said her colitis was caused by a tight anal sphincter. He proposed to cure it by using a graduated series of glass dilators. The patient experienced intense anxiety at the sight of the dilators, and she was aware that she was attracted to them. At this point she broke off her relationship with this physician. Each time, however, that anal rape fantasies began to emerge in the transference, the patient acted out by finding a new specialist to proctoscope her, and so forth. It was only after four years of analysis that she stopped splitting the transference.

In other instances of the splitting of the transference, I have had to give up the analysis, as the resistance was unshakable. These therapeutic failures occur especially in psychosomatic cases where the symptom is of long standing and a strong dependent transference has developed to the "family" physician, who in his behavior and examinations gratifies pregenital drives.

In psychosomatic cases when a good therapeutic alliance has developed, the analyst should suggest to the patient a consultant whom he knows. However, specialists who have faith in the emotional cause of psychosomatic symptoms are few. Often, I have found it sufficient to bring adult patients to the point where they insist that no medication be given, except for the diagnosis of organic disease. I have the specialist send me a report, which I discuss with the patient. Where I feel it is necessary, I will, with the patient's permission, talk to the specialist myself. I do not consider any of these procedures as parameters, nor do they contaminate analysis. If they are well-timed and used judiciously, they strengthen the therapeutic alliance, furthering treatment.

The material that follows illustrates problems of technique with psychosomatic patients and patients with characterologic disorders. The first case, Margaret, came for treatment because of her severe urticaria. Margaret's image of herself as a cute little girl was a part of her fear-of-being-fat body image disturbance. The other cases cited evidence characterologic resistances involved with mannerisms of speech.

All of these cases demonstrate a split in the ego and a regression from oedipal conflict. The techniques used involve selective focusing on certain defenses and confrontation. Both these techniques are also used in our approach to psychosomatic symptoms and are effective in bringing about a marked improvement in the severe psychosomatic symptom, before the specific etiologic fantasies and conflicts were uncovered and worked through.

TECHNIQUES OF INTERPRETATION AND THE PSYCHOANALYTIC INVESTIGATION OF THE SPEECH MANNERISM, "THE BOYFRIEND, THE GIRLFRIEND"

An understanding of the psychodynamic significance of mannerisms of speech was greatly enriched and clarified by the detailed psychoanalytic investigation of a specific speech mannerism, "the boyfriend, the girl-friend." This mannerism appeared with pathological frequency in the free associations of a group of analytic patients who evidenced a common characterologic conflict — a degree of psychopathy.

The following discussion presents the case material and psychody-namics of this specific mannerism and relates the results of this research to the general problem of the technique of interpretation of speech mannerisms in the analysis of characterologic disorders.

It is possible and may be clinically fruitful to subject the individual word components of a mannerism to analysis. In "boyfriend, girlfriend," the components boy, girl, and friend will have other dynamic meanings; however, for purposes of clarity of research, a mannerism must be considered as an entity or unit. This research does not focus upon the typical compulsive patient who has desexualized and idealized the object and who has a boyfriend or girlfriend with no sexual relationship. The patients in this study have a sexual relation with an adult man or woman and a degree of friendly object relations; but it is a condition of the relationship that they always refer to the man as "the boyfriend" or the woman as "the girlfriend." Diagnostically, these patients all presented what appeared to be a serious degree of psychopathy, which, however, was analyzable. I am also not presenting a study of a closely related subject, the use of first names by patients.

Mannerisms of speech have been explored at length by Feldman (1959) in his book, *Mannerisms of Speech and Gesture in Everyday Life*. Feldman has a short section on the importance of the first name, in which he summarizes the analytic literature on names. Particularly relevant to the subject of this paper are Oberndorf's (1918) paper on people who do not like their names; Stekel's (1911) paper on "The Obligation of Names," in which he discusses the hidden relation between names and professions and also between name and neurosis; and Abraham's (1911) paper on "The Determining Power of Names." Feldman himself points out some further meanings of the use of first names and pet names, emphasizing that they are used by people to show closeness or superiority, as with a child, or to express familiarity and equality. As far as I know, there has been no attempt to analyze a mannerism of speech in detail. In his book Feldman focuses on the total problem of mannerisms of speech and gesture and offers short psychodynamic formulations.

Case 1

The following material is from the case of Margaret, a 38-year-old married businesswoman, in analysis for symptoms of severe urticaria and hysterical neurosis. In analysis she always referred to her women friends as "girls" or "the girls." When I first called this to her attention, she got angry and told me that everyone used this term—it was just a way of talking. I pointed out to her that everyone did not do it—only certain people. For example, when writing an article on civic responsibility, a writer will say, "Women should assume political responsibility." If he says, "*Girls* should assume political responsibility," we feel he means adolescents. She resisted this, but suddenly burst out,

"You're right! I have always resented it when another career woman says, 'Girls, let's get a cocktail, or we girls should play bridge.' "

Further associations illustrate the nature of this speech mannerism in this patient and how it responded to interpretation.

Patient: "I really was not in love with B, no physical attraction."
Analyst: "What did you like about him?"
Patient: "As a boy" — pause — tension — "a man, I mean — what I mean is, as a boy he was spoiled."

Here the patient was all mixed up. What she meant to say was that *the man* was not spoiled but had been as a boy. He broke up with her because she was "spoiled," that is, was too much of a little girl.

Patient: "Father wanted me to marry him; he had a good rich family; he was a formal, pompous young man, he even wore a watch fob; but last time I saw him he was much more at ease and married to an attractive girl."
Analyst: "Girl? How old is the girl?"
Patient: "In her late 30s."

Here the patient could sense how inappropriate her use of "girl" was. She referred to the husband as a man, to the wife as a girl.

In a subsequent session the patient said: "I saw a photo of an old boyfriend of mine."

Analyst: "Boyfriend?"
Patient: "Well, he was 21."

Then, the patient started to think about what she was saying.

Patient: "Actually, he asked me to marry him."
Analyst: "What was your response?"

The patient blocked; then came material that revealed that the young man had been very aggressive — he had wanted her to go on a weekend trip with him and to have an affair. She was shocked and afraid of her attraction to him. She avoided her emotions and his by being a flirtatious "girl," not taking him seriously. The frustrated man then broke up the relationship, which she regretted.

A week later, the patient stated: "My husband and I had a disagreement about W.W." W.W., who was one of the patient's "girlfriends," turned out to be an unmarried businesswoman of 60. The patient then tried to explain: "This beautiful young girl had been given W.W.'s job and I think it is terrible."

Analyst: "How old is the beautiful young girl?"
Patient: (with anger) "Doctor, we are never going to see eye to eye" – pause – she thinks, "Well, she is 27 years old and I guess she is pretty smart, but it is terrible, a girl of her age should do this."

The patient was talking of herself and her fears of asserting herself. She had been offered a new job the day before but had been afraid to ask the older woman who offered her the position how much salary she would get. Further material led to her fear of castration from her mother, as well as her identification with her mother, who had always played the part of a little girl with the father.

DISCUSSION

This patient's speech mannerism expressed her nuclear conflict, the incestuous relationship with her father, which she expressed by being a sexy little girl. This role she repeatedly assumed in the tranference with me. Both the speech mannerism and transference behavior responded well to interpretation, with a marked improvement in ego functioning and object relations.

Case 2

A woman in analysis for severe phobias could not let her mother out of telephone reach. The patient, whose father was dead, talked of her mother's "boyfriend," a man of 55. The patient violently resisted any questions about the boyfriend and mother. She insisted her mother was too old and too sick to have any interest as a woman in the "boyfriend." When as a result of analysis the patient faced her phobias and permitted her mother to move to a place of her own, the patient was enraged to find that her mother and the "boyfriend" had begun an affair. In this case, the patient's speech mannerism hid her homosexual attachment to her mother and her denial of mother's and her own heterosexual desires.

Case 3

A 40-year-old lawyer with a serious compulsive neurosis revealed in the transference an intense wish to be treated like a boy. All the women he knew were "girlfriends." He was involved in an affair with a beautiful married woman, which he was unable to interrupt, although he knew that she was promiscuous, had had a career as a call girl, and was the mother of a three-month-old infant. A shrewd man with intact reality testing, he was blind where his mistress was concerned. He always called her by her first name, Rosalie, showing great love and tenderness. She appeared to return his feelings. They worshipped each other. Repeated interpretations of the incestuous oedipal and preoedipal sources of his conflict and transference interpretations made little dent in the problem, until I began referring to the mistress by her last name. I pointed out to him that he never thought of her as Mrs. X, and that this denial of her marriage repeated his denial of his parents' sexual relationship at the time of his younger brother's birth. Similar processes of idealization and denial of sexuality occurred and were worked through in the transference.

The resistances to this interpretation were strong, culminating in a session in which he was flooded with the guilt that he had been warding off. The tender, sensual split had been perpetuated by his use of the first name; Rosalie was lovely and beautiful like his mother, to whom he had denied sexuality in childhood; Mrs. X was dirty and sexual. When the patient could accept the fact that his mistress was a married woman with a child, he was able to interrupt the relationship. In this case, the use of the woman's first name, as well as the first names of all the "girls" he knew, had a fetishistic quality to it, and indeed in childhood he had utilized his mother's brassiere in masturbation fantasies.

A second factor was at work in this case to promote this man's conflict. He had once been a devout Catholic and had fooled the priest and himself about the actual nature of his relationships with women by referring to them as girls—a mechanism that probably was readily accepted by most clerics. This man had an excessively severe superego, from which he could escape only by seeing himself as a boy and all his friends as boys and girls. Everyone was fond of him, and he lived as if the world were a big, happy family. This situation forced him to be a hypocrite, a fact which was painful for him to face.

His loving adoration of the beautiful Rosalie also expressed the patient's wish to be a beautiful girl. He had been ashamed of his crude, virile father and, although potent, had always been disgusted with his own masculinity.

Case 4

An attractive 30-year-old married woman came to therapy for severe phobias. Her little-girl approach to life and the intensity of her anxiety attacks had convinced the first therapist, an eclectic psychiatrist, that she was schizophrenic. Analysis revealed an attempt to act out her emotions and to get me to treat her as a little girl. She told me that she always had thought of herself as a little girl, although she was the mother of two children and accepted much responsibility.

A sample session follows:

Patient: "My older sister is a very glamorous *girl*."

Analyst: "How old is sister?"

Patient: "Sister is 38 — isn't that funny, she is a woman. I never say woman. No one says I have a woman friend — they — I always say I have a girlfriend."

Analyst: "Women do have women friends; men do not usually refer to their boyfriends."

Patient: "Well, some do" — pause — (the patient was blocking).

Analyst: "Say it."

Patient: "Well, homosexuals refer to their boyfriends. It is odd, I never refer to boyfriends. I have men friends and prefer men very much to women. I really have few girlfriends. I am always guilty with other women and pretend not to compete. I am guilty dressing up, taking my time at the hairdresser and preparing to dress, and I always come later to sessions to avoid seeing any other women patients."

These associations led to the patient's central problem. She was a very precocious and sexually attractive adolescent and had been terrified of being prettier than her sisters and mother. She hid her intelligence and charm behind her little-girl facade. She was guilty about her wishes to seduce me. Her homosexual bond with her sisters was intense.

In this case, her use of the word *girlfriend* but *not* boyfriend pointed to her homosexuality, which was a major symptom.

Case 5

An ultrasophisticated professional man in analysis for a severe neurosis exhibitionistically recounted the guest list of his Saturday evening dinner party. He felt everyone there was unique and remarkable and was surprised that my questions revealed a lack of acquaintance with his brilliant social group. He made casual reference to a writer whom he liked very much, saying that X said that the writer who seemed so nice was a homosexual and that his lover, another guest, played the girl's part in their relationship. In answer to my question about what the girl's part could be, he said that he assumed it was fellatio. Further questions evoked strong resistance that screened the patient's denial of ideas of anal intercourse between his two guests. In this case, the use of the phrase, "girl's role," represented a characteristic defense of the patient. Everyone he knew was bright, but most of his friends, including the patient, pretended that to be sophisticated meant one could do anything one wanted. They were all bright children, exempt from the standards of others. The patient had a severe, latent homosexual conflict.

Case 6

A 41-year-old compulsive businessman, in analysis for a symptom of impotence with his wife, was talking about the women he had dated. He had liked a young woman who went to a religious school. At the time, he said, he presented himself to "girls" in the role of a carefree, young, rich businessman. The patient went on to state that his date told him she was interested in *another* boy who was at school. The patient then said, "That certainly sounds childish." What he was aware of was the reference to *another* boy when he had just told of his role as a businessman. Further material led to how much he felt like a boy then and now, particularly in terms of taking the initiative with women. He realized with a shock that he was as inhibited with his wife as he had been with the young woman eighteen years before. This patient's language was replete with references to the "boys" (boyfriends), and he had many "girl-friends" with whom he had casual sexual affairs. Although he was the chief executive of a company and a pillar of the community, he absolved himself of responsibility for his acts by the use of the mannerism.

DISCUSSION

The pathological use of "boyfriend, girlfriend" represents a split and a regression in the ego. When its use is pursued in therapy, the split and regression are maintained by the ego, with the assistance of the defenses of rationalization and denial, as well as by an appeal to authority, that is, everyone does it. This mannerism of speech wards off the criticism of the patient's superego as well as the listener's. It also deceives the reality-testing functions of the ego. The ego's sense of time is faulty in these patients.

The patients cited in this paper who use this mannerism of speech also like being called the "boyfriend" or the "girlfriend," or by what to them is its equivalent, his or her first name. Thus, these patients are able to permit gratification of instinctual drives, aggressive and libidinal, but not as full adults. All of them evidenced a degree of what appeared to be psychopathy. However, when the speech mannerism was interpreted and the regression in the ego ended, the patients were able to accept and differentiate between normal and neurotic guilt. The apparently ego-syntonic psychopathy became ego alien. These particular patients are adept at fostering this speech mannerism on others, who will refer to this patient's "girl" friend. The various meanings of this behavior, as listed below, have to be repeatedly interpreted in analysis.

1. It infantilizes the patient — actually repeats often a castration — the meaning being that the patient is not really a man dating a woman but is a boy taking out a girl.

2. It encourages avoidance of a mature object relationship and denial.

3. It promotes regression and avoidance of guilt. In the use of the "girlfriend" or the "boyfriend," the patients actually avoid their own superego guilt; they are saying to the superego, "I am only a boy, she is a girl, so it is not for real." Another meaning is to avoid rivalry as a man with the analyst (father) for his wife or other woman.

In both the male and female cases in this study, the analysis of speech mannerisms revealed a wide range of unconscious conflicts that varied according to the individual case. Common to all, however, were (1) superego conflicts, (2) a degree of psychopathy, (3) identification difficulties, (4) severe latent homosexual conflicts, and (5) intense castration fears.

The speech mannerism is more frequent in females than in males, and this finding is true, not only of analytic patients, but of men and women in general in our civilization. A complex variety of psychodynamic factors are responsible for this increased frequency in the female, the most significant being the longer and more difficult oedipal development in the female than in the male. As Freud (1933) pointed out in his "New Introductory Lectures," the girl's attempts to resolve the Oedipus complex are prolonged and difficult because she has to change the erotogenic zone from the clitoris to the vagina and change her object from mother to father to a lover. Another difficulty is that she is not subjected to as abrupt and incisive a castration threat as is the boy.

Techniques of Interpretation of Speech Mannerisms in the Treatment of Characterologic Disorders

In analysis it is necessary to analyze a specific mannerism of speech, only if it is used repetitively and inappropriately by a patient. As Feldman (1959) emphasizes, there are normal and neurotic uses of speech mannerisms. We have no precise data on when speech mannerisms appear in ontogenetic development. The use of the "boyfriend, girlfriend" mannerism would appear to be normal up and through adolescence.

In general, the interpretation of speech mannerisms in analysis has to be undertaken with care. If the mannerism is profusely utilized by the ego and there is no evidence of its being ego alien, it is wise to call patients' attention to it until the price they pay for using the mannerism has been shown to them. Gradually then, the speech mannerism becomes ego alien. The therapist needs both tact and directness. The rationalizations and denials offered by the patient must be patiently and repeatedly exposed. Examples and illustrations of what is normal are extremely useful. Telling examples of the misuse of this mannerism, "boyfriend, girlfriend," can be seen in the theatrical world, where everyone is everyone else's boyfriend and girlfriend, which allows them to be omnipotently free to do anything they desire, exempt from mature judgment.

The successful analysis of one mannerism may result in the defensive appearance of another. In these patients, as they began to give up the use of the "boyfriend, girlfriend," another mannerism appeared, "you know,"[1] which was an appeal to the group behavior and revealed a failure to internalize a mature superego. In the transference it actually did mean that the mother or father did thus and so, why shouldn't they? The interpretation of a mannerism of speech, if appropriately timed, is not a parameter but is an integral part of analytic technique.

In a communication, "A Note on the Magic of Names," Sharpe (1946) points out the impact on the unconscious of the words we use consciously. Her point was that we would do well to devise other terms to replace "good object" or "bad object" in our terminology, because to the *unconscious superego* "good" and "bad" have the static significance of *nonsexual* and *sexual*. The "boyfriend" and "girlfriend" have equally profound unconscious meanings to patients. The meanings involve the id, the unconscious superego, and the unconscious ego. However, it is primarily the unconscious (and conscious) superego that is fooled by this speech mannerism.

The repeated ego-syntonic use of a mannerism of speech impairs the development of a healthy therapeutic alliance in analysis, and true insight is not attained, no matter how intense the transference neurosis. Investigation of the mannerism, the "boyfriend, girlfriend," revealed that the regression in the ego presented a special resistance to cure because it affected both the therapeutic alliance and the transference relationship.

Since the neurotic use of mannerisms of speech deceives the reality-testing functions of the ego in both the patient and analyst and represents a serious threat to the therapeutic alliance, a failure to analyze the mannerism will be taken by the patient as a silent condoning of the defense and can result in an analytic impasse. It is not my experience that the neurotic use of speech mannerisms will be altered by interpretation of the defenses, of the transference, of the superego, etc., without the direct analysis of the mannerism itself. I agree with Feldman's (1959) conclusion that many cases fail to respond to treatment because the mannerisms of speech have not been analyzed. The analyst can uncover significant countertransference conflicts through an understanding of his unconscious reasons for avoiding the analysis of the stereotyped use of mannerisms of speech. If the analyst avoids analyzing the "boyfriend, girlfriend" mannerism, he will infantilize the patient and encourage acting out.

The stereotyped defensive use of mannerisms of speech represents a

---

[1] Feldman discusses the mannerism, "you know," at some length in his book (1959).

rigid ego defense that is typical of patients with character neuroses. As Fenichel (1945) emphasized in his chapter on character disorders, "It is particularly urgent that the personality first be released from its rigidity, because here is where the pathogenic energies are really found. Frequently, even in cases in which a vivid struggle between instinct and defense appears at other places, directing the attention to the rigid defenses may be of decisive importance" (p. 539).

Reich (1949), in his concept of character armor, also emphasized the importance of analyzing rigid characterologic attitudes of the ego. The detailed analysis of the specific mannerism of speech, the "boyfriend, girlfriend," revealed an intricate structure of defenses that masked psychopathic character traits. Further analysis of other mannerisms of speech should amplify our knowledge of the technique of character analysis.

REFERENCES

Abraham, K. (1911). On the determining power of names. *Clinical Papers and Essays on Psychoanalysis,* vol. 2, pp. 31–32. New York: Basic Books, 1955.

Atkins, N. B. (1968). Acting out and psychosomatic illness as related regressive trends. *International Journal of Psycho-Analysis* 49:221–223.

Feldman, S. (1959). *Mannerisms of Speech and Gestures in Everyday Life.* New York: International Universities Press.

Fenichel, O. (1945). Psychoanalytic technique and therapy in character disorders. In *The Psychoanalytic Theory of the Neuroses,* p. 539. New York: W. W. Norton.

Freud, S. (1933). Femininity. In New introductory lectures. *Standard Edition* 22:112–135.

Margolin, S. G. (1959). Psychotherapeutic principles in psychosomatic practice. *In Recent Developments in Psychosomatic Medicine, Bulletin of the Menninger Clinic* 12, ed. E. D. Whitkower and R. A. Cleghorn, pp. 134–153. Philadelphia: Lippincott.

Oberndorf, C. P. (1918). Reaction to personal names. *International Journal of Psycho-Analysis* 1:223–230.

Reich, W. (1949). Character analysis and character resistance. In *Character Analysis,* pp. 1–136. New York: Orgone Institute Press.

Sharpe, E. F. (1946). A note on the magic of names. *International Journal of Psycho-Analysis* 27:152

Sperling, M. (1961). Psychosomatic disorders. In *Adolescents, Psychoanalytic Approach to Problems and Therapy,* ed. Lorand and H. Schneer, pp. 202–216. New York: Hoeber.

———— (1963). A psychoanalytic study of bronchial asthma in children. *The Asthmatic Child,* ed. H. Schneer, pp. 138–165. New York: Harper & Row.

———— (1964). A further contribution to the psychoanalytic study of migraine and psychogenic headaches. *International Journal of Psycho-Analysis* 45:549–557.

———— (1967). Transference neurosis in patients with psychosomatic disorders. *Psychoanalytic Quarterly* 36:342–355.

———— (1968). Acting out behavior and psychosomatic symptoms: Clinical and theoretical aspects. *International Journal of Psycho-Analysis* 49:250–253.

———— (1978). *Psychosomatic Disorders in Childhood.* Ed. O. Sperling. New York: Jason Aronson.

Stekel, W. (1913). Ein Fur Feuillton Mench und Nam: An Editorial on Man and Name Die Verpflichtung des Names. In *Zentralblatt Fur Psychoanalyze und Psychotherapie* 3:460–463.

Wilson, C. (1968a). The boyfriend, the girlfriend: the detailed psychoanalytic investigation of a mannerism of speech. *Psychoanalytic Quarterly* 38:519.

———— (1968b). Psychosomatic asthma and acting out. *International Journal of Psycho-Analysis* 49:330–333.

Wilson, C. P., Hogan, C. C., and Mintz, I. L. (1983). *Fear of Being Fat.* Rev. ed. Northvale, NJ: Jason Aronson, 1985.

PART II

THE RESPIRATORY SYSTEM

10

AIR SYMBOLISM IN ASTHMA

Ira L. Mintz, M.D.

Specific dynamics related to the respiratory system have been commented upon by Fenichel (1953), Sperling (1968), Knapp (1960), Greenacre (1971), and others, but there is little mention in the psychoanalytic literature of the psychodynamic meaning of air. This neglect is perhaps surprising, since the asthmatic syndrome itself is concerned so intimately with the choking off of air.

Many psychoanalytic articles in the literature over the past fifty years have described the etiology, allergic manifestations, parent–child relationships, and intrapsychic conflict in asthmatic disease. Important contributions include those of Dunbar (1938), Gerard (1940), French and Alexander (1941), Jessner and colleagues (1955), Sperling (1949, 1963, 1968), Abrahamson (1961), Fenichel (1953), Knapp (1960), Coolidge (1956), Greenacre (1971), Reiser (1975), Mushatt (1972), F. Deutsch (1959), and L. Deutsch (1980, 1987) (see Chapter 13).

This chapter presents a broader view of the psychological determinents in asthma. It illustrates that unconscious conflict can be both a primary and a secondary factor in precipitating asthmatic attacks and describes the multiple aspects of the unconscious role of air in asthmatic disease. The unconscious importance of air, it is suggested, is derived from the infant's sucking, which contains a mixture of milk and air that can be incorporated as an unconscious fantasy of the early milk-air-mother. It is also suggested that the effect of a nebulizer or of dust, allergens, respiratory infections, and exercise can have psychological as well as physiological reactions in determining asthmatic disease.

History, folklore, and literature provide us with a number of illustrations of the unconscious meaning of air. Frazier's (1959) *The New Golden Bough* (1959) reveals the following:

> The custom of kissing the mouth of the dying in order to receive his soul—Joseph thus kissed Jacob on his death bed . . . Alexander Pope has Heloise cry out to Abelard: "Suck my last breath, and catch my flying soul"; while Shelley invokes Adonis: "O let thy breath flow from my dying soul, even to my mouth and heart, that I may suck." The Romans inhaled the breath of their dying friends to capture their souls. [pp. 214–215, 248]

Thus we see, amply illustrated, the respiratory incorporation of objects—specifically lost objects—through the inhaling of air.

Greenacre (1971) describes the expanding ego functions of a 4-year-old and comments upon his increasing awareness of the respiratory system and his experiments with inhaling and exhaling—blowing bubbles, blowing out a candle, holding his breath, and so on. These are movements of air that the child is able to voluntarily control. During other experiences the child recognizes that momentarily it has no control over the movement of air: a cold with a stuffed nose interferes with the free movement of air through the nasal passages; imprudent swallowing of food leads to choking; or one may be choked during wrestling games. These situations emphasize the importance of air because its impeded movement is associated with discomfort or anxiety. Greenacre comments further upon the relationship between the used-up food discharged as feces and the used-up air discharged into the environment. She also notes that the child is aware of the presence of air as an unseen powerful force. "As the wind, the air's force may be felt as evidence of an unseen giant who makes things go—a reinstatement, probably, of the dim perception of the parents in earliest infancy" (pp. 230–231). Silverman (see Chapter 14, this volume) notes the importance of breath holding in his asthmatic-child patient. When the breath-holding subsided at age 5, it was replaced by asthma.

Just as the child perceives the wind as the embodiment of the parents, primitive tribes and ancient ritual make use of a similar concept in regard to the perception of their own gods and religious practices. Reik (1946) makes the comparison between the ancient Greek rhombus, the bull roarers of primitive tribes, and the Hebrew shofar or ram's horn. The rhombus was a noise-producing instrument whirled through the air, akin to the bull roarer. The bull roarer is a flat piece of wood or stone with a hole in it. Attached to a string and whirled about, it emits a loud humming noise. It was found throughout the world and was used by primitive tribes of Australia and the Pacific, especially during puberty rites, the sound apparently representing the voice of ancestors, or gods, threatening the sons with punishment during circumcision rites.

The blowing of the shofar, or ram's horn, in Reik's view reflects God's injunction to Moses on Mount Sinai. The sound of the ram's horn is the sound of God's voice, and the blowing of the shofar serves to inspire the fear of God, the Father, and the punishment to be meted out for hostile impulses by the sons toward the father. Schlossman (1979) believes that its use suggests an attempt to control and to re-create the voice of God, echoing and reechoing through the forests and canyons mimicked by the sounds of wind.

In writing about the unconscious role of air in asthmatic disease, one must consider whether the preoccupation with air is primary (air is utilized to symbolically deal with unconscious conflict in an etiologic fashion) or secondary (as a result of repeated difficulties in breathing and fears of choking, the patient becomes absorbed with thoughts of air, which then can symbolize different kinds of conflict). One must certainly acknowledge Reiser's (1975) thesis that a patient repeatedly suffering from asthmatic attacks can develop a symbolic elaboration of the physiologic traumatic experience and become preoccupied with air. He feels that this experience could erroneously convey to the therapist that the symbolic meanings associated with the asthma are etiologic, rather than responsive to the illness. In other words, the question is, "Am I preoccupied with conflicts over air because I am fearful of choking from asthmatic attacks (secondary), or because I have the unconscious impulses to choke people, and I feel guilty and need to punish myself by choking (primary)?" Expanded further, the issue has been raised whether asthma or any other psychosomatic disease is primarily physical (genetic, allergenic, infectious, etc.), with secondary elaboration arising from distressing preoccupation with symptoms, or whether the symbolic manifestations are primary and in part etiologic.

The source of a symptom is described by F. Deutsch (1959) as the wish for a lost symbolic object that reawakens earlier memories of sensory perception. If substitute objects of repressed memories are not found, a conversion symptom may result. If the conversion symptom does not bind the anxiety, an organic symptom may be required to safeguard ego integrity. Mushatt (1972) concurs and concludes that "the argument as to whether clinical phenomena are psychosomatic or somatopsychic tends to become irrelevant if one utilizes Deutsch's concept of the mind–body–environment relationship. Loss or disharmony in human relationships (with depression) or anticipation of loss or disruption of relationships (with anxiety) may be expressed in physical terms. Disturbance of physical function may evoke a sense of loss or threat of it in relation to key figures in the environment."

In attempting to resolve the question further, L. Deutsch (1980) concludes the following: He points out that from a pragmatic point of view, it is not crucial whether the symbolic conflict is primary or secondary. If the secondary symbolic conflict can precipitate an asthmatic attack, then it becomes primary and etiologically meaningful. Moreover, he recognizes that analytically treating the symbolic conflict as a primary conflict can result in the resolution of the asthmatic attack. Emphasizing his perspective further, he adds, "Another important aspect concerns the fact that even postulating secondary symbolization, the fantasies created do not arise *de novo,* but are true representations of the preoedipal and oedipal conflicts: their analysis, therefore, would be highly desirable."

The case of Louise discussed below provides the clearest data that the impulse to choke was primary.

Case 1

Louise, a 12-year-old girl, was referred for analysis because of increasingly severe, incapacitating asthma over a period of four years, to the point where sometimes she had to be carried upstairs and had to sleep propped up on pillows. A detailed description of the technique of treatment and the underlying dynamics is presented in Chapter 11.

Asthma had begun at age 18 months, three months after the birth of a younger brother, following which the mother developed a severe postpartum depression that did not clear fully for at least a year. The parents volunteered that the depression markedly impaired the mother's ability to care for both children, so that Louise not only had to share her mother's attention but also may have blamed the brother for causing her mother's illness and withdrawal of interest. The mother remembered Louise's persistent interest in feeding the brother his bottle on the one hand and at the same time twisting the bottle so that the flow of milk was choked off at the twisted nipple. Louise was choking off her brother's milk and undoubtedly creating discomfort for him in sucking and perhaps in breathing. The mother also reported childhood photographs of Louise standing behind her brother with her hands around his neck as if she wanted to choke him.

Louise's preoccupation with choking came up repeatedly during the analysis, not in terms of the passive fear of choking, but rather in the active wish to choke. This was present in choking behavior toward a bird, towards inanimate objects, and in the transference. For reasons further elaborated in the case history, Chapter 11, Louise strongly identified with a bird, making birdlike sounds, unconsciously viewing her badly chewed nails as sheathed talons, and seeing her impaired asthmatic condition as that of a bird whose wings were clipped and could no longer fly (move about). In looking at childhood pictures, the mother described Louise standing behind her brother and was struck by her "clawlike" hands.

Louise recalled that the family's first bird (a projection of herself) was very aggressive, bit people, and eventually was given away. She remembered wanting to choke its neck when it got aggressive, unconsciously seeing it as her brother, as well as identifying with the bird and needing to choke back the aggressive impulses with an asthmatic attack in order to avoid being rejected, given away, and abandoned.

When Louise was angry, she made repetitive choking gestures, twisting an empty soda can back and forth until she ripped it apart. In more sublimi- nated fashion, she became an expert in the use of the Rubic Cube and was able to twist the numbers with extraordinary skill and speed—a consequence of endless practice in twisting the cube. It seemed clear to me that at times the cube stood for the necks of hated relatives, associates, or herself and, on occasion, stood for me in the transference.

The first six months of analysis produced considerable material, from which the subsequent data on the unconscious meaning of air is derived.

Thereafter a long, intense, negative transference emerged, the handling of which is detailed in the case report (Chapter 11). During bouts of intense anger with me, on more than one occasion she threatened to choke me by stuffing a tennis ball down my throat. This occurred when her verbal attempts to choke off what I had to say were not successful and she felt obliged to exercise more forceful methods. Here, too, she was the aggressive child who wanted to cut off the air upon which my words flowed out, as well as the guilty child who felt she should cut off her air to suffer punishment for her aggressive impulses. In other episodes she needed to choke with asthma to repress the emergence of violent impulses, as well as to punish herself for them. Most dramatic during the analysis was her need to choke back, repress, and suppress any feelings and thoughts about the imminent and then the actual death of her beloved grandmother in order to avoid the conflict over grief, separation, and loss. On occasion, asthmatic attacks replaced these conflicts.

I have focused upon Louise's active impulses to choke—recognized at age 2 and persisting into the analytic treatment in behavior and in transference—because it helps to validate the hypothesis that the impulse to choke may be primary. It is part of the person's aggressive drive system and not secondary to fears of passively choking derived from experience of impaired respiration during asthmatic attacks.

Louise's case also illustrates a second major point: the preoccupation with choking is intimately linked with thoughts about the movement of air and its symbolic meaning.

In the third session Louise reported having the flu as well as suffering from the consequences of her mother's persistent smoking. The cigarette smoke came up the stairs and began to suffocate her, even though she attempted to protect herself by putting the bed covers over her head. The mother smoked, even though Louise warned her that she could get cancer and even though Louise wheezed from it. She associated to the exterminator who came to the house "to exterminate me. He comes to exterminate the roaches." Louise's associations suggested that she viewed her mother as the exterminator who produced toxic gases (smoke) to destroy her. The smoke "suffocates like the air drowns you," a possible unconscious link to internal drowning by bronchial fluids during an asthmatic attack. Louise's ambivalent relationship to her mother is apparent in her preoccupation with fears of her mother's dying from cancer and fears of inhaling toxic substances that can give her the flu as well as destroy her from within.

A few months into the analysis, Louise was told that her beloved grandmother was severely ill and was expected to die momentarily. The other siblings were grief stricken; Louise completely suppressed all thoughts and feelings about her grandmother. Despite her father's repeated warnings of the grandmother's imminent demise, Louise refused to discuss her grandmother's illness in analysis. She claimed that she was getting better but revealed her conflict in repeated asthmatic attacks.

When I questioned her not revealing a severe asthmatic attack, instead of discussing it, she began to illustrate it through play by twirling her bracelet around and around. "It's like a tornado. The molecules are being moved around cut in half by electrons, and subparticles are coming out. Did you know that the Japanese are experimenting with tornados? They make model houses and they use a vacuum that sucks the houses loose. 'Eaak, 'Eaak.' " I interjected that I just couldn't figure out what she meant. She sang "Taps." "It's the end, if you get caught in a tornado." She continued twirling the bracelet. I added, "When you twirl the bracelet, you push the air." She agreed and continued, "Now it's a jump rope. The volcano, I mean tornado, destroys by sucking things up." I noted that she said volcano. "I made a mistake. It rhymes."

As she described the Japanese experiment further, she slipped twice more and called it a volcano. I pointed out the slips again, and she began to discuss volcanos. "A volcano is formed as the manta rock erupts from the earth, throwing out rock and dust. The dust covers the atmosphere and interferes with its functioning. Part of the rock is pumice with holes in it and it floats in water." I responded with a trace of surprise. "It has air in the holes?" The entire scientific description was accompanied by drawings, beginning with the Japanese tornado model houses and the vacuum that sucked them loose. She continued by drawing a volcano and then enlargements of pumice rock disgorged by it. She drew an amoeba that resembled the pumice rock, identifying each of the pseudopods as father pseudopod, mother pseudopod, and baby brother pseudopod. She then drew two bacteria that had nuclei resembling eyes wearing glasses and a large mouth. Both bacteria clearly resembled identifiable human heads.

It was my impression that the entire hour helped to clarify the unconscious meaning of her asthmatic attack. Informed of her grandmother's impending death, instead of responding like her siblings with emotional distress and feelings of grief, or anger, the patient defended herself against dealing directly with the stress by somatizing it into a severe asthmatic attack. She did not report the attack the next day in order to avoid having to uncover the feelings that precipitated it, nor did she discuss the grandmother's impending death, which would have directly led to her painful feelings. When I expressed surprise that she did not tell me how ill she was, she responded, "It's painful breathing in," a condensation of her painful feelings and her somatizing respirations. She then defensively attempted innocence. "Little girls like me aren't supposed to know." Not put off by her innocence, I continued to question her. Her response was to displace and externalize the conflict onto the twirling bracelet—an object not part of her own body, but closely in contact with it—which now symbolized an asthmatic attack and served as a substitute for getting one.

Identifying the twirling bracelet as a tornado, she revealed her unconscious preoccupation with the violent movement of air and with the tiny objects floating in the air that were being bombarded against one another in the process of destroying and being destroyed. These microscopic objects— amoeba and bacteria—clearly represent people. They are family members who are present in the dust produced by the sucking tornado or are belched forth with the pumice rock by the erupting volcano-self. Here she clarified the symbolic meaning of inhaling dust. It can unconsciously represent the incorporation of hated or loved objects into the lung with the air, in the same manner that eating can incorporate loved and hated people into the gastrointestinal system with the food. In describing the sucking up of model houses by vacuums, she made "Eaak" noises, which seemed to be associated with these destructive tornados. In previous sessions, after she made the "Eaak" noises, she sucked in air. She linked death to the tornados: "It's the end if you get caught in a tornado." She then made three slips, calling tornados volcanos. When she described the volcanic eruptions of rock and dust, she alluded to pumice rock as filled with air sacs.

It is reasonable to consider that the whirling of the bracelet represented an externalization of the movement of air in her own respiratory system, symbolizing her own volcanic, tornado self. These externalizations are further elaborated in the Japanese experiments that attempt to cope with destructive tornados that suck up and destroy people. This externalization represented the destructive aspects of asthmatic inhalation. Forcible inhalation of air symbolically contains people and other objects that are destroyed by the "sucking tornado-lung-child." Further associations led to descriptions of volcanic eruptions of rock and dust, which represent the destructive aspects of asthmatic volcanic exhalation from the lung. The pumice rock filled with tiny air sacs could well have symbolized her perceptions of coughed-up pieces of "pumice-rock-lung, dust, people" during paroxysmal coughing and violent asthmatic attacks.

She had noted in a previous session that dust precipitated her respiratory attacks. Her descriptions of dust-amoeba as having "father pseudopods and mother pseudopods" and her drawing of dust-bacteria resembling people suggest that these objects are sucked in with the dust and inhaled by her. Once inside, they destroy her from within as hated destructive "amoeba-bacteria-introjects." They can also destroy her from within when retained during asthmatic attacks in which she experiences difficulty in exhalation. Conversely, she can destroy these hated introjects during her sucking-tornado inhalation, or her explosive, volcanic exhalation. Inhaling and exhaling symbolize tremendous destructive conflict, during which ambivalently cathected objects are symbolically destroyed or can destroy by inhalation and exhalation. At the same time one can preserve them by becoming unable to inhale and suck up tornadolike or exhale and explode volcanolike. The valued object is preserved when the bronchus goes into spasm and is filled with mucus. It is of considerable significance that air becomes the vehicle for expressing these destructive and dependency conflicts.

Louise's identification with volcanos and tornados may harken back to Greenacre's comments about the young child's perception of and experiments with air as an unseen powerful force "felt as evidence of an unseen giant . . . a restatement of the dim perception of the parents in earliest infancy." Louise played games blowing away ripped-up papers as a young child would blow out candles.

Case 2

Willie was a 7-year-old boy originally in analysis in the midwest for symptoms of asthma, most of which subsided during a two-year course of treatment. Analysis was interrupted because of the father's promotion and transfer to the East Coast. At the time I saw him, he was left with only occasional slight wheezing when he exercised. As a consequence of the first analysis, Willie's conflicts became less intense and the asthma subsided. What he did develop after the asthma subsided was depression, enuresis, and self-destructive behavior. The underlying, unresolved conflicts, no longer expressed by asthma, resulted in the development of self destructive behavior and depression.

I have noted elsewhere (1980–1981) that unconscious conflicts can be expressed through behavior, psychological symptom formation, or psychosomatic illness, simultaneously or in sequence. Changes in psychological symptoms and psychosomatic diseases may result in part from changes in the stress levels, in defense patterns, in shifting intensity of drives, and in alternating levels of ego integration and regression. The underlying conflicts, fantasies, anxieties, identifications, and character traits may remain, though in attenuated form, relatively unchanged. At different times, these conflicts are expressed in different illnesses. It is not uncommon for an asthmatic patient to develop anxiety, depression, or neuroses, or for these and other symptoms to precede or to follow asthmatic illness. An error is made when a connection is not recognized between a behavior disorder and a psychosomatic illness (Sperling 1968). Incomplete resolution of a conflict can result in a subsiding intensity of the symptom, not through a complete solution to the conflict, but rather through a shift in the manner in which it is expressed. It may then emerge in different symptoms. I introduce these ideas here to clarify the importance of air symbolism in a patient who ostensibly no longer suffers from overt symptoms of asthma but whose partially resolved conflicts are basically the same, as if the asthma were still present.

Willie was the oldest of three boys born in the Midwest of conservative Protestant parents. Shortly after his birth, his father's job required them to move repeatedly. In the first consultation, Willie, who was big for his age, appeared well developed, and had a cocky, arrogant attitude. He was bright, verbal, and challenging. He spoke almost with pride as he volunteered that he had been thrown out of one private school and was well on his way to being asked to leave the second. Nevertheless, I detected a careful thoughtfulness underlying his shell of toughness.

Six months into the analysis, Willie brought in a large plastic bag filled with pussywillow pods that he had gathered from a tree and wrapped in ice to keep them moist. He added, as he displayed them proudly, that he was a pussywillow collector. When those pods were kept moist, they remained flexible, and he used them to rub against his cheeks like little furry animals or like his present wool blanket. He demonstrated by taking one of the pods, which indeed resembled a miniature animal pelt, and gently and rhythmically rubbed it along his cheeks and around his lips. He remarked on how much the pod looked like a little seal. It seemed clear that the pussywillow pods represented the security of a transitional object, a miniature furry animal, or in his own terms, his wool blanket that he rhythmically rubbed against his cheeks.

After a short while, he tired of this behavior, and, still holding the pods, he volunteered how he prepared them. He placed them all in a bucket and poured boiling water on them "to pasteurize them like milk and get rid of any bacteria." He then wondered if he might be able to use them for incense, by putting some in a cup, pouring boiling water on them, and inhaling the smell, which he described as similar to roasting prunes. He added, "Do you think I could eat them after I pasteurize them, or would they be poisonous?"

His comment about pasteurizing them to get rid of bacteria suggested that he unconsciously viewed the pussywillow pelts as the equivalent of milk, which could be ingested but which might contain bacteria dangerous to his health. He then suggested that the pussywillow contents might be incorporated by inhaling as incense. His fear of danger from the incorporated object again reemerged with his anxious query about whether it might now be poisonous. Thus, he demonstrated his wish to incorporate symbolically mother's milk by drinking or by inhaling and his apprehension that either route was dangerous because of his ambivalent feelings toward his mother. Sucking milk or inhaling incense illustrates the close relationship between respiratory and gastrointestinal systems. His unconscious needs both to incorporate the mother and to expel her reflect his conflict over dependency and closeness on the one hand and the need for distance on the other. As Knapp (1960) has pointed out, asthmatics whose symptoms increase during separation may have a major conflict over dependency, whereas those whose symptoms decrease during separation (hospitalization, a distant school), may have a major conflict over aggression as well as the need to avoid destruction of the object through distancing.

It also seemed plausible in Willie's case that the rhythmical rubbing of the furry animal-wool blanket against the cheeks and around the lips unconsciously represents a stage preceding or following incorporation via eating or inhaling. This rhythmical movement becomes transposed into the rhythmical in and out movement of sucking or breathing. Willie's fear of damage from the incorporated (inhaled-ingested) internalized object is strikingly similar to Louise's concern about being damaged by inhaling her mother's smoke or destructive objects in the dust, or the sucking-up of objects by her tornado-self. In both cases ambivalence is evident in the question of whether the incorporated object will provide security or destruction and in the projection of the patients' own feelings of love or destructiveness onto the external objects: mother, pussywillow, tornado, earthquake, etc.

A number of months later, similar manifestations of the conflict reemerged when Willie reported that his cat had four kittens. "You remember we talked about holding the pussywillows to my face. Now I hold the kittens like pussywillows. I rub the big cat's chin and she purrs. I hold her to my ear like a telephone. The cat is alive, breathing, furry." I commented that he had never said anything about the cat's breathing before. Mistaking my comment, he replied that "a pussywillow 'breeds' too." At that point, lying on the couch, he grabbed his penis. On numerous occasions before and after this episode, when situations arose during the hour in which Willie felt angry and did not verbalize his feelings or act them out with menacing behavior, he grabbed his penis. Often he had to run to the bathroom.

His mishearing of "breed" for "breathe" reflected the eruption of his conflict over the birth of his little brothers. One of the determinants for his symptoms was related to his sibling rivalry and wishes to kill his brothers, along with his guilty identification with his brothers' unborn, nonbreathing, dead state. Associations to the furry little pussywillows that he rubbed and inhaled led to the furry little pussies that he also held up to his face, rubbing and inhaling their aromas in his unconscious preoccupation with their life or death. These furry little babies stood for his hated siblings. His spontaneous comment that the cat is "alive and breathing" belied his unconscious wish that the opposite might prevail. He was aware that breathing was synonymous with living and that the rhythmical movement of air attested to the babies' live status. Holding the cat to his ear like a telephone reflected a displacement of the air waves from the mouth to the ear.

It should not be surprising that his symptom of enuresis, in part, is a result of viewing his penis as an aggressive weapon. Sperling (1963) has commented upon the frequent interrelationship between asthma and enuresis at night. Because of the sleeping ego's weakened defenses, a release of hostility occurs through bedwetting. During the day, as the aggressive drives build up, they are in part discharged by urinating.

A short while later, without any advance notice, the patient brought in his cat. He spent a good deal of the session holding it on his shoulder, next to his face, breathing in its fur, and rubbing it so that it would purr. He amply demonstrated what he had described previously: that he enjoyed rubbing the cat's fur next to his face, that he inhaled the smell of the fur, and that he induced purring and was conscious of the noise next to his ear.

On the following session he came in with a toy that he had built from a reclaimed toy pottery wheel. It consisted of the motor itself, a drive shaft, the batteries, and an on-off switch, all fitted into a leftover piece of styrofoam packing material. He proceeded to color a circle of paper and attached it to the drive shaft. When the switch was turned on, the paper whirled like a colored pinwheel.

After admiring the concentric circles of color as he slowed down and then speeded up the pinwheel, he slowly brought it close to his face, next to his shoulder. It appeared that he might cut his face with the rapidly revolving wheel. It suddenly became evident, however, that this was not his intention.

He began to inhale the air produced by the wheel's movement. The noise of the motor, and the vibration that it produced, were clearly reminiscent of the purring of the cat in the previous hour.

He had constructed an artificial cat, perhaps in part symbolic of his mother, perched on his shoulder, purring, vibrating, and producing air for inhaling. Moreover, with the use of the switch he had complete control over its functioning, which was not possible with his cat nor with his mother or siblings.

In a subsequent hour he brought in a small battery-driven fan. Again he brought it close to his face, ostensibly to demonstrate its cooling properties, but I saw that he was inhaling the air it produced.

These clinical data assume increasing prominence when one learns that both parents loved cats and always managed to keep two or three of them around, even with their frequent changes of residence.

Case 3

Carol, a single, 20-year-old woman, entered treatment because of increasingly severe attacks of asthma, one of which almost resulted in her death. She was a bright, introspective woman who had suffered from asthma since the age of 7.

She was brought up in a small town in the West and went to college there because she felt too uncomfortable being away from her family. When her father was transferred east, she moved with the family, which consisted of her parents and her older brother. The mother had experienced manic depressive episodes as long as Carol could remember. She remembered from early childhood apprehensively watching her mother swinging out of control, becoming less and less responsive to the little girl's needs and more and more impulsive and grandiose.

Carols' father, a lawyer, was very attached to her and in many ways unconsciously opposed her healthy independence, as well as covertly encouraging regressive activities. For example, after being in treatment for a while, the patient progressed beyond her previous infantile outbursts of temper when caught in a traffic jam. Instead, when she and her father were caught in traffic one day, she expressed realistic exasperation. Her father facetiously suggested that she get out and kick the car in front that was blocking her, like a little girl in a temper tantrum.

During the course of treatment Carol described many frustrating experiences. Some of the circumstances she encountered were exasperating and distressing, because of her regressed view of them and her limited ability to tolerate frustration. In frustrating situations she felt overwhelmed, unable to control the environment, and filled with resentment and anger, often culminating in a screaming temper tantrum. It became apparent that when she felt that she could not cope with a distressing experience, an ego regression set in and she became totally preoccupied with the experience. Nothing else mattered. If she felt that she would have to take action, and at the same time realized that her anticipated behavior was inappropriate and infantile, she repressed the episode and developed an attack of asthma. She became increasingly aware that she could not control many situations in her life, and also that she could not control her impulsive response to these uncontrollable circumstances – her urges to act out with what she recognized was regressive behavior. She began to dream extensively about problems of control over external objects and about the violent movement of air, for example, tornados.

One morning she reported the following dream. "I'm in a field with little airplanes that you can fly yourself. I was afraid to go up and fly around, because the plane would get out of control." Associations were to her fear of being out of control. "The planes look like little round pressure cookers, with the steam exploding out." At that point she suddenly moved her left hand from her mouth to an extended arm position. In response to my noting it, she replied that *she* was the pressure cooker, and that the steam spilling out under pressure is like the asthmatic attack as the air is expelled. She is afraid of what will spill out of her.

The patient identified with the pressure cooker-airplane that poured out superheated air that could burn and destroy, a projection of the accumulated burning rage that built up in her and threatened to burst out inappropriately because of the pent-up pressure. Additional evidence is the movement of her hand from her mouth with her association to her being the pressure cooker. The airplane flies by sucking in air and by expelling it through propellers and jet engines, a projection of her identification with the steam pressure cooker-airplane that also pours air out under pressure. This situation is not dissimilar to the wheezing, noisy asthmatic state, where the air is sucked in and exhaled under pressure through the narrow, fluid-filled, constricted bronchi. The violent expulsion of air symbolically represents the partial discharge of aggression, accompanied by self-punitive choking in punishment for this unconsciously perceived transgression.

Carol's aggression would explode in infantile, inappropriate temper tantrums, encouraged by her father, or in disguised form during asthmatic attacks where the air under pressure, but without words, would move back and forth in the respiratory system. Both types of discharge were regressed:

one was a recognized infantile burst of aggressive behavior and the other a regressed psychosomatic symptom. The resolution of conflict can be expressed with either or both types of activity, representing alternative forms of ego resolution of the same conflict. This concept was expanded further in the previous case of Willie. The present illustration serves to further confirm its validity.

Carol was reminded further of a comment that a girlfriend made: that whenever she spoke on the telephone, she sighed audibly. The girlfriend always asked what was wrong and why she didn't get it off her chest. The patient added that she was moving worries from her mind to her chest. The clinical setting in which the sighing emerged, together with her subsequent associations to it, suggest that the sighing reveals a mental attitude, displaced to the lungs and expelled with the air. It is a symptomatic act symbolizing an attempt to discharge pent-up frustration, disappointment, and aggression. The behavior may also be viewed as self-punitive ("let my breath flow from my dying soul"). If expelling all the air is dying, then the asthmatic's excessive retention of residual air in the lung on expiration may be determined by both physiological and psychological factors. When the conflict becomes intensified and cannot be tolerated, the patient regresses, the conflict is repressed, and the expiratory sigh is replaced by an expiratory wheeze of the asthmatic attack.

About six months later Carol reported that for a week she had had no asthmatic attacks. Instead she was aware of constantly thinking, feeling, and worrying about all kinds of problems that upset her, but she was able to tolerate doing so. She added that she noticed a return of the sighing, which had been gone for many months. "It means that I'm unhappy, but I acknowledge it and that others know it too. It's using breathing to express my feelings of unhappiness, and I have control over it. It reminds me of sobbing, but no tears, . . . expel all the air, . . . like dying." I suggest that the sighing reflected an intermediate stage between sobbing and asthma. It emerged as she renounced the asthma but while she still felt that she needed to express feelings symbolically with breathing.

This relationship was further clarified during a session when she spoke about her childhood finger sucking. It was present until age 7, when it ceased, and she developed asthma. She wondered about her habit of sucking on the third and fourth fingers, since most other children appeared to suck their thumbs. Further associations led to remembering that she would rhythmically rub the second and fifth fingers against her face while sucking, "almost like windshield wipers . . . to wipe the tears away." In thinking about the similarity of her finger sucking to the asthma, she added that when she had asthma, "I can feel the air in my throat . . . like feeling the fingers on my face . . . the air goes in and out . . . early you get security by being rocked — rhythmically . . . like the ticktock of a clock. Put the clock next to the little puppy to help it sleep alone without the mother. Then the air goes in and out." The ticktock of the clock may stand for the mother, or for the puppy just as the rhythmic finger movements symbolize the respiratory presence of the mother for Carol and Willie.

Here, the patient connected the rhythmic rubbing of her fingers against her face with the rhythmic movement of air in her throat during an asthmatic attack. Her comment tended to validate the similar suggestion that Willie's rubbing the pussywillow pelts against his face was also an alternate form of respiratory air movement displaced to the outside of the face. Carol also correlated termination of finger sucking with the beginning of the asthma. Again I suggest that the rhythmic sucking of the fingers was related to the rhythmic movement of air and was related to dependency conflict. This was further confirmed with associations to the security achieved by being rocked, like the ticktock of a clock that reassures and helps the "little puppy (patient) sleep alone without the mother."

In the middle of the treatment, Carol's husband was transferred to a different city, and she was forced to consider moving and separating from her family and from treatment. She was distressed about it for months. On one occasion she reported speaking to her husband about it on the phone. She felt well until he asked whether she had contacted a moving company. At that point she regressed. She felt that he was joking at her expense. It wasn't she who was moving; she had made no preparations. As she became increasingly upset and began to lose control of her feelings, she was aware of a conscious, forcible inhaling and exhaling, although there was no obstruction to her breathing. "It was like a temper tantrum . . . wanting to yell and scream and wave my arms in excited fashion, . . . breathing heavily." At this point, as she was concentrating on the breathing, the feelings of anger disappeared. She was aware that she shouldn't be doing this, that she should stay with the feelings and the experience. "It was like holding your breath . . . a temper tantrum . . . exploding with rage." The attack of asthma was beginning.

Patients ordinarily do not reveal an awareness of emotional conflict and its replacement by an asthmatic attack in such graphic, dramatic fashion. Carol had to be persistently encouraged to report her thoughts and feelings surrounding these distressing experiences before this type of material finally emerged.

Her reaction to the prospect of moving was clearly one of intense separation anxiety and rage. She felt helpless and unable to cope with leaving her family, friends, and the analyst. As the time of departure drew near, she experienced increasing fear and panic and felt more and more out of control. When confronted by the fact that she had not contacted the moving company, she regressed, became somewhat paranoid, and began to deny that it was really she who was moving. She described in detail her feelings that she could not face the separation, and that she was overwhelmed. The more she thought about it, the more upset she got. Then she stopped thinking about the world around her and instead concentrated upon her own body—her breathing. At first the breathing was normal. As she concentrated upon it, her thoughts, fears, and anxieties about moving retreated. She then became aware of the increasing difficulty in breathing as the asthmatic attack began. She was extremely reluctant to reveal this situation, even as it became known to her, because she recognized that seeds for the control of the asthma lay in renouncing this method of avoiding intolerable feelings and, instead, consciously and painfully dealing with them.

What is most striking is the patient's description of her almost consciously deliberate behavior aimed at avoiding what she perceived to be overwhelming conflict. She reported an awareness of sudden marked regression, sensing a developing paranoid reaction toward her husband along with the emergence of a primitive defensive denial: she really wasn't moving. The regressive somatization with the asthmatic attack may have prevented an even more severe regressive state with paranoid elements, the use of denial, and possibly a psychotic state. This is the only patient I have seen who has described so conscious a development of an asthmatic attack. It raises the question whether the account was retrospectively distorted, or whether a more careful persistent approach with other patients may yield similar information.

It was significant to hear her correlation between the beginning of the forcible inhaling and exhaling of the asthmatic attack and the presence of a temper tantrum: "wanting to yell and scream and wave my arms in excited fashion . . . breathing heavily. . . . It was like holding your breath . . . exploding with rage." I have yet to hear a more lucid description of the similarity between a temper tantrum and an asthmatic attack. Certainly the violent movement of air is present in both, as well as retention of air in the lung, by breath holding or explosive discharge in the tantrum and the noisy inhalations and expirations and retention of air in the asthmatic attack.

A few months after moving, Carol returned from Washington for a visit. She reported feeling free of asthma. Now when under stress she would get upset. She revealed a dream that occurred a few nights before the visit.

My mother was crying and depressed and said, "Dad is going to abandon me." I became so upset for her, and attempted to comfort her, and at the same time I was crying violently on her shoulder. I never got so upset as I was in the dream and I awakened sobbing. Two years ago I would have awakened with asthma, I know it. *[End of dream]*

Associations were: I'm thinking of going to visit friends. We used to smoke pot with them, and I always got asthma. I'm afraid I still might get it. The last place left to get asthma. You smoke pot . . . to inhale . . . to keep the air inside . . . mother inside. I used to suck my fingers and wipe the tears away with my fingers. Now I take it inside, and cry inside. It's like eating cream of wheat every night.

The inhaling of the air-mother is clearly apparent in these associations. Analogous ideas are expressed by little Willie's inhaling the pussywillow incense.

The sequence of the patient's associations was very revealing. She reported a dream of the mother crying because of fear of abandonment by the father. Preoccupied by fears of abandonment herself because of her recent need to move and leave her parents, she identified with the mother in the dream. In attempting to comfort her, she cried violently. "I never got so upset as I was in the dream and I awakened sobbing. Two years ago I would have awakened with asthma, I know it." Her ability to tolerate and absorb terribly distressing feelings resulted in her experiencing distress by sobbing instead of asthma. She continued to clarify the linkage between the two experiences: "You smoke pot . . . to inhale . . . to keep the air inside . . . mother inside. I used to suck my fingers and wipe the tears away with my fingers. Now I take it inside and cry inside." She made it clear here that the conflict over separation that produced internalized grief could be dealt with by external or internal expression. To express grief externally is to cry and sob openly with conscious turmoil. To express grief internally is to "take it inside and (unconsciously) cry inside." The secretion of fluid and mucus in the bronchial tree may be the symbolic equivalent of crying inside. Disguised internal tears produce the same bronchial dysfunction as the comparable secretion of fluid and mucus the nasal passages produce during sobbing. Less prominent, but still evident, is the presence of agitated movement of air during expressions of grief and sadness.

The patient's associations to smoking pot at her friend's house seem to reveal a series of symbolic substitutes for the mother. As a child she sucked her fingers, which represented the mother, very much as a comforting doll.

The thumb sucking was replaced by the asthma, where the tie to the mother was now present through an internalized air-object within the lung. The shifting of this object by ingestion to the stomach is evident in her associations to eating the cream of wheat cereal every night. Again one sees the coexistence of the processes of inhaling and ingesting.

When this patient could not control the external world, she regressed and symbolically attempted to cope with it through the manipulation of her own bodily functioning. The internalization of the conflict via the asthma represented a regressed autoerotic, symbolic, rhythmical, self-rocking to gratify dependency needs, an attempt to expel the pent-up aggressive tension through the pressured exhaling of air, a self-punishing choking for her forbidden feelings of hatred, and an obliteration from awareness of the original conflict. She returned to a regressed view of the world, perceived within her own body, rather than in the environment.

Case 4

Conscious and unconscious preoccupations with the movement of air are not restricted to asthmatic patients. Not infrequently they are present in other patients who also unconsciously associate air with their conflicts.

Billy was a severely disturbed 7-year-old whom his parents reluctantly brought for analysis because of the school's threat to send him to a school for retarded children. Besides doing poorly in his school work, he was depressed and suicidal; had severe phobias, obsessional thinking, compulsive rituals, and psychosomatic symptoms; and displayed very effeminate behavior. Billy's unconscious conflicts over aggression were related in large part to his four younger sisters and infant brother along with his intense anger toward his parents.

In the first five months of treatment, Billy spent a great deal of time building houses with Lincoln Logs and drawing pictures of homes and schools. Gradually, first "by accident" and then deliberately, Billy described fantasies of the buildings burning down and killing the children inside. The houses and schools were also destroyed by hurricanes and earthquakes, with all the children inside dying. As he gained confidence in describing his feelings, the fantasies were further elaborated. "A little boy set the fire. He hates his mother. . . . He loves her. . . . All the children get burned to death." There were repeated descriptions of fires starting and then spreading through the windows and onto the trees. The ensuing conflagration was spread by the wind and consumed the entire town. Everybody died. At another point he related that "the Empire State Building is in the middle of a sandstorm. . . . The wind blows and blows and the windows are covered with bricks to protect the people inside from the storm."

He revealed how frightened he was of thunder and lightning, how "it can kill you." He said he had called for his mother during a storm in the middle of the night and that she could not come to him because she was with his sister. During one session he became terrified by a thunderstorm outside and huddled on the floor under my desk, sobbing. His mother had previously reported this terror during thunderstorms, along with his demand that she shut all the windows in the house during the storm.

Billy's unconscious, burning, explosive hatred for his mother, siblings, and classmates was repressed and projected into fires, thunderstorms, hurricanes, and sandstorms, which he then feared as retaliatory punishment for his intense aggression. There is nothing unusual about this typical structure of a phobia. What I want to emphasize is the particular role in it of the movement of air.

The air-wind-hurricane-sandstorm is the vehicle by which the aggression is manifested. It is an essential ingredient in the waves of destructiveness. The fires consume air in order to burn and to destroy. "The fire goes out the window and spreads to the trees, and the wind blows it to the other houses." During the thunderstorm, the closed windows were Billy's attempt to limit the entry of the fiery destructiveness. His fears of hurricanes, earthquakes, sandstorms, and bomb explosions were also projections of his repressed explosive wrath. One can understand why Billy was afraid to speak up and yell and let the aggression spill out on the exhaled air. His conflict was also displaced below and somatized in bowel and bladder behavior. When he got angry in the sessions, he would run to urinate or to defecate. On one occasion he developed abdominal cramps and threatened to defecate on the floor or pass wind. Filled with exploding feelings, he identified with his projected self and symbolically became the windstorm-thunderstorm-hurricane creating destructiveness and debris (feces) through the somatic discharge of his explosiveness.

In this manner Billy's unconscious conflict is very similar to that of Louise with her asthma. Both patients are filled with unconscious aggression, fearful that they will be unable to contain it and will explode in violent behavior. Both are also filled with guilt and the need for punishment, achieved by both with somatization, and by Billy, with phobias. Both patients unconsciously use the violent movement of air-wind in expressing the destructiveness—Louise with tornados, volcanos, and earthquakes and Billy with thunderstorms, earthquakes, and sandstorms. In attempting to repress the outpouring of hostile verbal abuse, Louise somatically chokes it back with asthma, while Billy somatically explodes through the colon and bladder. Both identify themselves symbolically with the storms, tornados, and earthquakes that pour out the destructive air they are afraid to express through angry verbalizations.

Much later in the analysis, Billy became able to tolerate emerging conscious recognition of his violent feelings and was able to verbalize them instead of projecting or somatizing them. He then verbally expressed in an outpouring of air his intense hatred for his parents, his siblings, and the children whom he felt had wronged him. The episode occurred in very dramatic fashion. In the preceding two years of analysis, his behavior had been very passive and self-destructive. He looked, acted, and spoke like a miniature version of a very effeminate teenager. He acted gently with people, spoke softly in a high-pitched voice, and volunteered that he was afraid of sports and getting hurt. He said he was "delicate and a g" and twisted his shoulders, wiggled his hips, and pirouetted about on his toes in the session. He was sitting in a high-backed, revolving chair turned away from me so that I could not see him. Suddenly his soft, high-pitched, effeminate voice assumed a loud, deep, and angry tone. It rose in volume as he began to describe how he hated each of his sisters. By the time he reached his anger toward his mother he almost screamed out the words: "I'd like to kill her . . . I'd like to kill all of them . . . I hate them so."

Abruptly he swung his chair about, and I was startled to see an entirely different child sitting in front of me. His body was tense and coiled as he gripped the arms of the chair. His eyes blazed. His lips were drawn back to reveal bared teeth as he continued to spew out his hatred and rage. He leaped from the chair and marched around the room, stamping heavily on the floor, in marked contrast to his previous, delicate pirouetting. All the while, the anger poured out of him. The violent movement of air now erupted from his throat, no longer repressed, projected, or somatized.

Four additional brief clinical vignettes may serve to further illustrate the preoccupation with the symbolic meaning of air in nonasthmatic patients.

A 45-year-old engineer was in the second year of analysis for symptoms of work inhibition, depression, spastic colitis, headaches, and backaches. A partner in a large engineering firm, he had always made a point of subtly avoiding anyone's recognition that he was Jewish. After months of material relating to his conflict over his unrecognized aggressive impulses, he became increasingly preoccupied with memories and dreams about the Nazi era. In one session, he recalled what he had read about Nazi tortures of the Jews. He remembered a story of a group of laughing Nazis surrounding an old man strapped to a table, who was suffering excruciating pain from boiling water that was poured through a tube into his rectum. He had the fantasy of the boiling water-steam exploding back out the tube and all over the Nazis. Continued associations led to his recognizing the feelings of helplessness a victim experiences and then to the possibility of his identifying with the victims of the Nazis and "blowing them away." I pointed out that he might unconsciously feel that way when he exploded from his own bowel. Acknowledging the possibility, he remembered his father having lost control of his bowels at the point of death, thus associating loss of control over aggression with guilt, punishment, and death.

Two weeks later, after a long series of what he felt were unjust attacks upon his competence by a colleague, he described a confrontation: "[I] felt red-hot lava welling up in me . . . and I exploded, telling him that he was a contemptible nasty person." In response to my noting the choice of "red-hot lava" exploding, he associated to "feeling like a volcano . . . pouring out . . . hot gas and fumes" and to the colitis attacks.

This man did not have asthma. In his dreams, fantasies, and behavior, nonetheless, he clearly identified with both the conscious helpless victim and the unconscious sadistic Nazi. The associations to air, steam, and hot water exploding in and out of the body provided the vehicles for the expression of his conflict.

A 26-year-old lawyer in analysis had considerable separation anxiety and suffered greatly during the lingering death of a young colleague. He reported considerable guilt over competitive strivings, as well as genuine feeling for his close friend. An exacerbation of symptoms followed the friend's death.

On the morning of the memorial services for his friend, he awakened with the following dream: "I'm in a restaurant looking for a clean glass in order to drink some milk, but all the glasses are dirty. I search and search. . . ."

He got up, dressed, and put the tea kettle on for breakfast. As it began to boil, steam emerged from the spout, and he had the momentary thought that he heard a gurgling noise sounding like his friend's voice. He was shaken and wondered about the uncanny nature of his perception.

His associations to the dream had to do with the search for the lost mother's milk, related to ambivalence over the death of his friend and its connection to the anticipated death of his father. In the ensuing discussion he

clearly recognized that the gurgling "steam-tea-milk" represented the anticipated symbolic incorporation of his dead friend through a fusion of drinking
the milk and tea and inhaling the steam-air. A similar incorporation of
ambivalent objects through a fusion of drinking milk (gastrointestinal) and
inhaling air-steam (respiratory) was presented earlier in the cases of Willie and
Carol.

A 13-year-old girl, whose mother had severe asthma, suffered herself from
severe separation anxiety. When discussions arose that triggered the anxiety,
she would characteristically pull on her hair and inhale its aroma—a respira
tory incorporation of the mother. She would particularly seek the lemon scent
left over from the previous washing. When the scent was gone, it was time to
wash her hair again. This is not uncommon in other adolescent girls.

A 40-year-old dentist, severely depressed and preoccupied with suicide,
reported he had been carrying a cyanide capsule in his pocket wherever he
went for the past ten years. He wanted to have it available should his
depression become overwhelming. One of the main deterrents to his using it,
he said, was the fear that someone would think he was dying from a heart
attack and might attempt mouth-to-mouth resuscitation. Inhaling his air, he
was afraid his rescuer would inhale the liberated cyanide gas and die.

THE UNCONSCIOUS MEANING OF AIR:
AIR AS AIR

The clinical material in this chapter revealed a tremendous preoccupation
with air, both as itself and as steam. The early importance of air is
derived from the infant's breast or bottle sucking, which contains an
admixture of milk and air. Both of these have the potential to become
incorporated as the unconscious fantasy of the early milk-air-mother.
This sucking also provides the anlage for the close relationship between
the respiratory and the gastrointestinal systems (Mintz 1987a,b). This
relationship may partially explain why conflict in dependency, aggression, and preoedipal sexuality is expressed regressively through an
admixture of depressive, asthmatic, and anorexic symptomatology. The
frequent interrelationship among these symptom complexes has been
commented upon in Chapter 11, this volume (Mintz 1987a,b).
    After boiling pussywillow pods "to pasteurize them like milk and get

rid of any bacteria," Willie wondered whether they were poisonous or could they be used for incense and inhaled. He was describing a conflict reflecting his preoccupation with milk and air as the introjected and ambivalently cathected mother, through the gastrointestinal and respiratory systems: drinking the pussywillow-bacteria-laden-poison-milk-mother as well as inhaling the incense-steam-mother.

THE DISPLACEMENT OF AIR

It seems reasonable that Willie's rhythmical rubbing of the pussywillow-furry-animal-wool blanket against the cheeks and around the lips unconsciously represents a displacement onto the surface of the face of earlier conflicts over ingesting and inhaling ambivalently cathected introjects. The rhythmical back-and-forth movement of the objects against the face reflects displacement from the rhythmical movement of sucking and breathing.

Carol also reported a childhood memory of sucking on her third and fourth fingers while rhythmically rubbing the second and fifth against her cheeks "like windshield wipers to wipe away the tears . . . I can feel the air in my throat when I have asthma . . . like feeling the fingers on my face . . . the air goes in and out . . . early you get security by being rocked — rhythmically . . . like the ticktock of a clock . . . next to the little puppy to help it sleep alone without the mother. Then the air goes in and out." The associations are similar to Willie's. They strongly suggest unconscious connections between the infant being rhythmically rocked externally, the rhythmic movement of the fingers against the face, and the introjection of the object during the rhythmic respirations and labored asthmatic breathing. The liberation of the introjects can also take place in reverse order through the projection onto the skin described by Louise, along with the further projection into tornados, volcanos, and thunderstorms described by Louise, Carol, and Billy.[1] Displacement within the body can be present in gastrointestinal involvement with anorexia, bulimia, and colitis. Significantly, Carol also remembered that the asthma began when the finger rubbing and sucking ceased at age 7. Wilson in Chapter 13 emphasizes anal aspects of asthma. Here the

---

[1]The liberation of the introjects also occurs in schizophrenic children from introjected objects (radios, television) located inside the chest, projected with age out onto the shoulder or outer ear and finally out into the environment as hallucinations.

preoccupation with air and the respiratory system is displaced to the colon. He cited an asthmatic patient who was preoccupied with farting and who stated that "in an asthmatic attack, he could not breathe out dirty foul air, all air was flatus, and to breathe was to fart." He also described a patient with hyperventilation symptoms, who when angry, would swallow air and save it up to pass gas. In the transference, hyperventilation was killing the introjected analyst by poisoning himself with air.

Thus we see that the unconscious preoccupation with air in asthma is manifested in different locations and in different forms. It is consciously dealt with by normal breathing and by speaking when the words are carried out on the exhaled air. It is unconsciously represented by the respiratory system in asthma. It is displaced to another body organ: the colon, with farting. It is displaced to the skin or to the outside of the body in Louise's preoccupation with her skin that can't breathe. It is further projected into the environment in Louise's fantasies about the movement of air in tornados and volcanos; she adds the presence of introjected objects that are sucked up with the air or ejected from the lung. Willie sucks introjects from the environment into his lung, while Carol explodes out air from the lung into the environment in temper tantrums, dreams, fantasies, and asthma attacks. Air is changed into steam and is exploded out by Carol or is represented on the skin of the body by Willie and by Karol's patient described in Chapter 12. Willie was also preoccupied with the aroma from kittens and cats held on his shoulder, along with the pussywillow pelts next to his face, reflecting ambivalent feelings about his siblings.

Direct preoccupation with the rhythmical movement of air was also described by Carol. Feeling overwhelmed by separation anxiety at the prospect of moving to another city, and beginning to defend herself against it with denial, she stated that she became aware of consciously inhaling and exhaling forcibly, although she had no obstruction to her breathing. As she displaced her attention from moving to the movement of her own breathing, the separation anxiety diminished and the asthmatic attack began.

AIR AS STEAM

Most of the asthmatic patients discussed in this chapter referred to air and steam. Just as the air symbolism can be viewed as primary and causal, as well as secondary and responsive to impaired respiration and choking, so steam, its counterpart, can have a similar relevance. Thus arises a self-perpetuating system, where regressed sexual and aggressive drives and dependency longings initiate asthmatic attacks, and the asthmatic attacks themselves serve to perpetuate further intrapsychic representation. Louise's exploding volcanic-destructive-self can pour out hot-air-steam-lava in the service of destroying hated external objects, symbolizing the expression of repressed, regressed, aggressive drives. Concomitantly her primitive and punitive superego demands that the destruction wreaked upon others be visited upon the self: that her internal volcanic self be scalded from within.

To that end, we see clinical evidence of steam, wheezing, and burning in fantasy, dream, and accidental behavior. Louise reported being "accidentally" burned on the arm by an overturned steam iron. Willie reported fantasies of being branded on the arm by a red-hot branding iron. The adolescent girl analyzed by Karol in Chapter 12 reported detailed fantasies of slave girls having a hot rock placed upon their genitals as punishment, with steam arising from the area. Karol concluded that the noisy, wheezing respirations during asthmatic attacks reflected displacement upward of sexual conflict from the genitals to the lung. Louise's "accidental" burning with the steam iron and Willie's fantasy of being branded on the arm with a branding iron can reflect displacement onto the outside of the body of internalized sexual and aggressive conflict.

Willie's associations referred to castration anxiety. Conceptually one could consider Louise's accidental burning by the steam iron to be an externalized displacement from her volcanic respiratory system. Whether one of the primary determinants arose from a sadomasochistic view of coitus, as illustrated by Karol's patient, is not clear. Willie, by contrast, no longer having asthmatic symptoms, but with the underlying conflict still unresolved, displaced his castration anxiety onto the outside of his body, with fantasies of being branded. It is not clear whether the steam fantasy might also contain residual components of his past asthmatic symptomatology.

Steam also played a role in Carol's associations to her dream of the little airplanes going out of control. "The planes look like little round pressure cookers, with the steam exploding out." She also produced associations to her being a pressure cooker exploding superheated air out of her during an asthmatic attack, when the wheezing, noisy air is expelled under pressure through the narrow, fluid-filled constricted bronchi. One recognized alternative was her regressed, explosive out-burst during rage-filled temper tantrums, when a heated response would also pour out of her.

Added to Willie's branding fantasies was his preoccupation with boiling pussywillow pods. Among his associations was his inhaling the steam-filled aroma and wondering whether this would be beneficial or poisonous. Here he illustrated that the inhaling of air reflected his dependency conflict over introjection of the ambivalently cathected mother.

Finally, there is the importance of air-steam in the fantasy of a nonasthmatic patient. The engineer with spastic colitis described in a vignette a story of Nazis' torturing an old man by pouring boiling water into a tube in his rectum. His fantasy was that the boiling steam-water would explode back out the tube, scalding the Nazis. Subsequently, during a violent argument with a colleague, he felt "red-hot lava" welling up in him "like a volcano . . . pouring out . . . hot gases and fumes," as he exploded and insulted his colleague. Here the aggression is displaced to the colon, with volcanic eruptions of hot, toxic gases expressed during colitis attacks similar to Louise's volcanic attacks. The unconscious use of steam and air to represent conflict plays a considerable role in colitis as it does in asthma. Anal components in asthma have been described by others (Greenacre 1971; see Wilson, Chapter 13, this volume).

THE VIOLENT MOVEMENT OF AIR

Louise's marked identification and preoccupation with tornados that destroy through the violent sucking up of air, and with volcanos that destroy by explosive outbursts of air, clearly reflected projections of her conflicts over aggression, with regressive somatization to the bronchi and lungs. Her need to deny, repress, and regress in the face of intense conflict resulted in her severe asthmatic attacks. During the analysis, as the aggressive conflict became accessible to consciousness and to verbal expression, almost totally in the transference, the patient's severe asth-matic attacks began to subside. A marked verbal onslaught in the transference, together with repeated impulses to choke the analyst, was accompanied by the patient's choking less and breathing more freely. Repeatedly, during the many sessions when she was angry with me, she would tear up napkins, magazines, and newspaper into tiny shreds. At the end of the session she would hold all the paper up to her mouth and then, volcanolike, blow the pieces all over the floor and walk out cursing.

Problems of verbal aggression expressed by the violent movement of air were also illustrated by Carol with the exploding steam-pressure cooker-airplane. Billy, the nonasthmatic child, was also concerned with the violent movement of air. His fires, set by a little boy and killing all the children (siblings), were fanned by the wind through the windows into the trees, consuming the entire town with all its inhabitants. He was afraid to speak up and yell and let the aggression out on the exhaled air-wind. With a build-up of anger, displacement occurred to the bowel and bladder. Angry on one occasion, he threatened to defecate on the floor or pass "wind." Filled with exploding feelings, he unconsciously identified with his projected self and symbolically became the hurricane-earthquake-thunderstorm, creating destruction and debris (feces and gas) through regressed somatic discharge of aggression. Finally, with verbal expression available and eyes blazing, he spewed out hatred and fury against his family on the exhaled air-wind.

Wilson (Chapter 13) reports the childhood memories of a severe asthmatic adult. "As a child, he used to stick straws in frogs' anuses and blow them full of air. Then he would either float the frogs in water or step on them, bursting them. Later he learned that the Nazis had similar tortures for prisoners."

THE UNCONSCIOUS MEANING OF A NEBULIZER

In practice and in the literature the use of a nebulizer has been viewed solely in terms of its antiallergic properties, based upon the specific medication to be inhaled. Evidence in Louise's history and Luparello's research cited below suggests that additional factors may be playing a predominant role. Luparello and colleagues (1968) observed the narrowing of the airway in asthmatic subjects in response to suggestion. In a subsequent paper (1971) they reported a group of forty asthmatic patients and thirty-one controls who were told that they would be inhaling five different allergens previously associated with asthmatic attacks. Actually saline solution was used. Only the asthmatic patients developed respiratory difficulties, with twelve developing wheezing and dyspnea. They were then given another saline solution and told it was isoproteranol. The attacks promptly subsided.

Luparello vividly demonstrated the role of psychological factors in asthmatic disease. It was not only what was in the inhaler that was important, but also what the patient thought was in the inhaler. It is possible that inhaling the "allergens" might have been viewed unconsciously as inhaling destructive introjects, setting off aggressive conflict symbolized by the violent movement of air, while inhaling the "therapeutic drug" might have been viewed as inhaling loved introjects, the resulting sense of security being reflected in a change to quiet breathing.

THE UNCONSCIOUS MEANING OF SMOKE, DUST, ALLERGENS, INFECTIONS, AND EXERCISE

Smoke

Louise's rich fantasy life, intimately associated with her asthmatic symptoms, provides the opportunity to consider the effect of smoke, dust, infections, and exercise as psychological factors that played a role in her asthmatic disease. This view has not been previously considered. It widens our perspective in terms of considering relevant factors in the development of asthma. Louise had fantasies that when her mother was smoking, the mother was the exterminator producing smoke (toxic gases) to destroy her, the roach. This view represented her feeling about the mother's distant, abandoning, damaging relationship to her. It was also a projection of Louise's resentment and anger toward her mother, expressing the feared-wish that the mother might be destroyed by lung cancer induced by the toxic smoke. Louise's fear of inhaling the toxic smoke that could destroy her from within could have contributed to the asthmatic attack. Punitive superego retaliation required that Louise also suffer from respiratory damage.

Dust

In addition, Louise described her unconscious preoccupation with ambivalently cathected introjects, incorporated during respirations and symbolized by her projections onto tornados and volcanos. She described how tornados suck up homes in the debris and destroy people and buildings, while volcanos belch forth the same destruction upon people and the environment. While she utilized air as a destructive force in and of itself, a projection of her tornado-volcanic-self, she also described the introjects carried in the dust-air-steam-lava. The volcano would burst forth with pumice rock that had air holes in it (fragments of lung tissue). She drew and described the rock fragments as amoeba, having father pseudopod, mother pseudopod, and baby pseudopod. Microscopic people were carried in the inhaled air. She then drew bacteria, also carried in the air, clearly resembling human faces with glasses.

Talking about her asthmatic attack, Louise twirled her bracelet symbolizing the tornado, and spoke of the molecules in the air being "moved about and cut in half." Battles take place in the moving air between symbolic microscopic figures representing the ambivalently cathected introjects. These "dust people," who could be sucked up and destroyed by the "tornado Louise" or destroy her from within, or whom the erupting "volcano-Louise" could destroy or could retain within, by not exhaling to preserve the object, further confirm the unconscious fantasy about what is carried by the movement of smoke, dust, infection, and allergens in the air.

I was particularly interested in finding corroborative clinical data in an asthmatic paper by L. Deutsch (1987). He reported an asthmatic teenager's long-standing fantasy dating back into childhood, of a "spot of dust wandering in his lungs." He viewed the dust particle as himself, lost in his lungs, a concept accompanied by feelings of panic. At another time he stated that when he was furious and wheezed, "he was taking in the enemy" and hurting him inside. The dust particle then represented a microscopic internalization of both himself and a hated enemy that he wanted to kill or choke.

Allergens

L. Deutsch (1987) also described the case of a 6-year-old boy who would develop severe asthma when exposed to dog hairs. He was surprised to notice that the child did not develop asthma in his office, because, unknown to the child, his dog had been in the office many times. He concluded that the child remained asymptomatic because of the strong positive transference, which overrode the negative impact of the allergens. Although I agree with that concept, I suggest also that the positive transference facilitated the incorporation of positive loved introjects. The situation was very similar to that of Luparello's patients, who were told they would be inhaling a new antiasthmatic medication. Such psychic overdetermination would help explain the asthmatic attack of a hospitalized asthmatic patient exposed to a bouquet of artificial roses, or that of a patient of mine who was allergic to sawdust and developed asthma upon seeing the sawdust in a movie about the circus.

Infection

A multidetermined perspective on the role of infection in precipitating asthmatic disease may also be warranted. Is the truly toxic, infectious nature of the illness the sole factor that precipitates pathophysiologic changes in the respiratory system, culminating in the asthmatic attack? Or does the unconscious perception of being invaded by noxious, toxic, destructive introjects play an additional role? Willie's fantasies of inhaling toxins from the pussywillow incense were similar to Louise's fantasies of destructive bacterial-people introjects in the air.

The movement of harmful and deadly objects in the air has also been described by Karol in her treatment of a 13-year-old asthmatic girl (see Chapter 12). Preoccupied with displaced primal-scene trauma, which was dealt with by sadomasochistic fantasies, she was frightened by "sperm (that) could fly through the air and get in by the mouth, nose, or even eyes and you could go blind" (displacements from the vagina and lungs). These concerns were complemented by her mother's fantasies that it was "dangerous to cough, because the tubercle bacillus could fly through the air, invade the lung of an innocent victim, and kill."

We may therefore consider that infections may also have their own psychological consequences in asthmatic disease. If the asthmatic patient unconsciously perceives a developing respiratory infection as an invasion of toxic microbial bodies that could cause deadly harm, then the conflict and the anxiety engendered could contribute to the asthmatic attack. Presumably, a nonserious bacterial invasion could be viewed as lethal when associatively linked to conflicts of aggression and sexuality, linked in turn to the operation of a primitive and punitive superego.

Paradoxically, a different intrapsychic view of infection could have the opposite results. Louise reported that her asthma subsided whenever she had a fever, an upset stomach with vomiting, the chickenpox, or the flu. Wilson (Chapter 13) describes a 30-year-old asthmatic patient who was amazed that he never got asthma when he got the flu.

Exercise

Paradoxical effects of exercise have also been noted. Louise said that she wheezed badly all winter except when she was able to go skiing in cold weather. The benefits of skiing occurred during the same period that mild walking produced severe asthma and dyspnea, such that on occasion she could not walk and her father had to carry her upstairs.

A 14-year-old boy seen in consultation for severe anorexia also had severe asthma, to the degree that he was frequently unable to walk slowly without dyspnea. His internist reported seeing him running along the road symptom free in a cross-country race. The patient told me that he had to run and that life was not worth living if he was forbidden to run. He stated that he was almost always able to compete in cross-country races, although acknowledging his difficulty in walking.

Karol's patient (Chapter 12) reported an attack of asthma because she "became short of breath from running home from school." Her subsequent associations, however, uncovered a fantasy that immediately had preceded her asthmatic attack — a sadomasochistic fantasy of slaves who were punished by having a hot stone placed upon their genitals with steam coming out. Karol concluded that it was the first time the asthmatic attack was connected with the fantasies that had preceded it. She said nothing about the patient's allusion to the role that the exercise had played. I suggest that the heavy noisy breathing from the running liberated unconscious conflicted fantasies, possibly of a sexual nature, some of which were later recounted by the patient. These fantasies then contributed to the asthmatic attack. Whether the physiological changes caused by the exercise played a role in the attack is not clear. In my patient, the running freed him from the asthma. It would be interesting to know whether Karol's patient had been running home during cold winter weather, when the exhaled air would be visible and could contribute to the "steam" elements of her fantasies.

SUMMARY

Although the general focus of the chapter is on air symbolism in asthma, a number of other cases are presented to illustrate the frequent symbolic use of air in reflecting unconscious conflict. This chapter suggests taking a broader view of the psychological determinants in asthma. Unconscious conflict can be both a primary and a secondary factor in precipitating an asthmatic attack.

When Louise was told of her grandmother's impending death, she developed severe asthma. In response to my request to discuss the circumstances of the attack, Louise resorted to expression through play. She began to whirl her bracelet around and around. The fantasies associated with the whirling bracelet clarified the play. The whirling bracelet was like her tornado self, inspiring sucked-up houses and destroying them, or like her volcano self, exhaling the spewed out dust and rocks. Hidden in the rock and dust during respiration were microscopic little figures representing the family and the analyst. Inhaled dust can unconsciously represent the incorporation of loved or hated introjects in the air via the respiratory tract, just as eating can represent the same phenomenon in the gastrointestinal tract. In similar fashion, exhaling and vomiting may also represent the expulsion of loved or hated introjects.

What Louise illustrated in play with her associated fantasies was the unconscious symbolic meaning of the asthmatic attack. The precipitating event was feeling overwhelmed by the grandmother's impending death, to which she responded with denial: "She's getting better." She refused to discuss it and became increasingly angry at the prospect of having to face the painful thoughts and feelings that were habitually repressed. The asthma represented a regressed symbolic attempt to cope with the conflict. The wheezing attack with the violent movement of moisture-laden air through narrowed bronchi was illustrated in the fantasy play, where family members are introjected into the respiratory system to be retained or destroyed during expressions of anxiety, loss, grief, and anger.

Willie, the second patient, described his preoccupation with boiled pussywillow pods, which he could pasteurize and drink like milk, while retaining his concern that they might be poisonous. Concomitantly, he mused about the possibility of inhaling the steam as roasted prune incense. The fantasy derived from the play suggests preoccupations of ingesting or inhaling the ambivalently cathected mother and siblings reflecting dependency and aggressive conflicts towards them or unconscious attitudes about them, or projected into them. Also evident in his mind is a fusion of gastrointestinal and respiratory systems contributing in some patients to asthma and anorexia (Louise and Silverman's patient, Chapter 13).

Willie's continued preoccupation with the inhaling of air was elaborated in his comparing the pussywillow pods to his little kittens held on his shoulder and a cat he brought in breathing in its fur. The cat and kittens represented his mother and hated siblings that drained her affection. He subsequently made a pin wheel and inhaled the air produced by it, like the pussywillow incense and the cat's fur. Willie's absorption with air and steam in fantasy is similar to Louise's and suggests an attempt to deal with aggressive and dependency conflict through the ingestion and inhalation of ambivalently cathected introjects that can be retained or destroyed in the lung or gastrointestinal system.

Carol reported a dream of her fear of flying a little airplane and her losing control of it. Associations were to ". . . the planes' looking like little pressure cookers . . . to being the pressure cooker with steam pouring out that could burn and destroy, leaving me fearful of losing control and exploding." The asthmatic symptoms reproduce a symbolic enactment of this fantasy: pressured air bubbles pushing through constricted moisture-laden bronchi, destroying the hated introjects within the lung during inspiration or the external objects during expiration. Willie "accidentally" burned his arm with a steam iron, while Karol's patient had the fantasy of slaves having hot stones placed on their genitals with steam emerging.

Carol's alternative to a symptom resolution of conflict with asthma was to lose control by a regressed, screaming temper tantrum, jeopardizing her relationship with her husband. Thus we see a trajectory of ego solutions to conflict: dreaming of losing control, associations to losing control and exploding with destructive steam, having an asthmatic attack, and acting out by exploding with a temper tantrum. From this perspective, the asthma attack represents one method of ego resolution of conflict, with nightmares and acting out representing alternative solutions. Finally, analysis of thoughts and feelings, epitomized by her recognition that she is the exploding pressure–cooker–airplane fearful of losing control and hurting people, represents the most mature solution.

Carol later described the development of almost unbearable separation as a result of her husband's transfer to a distant city. Intense anxiety was followed by impaired reality testing — a denial that she was moving — and paranoid trends. At that point, she became aware of conscious inhaling and exhaling, culminating in an asthmatic attack, which she later compared to a temper tantrum. She was aware of a deliberate attempt at inducing the asthma. An alternate to the asthmatic attack might have been a paranoid decompensation.

With this viewpoint, asthma is not recognized as a distinct, separate, circumscribed purely organic illness unrelated to psychological factors. This concept will help explain how, during the course of treatment, one psychosomatic illness can change into another, or into purely psychological symptoms like depression or phobia, or into various forms of self-destructive acting out. My report of a patient in analysis—whose illness began with ulcerative colitis, followed by asthma, migraine, angioneurotic edema, sterile monoarticular arthritis, and nasorhinitis interspersed with severe bouts of depression, and various forms of self-destructive behavior and "accidents"—would fall into this category (Mintz 1980–1981). Too often a clinician can be satisfied with the subsiding of one psychosomatic symptom, without recognizing that another psychosomatic symptom, depression or self-destructive behavior, can replace it.

In Case 4, 7-year-old Billy was also preoccupied with the violent movement of air evident in his involvement with fires, which suck up the air and are spread by the wind, burn the town and consume its inhabitants. Projected into phobias, his terror of thunder and lightning as the air–wind–hurricane, becomes the vehicle through which his aggression is expressed; that is, a symbolic alternative to the outpouring of verbalized hatred. Aggressive hatred was also displaced with somatizing to the bowel and bladder. When he got angry in the sessions, he would run to the bathroom to urinate or defecate. On one occasion, after many such episodes of running to the bathroom, with my subsequent interpretation of his getting rid of feelings into the toilet, he planned another quick exit to the bathroom. I then said, "You are again running to the bathroom to get rid of your angry feelings; you must feel that you can't control your anger, so you have to explode it into the toilet." Misinterpreting the comment as a prohibition, he complained of abdominal cramps and threatened to defecate on the floor or pass wind. I chose not to clarify his view of my statement, adding "Why do you feel that you can't control your temper?" He became increasingly anxious and began to plead that he had to go. In response to my silence, he threw himself on the floor face down, and began to pound the floor with his fists threatening to defecate. I watched silently. After a few minutes of threats, screaming and pounding now including head banging, he stopped and relaxed. Looking up with a sense of exultation, he remarked, "I did it, I did it, I don't have to go." His ability to relinquish somatic discharge was in part a result of his general progress in dealing with aggression and also a consequence of increasingly angry threats of defecation on my rug, fist and head pounding, and kicking on the floor. Aggressive discharge in temper-tantrumlike fashion began to replace the more regressive somatic discharge by defecating and urinating. This pattern was also seen in Carol, where she could alternate between an outburst of temper tantrums or asthma.

Over a period of two years, Billy became more able to cope with his emerging aggression, culminating in a dramatic episode. Entering analysis, he appeared extremely effeminate with shoulder twisting, hip wiggling, and pirouetting. Speaking in a soft, high-pitched voice, he proclaimed that he was "gentle, and a g." In the session with the chair turned away from me, he became increasingly angry as he spoke about how he hated his family. His tirade culminated in screaming how he'd like to kill them all. Swinging about, I saw a different child: tense, furious, eyes blazing, and lips curled back. Leaping from the chair, he replaced effeminacy with masculine and aggressive posturing. The violent movement of air now thundered out of his throat, no longer repressed, projected, or somatized.

I have presented the possible unconscious meaning of a nebulizer, of smoke, dust, allergens, infections, and exercise. Luparello's (1968, 1971) research demonstrated that asthmatic patients, who thought that they were inhaling allergens and then medication, developed dyspnea upon inhaling saline, and cleared up upon inhaling more saline. Clearly illustrated is the psychological ability to produce asthma and then to eliminate it. When the patient thinks he is inhaling allergic bad substances (hated, feared introjects), he develops asthma. Inhaling good medicine (loved introjects) clears up the attack. There are many clinical illustrations that support this concept: the hospitalized asthmatic patient who began to wheeze after receiving a bouquet of wax roses; or my patient, allergic to sawdust, who began wheezing while she watched a movie about a circus.

Louise's concern that she was inhaling the mother's toxic cigarette smoke suggests that, in addition to what might be allergenic factors, is her unconscious anxiety about inhaling hostile introjects that can destroy her from within. Further evidence of the validity of this hypothesis is present in her rich fantasy life, marked by preoccupation with tornados and volcanos. During inspiration, her tornado-self can inhale the feared –hated dust-people whom she can destroy, or who can destroy her. Dyspneic and unable to inhale she precludes sucking up and destroying the introjects or being destroyed by them. During expiration, her volcano-self can belch steam and destruction upon the hated external objects or can rid herself of the destruction within. Inability to exhale during asthma can retain the introjects, be destroyed by them, or avoid destroying the external objects.

Unconscious fantasy may be stimulated when the patient is exposed to smoke, dust, allergens, and infection. Immunological response can be augmented by psychological response or even replace it in importance. Although dog hairs produced severe asthma, Deutsch's (1987) child did not develop asthma in its presence because of a strong positive transference. Psychological factors play a role in the paradoxical effects of exercise. The patient who wheezed while walking very slowly, was on the cross country team. Louise had severe asthma all winter, with remissions during skiing.

The unconscious importance of air is in part derived from the infant's sucking of admixture of milk and air. Both have the potential for becoming incorporated as the unconscious fantasy of the early milk-air-mother. The unconscious preoccupation with air is paramount and operates in the service of expressing aggressive and sexual drives, as well as dependency longings. Conflict centering about the violent movement of air represents both a primary and a secondary feature in the illness.

The effect of a nebulizer, of dust, and other allergens, of respiratory infection, and of exercise warrants reevaluation. Clinical data suggest that major psychological features are present and operative in each of these circumstances and that they play a role in determining asthmatic disease.

REFERENCES

Abrahamson, H. A. (1961). Psychodynamics of the intractably asthmatic state. *Journal of the Children's Asthmatic Research Institute and Hospital* 1(1):18.

Coolidge, J. C. (1956). Asthma in mother and child as a special type of intercommunication. *Journal of Orthopsychiatry* 26:165.

Deutsch, F., ed. (1959). *Symbolization as a Formative Stage in the Mysterious Leap from the Mind to the Body.* New York: International Universities Press, pp. 75–97.

Deutsch, L. (1980). Psychosomatic medicine from a psychoanalytic viewpoint. *Journal of the American Psychoanalytic Association* 28(3):653–702.

—— (1987). Reflections on the psychoanalytic treatment of patients with bronchial asthma. *Psychoanalytic Study of the Child,* vol. 42, ed. A. Solnit and P. Neubauer, pp. 245, 253–254. New Haven: Yale University Press.

Dunbar, H. F. (1938). Psychoanalytic notes relating to syndromes of asthma and hay fever. *Psychoanalytic Quarterly* 7:25.

Fenichel, O. (1953). Respiratory introjection. *Collected Papers of Otto Fenichel,* pp. 221–240. New York: Norton.

Frazier, J. (1959). *The New Golden Bough.* New York: Criterion Books.

French, T. M., and Alexander, F. (1941). Psychogenic factors in bronchial asthma. *Psychosomatic Medicine Monographs,* vols. 2, 4. Washington, DC: National Research Council.

Gerard, M. W. (1940). Bronchial asthma in children. *The Nervous Children* 5:327.

Greenacre, P. (1971). *Emotional Growth.* New York: International Universities Press.

Jessner, L., Lamont, J., Long, R., Rollins, N., Whipple, B., and Prentice, N. (1955). Emotional impact of nearness and separation for the asthmatic child and his mother. *Psychoanalytic Study of the Child* 10:353.

Knapp, P. H. (1960). Acute bronchial asthma: psychoanalytic observations of fantasy, emotional arousal, and partial discharge. *Psychosomatic Medicine* 22:88–105.

Luparello, T., McFadden Jr., E., Lyons, H., and Bleeker, E. (1968). Influences of suggestion on airway reactivity in asthmatic subjects. *Psychosomatic Medicine* 30:819.

—— (1971). Psychological factors and bronchial asthma. *New York State Journal of Medicine* 71:21–61.

Mintz, I. L. (1980–1981). Multideterminism in asthmatic disease. *International Journal of Psychoanalytic Psychotherapy* 8:593–600.

—— (1987a). The Clinical and Theoretical Association between Anorexia Nervosa and Bronchial Asthma. New Jersey Psychoanalytic Society, Hackensack Medical Center.

—— (1987b). Discussion of Dr. L. Reiser's paper, The Oral Triad in Bulimia. Meeting of American Psychoanalytic Association, Winter Meeting. New York. 1987.

Mushatt, C., and Werby, I. (1972). Grief and anniversary reactions in a man of sixty-two. *International Journal of Psychoanalytic Psychotherapy* 8:83–106.

Reik, T. (1946). *Ritual.* New York: Grove Press.

Reiser, M. (1975). Changing theoretical concepts in psychosomatic medicine. In

American Handbook of Psychiatry, vol. 4, ed. M. F. Reiser, pp. 477–500. New York: Basic Books.

Schlossman, H. (1979). Personal communication. New Jersey Psychoanalytic Society Presentation at Hackensack Medical Center.

Sperling, M. (1949). The role of the mother in psychosomatic disorders in children. *Psychosomatic Medicine* 11:377.

———— (1963). A psychoanalytic study of bronchial asthma in children. In *The Asthmatic Child,* ed. Henry Schneer, M.D., pp. 138–165. New York: Harper and Row.

———— (1968). Asthma in children: an evaluation of concepts and therapies. *Journal of the American Academy of Child Psychiatry* 7:52–53.

11

Treatment of a Case of Anorexia and Severe Asthma

Ira L. Mintz, M.D.

Like many illnesses, asthma has a long and illustrious history. It was described by Hippocrates, who recognized its psychogenic elements with the caution, "Asthmatics must guard against anger" (Lieberman and Lipton 1963). A host of physicians treating psychosomatic disease have lent this dictum their support, epitomized by a warning that psychiatric intervention during the acute stage of psychosomatic illness is contraindicated. The implication is that, if the physician upsets the patient, the symptoms will get worse. Worsening may occur, however, not because of the psychiatric intervention per se, but as a consequence of the type of intervention. A nonanalytic, ill-timed, inappropriate interpretation may well set off an attack. The attack may then represent, in part, an attempt to intimidate and punish the physician for intruding into areas of conflict where the patient felt unable to cope.

This chapter illustrates a psychoanalytic approach to a case of very severe asthma in a 12-year-old girl, whose symptoms began at age 18 months and were increasing in severity over the four years prior to entry into analysis. The importance of aggressive conflict is highlighted by the degree of hostility evident in her resistance, defenses, identifications, and transference reactions. The analysis lasted for two and a half years and was terminated before it could be completed. While incomplete, the analytic treatment did accomplish symptom resolution. I shall present detailed clinical data revealed by the patient as well as a detailed description of the analyst's attitudes and responses to it. Although the focus is on the aggressive component of the conflict, I do not mean to minimize the importance of other conflicts: the parent–child relationship (Abrahamson 1961, French 1941, Sperling 1949, 1963, 1978), separation anxiety (Dunbar 1938, French 1941, Jessner 1955, Knapp 1963, Sperling 1949), primal-scene trauma (Karol 1981; see Chapter 12), overstimulation (Deutsch 1987, Wilson 1980–1981, 1988; see Chapter 13, this volume). The complex relationship between psychogenic and nonpsychogenic factors is highlighted by Deutsch (1980, 1987, 1988) and Mintz (1980–1981).

LOUISE

Louise, a 12-year-old in four-times-weekly analysis, was referred because of increasingly severe asthma. Present since age 18 months, the symptoms had become more frequent and severe over the past four years, despite the use of all kinds of medication. Seen in consultation, the parents stated that Louise had had sporadic attacks of asthma since she was a little child, but recently the symptoms had grown worse and she required frequent visits to the hospital for shots of adrenalin. The asthma was almost continuous. Her shortness of breath was so marked that sometimes she had to be carried upstairs and had to sleep sitting up. The mother also felt that Louise had seemed more depressed over the past two months, wearing a sad expression.

Elaborating on her current functioning, the father indicated that she was an excellent student, had many friends, and was a good athlete. Both parents felt that she always was an easy child to rear: pleasant, smiling, obedient, and never giving them any trouble but for the asthma. The mother added that they were a close family and that Louise was especially close to her younger brother, although she also got along well with her two older sisters. The father emphasized that she loved athletics and at times insisted upon playing ball although her wheezing was marked. He added, with the mother's agreement, that she was particularly attached to his mother, who delighted in playing with all the children, but especially with Louise.

Significant features in the past history revealed that the patient whistled when she breathed at age 1. She was not a good eater and used to throw up her bottle about every other day, although she gained weight normally. The mother added that, because she wanted things to be perfect, the first few months of the patient's life were very stressful. The mother attempted to keep Louise always neat and clean and changed her outfits frequently. She volunteered that she felt burdened by Louise's birth. Having two girls already, both parents had hoped that Louise would be a boy, and they acknowledged some sense of disappointment at her birth.

When her brother Christopher was born 18 months later, Louise reacted markedly. She seemed to withdraw and appeared sad. A picture of her holding him during a Christmas celebration when she was 6 suggested that she was gritting her teeth. At age 3 she had pneumonia and was hospitalized for a week.

At 18 months, two weeks before Christopher was born, Louise developed a severe allergy to what was later determined to be sesame seeds. Her eyes and face were markedly swollen, and this reaction lasted almost until the day the mother gave birth. Three months later her breathing became so difficult that a shot of epinephrine was required. The mother had a vivid impression of the episode, because it took place on the father's birthday.

The mother added that she had always felt comfortable cuddling Louise, but that the father was never able to do so with any of the girls. The father appeared irritated at the indictment, interjecting that he always enjoyed playing with them and would "tickle them all until they couldn't breathe." Toward the end of the second session the mother revealed that after the birth of Christopher, much to her surprise, she became quite depressed, requiring a course of antidepressive medication.

The family history revealed lifelong asthma in the mother and in her mother. The parents both were of Spanish descent, having arrived in this country when they were children. The father, an executive for an international corporation, had to make frequent but short trips back to Europe. Both parents were religious Catholics, although the paternal grandfather was not. The mother volunteered that while she liked to be sociable, it had always been difficult, because the father was frequently transferred from one city to the other. The family had lived in San Francisco, Dallas, Chicago, and Baltimore before arriving at their current location.

Initial consultation with Louise revealed a tall, thin 12-year-old with almost waist-long blond hair and large blue eyes, who initially appeared quite wistful and sad. She was verbal, however, and described her asthmatic condition in a matter-of-fact manner. She revealed that she was "allergic to dust, pollen, cold, her brother, and nuts. He's a nut and the whole family is nuts." She also got attacks in cold weather, after she got a cold, when she ran, and when she got excited playing in athletic events, especially football. In the winter she had to sleep propped up in a sitting position, because lying flat when wheezing made breathing difficult. She repeatedly mentioned her brother Christopher as a competitor and as a pest, who took items from her room without permission and who constantly teased her.

I asked about the worst asthmatic attack she had ever had. She replied that it happened almost a year ago when she was working on a science project. She had prepared an exhibit of a volcano, and just as it was being judged, she began to wheeze so badly that she had to be rushed to the hospital to get two shots of adrenalin. She had worked hard on the project and had been looking forward to the exhibition. She had found out that mixing baking soda and vinegar would make the volcano explode and produce an eruption of lava from the inside. She never had a chance to demonstrate it.

In the second session she spoke about her strict Catholic parochial schooling. She hated the school, the uniforms, and the nuns, who ran it like a prison. She told her mother "80 million times" that she hated it and wanted to transfer; but her mother said that when she was little she also hated it, but she grew to like it, and later Louise would thank her for it. When she saw her C grade in a history test, she began to wheeze and thought that she needed her medicine, or should study more to avoid getting another C. Her only consolation was that same day, her brother brought home an F.

In the third session she said she thought that she had the flu and had gotten it from her brother. Her mother smoked all the time, and she hated it. "I told her not to, that she could die from cancer, but she won't stop. Mother always sits in the den smoking, and at night when I go to bed, the smoke comes up the stairs into my room. . . . I make an artificial gas mask by putting the covers over my head, but it suffocates . . . ugh . . . like the air drowns you. She won't stop. I threw her cigarettes out, . . . it makes me wheeze. . . . The exterminator came to the house . . . to exterminate me." When I indicated that I was puzzled, she repeated, "He comes to exterminate me. He comes to get rid of the roaches." She then spoke of her Sunday school classes and observed that "the Bible is chauvinistic, because it speaks of being 'weak like a woman.' "

Notice that in this third session the patient associated the mother's smoking with suffocating external toxic substances that require a gas mask, to the "air that drowns you,"—a possible link to the internal drowning bronchial fluids during an asthmatic attack. The subsequent association linked the man who came to exterminate her to a displacement of her perception of her mother's rejecting, exterminating attitude toward her, and her own identification with a devalued self image; a roach.

In the fourth and fifth sessions Louise spoke easily, describing her fussy attitudes about foods. She avoided all green vegetables. She hated the school lunches and, although they were paid for in the tuition, she refused to eat them. Frequently she ate no lunch or just an apple.

I commented that she didn't seem to be wheezing today. "That's because I think I have the flu. Whenever I get a fever from the flu or from chicken pox, I don't wheeze. I had pneumonia when I was four. My mother said, 'Don't run outside.' My grandmother and grandfather came to see me then. She had a lung taken out when I was six, because she had pneumonia. She's no athlete so she doesn't need it." I commented that I could understand that athletes certainly could use two good lungs. She replied, "I could use three." In these remarks her attitude was joking and ingratiating.

I chose not to comment at this time upon her distortion that the grandmother lost her lung because of pneumonia. Owing to her own pneumonia and its associated linkage to her current asthma, Louise had obviously identified with the grandmother, and I did not wish to introduce an anxiety-laden circumstance that might interfere with the emerging associations and the early developing analytic climate.

In the fifth session the "flu" was gone, and her wheezing had returned. She continued describing how she hated the food at her school and said she hadn't eaten lunch there since she was 7. "I don't like many foods. School food is injurious to your health. I'm allergic to seeds and my eyes swell. . . . My father doesn't sleep in pajamas. He sleeps in underwear and comes in every morning to wake me for school." The sequence of these associations suggests a sexual conflict related to the asthma, but represented in oral terms, with avoidance of foods linked to displaced pregnancy fantasies. "I'm allergic to father's seeds, which will

cause a part of my body to swell up." These associations were also left
untouched, especially since sexual conflict in these patients ordinarily
should not be dealt with early in the analysis.

In the sixth session the patient came in with increased wheezing. She
had not taken her asthma medication because she ran out of it, and it took
her father three weeks to renew it. Then she forgot to bring it to school,
because, she said, she was stupid. I suggested that she did not just forget,
and that she was not stupid, but that there might be another reason. She
had a need to hurt herself, and in the back of her mind, she felt that she
should suffer. She countered that she was told that her bronchi were too
small. I pointed out with the use of a diagram that her bronchi were of
normal size, "but something makes them get narrow and produce mucus,
and if we can figure out why, you can stop it and get rid of your asthma."
She then complained of feeling sleepy. I indicated that the back of her
mind did not want to hear what I had to say. Looking down at the chair,
she commented, "Someone tore a hole in the chair. They must have had
long fingernails." I added, "They might not have wanted to hear what I
had to say." She retorted, looking at her well-bitten fingers, "I have no
fingernails."

This was the first session in which I attempted to interfere with her
use of asthma as a solution to aggressive conflict, by not accepting her
excuses of poor memory and stupidity as reasons for not using medication. In pointing out that she had a need to hurt herself and to suffer, I
was interfering with her somatization process, which heretofore had
relieved her of conflict at the expense of symptoms. The emerging anxiety
was dealt with first by rationalization: her bronchi were too small; then by
a defensive attempt to leave the discussion behind: feeling sleepy; and
eventually by the emergence of the underlying aggression as a transference phenomenon: "Someone tore a hole in the chair, they must have had
long fingernails"; and finally by the denial of aggression: "I have no
fingernails." The issue of her well-bitten fingernails came up later in
treatment in an identification with a very destructive bird with dangerous
talons.

That night the patient's asthma increased so that she was unable to
walk and had to be carried up the stairs. In the next session she reported
that her father had a large collection of statues of birds. Her uncle had a
bird that he named Henry Harrigan, and it talked so well that everyone
loved it. Once it flew away, but it was brought back because it spoke so
well. She commented sadly about some birds in a local pet store who had

their wings clipped and who couldn't fly at all. I tentatively considered that the patient had identified with the birds, that her unusual verbal ability was in part an attempt to win the parents' approval, that the male bird represented the parents' preferences and her partial identification, and that she was the bird who had its wings clipped by the asthmatic defect and was unable to fly about but had to be carried upstairs on the previous evening. I noticed also that Louise was a particularly verbal and expressive child who continued to maintain a smiling, joking attitude in almost every session in spite of her frequent wheezing.

In the session that followed, she again reported having the "flu" and noted that the wheezing had subsided. She was able to sleep lying flat and not propped up. "The flu puts a protective seal all around me and prevents the wheeze from getting in." Here she clearly alludes to the wheezing as an external noxious substance, similar to the mother's smoking, which enters her body and damages her. The unconscious relationship between asthma and the inhaling of toxic substances is further elaborated in this case; it is also discussed in Chapter 10 on air symbolism.

Responding further to the interpretation in the previous session that in the back of her mind she needed to suffer, she remarked: "I have no back of my mind. A little bird takes messages between the front and the back." She reported her first dream: "I watch myself sleeping and someone downstairs is hammering." She added, "I need noise to sleep. Sometimes I put the radio on. I have trouble falling asleep. The other night when I was lying in bed sitting up, it took me over an hour and a half to fall asleep. At times I wake up wheezing from a dream."

In the next session she returned after having been confirmed, which she resented, with noticeable wheezing and with manifestations of muscular inhaling above the sternum. She stated that she had run out of the vaporizer. Even if she had it, she was afraid to take it to school out of fear of losing it, as she had lost her pencils. In addition, she did not take her pills. She further described her asthmatic condition. She wheezed badly all winter except when she was able to go skiing in cold weather. This, I noted privately, was physiologically inconsistent. Since mild exercise like walking about the house increased her wheezing, and she was unable to walk upstairs, one would expect that intense physical activity during skiing should further compromise her ability to breathe.

Another patient presented a similar physiological inconsistency. He was a 16-year-old referred for severe anorexia nervosa. During the initial evaluation I became aware that he suffered from severe asthma. Despite medication, the asthma appeared uncontrolled to the degree that he was unable to walk without severe wheezing. His internist reported that one day, while driving along a local road, he was shocked to see his patient running in a cross-country race with no apparent respiratory impairment. When I brought the episode up, the patient remembered it. He added that it was so important for him to be a good runner and to control his fear of getting fat that he did not tell the doctor of his activities. He was enraged at the possibility that, because of his emaciated state, his doctor might attempt to curtail his running.

Although Louise was quite thin, very fussy with her food, and involved with athletics, she did not express a fear of getting fat. It was my impression, however, that she was a subclinical anorexic.

She again chronicled the history of her wheezing. She wheezed all winter except when skiing, or had a fever, or chicken pox, or a stomach upset with vomiting. In April she began to sneeze, and had watery eyes. In May the wheezing stopped. All summer she sneezed. In September there was no sneeze, and in October she wheezed again. Again identifying with the bird, "When the wheezing disappeared, it just flew away."

In the thirteenth session she described two different types of noises. The first, "Eaaak, you make it when someone bugs you . . . about school lunches . . . they're awful, fatal . . . the meatballs are like bombs. Eaaak." I commented that it was a sound that tried to get out, but something blocked it from getting out. She agreed. "Eaaak." She then made a new sound like crinkling, bubbling plastic, "th th th." I tried, with difficulty, to imitate it, and she repeated it. "You push the air into the cheeks and past the lips." She then took off her confirmation ring "to let my finger breathe." As she spoke about the ring and the other confirmation gifts, coughing from the asthma interrupted her attempt at perpetuating her "th th th" sounds.

It seemed reasonable to consider that her conflict over expressing aggression toward the school lunches was linked to the condensed noises without content, "Eaaak" and "th th th." She acknowledged that something prevented the sounds from getting out. The second sound, the crinkling, bubbling "th th th," more closely resembled asthmatic sounds. At that point the conflict, expressed by noises in the throat and verbalized by her as the expulsion of air, was displaced to the finger that was choked by the ring, as she removed the ring "to let my finger breathe." The residual conflict located in the throat was then expressed by coughing, another manifestation of the forcible expulsion of air. The accuracy of these ideas was confirmed in sessions that followed.

In the next session, Louise complained that her shoes were too tight and that "they were choking the circulation of my toe." She then drew a picture of a weird boy and spoke about how weird her brother was. He would say all kinds of things to her that didn't make sense and was preoccupied with collecting spiders and ants. He was heavier than she, although at that time she weighted 68 pounds and looked like a 10-year-old. She also volunteered that ever since she was little, because of the way she sang, the family had nicknamed her "little bird."

At that point a crisis arose. Louise's father phoned to advise me that his mother had advanced carcinoma and was not expected to live more than three months. This was particularly distressing to the parents because Louise was especially attached to her grandmother. Louise was her favorite. All the children could anticipate lovely gifts whenever she returned from a vacation. Louise's father told her that her grandmother was very sick but did not mention that her death was imminent.

In the next session the patient said she had been told her grandmother was very ill. She added that her family had lived with the grandparents for two years when her father was transferred to Dallas. They had lived in a big house with servants and a tennis court and a swimming pool. "They usually come up for Christmas, or they send us money to visit them. Once they took us on a cruise." There was little obvious concern in her attitude. She added that she was going to a party after the session. That was why she was all dressed up and wearing stockings. She pulled at the stockings, making tentlike projections: "They are too hot and my feet can't breathe. I can't get fresh air in there." I acknowledged that she seemed to be having trouble getting the air in there. She added, "Well, you can, but you can't get enough air in." Her preoccupation over the conflict of getting air into the bronchi, with a sense of choking, had now been displaced to the finger that was choked by the ring, to the foot choked by the shoe, and to the leg choked by the stocking.

She pointed to a scar on her inner forearm. "I got this when I cut myself getting out of my grandfather's pool. The cut didn't hurt until they sprayed it with antiseptic. It's like Martian juice. They take tomato or grape juice and spray it in their throats (she gestured as if using a spray can). They don't worry about fluorocarbons and ozone up there." I interjected that it was just like a nebulizer. "I didn't think of that. They might also use cactus juice, ugh, and it will make the blood turn green. I sound weird when I say things like this. My father has statues of birds all over the house. I have two: one of them I call 'Momma,' a big pelican that watches over me."

Here her preoccupation with choking has been followed by association to body damage and concerns over inhaling and drinking beneficial or toxic substances. These concerns are related to her ambivalent attitude towards "Momma," the bird who watches over her. Allusions are made to the inhaling of the good and bad mother via the beneficial or toxic juices. These ideas are expanded further in Chapter 10 on air symbolism.

The patient arrived at the next session on crutches. She had tripped while talking with an obnoxious woman teacher, who wanted to know personal things about her family. She began to fan the injured right foot and blew on the ace bandage. This was the same foot that in the previous session had not been able to "breathe." She repeated, "Eaak, Eaak, Theaak, Theaak the world," without further revealing what it meant other than providing alliterative clues. She continued with clicking sounds like a dog drinking water, then made audible sounds of sucking air in. Grabbing the crutch, she pointed it like a gun at a breastlike projection on the ceiling, "Pow."

That night the father phoned, advising me he had told Louise that her grandmother was very ill and could die shortly. In the next session the patient behaved as if nothing had happened and became completely immersed in drawing various objects: a car, a mixed salad floating in space, a man, a black witch with visible teeth and with a broom sticking out between her legs. She did not associate to any of the drawings. Toward the end of the session, when I openly wondered about the drawings, she said, "I don't like to find reasons. "During the session she did volunteer how allergic she was to dust.

In the next session, on a Saturday, she arrived wheezing noticeably. When I remarked upon it, she added that she got it all out of her system Thursday night (the night her father told her that her grandmother could die soon). She wheezed and choked and couldn't sleep and was so sick that she couldn't go to school Friday. I responded with surprise that she hadn't told me on Friday how ill she was. "It's painful breathing in," she said. I expressed puzzlement, and she responded, "It just is." Again I didn't understand. "Little innocent girls like me aren't supposed to know." I repeated, "Little innocent girls like you aren't supposed to know? Now I really am puzzled." She began twirling her bracelet around and around and began talking about Japanese experiments in which model houses were sucked up by vacuums that simulated tornados. Tornados led her to the topic of volcanos. I have discussed this part of Louise's analysis in detail in Chapter 10, this volume.

THE GRANDMOTHER'S ILLNESS

In the next session the patient reported having had a severe asthmatic attack at 12:45 that day in school, "when my medicine stopped." This was a euphemistic description of her masochistically having left her medication at home. "I had to leave the classroom, and I walked so slowly that it took five minutes to get to the office instead of ten seconds. The taxi drove me to the door, so I didn't have to walk up my driveway. It's Wednesday and the doctor's off. I needed a shot, but my parents don't like me to take a cab to the hospital." Her wheezing, as she told me this, was not as marked as it had been in the previous session.

In reply to my wondering why she had had the attack, she had no awareness of any reason. She denied that anything had worried her, or that she had been told anything that upset her. She thought that it might have been the bad weather, since the day was overcast. I pressed further, asking how she felt her grandmother was coming along, since she had told me that she was very ill. She denied any concern, but almost immediately she developed an itching in the left eye, which she said had been present throughout the session, obviously was not. She volunteered that although this attack was bad, it was not as bad as her worst one, which had occurred at the science fair the preceding year. I acknowledged that she had told me of that attack in her first session. It also occurred to me that the project she had been working on was a model of a volcano, using vinegar and baking soda to simulate eruption. I asked if she could remember the date of the science fair. "It was December 16. I remember. I was asked questions about my project which I couldn't answer, and right after that, . . . two minutes after, I got such wheezing that they had to take me to the hospital. I needed oxygen and two shots of adrenalin and a long-acting antihistamine." I asked what time the fair had taken place. She replied that it had been on a Sunday from 12 to 3 and that she was questioned by the judge at 1:00 P.M.

This session was taking place on December 16, and her asthmatic attack at school earlier in the day had occurred, she had told me, at 12:45. After the session was over, I checked the calendar and found that the Sunday of the science fair she referred to had been December 15. Anniversary reactions of this type are not unusual, particularly with psychosomatic diseases. Another asthmatic patient had entered treatment following a very severe attack of asthma, precipitated by a fight with her father between Christmas and New Year's. The following year, while still in treatment, she developed another severe asthmatic attack between Christmas and New Year's. I have seen anniversary reactions in cases of migraine and ulcerative colitis and have reported anniversary reactions for anorexia nervosa.

It is also reasonable to consider that the very detailed material on tornados and volcanos in the preceding session had been in part (Chapter 10, this volume) determined by its being nearly the anniversary of the volcano exhibit of the previous year, as well as by her having heard the traumatic news about her grandmother.

In the next session she continued to avoid dealing with her concern about her grandmother. When I encouraged her to talk about the severe asthmatic attack at school, she changed the subject. She also minimized the attack at the science fair a year earlier, although previously she had called it her most severe attack. I pointed out that she might have been upset at the possibility of not winning the science award when she could not answer the judge's questions. I suggested it might have something to do with her saying that she did not want to win: that she was weird like the rest of her family. She said that her father carried her upstairs upside-down. She added, "Three of my toys breathe fire." I inquired, "Like human volcanos?" She replied, "Let's talk about volcanos instead of asthma."

When she did not follow her own suggestion and lapsed instead into silence, I asked further about the asthma. She said that she had to go to the bathroom. I observed, "When I ask about your asthma, you need to go to the bathroom." After returning, she began to rub her suede shoe back and forth, commenting that when you rubbed it, it changed color, and that her finger hurt from the friction. Her rubbing of the pelt-like shoe was strikingly similar to the behavior of an 8-year-old asthmatic boy who would bring in peltlike pussywillow shoots and become preoccupied rubbing them. The dynamics of his conflicts are discussed in Chapter 10.

In the next session, at the end of three months of analysis, similar behavior continued. She played with air sounds: "Geaak . . . Thuck." She commented that air got pushed through her teeth. She twirled her bracelet and called it a *he*. "As it gets twisted, he dies": a symbolic reference to later conflict.

During one of my infrequent consultations with her parents, Louise's father volunteered that he thought the grandmother would probably die this month. He and his wife had discussed this eventuality openly at home in front of Louise in the hope of preparing her for it. She still had said nothing about it and had shown no feelings referable to it. Louise's father volunteered for the first time that he felt that Louise's grandmother, his mother-in-law, was one of the worst people he had ever met. She was mean, distant, thoughtless, and very critical of her daughter, his wife. Every time Louise returned from a visit to their home, she returned sick or with an attack of asthma.

Louise's mother then revealed that, although she had four children, she had never felt that competent to be a mother. In a crisis, her husband always had to do everything, including diapering a messy baby. She was never able to care for the house. She was unable to cook and clean. If it weren't for the maid, she felt that everyone would starve. Things had grown much worse after her postpartum depression with Louise's younger brother, Christopher. When she accidentally became pregnant with a fifth child, she was so overwhelmed that, although she was a strict Catholic, she had an abortion.

Two nights later the father phoned to advise me he had again told all the children that the grandmother was close to dying. While the other three became very upset, Louise reacted in stony silence. She didn't get upset and didn't cry. He was concerned because he felt that she wasn't accepting the probability of her death.

In the next session she discussed varying topics but did not mention her grandmother. She described different functions of various parts of her body:

> The function of my food is to get fractured.
> The function of my nails is to get bitten.
> The function of my arm is to break.
> The function of the ends of my fingers is to be ripped.

She laughed in a self-deprecating way. I commented that I thought she was feeling hurt. She offered no response.

In the next session I confronted her more directly. I pointed out that she was avoiding talking about things that upset her. Her doing so left her with the feeling that she couldn't cope. I added that people with asthma tend to do this and that they get asthmatic attacks as a consequence. If she were to talk about what disturbed her, she could see things more clearly. She replied that she couldn't see without glasses. I told her she was joking about what I was saying and not thinking about it seriously. For a moment she became serious, remarking that her mother got cortisone injections in her nose for her asthma. Then, instead of her bracelet, she whirled her glasses to make a tornado.

Was I wise in directly confronting her with her denial of the grandmother's imminent death? Under other circumstances I might have chosen to wait, gather more information, and interpret the later consequences of the denial. I chose to intervene more actively, however, because the patient's asthma was so severe. I was concerned that the grandmother's death could precipitate an attack with unpredictable consequences. Intervening earlier and more directly is necessary when treating potentially fatal psychosomatic diseases.

A few sessions later she reported wheezing all day. She had no medicine in school, didn't take any at home, and often "lost" it in her bookbag. I pointed out that if she really wanted to have it, she wouldn't lose it: she "lost it" because part of her needed to suffer with the asthma. She replied that I was crazy. The next day she reported that the asthma got worse and she needed two shots. Nothing was bothering her. The doctor had talked about giving her different shots that might work better. She was having to use the downstairs bathroom because her grandparents were using the hall bathroom.

THE INCREASE IN RESISTANCE

Her father phoned the next night to state that Louise was very upset about having to continue treatment. She felt that it was interfering with her being in sports and was ruining her life. She had sobbed and cried for thirty minutes about having to continue analysis. He added that the grandmother was still deteriorating. He had told Louise again that her grandmother would die shortly, but she had not said a single word about it. The other children talked with the grandmother and were close to her, while Louise had become increasingly aloof and stayed away from her.

In the next session she made one of her few allusions to her grandmother's illness. After speaking about being with her grandfather, she said, "My grandmother is still sick, but she's getting better. She told me so. I didn't ask anyone what's wrong. I don't butt in. My father didn't tell me." (The last statement was untrue.) At the end of the next session, after Louise had walked out, her father stopped in momentarily to state that his mother would expire in the next thirty-six hours. Louise had not discussed it, but she saw him speaking to me. On the day of her next session, five months into the analysis, her father phoned before she arrived to tell me that Louise's grandmother had died over the weekend.

She arrived for her session on roller skates, casual and nonchalant as ever. When it appeared that she would continue indefinitely with small talk, I interjected that I had heard from her family that her grandmother had died. "Yes," she replied. "Did you see I got the tornado back?" She took off her bracelet and swung it around and around. After playing in various ways with the bracelet for ten minutes and discussing it, she said, "This stands for the tornado," and made audible sucking noises with her mouth. I said I was puzzled that she didn't say anything about her grandmother's death. "Why should I?" she replied, and she went back to playing with the bracelet.

I chose to confront her directly about her avoidance of discussing her grandmother's death, because I was worried that the denial might precipitate a severe asthmatic attack. I had also decided that I should not interpret any aspect of her bracelet-tornado-volcano fantasy. I was concerned that, especially in the face of her increased resistance, the productions would cease. Her reply to my comment about her grandmother's death had been to abruptly return to the bracelet-tornado play. That was how she felt about her grandmother's death. Although it might not have been appropriate to interpret the bracelet-tornado play as an externalization of an asthmatic attack, connecting it causally in form rather than in content might have been warranted: "I say something about your grandmother's death and you begin twirling your bracelet."

As she continued to avoid the topic, I asked about the funeral. It had taken place at noon, the burial had been in the afternoon, and she had attended both, including the lowering of the coffin into the ground. She also had attended the evening memorials. She related all this with no expression of feeling. She also acknowledged that during all that time, she had expressed no feelings. Responding to my question, she said she hadn't seen whether anyone else cried; she hadn't been able to look around. "You can't move when you pray, even if a snake crawls up your leg. You die for your religion."

It was curious, I pointed out, that she showed no feeling about the death of a person she loved. She kept her feelings in. Although she must have been upset, she did not cry. She replied angrily, "That doesn't mean I don't have feelings!" I asked how she showed them. "There are personal feelings that I have, that I don't tell anyone and I'm not going to tell you. I don't like your poking at me." I tried to clarify that I was not thoughtlessly poking at her. I was trying to help her get rid of her asthma, and the best way to do so was to help her understand how she felt about important events that happened in her life. She replied that I had said she got asthma attacks when she got upset, but she didn't have asthma now. She wondered why that was. The time was up. I suggested that, while that was a very intelligent question, we would have to wait to answer it.

In the next session she was playing with a baseball, still ignoring what had upset her. I said I had been thinking about what she had told me, that she didn't show her feelings. "I don't have to show any feelings. . . . I was told by my mother and by my father and the allergist doctor that the asthma will go away soon." I acknowledged that I understood now why she wasn't talking. No one, however, could definitely predict that the asthma would go away. She said plaintively that they had been telling her that for ten years. "How would you feel if you were lied to? It's no joke." I suggested that no one had deliberately lied to her but that it was impossible to accurately predict that her asthma would just disappear. "They said it would at least go away by the time I was 20." I asked if she were willing to suffer for the next eight years the way she had been suffering for the past four, when she was choking so badly that she couldn't walk upstairs by herself.

"I hate coming here. . . . I have no friends, well, just three. How would you feel about that? Maybe that's why I have asthma. I hate school. I hate Mother Loretta. Even my mother wishes Mother Loretta was dead. I dislike all the other teachers too, I hate them. You see I can talk." I replied that I had always known that, and that she was an excellent talker.

I noted here a development first described by Freud. When the associations of anger get closer to the hated objects, at that point they defensively become displaced onto the analyst in a transference reaction.

In order not to have to deal with her feelings of hatred toward others, Louise began to hate me.

Her talk in the following session was filled with feelings of hatred for her parochial school. She complained that she had no friends, that she hated the food, that she hadn't eaten lunch there in seven years. "I didn't have much asthma from 3 to 7. I've been trying to get out of that school since the third grade, when the asthma began again. Maybe it's (father's) fault that I have the asthma, . . . that I have no friends. He thinks it's a joke. I told him a hundred times."

In the next hour she described an anticipated ball game that night. "I'm going to hit a double . . . then a home run . . . catch a fly . . . and strike out . . . and pitch a great game." I noted that she seemed to have it all planned out. She continued talking about baseball, her attempt to control the game possibly being related to controlling the material in the hour. I said I was still wondering about what she said last week about keeping her feelings to herself. She replied that she had already told me: it was about school. She had told her father thousands of times that she hated it, and he just didn't listen.

I suggested that she might have felt there was no point in telling me things, because I wouldn't understand either. She immediately corrected me: "I said not *listen!*. . . that you won't *listen* either." I responded that I would listen to her very carefully. "Some things you just have to keep to yourself. Why should I tell you?"

I repeated that I didn't wish to just pry. Certain experiences that upset her were related to her attacks of asthma, and in asking about them, I wanted to help her understand them. She countered, "It's not that I'm going to die from it." Some people did, I told her. She accused me of trying to scare her. That was not so, I said, I was simply telling her the truth. I would not try to scare or upset her. "But you are!"

I observed that it was better to be upset, and to decide to figure out what was troubling her so she could get rid of it, than to push it away and be stuck with the asthma. There was a long period of silent thinking as the hour ended.

In the next session she reported that since her girlfriend had betrayed her and her father didn't listen, she didn't trust anyone and that included me. After the session the mother phoned to report that Louise had had a fight with her best friend, Josephine; that she was arguing with the maid; that she had blown up at the girl next door; and that she was very angry at her father about being kept at her school. The mother said Louise was much more angry than she had ever seen her.

In the next hour she complained that the boys at a party were obscene. One of them had climbed under a girl's dress; another had asked a girl to open another button on her dress. She was glad that the boys didn't like her and that she wasn't even second choice.

It was now spring. A number of sessions later, the patient complained about her sniffing allergy, because no one had time to take her for her shots. She added that she was allergic to "rugs and dust . . . father too." It was not clear whether she meant she was also allergic to her father, or whether he was also allergic. Given her attitudes toward him, I suspected both. She declared that she didn't like perfume, and she smelled her wrist. Perfume had gotten on it, and she didn't know how. She had hated all kinds of perfume ever since she was little. Mother's parents used to bring it to her as a gift. She also didn't like to eat anything green. Her mother had told her that she hadn't liked peas ever since she was little. She used to spit them out at her mother. She still didn't eat peas, lettuce, broccoli, green peppers, asparagus and cucumbers. Again one sees the combination of inhaling (rugs, dust, perfume) and ingesting what she perceives to be toxic substances, associatively linked to her asthma and to her subclinical anorexia.

In the next session she became more openly defiant and angry. "You stinker, I'm missing my ball game because I have to come here." I suggested she could make the most of the session. Then she wouldn't feel that she had wasted it and hadn't gone to the ball game either. A long period of silence followed, during which I interjected a number of comments. I noted that she was doing a lot of thinking, that I understood it was difficult for her to talk, that I knew that what she was thinking about was important, and that she really didn't believe that I'd listen carefully to what she had to say. "No, the only thing I want to do is to play ball. Why don't you leave me alone." If I thought I could help her by leaving her alone, I said, I would. The only way I could help her, though, would be to help her figure out the worries that contributed to her asthma. "I just want to play ball."

I suggested that she was too intelligent a person to think that playing ball came before getting well. "If you're so smart, why don't I wheeze in the summer?" I acknowledged that I didn't understand that yet. If she told me about her worries, maybe we could find that out. "Well, why don't I die from it?" I reiterated that some children do. "Well, what do you want me to do, disassemble my room when I get mad!" I expressed my puzzlement. "That's clear, what to you expect?" she said in an angry tone. I explained that I had an idea what she was saying but I wanted to be sure. I didn't like to decide things unless I really understood what she meant.

"I can figure out things myself. I'm not wheezing anymore." I asked if she felt she would be able to say that next November, December, January, and February. "You say I'm smart, so why can't I figure it out myself?" I acknowledged that she was smart. She didn't, however, have the training and experience to figure out how to solve problems causing asthma, and she could use some help. I then made a joke that broke the tension and she laughed and began talking about her bird. "It wakes up early in the morning talking and I'd like to choke it. We had to give back my first bird because it was crazy and bit me. This one has a sharp beak and long claws and acts crazy too by hanging upside-down."

Here Louise revealed her reluctance to confide in me through the description of the behavior of the bird—a projection of herself, the little bird, who used to be carried upside-down by her father. The first bird was crazy and so hostile that it opened its mouth and bit and therefore was gotten rid of: abandoned. The second, crazy too, also has a sharp beak and long claws and is filled with aggression, but it is able to keep the claws sheathed and the beak shut.

Louise's incessant biting of her nails and picking at her cuticles, an extension of the nails, serves to symbolically keep her claws sheathed. Terrible fear of her aggression is evident as she identifies with the overaggressive bird, verbalizing impulses to choke it in order to contain the aggression. Indeed, she chokes her bird-self with asthmatic attacks to contain her explosive rage, and she remains silent, suppressing her aggressive thoughts and feelings out of fear of abandonment. Silverman (Chapter 14) comments that his asthmatic-anorexic-child patient also identifies her helplessness, vulnerability, and rage with a little bird.

In retrospect, I might have, at this point, interpreted to her one of the reasons that she was silent and reluctant to confide in me: she feared that if she revealed all her angry thoughts and feelings, I would think she was a bad person and no longer be interested in helping her.

The next session was filled with resistance, suppression, and repression. As she spent time fooling around with her school papers, I asked how she felt about the previous session. "I fell asleep. . . . I don't remember anything about it . . . I'll do it myself. I can only trust my two friends." I added that they weren't trained to help her.

The next session again preceded a ball game, and she revealed a fantasy of predicting everything that would happen. She went through every inning, describing events in detail as they would affect her: catching a line drive, missing a grounder, getting a certain number of hits, hitting the ball to certain areas of the field. I commented again on her need to have complete control of the game. To myself I reflected that she was attempting to achieve a similar control over the analytic game that she perceived was being played out between us. We were in competition: I was encouraging her to reveal her thoughts and feelings, and she felt a need to keep them all to herself. I chose not to reveal the analogy, because she might become distrustful and suspicious that I could see more in her words than she realized she was revealing. She might then speak even less. Further reflection suggested that she was also daydreaming the game to compensate for not being there.

She continued, "My father got me up at 6:30 A.M. to make early mass today, and I resented it. I'll kill him if he wakes me tomorrow." As she discussed the episode, she took off the bracelet with the comment, "The return of the volcano. Look at the tornado." She swung it frantically. As she stopped the whirling, she exhaled pointedly. Here, as the anger toward her father was further mobilized by her discussion, she felt unable to cope with it. It was then externalized into the destructive volcano-tornado. As that symbolic aggressive discharge ceased, she reidentified with the explosive volcano with an obvious exhalation.

A SUBCLINICAL ANOREXIA

A few sessions later, Louise arrived on crutches. She had fallen playing kickball and strained her knee ligaments. Discussion of the injury brought up the previous episode on crutches three months ago, as well as a third episode in the third grade.

She discussed the ball game in great detail and then casually added that she wasn't coming tomorrow. When I inquired about the reason, she came up with a vague, complicated story about coaching tomorrow's game. She also implied that her mother was willing for her to miss the session. When I questioned the relative importance of coaching a game versus missing her session, she burst out with an angry diatribe. "I don't want to be here anyhow . . . I want to be left alone. I can figure out things myself . . . never mind how. I won't talk to you anyhow."

I suggested that her attitude might lengthen the treatment and that her reluctance might stem from not wishing to discuss some of the topics that were coming up. "I know. I don't have to . . . and you can't make me. I don't want to be here and waste my time." Her response to my comment about wheezing all winter was that it was her business.

I pointed out that she was getting increasingly angry in the sessions. She replied, "I probably get angry feelings at others out on you." I told her that was pretty good and that I didn't mind her getting mad at me. "Why should you! Like when my friend gets mad at me and she's really mad at her little brother. I understand what it's like to have a little brother." I indicated that I bet she did.

She began tapping on her inner thigh with her forefinger. I wondered about the tapping. "My thighs are too fat. It's like an earthquake here with the P waves spreading out around the earth's crust." I thought it sounded like an interesting experiment, but it didn't seem finished. "Nothing," she replied. As the session ended, she was much friendlier and left on the crutches.

During the session she had become furious at the thought that I would charge for missed sessions and badgered me about whether I would charge if this happened. In the midst of her anger, Louise began tapping her thighs and claimed that they were too fat. The rippling of the flesh as it was tapped was associated to rippling earthquake waves of destructiveness spreading across the earth, and directed toward me in the transference. While I have indicated that I felt Louise was a subclinical anorexic, these characteristic preoccupations with fat thighs, especially inner thighs, when actually she was quite thin, lend additional confirmatory evidence to that supposition. Most anorexics are preoccupied with their thighs being too fat, and they point to them. I do not remember any of them tapping their thighs. Without that association of hers, however, the additional dynamic significance of the touching or tapping would have been lost on me.

It seems reasonable to assume that for Louise, the presence of flesh that can ripple or shake is associated with earthquake convulsive movements identifying with aspects of her tornado-volcanic self. It also appears plausible that there is also a sexual component. The patient's experiencing convulsive tremors emanating from the regions between her inner thighs suggests unconscious orgastic linkage. Touching or tapping the area would also suggest masturbatory preoccupations. Finally, the association of all these convulsive reactions with P waves indicates preoccupation with the penis as the initiator of the convulsive sexual experience, or indicates that the flesh between her thighs symbolically represents an unconscious perception of a penis. I (1983) have previously described that in anorexic women, the frantic need to rid themselves of flesh from different parts of their bodies, but especially from their inner thighs, represents a manifestation of conflict over psychosexual identity. Preoccupation with the loss of flesh represents multiple symbolic penises in all parts of the body: As stated by one patient, "I can't stand that flesh hanging between my legs."

On the phone that night, Louise's mother acknowledged that she had made an error by not discussing the session with me in advance and then by thinking of letting Louise miss the session. She would correct it on the following day. Louise arrived in a rage, claiming that she was not going to talk to me for the rest of her life. She turned the chair around, plugged her ears with her hands, and agreed that she was very mad at me. Surprisingly, she volunteered that it really was not my fault and that she was taking it out on me. She hated her parents. However, she added that she didn't have to talk to me even if she didn't hate me. I suggested that she was putting her sense of fairness on the shelf. I told her I understood how she felt; she was using being mad at me as an excuse not to talk about what she really didn't want to discuss anyhow, and I would accept her anger.

I did not think that the mother had made an innocent error in judgment. I suspected that the treatment was distressing the mother in two main ways. First, she was increasingly troubled by Louise's absorbing involvement with me in the analysis, and she was experiencing a sense of alienation and separation from Louise as a consequence. Second, rumblings of assertiveness and anger may have begun to emerge, and the mother felt ill equipped to cope with them. Both sources of anxiety were unconscious, however, and the mother's behavior was not motivated by a conscious attempt to destroy the treatment. What the mother did was to agree to cutting a session for a spurious reason and then to require me to question the reasons for her absence. By encouraging Louise to face the responsibility of working in the office rather than playing at the ballfield, I would antagonize her and increase her resentment toward me.

In addition the mother had clearly sent a signal that ball playing was more important than analysis, so who was Louise to argue with that conclusion, especially if it meant choosing between me and her mother. The mother then consciously attempted to undo the sabotage by springing on Louise in the car that she was going to treatment anyhow. Louise went into a rage and took it out on the analyst. This type of threat is frequently experienced also by the mother of an anorexic patient. As indicated, I had become increasingly convinced that Louise was a subclinical anorexic child. Coexistence of asthma and anorexia is not uncommon, either in sequence where the patient is asthmatic until adolescence, when the asthma subsides and is replaced by the anorexia, or simultaneously as seemed to be the case with Louise. I have noted about a dozen cases of both asthma and anorexia.

In the last week of analysis before her summer vacation, Louise remained angry at me, was less communicative, and frequently spent time reading in the office. I felt that she was still preoccupied with her difficulty in talking about her conflicts over aggression, and her anxiety over the separation for the summer, although she denied it. At the end of the last session before the summer vacation, when she was about to leave, she said that she could not get out of the chair (to leave).

During Louise's summer vacation I saw the the parents individually. For many years the father had felt that his wife had chronic subclinical anorexia. He was familiar with it because his youngest sister had anorexia, and his wife's symptoms and behavior were strikingly similar to hers, though not as severe. For long periods she was amenorheic. She had always "eaten like a bird." This simile was not without relevance. Louise was nicknamed "little bird," having identified with her mother, whom she specifically named "Momma, a *big* pelican who watches over me." In subsequent sessions, Louise's identification with the aggressive aspects of the bird became increasingly clear. The father reported that his wife pushed food about on her plate and picked at it, after cutting it up in little pieces just as his sister did. She had always been preoccupied with how her clothing fit, because she was concerned that she was too fat. He noted also that she had been hypochondriacal and accident prone for many years. She had broken her ankle twice and had three automobile accidents. She also had a chronic depression when the children were young. She had great difficulty in getting out of bed in the morning. This depression occurred after the birth of each of the four children. He would come home at 8 P.M. to find his wife still in her bathrobe. She had constant stomach symptoms and had been diagnosed by one physician as having mucus colitis.

The father felt that during the six months of analysis, Louise had changed considerably. She was much more assertive and on occasion even would argue with her older sisters, something she had never done before. Most of her anger, however, was reserved for her younger brother. He also noticed that although she had injured her leg twice this spring, she had less physical illness. She was still very hypochondriacal, however, and had constant vague complaints about her body similar to her mother's. She also tended to pick at her food and push it about on the plate. He acknowledged that he probably did baby her and that he would attempt to give that up.

In August I saw Louise's mother, who reported that during the past six months in treatment, Louise had been healthier physically. She thought that the asthma was a little less severe. Her typical allergic rhinitis during the summer was much improved, with little eye rubbing and sniffing. She behaved in a much more direct and challenging fashion. While Louise and her brother both complained that parents didn't care about children's feelings, it was Louise who threatened to get a lawyer to sue for her rights. While the mother was willing to transfer Louise from her Catholic school, the father was not, and Louise was very angry about it.

When I raised the topic, she discussed Louise's eating habits. She felt that my concern was exaggerated and that Louise was well nourished. She acknowledged that Louise was extremely fussy and did not eat any of the usual foods that children ate for lunch. Since treatment, however, she had been more experimental in her eating habits. As a baby, she had eaten everything without any pressure. The mother stated that since she herself had been pressured to eat as a child, she would not pressure her own children. Louise used to wolf down the bottle as an infant and then vomit. Her eating difficulty became more noticeable around 8 years of age, although she became less interested in eating at about ages 3 and 4 and dropped out some foods.

The mother reminisced that about the time that Christopher was born, the father took many pictures of the children. In many of them Louise appeared very sad with gritted teeth. Her first allergic reaction occurred two weeks before the mother gave birth. "She was about 18 months old. She ate sesame seeds and swelled up all over. Her eyes were like ping-pong balls. She may have become difficult in her eating then. I remember pictures of Louise holding her brother with almost clawlike hands." The "clawlike" hands must have been striking to the mother, because she also noticed Louise's "clawlike" hands in a picture of her and Louise. During the spring, Louise bought her mother a T shirt with the inscription "When God created man, She was only joking."

It is of some relevance that the father described Louise as eating like a little bird, that he had statues of birds all over the house, and that the mother commented upon her gritted teeth and clawlike hands. You will remember Louise's own description of her birds. She wanted to choke back what was coming out of the mouth of one, and the other bit and was given away. Her current bird had a sharp beak and long claws and acted crazy. We may presume not only that Louise identified closely with her bird, including making birdlike aggressive sounds when frustrated, but also that her mother unconsciously recognized the same identification in her emphasis upon Louise's specific characteristics. Louise was the bird with the sharp beak (gritted teeth) and long claws (that had to be bitten to be sheathed), filled with sucking (tornado) and explosive (volcano) rage, fearful of erupting and requiring that the aggression be constantly choked back out of fear that she would otherwise be given away (abandoned). The bird symbolism also expressed the unconscious meaning of her subclinical anorexia. The biting bird, filled with aggression, had to contain its oral destructiveness or face being abandoned: given away when it bit. The associated impulse to rip and tear in conjunction with destroying while eating had to be contained by sheathing the claws. Subsequently we will see more overt evidence of the underlying cannibalistic impulses.

SADOMASOCHISTIC SEXUAL CONFLICT

Louise returned in the fall subdued and quiet. In the third session she brought in a book about a girl who was an orphan, who wrote to a man who sent her to school, but he never wrote back. She spoke about how much she hated her brother's rabbit and how allergic and stuffed up she was. The pollen count was 304. She began tapping her fingers on her thigh, singing "Heart and Soul." She read during the rest of the hour. During the following hour she attempted to doze, giving the excuse that she had been up late.

At the end of the month she brought in a book entitled *Are You Alone in the House*. It was about a girl babysitter sitting alone in a house, who got hit on the head with a poker and raped. No one believed her when she told them who did it, because he came from a powerful family — not even her girlfriend, her parents, or the doctor. In response to my encouragement, she continued. In the beginning the girl got phone calls in a shrill, weird voice. Then, when she opened the door because she knew the boy, he tried to pull off her clothes, saying that she wanted it. She tried to hit him with the poker, and he hit her on the head. She was unconscious until she woke up in the hospital. We discussed how no one believed the girl, but they all believed the boy. I commented that her nose appeared more stuffed up at that moment. She replied that her new medicine wasn't working, just like the old one. As she finished reading the last two pages, nothing happened to the boy. "He should have been thrown off the Empire State Building. I fell off my bike when I was eight. The brakes didn't work. I flew over the handlebars and landed on my head. They found me unconscious in the street with blood on my head and I woke up in the hospital as they were stitching my head."

Her description of the rape was immediately followed by her identification with the rape victim, along with an immediate increase in nasal congestion characteristic of the summer phase of her respiratory illness. Karol describes (in Chapter 12) the important aspects of sadomasochistic conflict in contributing to asthmatic disease, where the sexual conflict is displaced from the vaginal vault to the lung. In the winter months Louise developed asthma; in the summer months, nasorhinitis. The underlying conflict is the same, as the ego finds different ways of expressing it.

Louise became increasingly resistant in the next few sessions. Silence, sleeping, and uncooperativeness alternated with occasional bouts of talkativeness. Although she acknowledged that she was willing to talk about her life in order to get rid of her plugged-up nose, her attempts were meager. "I woke up with a stuffed nose. Maybe I had a dream. I don't remember dreams. I don't care about dreams. My mother sneezes so much, she gets cortisone injections in her nose." The comment about nasal injections tends to clarify the nasal cavity as an unconscious vaginal equivalent similar to the lung. In the next few sessions, Louise continued reading, offering me monosyllabic responses. Her anger toward me erupted more visibly, with sarcastic comments, such as "You are so thick!" Attacks on herself increased: "I'm stupid because I left my book home . . . stupid because I stuck my finger with a fork."

In mid-October, angry at losing a class prize that she would not discuss, she quietly read the newspaper. As a consequence of my comments, she found the disappointment more difficult to push away. Stating that she would not discuss it, she began to exhale noisily, threw her jacket over her head, and remained silent for the rest of the hour.

Louise did not show up for the next session and did not call. I saw her mother before the following session. She stated that when Louise lost the prize Wednesday, she developed a severe asthma attack Thursday morning in school and had to leave. "I took her to the allergist and forgot to call you." The mother volunteered that she realized that forgetting was not a simple mistake and she was visibly upset. She said she had been feeling overwhelmed recently, to the point that it interfered with her working effectively in her law practice. She added that it had been increasingly difficult to get Louise to the analytic sessions. "Since the summer she has ranted and raved about not wanting to go. She said she was not going to talk with you and that it was a waste of money." The mother's conscious recognition that forgetting the analytic hour was a sign of her own resistance to Louise's treatment was followed by her unconscious recognition that Louise's reluctance to continue was in part a response to the mother's behavior.

That afternoon Louise arrived with math homework and did it the entire hour, unwilling to discuss anything about the asthma attack. There was no reply when I wondered whether it had anything to do with the prize. I indicated that I was sorry to hear about the attack, especially since she had missed that session. By not talking this session, I added, we didn't have the chance to figure anything out. She was almost mute for the entire session, reflecting, I felt, her unconscious awareness of her mother's attitude toward the analysis as well as her reluctance to trust me while facing painful conflict. This increasing resistance and uncooperative behavior heralded the beginning of an eruption of tremendous hatred in the transference, which was to persist for many, many months.

During the next few sessions she continued to read or to do her homework. My attempts to interpret her behavior or to encourage her talking were met with increasing hostility. "Why don't you shut up. . . , stupid. If you were dead I wouldn't have to come here."

Because of her continued asthma and lack of response to medication, her allergist took additional tests and told Louise that her pulmonary function was decreased. Discussing the tests with me, he indicated that while the pulmonary functioning was impaired, he felt that the condition was still reversible. However, with persistent asthma he thought that she would be impaired permanently. As Louise listened to my elaboration of the testing, she either was silent, continued reading, or responded with a vitriolic attack. "I never met someone that I detest so much." Accepting her attack, I continued to point out how worried she must be about permanent lung damage and how difficult it was for her to talk about problems. She remained silent. I indicated how puzzled I was that she could contemplate permanent lung disease rather than talk with me. She replied that she would not talk with anyone who was so stupid and idiotic and whom she hated so much. I pointed out that she didn't have to like me, that she could hate me if she felt like it, but that it was very self-destructive of her to suffer from asthma rather than talk with me. She countered, "But I hate you."

I asked whether she was coming here to like me or to get rid of her asthma. I added that I thought she knew some of the reasons why she had the asthma. "I know, and I can handle it myself." I replied that I saw what a good job she had done the previous week, ending up in the hospital with shots. "You know I never hated anyone like I hate you. I never spoke to anyone like this before." I observed that she was acting like the high school students who say that they won't learn because they hate the teacher. People go to school to learn, not to like the teacher. "You're not my teacher. Why don't you just shut up!"

I persisted, indicating that I could help her get rid of her asthma if she let me and I didn't care if she hated me. She ended the session with "I'll bring my radio so I don't have to listen to your idiotic nonsense."

This somewhat vigorous interchange initiated a period of months of similar involvement, in which Louise poured out verbal volcanic eruptions and found that I survived, that I accepted her aggressive outbursts, that I did not attack in kind, and that I did not abandon her. The sessions were significant for her, because she was able to express so much hatred for the first time and to express it by talking rather than with an asthmatic attack. She recognized this with her comment, "I never spoke to anyone like this before." In my responses, besides accepting her aggression, I attempted to convey my recognition that she could take my comments and not fall apart, that she was not fragile and weak and susceptible to illness at the slightest misadventure. I also used humor to break the tension and to indicate that these were not life-and-death confrontations between us. After this session her father called, saying that he had increasing reservations about continuing the analysis in the face of all the pulmonary testing and medication changes that were necessary.

The patient was still furious in the next session. "I don't talk to you because you're stupid. You can't help me. I don't trust you. I can't talk to anyone I hate and don't trust." I acknowledged that it was difficult for her, but that it was difficult for her to talk to anyone and that's why she had the asthma. As she remained silent and occupied herself in reading, I remarked on how self-destructive her behavior was, because she was wasting time and not working. "You're just trying to scare me and it won't work." I replied that I was not trying to scare her; she had enough problems without my adding any more. "The allergist said that you could have permanent lung changes, not I, and if you don't believe me, call him." "I just hate you." I asked when she had given me a chance to help her. "Last spring I talked. Now I'm doing well on my own." I replied that she was doing so well that she had just ended up in the hospital. "There's nothing wrong with me. . . . I'm a nice person . . . people like me in school . . . lots of friends." I replied that she was afraid that if she told me her thoughts, I might not like her. "I don't care about you, stupid."

Here Louise revealed her fear that the release of her stored-up aggression would damage her inner picture of herself as a nice person and result in people abandoning her. Her statement, "I don't care about you, stupid," had two determinants. One was the obvious displaced hatred on-to me. The second, forged of a very tenuous, developing therapeutic alliance with me, was her protecting herself from abandonment, if indeed she continued to express her rage and I did not keep my word and abandoned her. Despite and because of all this expression of hatred, I felt that a bond was developing between us, based upon her awareness of her ability to express aggression and my ability to accept it.

During the next session, she did homework out loud so that she could not hear what I was saying. She interrupted the homework to hurl insults at me. "I hate you and I hate the school I go to. What have you done about it?" I observed that choking with her asthma was worse than going to her school, and she wasn't letting me help her with it. "You're too stupid to help me. Prove you could do it." I told her that I would. If she told me what her worries were, I'd help her with her asthma.

"No, you do it yourself if you're so smart!"

"Why should I! I can't do it alone. Besides, if you want to get rid of the asthma, it's your business. If you don't and want to consider permanent lung disease, that's your choice."

She said she was not going to tell me her "decent, interesting ideas."

I told her I wasn't sure she felt her ideas were all so decent, because she had a lot of angry thoughts. "Shut up, stupid. I'd like to see you dead." I asked how she'd do it. "Blow your brains out."

While the aggressive intent here is obvious, the choice of the word "blow" is overdetermined. "Blowing air" for the asthmatic is the vehicle by which the aggression is expressed. Louise has already identified with tornados, volcanos, and earthquakes, all of which contain violent movements of air and steam. Later in the analysis, when she was furious with me, she would shred endless little pieces of paper and save them until the end of the session. Then she would hold them in front of her mouth, "blow" them all over the floor, and leave.

Louise's blowing debris all over the floor for me to clean up was one manifestation of anger, expressed by blowing air containing anal-wind components. Urethral aggression was also evident in her threats to spill soda all over my couch when angry about an interpretation. Wilson in Chapter 13 describes both anal and urethral components of aggression in his asthmatic patients. One patient spoke of all exhaled air as flatus and of breathing out foul air. Another fantasied blowing up people by filling them with urine. This patient recalled childhood behavior of placing a straw in a frog's rectum, blowing it up with air, and stepping on the frog and bursting it. Louise's projection of her explosive self by identifying with volcanos that spew out hot foul gas and debris reveals another component of her anality. Characterologically, she would spitefully withhold all kinds of information she recognized as helpful. She also stubbornly refused to openly acknowledge the value of her treatment, while ascribing the improvement to invalid reasons.

As she continued doing her French homework out loud in order to avoid speaking with me, I told her that she probably thought I didn't speak French. "I know so, you're too stupid." I asked if she would care to bet, and she agreed. I asked her what she'd do if she lost. "I'll give you one hello." I told her to forget it. It wasn't worth it, for one crummy "hello." "All right, if you translate it, I'll talk three sessions," and the hour was over.

In the next session she spoke for the entire session, ascribing the asthma to the weather and to its being a physical disease. She denied that losing the class prize had anything to do with the subsequent attack.

I asked her, if she had the choice of having asthma or feeling upset, which would she choose?

"How upset?"

"Pretty upset."

"How severe would the asthma be?"

"It would be severe asthma."

"I'd rather be upset, but what about medium asthma?"

Her bantering would be funny if it were not both characteristic and tragic. Sperling (1963) has stated that psychosomatic disease is suicide in stages. Asthmatic patients often toy with their attacks as they choke, meting out the punishment proscribed by their strict consciences for alleged aggressive and sexual transgressions. Often they do not mean to die, but like the anorexic, occasionally they miscalculate.

I saw her father in consultation, because I was concerned about his reservations about further treatment. He said he had doubts, because the allergist had told him that the asthma was organic with few psychological features. In attempting to illustrate the psychological relevance, I pointed out what he already recognized: that a considerable number of attacks followed upsetting experiences. When he finally agreed to continue the analysis for another year, I emphasized two points. First, it was important for him and his wife to tolerate any increasing expression of anger on Louise's part. Second, he should not discuss his reservations with Louise, because it could ruin the treatment.

In the next session, the patient appeared very sad and quiet. After she failed to respond to general comments, I suggested that she might feel she could get rid of the asthma, and why didn't we work together. "First I have to get rid of my headache. It's killing me. I woke up with it. It's from a sore throat." I replied that the throat might have something to do with it, but it also might be caused from tension and from the angry thoughts that she had toward me. She recognized that I didn't deserve all the anger and maybe she felt guilty about it. "You spoke yesterday about blowing my brains out, so maybe you hurt your brain from the guilt instead." She did not reply but appeared very sad, almost about to cry, but it passed. I had never seen her that sad. I suspected that my interpretation had reached her and some of the previous guilt that was somatized became conscious.

The next day the mother phoned. Louise had had a severe asthma attack and had to go to the hospital for adrenalin and oxygen. When Louise arrived for her session, she spoke about how she had to care for her nails. She cut them and polished them. I noted that her mother had called about the asthma. "My father had a big corporation party and it was the smoking, especially my mother's. I told her to stop. I'm not going to tell you things because you're just in it for the money and don't care about me. My father said that he pays you a fortune."

Feeling bad, guilty, and depressed over how she treated me, she punished herself with an asthmatic attack. Unable to believe that I could really accept and care about her in the face of endless hatred expressed toward me, she voiced her doubt by saying, "You don't care about me." While my notes do not indicate my reply, I certainly felt that it was an important statement. Normally, I would surely have replied to it, with either, "Why do you think that I don't care about you?" or more probably in this case, "You just can't believe that I could possibly care about you after you get so mad at me, especially when part of you might feel that I just don't deserve it." I also indicated that wasting her time here must make her feel guilty. "I'd like to punch you in the nose. I hate it that you're alive." The angry outbursts continued during the next half dozen sessions.

In mid-December she spent the beginning of a session playing with her calculator and ignoring me, except for expressions of contempt and insult. I pointed out that she didn't want to talk because she knew that I was right. She knew she didn't want to talk about upsetting ideas and she choked herself instead. She denied it with a series of insults. I added that she must feel guilty at wasting her father's money at a dollar a minute and that she had just wasted fifteen dollars. "I don't feel guilty, and I tell him that I waste his money and he understands, you jerk!" I replied that I was sure that he understood.

"You must feel quite angry with him to waste his money that way. Then you feel guilty and choke yourself."

"Shut up! I'd like to take a tennis ball and shove it down your throat."

I acknowledged that then I'd choke. I said that she must feel guilty and choke herself when she thought of choking others.

From this interchange, it seems clear that, as the repressed aggression emerges in the transference, various manifestations of the aggression are expressed in terms closely associated with respiratory symbolism: tornados, volcanos, and the violent movement of air. The patient blows papers all over the floor as an expression of contempt. She wants to "blow my brains out." Now she wants to take a tennis ball and shove it down my throat. Aggression emerges in impulses to choke me, and then she chokes herself with asthma.

Reiser (1975) feels it is not surprising that a patient suffering from choking should be preoccupied with choking and manifestations of respiratory symbolism. The question arises whether the unconscious aggressive impulse to choke is primary and sets off the asthmatic attack, or whether choking fantasies are secondary to the choking asthmatic attack. This issue is discussed in Chapter 10.

In the next session, before the Christmas holidays, I gave her a bracelet. She accepted it with a flat-sounding thanks and put it on without any comment or expression of pleasure. She continued playing music from her tape recorder and doing homework. I pointed out that she had lost the previous bet and yet she wasn't talking, though she had promised to do so. "I'll talk in three years, I didn't tell you when." While the retort was hostile, the hidden transference implication was that if I could tolerate her aggressive behavior, and keep her in treatment for three more years, then she would talk. In retrospect, the transference interpretation would have been more helpful.

I noted again how puzzling it must be to her to be willing to suffer with asthma and choke instead of talking. "The allergist said that my asthma is less, and it's his medicine that is helping and my method that I'm using." Earlier she had said that she had her own method for getting better and that she wouldn't tell me what it was. I had countered that she probably was using my method and that was why she wouldn't tell me what it was: she was so stubborn that she just wouldn't admit that I could help her.

At this point it was becoming apparent that the asthma, which had been present almost continuously, was abating. As Louise recognized the improvement, it may have played a role in her presenting her secret plan for getting better. I remarked that if she were getting better, it might be related to all the anger that she had been pouring out at me for the past five months, instead of choking it back as she had done in the past. This prompted another attack in the form of an embellished note resembling a card.

> Louise Rose Dwight hates Dr. Stupid Jerk Mintz and will never talk to him again because he talks Bullshit with a capital "B" and she is doing fine on her own with her OWN method which will not be revealed to untrustable types.
> — Louise Rose Dwight
> P.S. With her OWN method she will smile awhile.

She then wanted to know what I would do if I lost the next bet. I replied that I would keep trying to help an uncooperative little girl with her asthma, even if she continued to insult me. She responded with disgust. During the next few weeks her anger and insults continued unabated. She again proclaimed that her secret method was getting her better and that I didn't deserve to know what it was. Her need to create a secret method of improvement suggested that she could not believe that changes in the medication were suddenly playing a decisive role after six or seven years; she recognized that psychological forces were responsible but was unwilling to acknowledge that they could in any way be attributable to the treatment. Also her repressed rage was so strong that it required continued expression, for which she needed an object.

In the last session before her Christmas holiday, she continued spewing hatred toward me. I pointed out again that her ability to express anger helped to diminish the asthma, because she no longer felt compelled to choke back her feelings. Those feelings, I added, were inside her long before she started her analysis; she used to be afraid of them and did not want to recognize their existence, and she used to feel so guilty that she would punish herself by choking. Toward the end of the session she acted as if she were going to get up and walk out in disgust. I observed that if she walked out, it was because she was anxious about being away from the analysis; she wished to show me that she didn't need me and could leave me rather than being told when to leave. In addition, if she got an asthma attack while on vacation (she was visiting relatives in Spain), it meant that she missed me. Finally, I added that she really knew that the asthma was better because of the treatment—because I was the only one whom she felt would accept all this anger and say, "Have a good holiday in Barcelona." "I will as long as I don't see you, stupid."

Two weeks later she returned and continued her hostile attacks. She said it was great to be away from a stupid person like me, and she had had no asthma attacks. I pointed out that she must have needed to get back here to get rid of all the accumulating anger, so she wouldn't have to choke it back with asthma. She responded with a look of disgust.

A few sessions later she arrived singing and chanting, putting her fingers in her ears when I attempted to speak. "Shut up, idiot, I can't learn this song." I told her that this was not a hard-rock singing studio and that she was chanting because she was afraid to hear what I had to say.

"It's not true. You're stupid and I don't listen to stupid people."

"If a person has asthma and doesn't try to get better, it isn't I who am stupid."

I felt she could tolerate those rather direct remarks, which implied to her that I did not think she was fragile. "When asthmatic patients have thoughts and feelings they feel they cannot cope with," I explained, "they bury and cover them up, shifting the feelings to the throat and lungs." She screamed, "Will you stop it! How would you like me throw these jelly beans at you?" I said she could *say* whatever she chose, but that didn't mean that she could *do* whatever she chose. That included throwing things at me or damaging the office. She persisted, "What would you do if I threw them?"

"You are acting as if you should do whatever you think. That's why you're afraid of what will come out of you and why you have to choke it back. You have all those angry feelings inside and you are afraid that if you talk about them, that means that you have to do it, so you don't want to talk to me."

"That's not so, idiot."

"If you're not afraid of losing your temper, why won't you talk?"

"I'm not. If I threw these, what would you do?"

"I'd have to take the jelly beans away from you."

"You can't. They're my property."

"They're your property to eat, not to throw at me. That's why you have asthma—because you don't believe that you can control yourself. You have all these angry feelings and you choke them back."

"You mean that I choke because I'm afraid of what will come out?"

"Yes."

This was an important statement. For the first time during months of increasing levels of transference aggression, accompanied by an almost total unwillingness to consciously respond to interpretations, Louise was willing to consciously consider an interpretation about one of the causes of her asthma and respond appropriately to me and permit me to know it.

Her ability at last to contemplate this interpretation was, I thought, a result of two factors. First, her previous aggressive outbursts had been confined to verbal abuse. Now the level of violence had escalated to threats of throwing things at me. This could have made her anxious over actually losing control, and she might also have been frightened as she recognized the increased inappropriateness of her behavior. She had a more acute need to come to terms with the anxiety. Second, this was the first time I had suggested that I would actively intervene and help her control her temper. I did so with the statement that I would remove the objects of violence. Also important was the manner in which the statements were made. I spoke quietly and directly, looked at her, and conveyed that I meant what I said. I also indicated that I was not anxious or fearful of her threats, nor did I respond with feelings of anger or alienation toward her. My goal was to help her understand what was going on between us. Her reaction to her own behavior, and her reaction to my behavior, both contributed to the response.

Insight was momentary, however. "It's not the treatment that got me better, it's the medicine. I haven't wheezed in a month. I just want to get out of here. I'll do what I can to get you to throw me out." I told her that I was very patient; I knew another person with asthma who did that and it took him nine years. "I'm 13 and I'll be on my own by 18." I suggested 21 and that she had eight more years. "I won't come. I hate you." I told her I knew that, and that was what we could talk about. "I won't talk." I said I had time; I got paid whether she talked or not. I tried to get across that her procrastinations and defiance did not trouble me and that she might as well talk now as later. "I know you. You're just interested in the money." I told her I knew she'd say that. "Prove it." I told her I would if she'd listen. "Who said I wouldn't listen. I'm not chanting."

She then threw the jelly beans, but not in a way to hit me. "They're half-eaten and sticky. You want to hear a joke? About why the dead baby crossed the road? Because it was tied to a chicken. . . . How can you get 100 dead babies in a thimble? . . . 'La Machine.' . . . What does a baby do at the bottom of 100 dead babies? Eat its way out." Then I told a joke, and she waited beyond the hour to hear the ending.

I am indebted to Gehl (1985) for pointing out that the patient's joke about "La Machine," where the whirling blades are used to cut up the babies and reduce them to liquid mucus, is a reenactment of her earlier fantasy of the tornado, where the "molecules are being moved about, cut in half by electrons," and that she is the tornado that sucks up and destroys the microscopic people in the dust. She is "La Machine," the volcanic-tornado who whirls, sucks, and destroys and is only prevented from doing so by the choking off of the violent movement of air by an asthmatic attack.

Here, she further confirmed the supposition that she had responded to the interpretation, as well as indicating that she accepted my direct comments. The jokes that poured out reflected some of the themes that she had previously been afraid to face in their more violent forms, although she had alluded to them in subdued fashion from the beginning of the analysis. The jokes suggested a tremendous amount of underlying hatred toward her younger brother.

She was 18 months of age when Christopher arrived. Two weeks before his birth she had become allergic to eating sesame seeds and developed severe swelling of the face and eyelids, which lasted until her brother was born. Her mother then developed a postpartum depression. Three months later, Louise developed wheezing attacks that required epinephrine injections. The early allergic swelling was linked to the later wheezing difficulty: both involved an outpouring of fluid into the tissues. The linkage between one psychosomatic disease and the other is further discussed in Chapter 10. It was my impression that Christopher's birth was traumatic to Louise because he required a great deal of the mother's time. In addition, the mother's postpartum depression focused her interest upon herself instead of on the children and sapped her ability to cope with their needs. Louise may have blamed Christopher for all this. Ever since his arrival the mother had been depressed.

Aside from the obvious hatred for Christopher, the jokes reveal an additional element: their strikingly oral cannibalistic quality. The jokes followed her expression of transference hatred toward me in the form of an urge to throw jelly beans at me. She then threw the half-eaten jelly beans and told the jokes. Her eating spawned the jokes about babies being destroyed and eaten. It is my opinion that the jelly beans stand for babies and that they may symbolize the earlier sesame seed–egg–jelly bean–baby. Of additional interest is what appeared to be her subclinical anorexia nervosa, an eating disorder with underlying cannibalistic destructive fantasies often involving babies. Cannibalistic fantasies to kill, cook, and eat a younger sibling have been reported elsewhere (Mintz 1983a).

When I saw the mother in consultation, she reported a major improvement in Louise's asthma. She indicated that the father still felt it was all physical. She clarified for me that, contrary to Louise's statement, the allergist had said that the cause of the asthma was both psychological and organic.

The mother spoke of how angry and burdened she had felt in the raising of four children. She clarified Louise's relationship with Christopher. The asthma began when Christopher was 2 months old. Louise always wanted to feed him the bottle, but she had to be watched closely, because she would twist the nipple in his mouth and choke off the milk. The mother brought in some early pictures. One showed Louise grimacing, her arms almost choking around Christopher's neck. In another she was grimacing and smiling while he was crying.

The conflict over choking emerges repeatedly in Louise's history and behavior, beginning with the mother's recognition of Louise's attempts to twist Christopher's nipple in his mouth and choke off the milk supply, continuing in the early pictures of Louise making choking gestures around Christopher's neck. In the next few months of treatment, the choking impulses reemerged when she twisted and destroyed soda cans whirled her bracelet, and obsessively twisted and turned the Rubic Cube for hours. Her tenacious pursuit of excellence with the Rubic Cube may have been fueled by an externalization of her impulse to choke herself, or by a sublimation of her unconscious impulses to choke her brother or me. The impulse to choke her family emerged early, suggesting that the asthma was a response to it, rather than the reverse. Unfortunately, at the time when Louise was twisting the can or the Rubic Cube, I had no opportunity to show her a link between her twisting, choking behavior and her previous impulses to choke Christopher, since I had received that information from her mother and not from the patient.

In the next few weeks Louise continued her provocative, testing behavior, threatening to walk out of the sessions and quit. I pointed out that no one knew what went on in the sessions, but if she quit, her parents would realize that she was not cooperating and hand her her head, since they saw that she was much better. She stopped talking about leaving and just read, sang songs, or listened to music.

In one session she played the radio very loud and, when I objected, asked me to make her turn it down. As I got up, she turned it down. The rest of the session she spent tearing up the napkin on the couch into little pieces, which she held in front of her mouth and blew onto the floor for me to pick up. I pointed out that she was expressing hatred toward me by blowing air without words. When she exhaled angry words on the air, she became frightened, and previously she had choked them back in an asthmatic attack.

I added that while she kept accusing me of being stupid, it was she who was acting foolish; she was making believe that she did not have problems, and risking asthma, instead of realizing that people could die from it. "Prove it." I told her that a patient in a local hospital had died from it a few weeks earlier. "I'm not that sick." I reiterated that she had all those feelings of hatred long before she met me and was spilling it out on me when it was probably meant for her family.

Having been advised that I would be out of the country the following week, she asked where I was going. When I told her, she replied, "Good, I'll be glad to get rid of you." I wondered whether she would miss being here. "Bull, I hate it here. Will you send me a telegram?" I said that I'd write her.

In the next session she continued ripping up paper, threatening to throw it in my face. If I tried to stop her, she warned, she'd yell rape and get me in trouble. She seemed to be acting out a sadomasochistic fantasy in which her provocative behavior of throwing something into my face would bring retaliation by my shoving something into her body, with a displacement from the oral cavity to the genitals. In asthmatic attacks it is often the reverse. Karol explains this quite well in Chapter 12.

On one occasion in the following weeks, the father called to report that the patient had suffered an asthmatic attack one night that required a hospital visit and adrenalin because she "forgot" to take her pill. In the session that followed she did not refer to it. When I remarked that her father had phoned about it, she refused to discuss it.

For a number of sessions, while she continued to be silent and angry, our disagreements took the form of betting. I suggested that if I won the bet, she could talk about her worries, and that if she won, she could talk about anything she wished. "You're so stupid. If I win, I don't talk, and if you win, you don't talk." I added, "Then we would never talk and you wouldn't get better. I still wouldn't be able to understand why you need to suffer. Even your nose is plugged. Do you want a cough drop?" "OK."

Following an episode of the flu, the patient returned to our long-standing bet, but it couldn't have anything to do with talking. "You have all those diplomas about thinking—think of something." I finally suggested that if she won, I'd get her any kind of ice cream at the ice cream parlor. If I won—"Then *I* buy it for *you*," she said. She came over and shook hands. She won. At the ice cream parlor, she was silent but affable. She complained of the residue of the flu. She was particularly bitter that her mother sent her for the sessions while ill, thinking that she was using the flu symptoms as an excuse. When I tried to discuss the issue, she told me to shut up or she would vomit on my couch.

In mid-March, after many sessions during which she did homework, she advised me to shut up because she was studying for her French test. I pointed out that she was acting as if this were a study hall instead of her analytic hour. I was not unduly concerned about her grade, I told her; I was aware of her various excuses not to talk, and my main interest was in helping her with her asthma. "If I don't talk," she said, "it's tough on you." I said it was an interesting idea and that she probably believed it. I suggested it was similar to her idea that when she had an asthmatic attack, she was hurting someone else and not herself. This was an important point, which I emphasized repeatedly. Patients with asthma and anorexia have grown up focusing upon achieving approval from others at the expense of dealing with their own self-interest. As a consequence they are primarily concerned about how their behavior affects others, giving little or no attention to how it affects themselves. Only by becoming increasingly aware that they focus upon the "other" at the expense of self-interest are they able to reverse the process. Louise really was concerned with the effect of her self-destructive behavior upon others, and not with how damaging it was to her.

She became increasingly angry at my comments. "Will you shut up, or I'll spill this soda all over you. I have to go to the bathroom, or I'll explode all over you." Upon her return, I said her comment that she would explode all over me was interesting; because the fluid pouring out of her bladder was like the fluid pouring out of her bronchi in an asthmatic attack.

That interpretation was a condensation of a more elaborate dynamic formulation, and was presented to focus upon the further understanding of her asthmatic attacks. So furious at that point, she was unable to concentrate upon a more detailed explanation. An expanded conceptualization, however, would include the clinical sequences and their underlying meanings. Feeling unable to contain and control her emerging verbal temper tantrums, she displaced it into the acting-out impulse to pour soda over me. Feeling that discharge blocked, she regressively somatized with an impulse to urinate over me—that is, pouring urine instead of soda. She then ran to the restrooms to discharge the urine. All three types of behavior were ego solutions to dealing with perceived uncontrollable aggressive impulses: screaming abuse, spilling soda, and spilling urine. The urge to urinate on me would be a most clear illustration of urethral components in asthmatic patients described by Wilson in Chapter 13. The fourth solution to the uncontrollable aggressive outburst would be to regressively somatize with an outpouring of fluid into the bronchi in an asthmatic attack. Here the attack is directed against a body organ with the fluid pouring inside instead of outside; against the self, rather than the external object—examples illustrative of the typical psychosomatic solution. The asthma attack is just one of four regressive solutions.

As I discussed her willingness to choke herself and to think that she was really hurting someone else, she felt that I was insulting her intellect. I replied that I thought that she had a good brain, but she didn't always use it, especially when she hurt herself and thought she was really hurting someone else. Increasingly resentful at what I said, she took the empty soda can and began twisting it back and forth until she was able to rip it apart. I suggested that when she was angry, that was what she did with her bronchi. "When you have asthma, it's almost like taking your hands and twisting them around your neck back and forth until you choke." In retrospect, I should have interpreted her impulse to do that to my neck. Then, she would not have to listen. "You see how strong I am, stupid." She did not challenge the interpretation.

The next day the mother phoned to indicate that Louise was acting much more assertive with everyone. She had insulted her sisters, picked a fight with her brother Chris, and got her father a hat with horns for his birthday. The interpretation had contributed to the sublimation of some of the raw aggression into assertiveness, insulting comments, and disrespective behavior.

In the next weeks the patient continued her angry tirades, played her radio and tape recorder, brought in food, and did homework. In one session, as I attempted to talk, she put her fingers in her ears. I suggested that she was blocking out the truth, just as the Russians blocked the "Voice of America." She got furious, protesting that I was accusing her of being a Russian and that she hated the Russians. Because I had insulted her, she was leaving. A spirited interchange ensued. She said, "I get asthma from smoke, not worries. You're full of shit. If I died, my parents would sue you." If she died, I retorted, it might be because she did not cooperate here and because she wanted to die to spite me and other people. She then ripped up her magazine into little pieces and blew them all over the rug. "I'll be back with more garbage for you next time" — a clear illustration of anality in asthma and involvement in treatment.

By spring, Louise had been in treatment sixteen months. She continued to be resistant: not talking, reading, doing homework, playing her radio, eating, and chanting.

Provocativeness persisted; she threatened to spill soda on the couch, cut the couch with the soda can, and mark up the walls with Magic-Marker. On occasion, as she was about to mark up the wall, I felt obliged to take her Magic Marker away from her. I found it sufficient to get her to refrain from spilling the soda, to indicate that what went on here was confidential, but if she spilled soda all over the couch, a bill to her parents to replace the couch would probably reveal her activities here. Continuing to twist soda cans and the Rubic Cube was intrepreted as a sign of progress: twisting objects other than her neck.

At one point she reported to the father that if Dr. Mintz were smart enough or cared enough about her, he would get her to talk. In the service of attempting to quit treatment she had already told her parents that the treatment did not help, that she hated me, and that she was wasting her time by not talking. The parents continued to report sporadic asthmatic attacks, which the patient would deny. I pointed out that even the changed medication, which she felt had greatly reduced the asthma, had failed to prevent her attacks. I also stated that her parents indicated she was acting thoughtful and very considerate at home, so that the only person she showed anger toward was me. I took it as a compliment that she trusted me enough to be able to be angry with me, knowing that I understood her well enough not to reject her for it.

In one session she said her father had told her to show me how the Rubic Cube worked. "I'm showing you because I keep my word." She instructed me impatiently but would not let me touch it.

Later, as she was reading, I remarked, "You must have told your father that you don't tell me things, because he called to tell me that a memorial for your grandmother was taking place Sunday. It might be a difficult time for you." "I thought you said you'd be quiet," she said, and went on with her reading.

Her mother phoned on Monday to report that Louise had had a severe asthma attack Sunday night (after the memorial for her grandmother), and that she had had to go to the hospital. Louise had told her mother that she wanted to try and stop the attack herself. She said she had been successful in stopping three previous attacks that were not as severe. She arrived Monday afternoon, hostile and provocative. After a while I informed her that the mother had told me of the asthma attack. I added that we probably could have predicted the attack because we did not discuss her grandmother's memorial, and she covered up her upsetting feelings and got asthma instead.

The idea of writing a poem came up, and she asked, "What kind of a poem shall I write?" I suggested a poem about asthma, trust, or friendship.

As I sit in the sun, I hear a lonely bird chirping
I think he is only singing to make his day worthwhile,
Otherwise if he hadn't had such a lovely voice
He would have stayed asleep.
Little did he know, that his lovely song
Was not only for him, but for me, too.

While my suggestion about the poem was an attempt to encourage her to focus upon her asthma and upon the possibility of trusting me with her thoughts and feelings, I did not expect the poem to incorporate those concepts; I thought she suggested the poem as another diversion. Unconsciously she did not view it this way. The poem revealed her overdetermined identification with the masculine bird, her sense of loneliness, and her search for warmth and understanding, with the accompanying thought that no one was listening to her chirping. The last lines expressed her surprise in recognizing that someone else was really listening.

During the next two sessions she did more singing, but I chose not to connect it for her to the bird in the poem. Instead, I told her I liked the song she was singing. Would she sing it louder? "I'm not here to make you happy." During one of her silences I mentioned again that I would be away during the Easter week and I hoped she would not miss me too much or get asthma. She responded by faking a spell of choking. She had been doing this with increasing frequency to indicate incredulity and anger. In spite of her conscious denials, evidently she had accepted the concept that choking communicated a message, and she was willing to consciously use its symbolism herself. While consciously she continued to protest everything I said, unconsciously she agreed with it and related in the same symbolic medium. She continued to talk, but now in hand sign language, and asked what part of New Mexico I was visiting.

When I returned from my vacation, she refused to tell me what had gone on. I mentioned that when I had returned a phone call from her mother, and Louise answered, I was surprised to hear a considerate, thoughtful, polite and intelligent person on the other end of the phone. I realized that she hadn't spoken to me that way for over eight months. "I didn't know that it was you, stupid." She added that the family was attending a big celebration in Montreal over the weekend and she would miss her Friday appointment. "I thought you'd be glad that I wasn't here."

I replied that it was an interesting comment, and I wondered why she made it. Silence. I added that after all the insults she had given me, she might have felt that I might be glad to be rid of her. It might still surprise her that I was not mad at her. Silence. Then as she renewed the insults, I remarked that she had experienced relatively little nasorhinitis this spring, and much less asthma during the past winter. I suggested that if we both worked, she'd make more progress. Silence.

In an interview with the mother, she volunteered how guilty she felt about forgetting another of Louise's sessions. She thought it was related to her own feeling that no one was taking care of her, which made it very difficult for her to take care of Louise. She added that she felt filled with rage and never was able to express it to anyone. At the end of the session, with great embarrassment, she stated that she carried around in her purse the bracelet that I had given Louise for Christmas. Evidently, the mother was in competition with Louise for my attention and unconsciously resented Louise's opportunity to get well, while she herself was still asthmatic and had no one concerned about her. This resentment was unconsciously communicated to Louise by events such as the mother's forgetting the session. Getting close to the analyst would make Louise feel that she was depriving her mother, and this feeling would fill her with guilt. It was also evident that Louise did not buy the mother's explanation that she was holding the bracelet out of fear that Louise would lose it. Finally, Louise, who identified with her mother, recognized the mother's inability to express her frustration and anger out of fear of rejection. Louise was able to express such feelings without fear of rejection or retaliatory anger only toward the analyst. In spite of the mother's problems and her asthma, she refused to consider any treatment.

A number of sessions later, still silent, interrupting whenever I attempted to talk, Louise began reading a book. I continued my efforts to interpret her behavior to her, anticipating an eruption of singing or chanting to drown me out. Instead she remained silent, and occasionally she put down the book and listened. Lying on the couch, she bent her knee so that it obscured my seeing her face. As I swung my revolving chair to get some slight view of her face, she imperceptibly moved her knee to obscure it. Swinging my chair in the opposite direction produced another slight movement of her knee. I continued to speak as I had in other sessions, but for the first time I emphasized different aspects of her sadism. I quietly pointed out that she acted mean, nasty, and spiteful and that she knew it and I knew it. She was afraid, however, for anyone else to know it, so she acted like a good little girl with everyone but me. This was a side of her she didn't want to know about, because she felt guilty when she acted that way — so guilty that she had to punish herself with asthma. She knew that she acted mean to me when I didn't deserve it, but she knew that I understood her and wouldn't reject her for it.

The healthy part of her, I continued, was thoughtful, intelligent, considerate, and wanted to get well, but the sick part of her was mean, spiteful, and nasty. She knew that the mean side of her was there, because she had been continually demonstrating it to me, but she didn't know how to get rid of it. While she was afraid to talk to me about it, she knew that she certainly couldn't talk to anyone else about it.

I added that I could help her get well, but I couldn't make her well. If I could, I would, in spite of how nastily she had acted, because I knew that she couldn't help what she was doing. She didn't know how she had gotten this way or how she could get rid of being this way. I added that she was bright and she could get well. She would not have to stay asthmatic or mean, but she had to work and talk with me about her thoughts and feelings.

As I spoke, she played with her crutch, dangling it close to one of the pictures on the wall. I pointed out that she was toying with the idea of damaging the picture. That would be inadvisable, because when the parents got the repair bill, they would find out about all this spitefulness that she was afraid to show them. She thumped the crutch down hard against the couch, and I told her I thought she was thinking of hitting me with it. "I could, you know." I acknowledged that she could, but that was not the issue. The point was that she was thinking of hitting me even as I was trying to help her.

During that session, she listened, despite her attempts to defend herself by reading, which did not work. She was upset enough so that she did not want me to see her face. She did not sing or blow up, and she left with a look of sadness on her face.

The respite was brief, however, as Louise returned to the attack in the remaining sessions before the summer vacation. She threatened to shove her sneaker down my throat and walked over to me with it, asking what I would do. I said that I would stop her, and I pointed out that her impulse to choke me contributed to her own choking. Thus finished eighteen months of analysis.

In the fall the mother reported Louise had had her best summer ever. She was bursting with energy, talking about telling off all the nuns at school, and arguing with her siblings all the time. In the first session of the fall, Louise was reasonably friendly, apologized for being late, and offered me some of her potato chips, which I accepted. At the end of a subsequent session, she volunteered, "I hope that you're not going to try and get me to talk. My mother used to try, and when I didn't, she would explode and scream at me . . . lots and lots of times." Additional transference aspects of her uncooperativeness were thus further clarified.

In the next two months she continued her hostile, provocative behavior, admixed with an underlying acceptance of me. It became increasingly clear, however, that one of the major impediments in Louise's inability to develop a closer working alliance was her parents. She recognized that both of them resented her closer relationship with me, viewing it as a rejection of them. A major need to fight with me was to reassure her parents that she would not abandon them in order to be close with me. Therefore, they need not abandon her.

In further provocative arguments, she threatened to vomit on the couch if I did not shut up. Then she accused me of being nasty to her.

In one session she suddenly asked, "Do you forgive me for everything?" I pointed out her guilt for her aggression, my understanding, and my thoughts that she was not the terrible person she thought she was.

In one session I suggested that she did not wish to admit that maybe she liked me or wanted to get closer to me, because she was afraid that something would happen. It was important for her to tell her parents that she hated me. In subsequent sessions I repeated the suggestion that she was afraid to acknowledge that she liked me. She cursed at me and left me "Fuck you" notes. After writing me one such note, she asked when my birthday was. I wondered what kind of a gift she was planning; she violently denied she was planning any. "You'll never get close to me." I suggested that under that outer shell of an impossible little creature was a heart of gold. She defended with, "You'll never get close to my heart . . . I'll tell my father on you."

I felt I needed to see the father because of Louise's continued resistance. During the course of two sessions he acknowledged that he didn't like anyone getting between him and his children. When they visited Spain, he even resented the relatives' attempts at getting close to his children. He didn't like to share them with anyone. He originally had told himself that I was working for him as his employee, just doing a job that he couldn't do, and therefore he should not be jealous, but it didn't help.

I explained that if she unconsciously sensed he did not wish her to get close to me, she would have a need to obey him out of fear of his disapproval or of losing him. The closeness was a necessary prerequisite for trusting and working out problems, I said, but when the analysis was over, I would play little role in her life. This seemed to reassure him. He agreed to try harder to encourage her involvement in the treatment.

When later, without calling me, he canceled a session so that Louise could go on a religious retreat, I saw him for two more sessions. His excuse was that they were a religious Catholic family, and he did not wish to interfere with her enjoying life. I reemphasized the seriousness of her illness, and he unleashed an antipsychiatric tirade. His sister had undergone psychiatric treatment, he said, and as a consequence became very angry with her parents and did not speak with them for years. Was this his worry, then? He acknowledged that it was. He said again that he would try.

Meanwhile the mother phoned to indicate that Louise had had another asthmatic attack. While at the hospital, Louise told her mother she felt like a bomb about to explode, and she might be mad at her father, who still insisted that she remain at the Catholic school. She told her mother that she was able to fight better with her father about it, "because I fought with the best . . . Dr. Mintz." The father phoned the next day and told me:

> You'll have a new patient today. I spoke with her and told her that you cared about her, and I cared about her and that she has to get better. It can't go on this way. I told her how much she loved her grandmother, and that if she were alive, she would want her to cooperate and get better. I asked what she did in the sessions, and she told me all the ways she wasted time, and she wanted a woman psychiatrist. I told her that we weren't starting over, that she was much better . . . and I wanted her to get well. She began to cry and sob and didn't say anything, but she acted as if a weight was taken off her shoulders.

In the next session later that day, Louise arrived with a note:

> Take note:
> I have given up.
> I am too tired to fight anymore.

I am willing to cooperate, beginning Friday, not today.
Please don't ever mention this note to me or to anyone else
or you can forget it.

Louise missed the next session, because her father forgot to phone
the cab, so it was evident that his problems persisted. While Louise
renounced open resistance, it persisted in different forms. She no longer
brought in homework, radio, books, and knitting, but she was still
uncooperative and provocative. She would sadistically ask me what she
should talk about, hoping to get me to make a suggestion, to which she
could then reply in one or two words. "I have lots of interests, why don't
you ask me to talk about one of them?" Anticipating that I would see her
father soon, she wondered if I would tell him that she was not cooperating, because she was. I reflected that she was cooperating on the surface
and was uncooperative underneath, mirroring the father's behavior. His
unconscious resistance to her involvement in treatment was reflected in
her resistance: a major therapeutic problem without his being in treatment. I replied that she was pretending to cooperate, but she was really
giving worthless information. Later in the session she asked, "Tell me
what I could do to get better without having to yell at you forever, . . .
yell at someone else?" I replied that it certainly was a subject worth
discussing. "But what do others do? If you really cared about me, as you
say you do, you'd tell me." As I explained that the solution was not
available in one or two sentences but required that we work together, she
replied, "Bullshit."

In the next session she insisted that if I didn't pick the topic, I didn't
care about her and didn't want to help her. If I didn't want to help her,
I responded, would I tolerate her nonsense for so long? She continued
fencing. I suggested that she had been angry at me for a long time and
perhaps she could talk about it. "I hate you!" Silence. I pointed out that
she had been angry at me for over a year and she could only come out
with three words.

"I'd like you dead . . . why don't you ask me why?"

"Why?"

"That's all you can say? Can't you think of an idea of your own?"

I discussed again her having all these angry feelings toward other
people, like thoughts of their being dead, and her having switched the
feelings to me. I explained that she felt guilty about it and thought of
choking herself with an asthma attack. She denied having the idea.

EMERGING COOPERATION

At last, and for the first time, Louise began a session with "hello." Then, defensively, she asked me what she should discuss. Later, when I asked why she hated me so, she professed ignorance and immediately declared, "I have to go to the bathroom before I explode." Upon her return, I pointed out that people who hold their feelings in often go to the bathroom and let their feelings out that way." I added, after a period of silence, that when she first began to yell and hate me, I felt that it was all right. She was getting some of the angry feelings out at me instead of hurting herself by choking with asthma, and the asthma attacks had stopped 90 percent. But now we had gone through more than a year of her yelling at me without her attempting to figure out why she was so angry and how she had gotten so sick. She had stopped making progress. "OK, but if I don't yell at you, what should I do?" With the session over, I suggested that we could continue the next time. For the first time she cleaned up her five gum wrappers before leaving.

In the next session, she again asked me to bring up topics, because she didn't know what to say. I explained that I was not impressed with her attempt to act stupid, because I knew that she was bright and that she was acting dumb just to be uncooperative. "All right, let's talk about yesterday. What can I do if I don't act angry at you?" I indicated that she must be angry at someone. "I could yell at my friends, but they'd all leave me. You want me to say my family, but I can't." I told her she had already acknowledged how angry she was at her father and brother, but she hadn't mentioned her mother. "She's a bitch. She doesn't bring clothes to school that I forget, . . . or notebooks that I leave home."

In the next session she continued berating her mother. She said she was afraid of screaming at her, because her mother screamed back and frightened her.

"Like 'Eaak'?"

"That's not funny. What should I do?"

I explained my understanding of her plight. When she was filled with angry feelings and fearful that she couldn't keep them in, she would have an asthmatic attack, choke the feelings back, and punish herself for them.

"That was the way I was doing it. You are supporting my idea. You're supposed to be showing me a different way. If she screams at me, I get all frustrated."

I said I could well understand just how she felt. She smiled. "You're not supposed to say that." I suggested that she screamed at me the way she felt that her mother screamed at her.

The next several sessions were filled with provocative insults and with attempts to get me to talk about other patients or tell her what to do. She showed no realistic willingness to discuss any of her many asthmatic attacks or the events that preceded them. A number of times she voiced a concern that if she did not scream at me, she was afraid of getting asthma. "I realize that when I scream at you, I don't wheeze, but when I don't scream, I start wheezing, and I'm afraid to stop screaming." Nevertheless, she still was extremely manipulative, and she was unwilling to discuss events leading up to attacks, what was bothering her at the time of the attacks, or alternative ways of avoiding attacks. She did acknowledge, however, that when she awakened one night with asthma, she could not remember having had any dream. On other nights she had repeated dreams "of my contact lens breaking," but she was unwilling to think about what that might have meant to her or to associate to it. Because of her extreme uncooperativeness, I did not attempt to consider with her that the broken contact lens might have had something to do either with not wanting to see or with concerns over losing contact with someone.

In January, after 18 months of constant attacks upon me, she became a little more cooperative. The topic of fighting between her father and mother came up, and I acknowledged how she must have felt, caught in the middle. Her mother would cry and run to visit the priest, and her father would then attack the church. When little, she would lie in bed and listen to noises of the fighting drift upstairs into her room. She never knew what was going to happen next, and she was afraid. I empathized with her. It must have been difficult for a little girl in bed, not knowing what would happen. She must have kept so many upset feelings inside. Her eye began tearing, and she reported that it came from her allergy shot. I suggested that tearing eyes sometimes come from holding tears back when a person is upset inside. "But what could I do? I can't kick the door down . . . or yell at people . . . and have no friends."

I acknowledged her dilemma. Now that she had recognized that yelling at me made her feel better, I wondered what else might be possible. "Well, I don't want to change my personality. Everyone likes me this way." I agreed that if she blew up at her friends and lost them, it wouldn't be good for her.

"Well, I'm more assertive than I used to be, but if I get stale bread in the bakery, I don't want to bring it back. If someone gets ahead of me in a line, I don't say anything. Someone else says, 'That girl was ahead of you.' " I agreed that being assertive was difficult for her. However, I added, she seemed, to know the different ways that she could be assertive, so that the feelings of resentment didn't build up like a reservoir until she was afraid that they'd spill out of her. Then she would have to yell and scream at me, or choke them back with asthma.

"I think that the asthma is crying inside. I was wondering if twisting my knuckles would damage them?" I suggested that it was safer than twisting her throat. "If I cooperate 1010 percent, will I have to tell you everything?" I replied that all super secrets had the most important information. She picked up her gum wrappers and, for the first time, said goodbye.

Further exploration and trust emerged in the next few sessions. In one, she again lamented, "Either I lose friends or I don't breathe." Fears of the consequences of assertiveness intermingled with thoughts of cracking her knuckles, her back during gymnastics, and her toes, with my suggestion that she had cracking someone on her mind. She produced a hit list that included her mother, brother, two girlfriends, three boys in school, and her uncle. When she discussed her anger with one of her girlfriends, I wondered whether she smiled. "No, the smile is at you. . . . Do you want me to call you great grandmother? . . . That's how you act toward me." (Great-grandmother was a favorite relative.)

In another session she volunteered that she was a good poet. "Do you want to hear a poem?" "Yes." "Inspire me." She replied.

Inspiration
A warm spring day
With flowers blooming
A sunrise
A newborn baby
A birthday cake
Inspiration.

These sessions clearly reflected more cooperation, an emerging willingness to converse, and self-reflection. She manifested a more positive transference and saw the analyst as her "inspiration." Just as her earlier hatred toward the analyst was replaced by feelings of affection, so the previous tornadolike destructive inhalation was replaced in her poem by a more peaceful "inspiration" of rebirth, hope, and enjoyment. Her request, "Inspire me," can be taken as her wish for me to inhale or "inspire" her, to keep her inside me, with me as her protector, as her great-grandmother. Conversely, it also can represent her identification with me, "inspiring me" inside her body. She would keep me with her as a positive introject to counter all the previous negative introjects, which either she destroyed with her sucking-up tornado inhalations, or she feared would destroy her. Again it emphasizes the importance of the movement of air.

In the next eight sessions, her sarcasm seemed related to distrust of the treatment and her fear that asserting herself would result in rejection by all her friends. I pointed out that assertive people had friends. In playing a board game that she brought in, she stated, "I'd like to kill you with this dagger. If I blow on you, you die." We had spoken earlier about her constant gum-chewing and blowing of bubbles, which I interpreted as exhaling air without any angry words. She refused, however, to reflect further upon, "If I blow upon you, you die." It was a very clear reference to the destructive, lethal impulses unleashed by the exhaling of air. She had previously demonstrated these impulses through projections into tornados and volcanos, and in the transference with the "blowing your brains out." This time there was not the slightest ambiguity. "If I blow on you, you die." What better reason to choke back the respiratory movement of air.

Louise spoke about her nasorhinitis, which seemed to have replaced her asthma. She confided that five years of shots did not seem to have helped either group of symptoms. This observation reflected the principle that progress in treatment without full resolution of the basic unconscious conflicts often results in a shift from a serious psychosomatic illness to a less serious one. This concept is elaborated in a previous paper (Mintz 1980–1981).

Louise's further references to chewing gum led me to comment about her impulses to chew out people. "I also used to bite my nails. I had a fight with Gregory in the back of the church, and I wanted to sink my nails into his neck." This is again a clear reference to her identification with the destructive bird who rips and claws and is punished by being given away. I commented that she probably used to bite her nails to keep them from growing sharp, so that she would not be able to sink them into someone's neck when she got mad at them and was afraid of losing her temper. This interchange was accompanied by Louise's sudden heavy breathing.

In the next session she reminded me of the baby jokes, including the one about the live baby under a pile of dead ones eating its way out. Regressive cannibalistic fantasies associated with her anorexia were again mobilized as she attempted to deal with her aggression.

Louise continued her provocative behavior, interspersed with periods when she was cooperative and insightful. After endless denial about the cause of one of what now had become very infrequent asthmatic attacks, she finally burst out with a diatribe against her mother, who had insisted that she go to a summer camp she hated. The understanding emerged via the transference, where Louise screamed at me that she didn't know what had caused the asthmatic attack. I suggested that she really wanted to scream at someone else. "So what. If I screamed at my mother, she'd kill me. . . . She once punched out a 300-pound woman. She has hit me, but this way if I hurt myself, I control the amount I get hurt." I acknowledged her dilemma, and I suggested trying a solution in which she did not have to get hurt by herself or by her mother.

In the next session she voiced her fear that any yelling at her mother would provoke her mother to scream even more. She seemed to accept an interpretation that she choked off her throat at the point when angry thoughts and feelings were going to pour out of her. She remembered an episode when her mother was screaming at her and she began to wheeze. Her mother said, "Stop that," and she did. She was unwilling to discuss the episode further.

The following month she drew "bubble letters," which she associated to blowing air into bubble gum. She drew a peaceful rainbow scene, which she changed into a windy, thunder-and-lightning storm. Then she drew a cartoon where an elephant jumped upon a giraffe's neck and twisted it out of shape. In the next day's cartoon, a cow fought with an elephant and twisted its trunk in a knot so it couldn't breathe, and the elephant pulled off the cow's udders. The cartoons suggest a peaceful rainbow scene with a storm surging underneath. Identifying with both the choked giraffe and the elephant, she pulled off the udders of the nonnurturing mother.

In one session, after a great deal of her arguing, I attempted to paraphrase what I thought she had said: that she had a great deal of difficulty in confiding in people, that she kept upsetting feelings inside and stayed upset, and that sometimes the upsetting feelings set off the asthma. "That's the first time you ever said anything correct." Those ideas, however, had been spelled out for her for the past two years without acceptance. I told her how I had known that she was upset over her grandmother's death, and I had tried to help her with her feelings about it so that she would not get asthma, but she must have been so unhappy that she just couldn't talk. "Yes."

At that point the patient had been in analysis for two and a half years. The father called for an appointment, and he described Louise's improvement. There had been almost no asthmatic attacks all winter, a further improvement over the previous winter. This spring, too, her severe nasorhinitis had subsided markedly. The father was particularly delighted by her improvement, because he had been just offered an important promotion that he felt he could not refuse. It involved moving the family to Chicago in the fall.

Louise continued her sessions in the month prior to summer vacation. We discussed termination. Louise again visited her relatives in Spain for the summer. I saw her for a week in the fall, and we stopped.

SUMMARY

A detailed description of the psychoanalytic treatment of a 12-year-old girl with a case of anorexia and severe asthma was presented with emphasis upon the dynamic features and techniques of treatment. Although the asthma began at 18 months of age, a clear-cut genetic component was present, and well-established allergic and infectious factors existed. The asthmatic illness subsided during an incomplete psychoanalytic treatment. The outcome highlights the concept that the illness is overdetermined and multidetermined. Modification of psychological factors during the analysis resulted in the clearing up of the illness.

Over the years I have reflected upon the course of the two and one half-year analysis. I felt satisfied with the symptomatic relief in a teenager who was so ill for so long. When Louise began treatment, I had doubts about whether an analysis could effect symptomatic resolution in so sick a girl. I was also aware that during severe attacks, her respiratory reserves were almost exhausted, so that she was unable to walk, and had to be carried up the stairs to the bedroom. Under those circumstances, any experience that suddenly and markedly impaired her respiratory functioning, might well result in her demise. At the same time, however, I was also acutely aware that for Louise to be this sick, the degree of infantile sadistic aggression must be intense. In a regressed, sadistic fashion, she was controlling people and situations that she could not deal with directly by threatening to die. Furthermore, her concern was entirely focused upon controlling the external object, with little awareness of the dire consequences to herself. It was important, therefore, for her not to feel that she had to control me with the threat of choking. Otherwise, her sadistic impulses to control me by choking might outweigh her attempt to get well. I discussed this mechanism in an ulcerative colitis patient in Chapter 9.

The dilemma was to avoid inappropriate, ill-timed interpretations that would set off a regressive, potentially fatal illness. Concomitantly, I had to indicate that I was not afraid of her sadism and could truly accept all forms of her aggression, so that she would not feel forced to regress and sadistically express it against her respiratory system with asthma. The anticipated death of her beloved grandmother precipitated a crisis early in the analysis before a working alliance was fully established and before she had progressed in treatment to the point that she could experience very painful feelings and express them in my presence. I was concerned that the grandmother's death might set off a severe downhill course that could not be interrupted. Her total denial of the situation, and absence of thoughts and feelings with isolation and reaction formation was an additional bleak feature. I felt that it was crucial to deal with the impending death, in spite of her strong resistance and the beginning of intensely negative behavior. Under less dire circumstances, had it been possible to wait, I should not have pushed discussion of a so desperately defended conflict.

I also thought that there were indirect but positive feelings expressed during those two years. I wondered whether the transference might have been negative, even without the turmoil related to the grandmother. Silverman (Chapter 14) reported intense negativism for eight months in his asthmatic patient, with an analysis lasting seven years. The aggression was extreme in this patient, resulting in self-destructive life-threatening symptoms. Perhaps, if the analysis had continued into the third year, a more exploratory and a less chaotic experience might have evolved.

It was also clear that both parents unconsciously opposed her working in analysis, in spite of their conscious wishes for her to get well. The father strongly opposed her close relationship with me at what, he felt, was his expense. The mother resented Louise's opportunity for a close supportive relationship: one that she herself cherished. Neither were willing to enter treatment. At some level, Louise must have recognized the parents' ambivalence, which fed her own resistance.

I think that this case highlights the importance of psychological factors in this patient's illness. In the face of asthmatic disease beginning at 18 months, complicated by genetic, allergenic, and infectious factors, marked parental ambivalence, severe asthma for four years prior to analysis, a marked crisis early in the analysis, the analysis was still able to clear up the asthmatic symptoms in a two and one-half year incomplete analysis that primarily focused upon the aggressive component of the disease.

In the years following treatment, her uncle was kind enough to phone me during Christmas holidays to inform me, that for the past seven years, Louise has been relatively asymptomatic — occasionally requiring an inhaler — but has had no asthma attacks that were interfering with her functioning. She was off all medication, which she had been using for years without being able to control the asthma. There was also no obvious anorexia. In subsequent years, I lost contact with the uncle.

REFERENCES

Abrahamson, H. A. (1961). Psychodynamics of the intractably asthmatic state. *Journal of the Children's Asthma Research Institute and Hospital* 1(1):18.

Deutsch, L. (1980). Psychosomatic medicine from a psychoanalytic viewpoint. *Journal of the American Psychoanalytic Association* 28(3):653–699.

———— (1987). Reflections on the psychoanalytic treatment of patients with bronchial asthma. *Psychoanalytic Study of the Child* 42:239–260.

———— (1988). Psychosomatic medicine: a psychoanalytic dilemma. Unpublished manuscript.

Dunbar, H. F. (1938). Psychoanalytic notes relating to syndromes of asthma and hay fever. *Psychoanalytic Quarterly* 7:25.

French, T. M., and Alexander, F. (1941). Psychogenic factors in bronchial asthma. *Psychosomatic Medicine Monographs,* vols. 2 and 4. Washington, DC: National Research Council.

Gehl, R. (1985). Floor discussion, New Jersey Psychoanalytic Society. Hackensack Medical Center, Hackensack, NJ: September 1985.

Jessner, L., Lamont, J., Long, R., Rollins, N., Whipple, B., and Prentice, N. (1955). Emotional impact of nearness and separation for the asthmatic child and his mother. *Psychoanalytic Study of the Child* 10:353.

Karol, C. (1980–1981). The role of primal scene and masochism in asthma. *International Journal of Psychoanalytic Psychotherapy* 8:577–592.

Knapp, P. (1963). The asthmatic child and the psychosomatic problem of asthma: toward a general theory. In *The Asthmatic Child: Psychosomatic Approach to Problems and Treatment,* ed. H. Schneer, pp. 234–255. New York: Harper & Row.

Lieberman, M., and Lipton, E. (1963). Asthma in identical twins. In *The Asthmatic Child,* ed. H. Schneer, pp. 258–274. New York: Harper & Row.

Mintz, I. L. (1980–1981). Multideterminism in asthmatic disease. *International Journal of Psychoanalytic Psychotherapy* 8:593–600.

—— (1983a). Anorexia and bulimia in males. In *Fear of Being Fat: The Treatment of Anorexia Nervosa and Bulimia,* rev. ed., ed. C. P. Wilson, C. C. Hogan, and I. L. Mintz, pp. 263–303. Northvale, NJ: Jason Aronson, 1985.

—— (1983b). The psychoanalytic therapy of severe anorexia. In *Fear of Being Fat: The Treatment of Anorexia Nervosa and Bulimia,* rev. ed., ed. C. P. Wilson, C. C. Hogan, and I. L. Mintz, pp. 217–244. Northvale, NJ: Jason Aronson, 1985.

Reiser, M. (1975). Changing theoretical concepts in psychosomatic medicine. In *American Handbook of Psychiatry,* vol. 4., ed. M. F. Reiser, pp. 477–500. New York: Basic Books.

Sperling, M. (1949). The role of the mother in psychosomatic disorders in children. *Psychosomatic Medicine* 2:377.

—— (1963). A psychoanalytic study of bronchial asthma in children. In *The Asthmatic Child,* ed. H. Schneer, p. 138–165. New York: Harper & Row.

—— (1978). *Psychosomatic Disorders of Childhood.* New York: Jason Aronson.

Wilson, C. P. (1980–1981). Parental overstimulation in asthma. *International Journal of Psychoanalytic Psychotherapy* 8:601–620.

THE ROLE OF PRIMAL SCENE AND MASOCHISM IN ASTHMA

Cecilia Karol, M.D.

The word *asthma* comes from the Greek word for *panting,* and the Greeks defined *asthma* as a difficulty in breathing, accompanied by sound (Peshkin 1963). According to Lieberman and Lipton (1963), Hippocrates recognized the psychogenic aspects of the illness when he stated that "asthmatics must guard against anger." Immunobiologists, pharmacologists, and pulmonary physiologists have all agreed that whether the etiology of asthma is primarily hereditary or allergenic, the final common pathway in asthma is the same (Austen and Lichtenstein 1973). In spite of the increased drug armamentarium, death from asthmatic illness has increased in the past years (Siegal 1967).

HISTORICAL REVIEW

According to Trenting and Ripley (1948), in 1926 Ziegler and Elliott studied asthmatics without a history of protein sensitivity and concluded that asthma attacks seemed to be induced by psychic stimuli.

Faulkner (1941), looking through a bronchoscope, found that

bronchi dilated when pleasurable topics were brought up and constricted with unpleasurable ones.

Freud postulated early in his work (1925) that fantasies played a major role in the etiology of mental illness. He wrote that "unconscious fantasies are the immediate precursors of a whole number of hysterical symptoms." He attributed the formation of symptoms to reactivated fantasies and he postulated that a fantasy could be used defensively to either decrease anxiety or engender it further.

In "A Child Is Being Beaten" (1919), Freud described at length the psychological relevance of beating fantasies and showed how these fantasies were related to feelings of punishment for forbidden genital strivings representing, as well, a regressive substitute for sexual intercourse with father. The importance of these sadomasochistic fantasies are particularly relevant to the theme of this chapter.

Bacon (1956) postulated that asthma is a response to unconscious fears of damage of the respiratory system.

French (1939) observed that each of his asthmatic patients was exposed to sexual temptation that threatened his relationship with a parental figure—usually the mother. These patients subsequently confessed their forbidden impulses in an attempt to regain their mother's love. French also emphasized how asthma may be an equivalent of repressed rage related to the fear of loss of maternal love. The asthmatic attack was used to regain this affection. Finally, he stressed the importance of the mother–child relationship, especially aspects of the mother's unconscious hostility, overprotectiveness, and conflicts over separation anxiety.

Sperling (1949) emphasized specific parental relationships, not only between asthmatic children and their mothers, but in children with ulcerative colitis and other psychosomatic illnesses as well. The child is rejected by the mother when he is healthy and is rewarded by the mother when he is sick and helpless. She also stressed the continuum between asthma, phobias, and aggressive acting-out behavior. The aggressive behavior is unacceptable to the parents, who by now catalog their child as a "bad" child instead of a "sick" one, so that aggression is often replaced by asthmatic symptomatology.

In 1946, Brown and Goitein pointed out how early traumas such as birth of siblings, miscarriages, serious illness, primal-scene experiences, and death within the family may precipitate an asthma attack. Later in life, every crisis and stress may reactivate the traumatic event of early childhood, "repeating a patterned response of the organism via its particular organic safety valve of release in the 'oral' subject (the lung)."

Knapp and colleagues (1970) hypothesized that "the asthmatic state consists of conflicting fantasies, regressively mobilized, in which destructive urges and affects are inhibited by guilt and fear, while primitive urges to take in, retain, and eliminate through the respiratory apparatus, are accentuated."

Wilson (1968) reported the analysis of a woman whose dreams preceding her asthma attacks expressed primal-scene and pregnancy fears.

These authors have all emphasized sadomasochistic fantasies, a disturbed mother–child relationship, primal-scene experiences, and the importance of aggression in the development of psychopathology in asthma.

Through the presentation of the detailed clinical case that follows, I shall attempt to link these factors to the development of asthmatic attacks during the course of puberty and early adolescence.

CLINICAL EXAMPLE

Susan was a 13-year-old girl, slightly overweight, with fuzzy hair and glasses. She was referred because of considerable difficulties in completing homework assignments and her complaints about not having friends and being made fun of in school. She also acknowledged difficulties in falling asleep. Her parents reported that at one point, she had told them of a fantasy of wanting to hit and bite the penis of a neighborhood boy. On occasion, when angry, she would punch her thigh with her fist and wish that she were dead.

My impressions were that Susan had an obsessional neurosis with hysterical features. Shortly after her analysis began, her mother phoned and told me that Susan just had a mild asthmatic attack. It was then that I learned that she had been having asthmatic attacks since the age of $4\frac{1}{2}$, although this had not been presented during the initial evaluation.

Salient features in Susan's early history included the mother's recognition that she consciously rejected Susan when she was a baby, and the birth of a sister when Susan was 2 years of age. The mother acknowledged the preference for her second child, who was so much less demanding. Susan was reported to be a "colicky" baby who sucked on a pacifier until age 7. Although the mother provided her with the pacifier, she simultaneously told Susan that she shouldn't use it. Whenever at night Susan used the pacifier, she confessed as much to her mother the following morning. This compulsion to confess, and then be forgiven, regained parental approval, persisted throughout her analysis.

Although Susan's mother had graduated from college with honors, she had great difficulty in expressing herself. She appeared vague, guilty, and unsure of herself. The patient's identification with her mother was evident. She, too, suffered from an initial difficulty in communicating and establishing friends.

Susan's father, a brilliant academician, suffered from a severe obsessive-compulsive neurosis, which played a role in his need to control and tyranically rule the family. Interestingly, Susan's initial complaint to me was that her frizzy hair, inherited from her father, was the cause of her lack of popularity in school.

During the interview, I commented about her asthmatic attack. She stated that she had heard it was psychological and that she hated taking medication or receiving shots for it. An early development of a therapeutic alliance arose with our mutual agreement that we would work toward the resolution of the asthma as well as the elimination of the medication. Both Susan and her parents agreed to consider discontinuing the medication, and although she had asthmatic attacks during the course of the analysis, Susan made a conscious attempt to analyze the asthmatic attacks rather than use the medication.

Course of Treatment

The analysis ran for four and a half years. I will focus on the analysis of screen memories, fantasies, dreams, and the recovery of the memories directly connected with the initiation of her asthma and the triggering of subsequent attacks.

After Susan's initial visit, she had her first period and then was amenorrheic for a few months. At the time of the month when she was supposed to have her period, she was invariably euphoric and talked endlessly in an attempt to ward off intense castration anxiety. She felt that her body was falling apart, and she overate. She indulged with pleasure in displaced castration fantasies of breaking a leg or an arm, walking on crutches, or suffering an attack of appendicitis. In her fantasy, she attempted to arouse the desperation of her parents and the sympathy of her friends. She fantasized that something in her body would be broken or cut off, but only through an accident or an illness. By creating such a fantasy her ego was attempting to bind and control her anxiety, preventing the actualization of her fears in reality.

During the initial phase of her analysis, Susan, like a typical obsessional neurotic, talked endlessly about her school, classmates and teachers, describing ad infinitum each one of their characteristics, what they said, and how they looked. She was extremely vivid and sometimes brought drawings to illustrate her lengthy descriptions as well as her fantasies, in which she invariably ended up as the victim. During the first two years of her analysis, I had to interpret repeatedly, and make her aware of how provocative she was with her classmates and parents. She maintained a positive transference with me, although she constantly tried to provoke me into either feeling sympathy or scolding her for not doing her homework and for fighting with her sister. She gradually uncovered an increasing number of sadomasochistic fantasies, which she slowly began to recognize as playing an intimate role in setting off her asthmatic attacks.

One of these fantasies emerged quite early in her analysis. At one point she reported that she had an asthmatic attack earlier in the day because she became short of breath from running home from school. Her subsequent associations, however, led to uncovering a fantasy which immediately had preceded her asthmatic attack.

There were two girls. They were Hawaiian slaves. There were also two men, one a slave, and the other a master whose mistress was there. The male slave sexually attacked one of the Hawaiian girls, who promptly told the master about it. The attacker was punished by having a hot stone placed on his penis. He screamed and a girl threw water or mud at him. She in turn was punished for having helped him, and a stone was placed on her genitals until steam came out. The girls by now were twins, and one fell in love with the son of the owner of the farm. He was a white man, and therefore the master, and he did not allow her to go with him. The slave wanted to go to bed with her but did not, "although they were both naked."

Her associations led to the theme of oedipal rivalry. She remembered a book which her mother had forbidden her to read, *God's Little Acre*. She said that in the book, a girl went to bed with a man who was married and who said that he would get her when she was drugged. The wife came in and shot the man between his legs with his mother-of-pearl gun and hit the girl with a hairbrush.

Recounting this story filled her with disgust, because it reminded her of her feelings that sex was dirty unless the person was married.

This was the first time in the analysis that we had a direct link between an asthmatic attack and the conscious and unconscious fantasies that had immediately preceded it. The sadomasochistic fantasies associated with sexual relationships were so filled with recrimination and guilt that the patient felt the need for immediate punishment. Her harsh superego's attack was elucidated later in the analysis. In this case, the additional recounting of the story of the girl who went to bed with a married man mobilized Susan's own oedipal impulses and her guilt feelings to the degree that she experienced feelings of revulsion and disgust in the analytic session. The oedipal fantasy, in which she competed with the mother for her father, mobilized regressive sadomasochistic conflicts in which she punished and was punished.

It was my impression at this time — and this impression was confirmed later in the analysis — that the fantasy about the hot stone on the genitals and the emergence of steam appeared to be a displacement of a body organ function from the genitals upwards to the lungs. That traumatic insult to the genitals and the noisy emission of steam was symbolically represented in the asthmatic attack.

Another conflict was revealed that provided a connection between her asthma and primal-scene experience. This emerged after a boy had given her a ring as a gift. Interestingly enough, just as there were many manifestations of body-language symptomatology associated with the sadomasochistic fantasies, for example, experiencing disgust in the session, on this occasion she reported feelings of nausea on her way to the session. She was aware of her desire to remain home and eat. Additionally, she developed a headache and thoughts of not wanting to remember things. Her associations had to do with hostile feelings toward me, including impulses to hit me on the head with an axe. It was clear that the intense anxiety associated with emerging material provided the impetus for the somatic symptoms. Also it masked hostile feelings toward me as a transference object and secondary manifestation of hostility as a result of feeling coerced about revealing anxiety-laden material in the treatment. In the same session, she revealed that she was afraid of boys, because once she heard her father make love to her mother and thought that he was hurting her. Additionally, she expressed the fear that if a boy was on top of her, he could smother her and she would not be able to breathe.

It seems plausible that the somatic symptoms are closely related to the inability to cope with primal-scene conflict and particularly with the auditory aspects of the primal scene, since she reported hearing sounds of wheezing. It also seems plausible that the headache reflected feelings of guilt about her hostility toward me in wishing to damage my head, and also her identification with a sadistic father who penetrates the mother during coitus. Some aspects of her inability to accept the emergence of femininity, as manifested by her early adolescence and by feelings of smothering, were also clearly evident by her amenorrhea.

The comments about the primal-scene experience were followed by a series of memories that led to the description of her first asthmatic attack at age 4. She was spending the summer at a beach resort in the company of her parents and sister. The sister had been ill, and while she was not clear as to what the circumstances were, she did remember having slept briefly in each parent's bed. At that time, she remembered seeing the parents having intercourse and also remembered that her parents discussed her mother's recent miscarriage. One day, at the beach, she was told not to go into the water above her knees. When father walked away and mother was not looking, she remembered falling under the water, looking up, and being pulled out of the water by the father. He admonished mother for not looking after her. Shortly thereafter, Susan developed pneumonia and, subsequently, her first asthmatic attack. Susan associated it to her being under the water and being smothered by her asthma, and as she talked during the session of her mother's miscarriage, she again felt nauseated and had fantasies of being pregnant and of getting an artificial penis by means of an operation.

Susan's comments about being smothered by the water seem to be related to her similar feelings about a boy being on top of her during intercourse. One might consider that the asthmatic's feelings of being smothered by exuding fluid in the bronchi during an asthmatic attack is closely related to fantasies of being smothered in the water and, in Susan's case, with the sensation of someone lying on top of her during sexual intercourse.

Just as many psychosomatic patients deny the realistic possibility of death from severe psychosomatic symptoms, asthmatic patients also do not accept death as a finality. They deny the realistic possibility of

suffocation through smothering by fluid in the bronchi with an unconscious intrauterine fantasy of life under water and regaining of the
long-lost and still-desired reunion with the mother. It is fair to presume
that one aspect of this fantasy is represented in the memory of being
under the water, looking up, and being pulled out of the water. (Two
years later in the analysis, when she again recalled this memory, she
added, "It felt safe to be under water; it was like being in my mother's
womb.") Her associations to the miscarriage seem to relate to feelings of
sibling rivalry with her sister, as well as to the ambivalent feeling about
the dead sibling and the miscarriage. The sibling rivalry was previously
alluded to in the fantasies about the twin sister and the girl who was
tortured by a hot stone placed on the genitals. This conflict was
additionally overdetermined and evidenced by revived feelings of
nausea, where she identified with her mother in her fantasies of
pregnancy, while also serving as the recipient of punishment for her
hostile feelings toward her mother and wishing that her babies would die.
These conflicts additionally determined her anxieties about sexual
relationships. The fantasy about obtaining an artificial penis by means of
an operation seemed to reaffirm her continued ambivalence over
accepting the emerging feminine role and an unconscious desire for
masculine strivings.

The patient continued to provide additional clinical material in the
same session. It is my feeling that adolescents characteristically can
provide tremendous outpourings of clinical material from time to time,
because of the fluidity of their psychic structure and the momentary
relaxation of defensive structures. This is not to suggest that the
associations and the symptomatology are not molded by both unconscious
drives and the defenses against these drives. She further recalled that
when she was 4, a neighbor's boy had shown her his penis, and she had
wanted to expose herself also but felt unable to do so. The penis envy
persisted and was now represented by regaining it through the fantasy of
biting it off. Again we see persistence of the inability to accept her
femininity and of the continued envy which arose in childhood, when she
felt so depleted that she was unable to express herself. The conflict over
her sexual identification seems therefore to serve as one of the determinants in the formation of her sadomasochistic character structure.

Additional associations led to the recovery of further memories while
on vacation at the beach. "There were two old lesbian ladies who
vacationed there. One went crazy and one died." Susan associated going

crazy with pregnancy and death with asthma. Her going crazy was linked to her identification with the lesbian lady, her renunciation of her own femininity, and her unacceptable sadomasochistic fantasies of wanting the penis by biting it off, which set off attacks of asthma. The sadomasochism here seems to be intimately tied to feelings of guilt over masculine strivings, hostility toward siblings — both born and unborn — and toward her mother, and fears of retaliation through death for this aggression.

Susan reported having had two repetitive dreams whose analysis provided additional understanding of the relationship between her primal-scene experiences and her asthma attacks. In the first dream, "I used to go up a staircase and there were people, but instead of people, there were carrots or maybe balls with eyes in them." The second dream: "I dreamed of going to the eye doctor — into a dark room."

Her associations to these repetitive dreams were as follows: "I was scared of these dreams, which kept repeating time and again. I still go to an old-fashioned eye doctor who has a long nose with a wart on it. He puts drops in my eyes which blur my vision. During summer vacation, I used to sleep with my parents in the same tent, and had to turn around so as not to see certain parts of their bodies when they undressed. At home sometimes, I lay in the dark on my bed and feared that I would hear my parents having sex or that I would see them through a crack in the closet door. Sometimes I felt that if I was blind I would be safe."

The patient appeared to be displacing conflicts from the genitals upwards to the eyes. The eyes, which were capable of penetrating the environment symbolically, stood for the phallus and her repressed masculine strivings. The fear of going blind represented displaced castration anxiety, already alluded to in previous fantasies and associations. In addition, the fear of the doctor who penetrates her eye with a long tube from which fluid is ejected, clearly appears to be sexual in nature and representative of her conflict over femininity. Her sadomasochistic interpretation of coitus is evident in her fears of seeing or hearing the activity, and the wish to be blind seems to reflect her defensive attempt to cope with these fearful sadomasochistic experiences. Further, her identification with both the victim and the attacker emerged more clearly in the analysis of an additional asthmatic attack. It occurred after her father screamed at her for not having helped her mother in the kitchen. In speaking about the asthmatic attack in the following session, she remembered that the night before, she had an apprehensive feeling that she could hear her parents having intercourse. She then commented about her desire to see the movie, *Oliver,* for a second time, because she was attracted to the episode where Jennie, the protagonist, made a peculiar sound when she was killed by her lover. "Oh! Oh!" Jennie screamed. The patient commented: "It sounded as if she were being raped."

It seemed clear from the associations that her preoccupation with parental intercourse viewed it as sadistic, and this concept was reaffirmed by the subsequent association of Jennie being killed, recognized by the patient as a rape. The sound that caught her attention was respiratory in nature and equated with breathing. This reflected thoughts of the parents' heavy breathing during coitus, where both killer and victim were present. It also reflected her own dyspnea, where she is ambivalently identifying with both the sadist in her masculine strivings and the victim in her feminine identification. This interpretation achieves added validity from her comment in a previous session of the fantasy of growing a penis and the thought that she could then rape me. These sadomasochistic sexual fantasies evident in her oedipal conflicts, as well as in the transference toward me, were so distressing to her that she fantasized killing both parents, a hoped-for solution to her torturing self-preoccupation.

Additional material, which shed further light on her breathing difficulties, followed the analysis of a dream. Susan's bedroom was separated from the parents' bedroom by a closet having two doors— essentially a corridor between the rooms. The door in the parents' room had no lock and could not be completely closed. In spite of Susan's repeated requests to the parents that the door be fixed, the parents' either postponed or ignored doing something about it. This behavior in which the parents unconsciously play a role in traumatizing the child with sexual activities, tends to confirm M. Sperling's (1949) comments about the role of the parents in activating psychosomatic symptomatology in their children. The dream was as follows: "A man or me or some people were running away. There were racks and closets. A person was hiding. I was breathing so hard that they found me."

Her associations to the dream were that on the previous day, she had a fearful fantasy that her father would attempt to rape her, and that she would refuse his overtures. Susan then commented about her fears of her headache and the fantasy that she might develop a brain tumor. She continued elaborating upon a whole series of hypochondriacal preoccupations. She was fearful of bleeding, of death, and of a deformity and bulge in her tooth. During this time in the analysis, she suddenly became amenorrheic, after having had normal regular periods. She became frightened and developed fantasies of something growing in her uterus, "maybe cancer." On one occasion, after a fight with her mother, she inadvertently licked the crayon that she had been using in her art sketches and immediately became fearful that she could be poisoned. Subsequent associations to the fantasy reverted back to memories, when she was 6 years old, of having given her sister a solution of chalk to drink, thinking that perhaps she might die.

The material seems to indicate a tremendous preoccupation with oedipal fantasies and their consequences. By leaving the door open between the rooms, the parents exposed the patient to the temptation to experience primal-scene activity. The dream where a person was hiding seems to be the patient who was breathing hard when she was discovered. The breathing represents a coalescing of breathing from sexual excitement, from terror at witnessing what to her was sadistic behavior and identification with both the mother and father, and the asthmatic attack. The associations seem to confirm this supposition, in that she reported a fantasy that her father would attempt to rape her and she would then refuse him. However, the ambivalent attitudes about her refusal seem to be demonstrated in the subsequent associations and in her behavior in the following weeks. The sudden amenorrhea, the fantasies of something growing in her head, and the fears of bleeding and death and of a deformity and bulge, all seem to indicate pregnancy fantasies. She confirmed this with the fear of a cancer growing in her uterus. These sadomasochistic, primal-scene conflicts played a major role in her asthmatic attacks, which grew worse during these weeks in the analysis. These conflicts were also supported by sadistic death wishes toward the sister. Susan's fear of being poisoned was linked to her childhood wishes to poison her sister. The aggression toward the sibling was also reported earlier in the analysis, and repeated itself during the subsequent analytic material.

These conflicts would characteristically erupt after violent arguments with the mother. She remembered thoughts of wanting to kill her mother, which would then be followed by breath-holding. She also recalled an interesting warning that the mother used to mention. Her mother's father had died of cancer of the lung. She told the patient that she should not cough in front of her, because "a person could kill someone with one's breath." She was referring to the ability of a tuberculosis patient to infect an innocent victim by coughing in his face. This seems to clearly indicate a threat that the exhaling of air or coughing is destructive and could kill. In the asthmatic attack, when the patient is filled with violence, the outpouring of air and anger is strangled and retained by the asthmatic state and the difficulty in the slow exhaling of air.

When she felt the impulse to kill the mother, two major defenses were mobilized: identification with the mother and turning the aggression against the self. The asthmatic attack represented a defense against a desire to kill the mother through the outpouring of the infected, contaminated air; at the same time choking herself by not being able to breathe.

These psychosomatic patients with frequent obsessional mechanisms typically associate thinking with doing. The unconscious belief in magic and the omnipotence of thoughts engenders great anxiety and fears that the destructive thoughts would result in the actual death of the hated object. As the analysis proceeded, a great deal of pregenital material emerged, particularly related to intrauterine sadomasochistic fantasies having to do with herself and her sister. These fantasies were closely related to the development of her first asthmatic attack. She again recalled the experience at age 4 of falling into the water. This time, however, she emphasized memories about the mother's miscarriage, her having viewed the mother's bleeding, and her fears of her mother's death. The hostility toward the sister, and toward the mother who was trying to replace the patient with a sibling, as well as the fears of retaliation for this aggression, were evident in her anxious anticipation of her menstrual periods.

She recalled a movie about a snake eating a lion cub and a fish. She associated it to the fantasy that she had about being inside the mother's womb and of being hurt by the father's penis during parental intercourse. These pregenital intrauterine fantasies were frequently elicited following the asthmatic attacks. On one occasion, she reported: "When I was inside my mother, I was in her stomach, and that reminds me of eating and sex. . . . I am afraid of falling asleep in the dark for fear of going blind. A sperm could fly through the air and get in by the mouth, nose, or even eyes, and you could go blind."

At another time, she read that in a prison a man introduced a rod into a woman's vagina, which went all the way up to the woman's lungs, and the woman died. After reading this, she developed a fantasy about a penis reaching all the way from the vagina into the lungs and she added:

"At the time I fell under the water at the beach, I had seen my parents having sex. When I was inside of my mother's uterus, I was surrounded by fluid, and fluid has to do with fluids in your lungs and asthma."

The clinical material indicates a continued preoccupation with preoedipal intrauterine fantasies of a sadomasochistic nature, where death and destruction predominated. She identified with her intended victims, the sibling and the mother, and she was fearful of being destroyed by the paternal phallus in the very way she hoped to destroy the victims. The patient emphasized again the fear of going blind. At this point, however, she provided additional material having to do with a sperm that could fly through the air and penetrate all body cavities.

On another occasion, she recalled having seen her parents having intercourse in the dark. The fear of the dark became clearer. She commented that she feared the dark "because a needle could get into your eyes and blind you." She equated the eye to the vagina with a comment: "If a needle, a penis, or a rod goes in there, I could get hurt."

It seems plausible that in her fantasies, the penis that attacks her vagina was the equivalent of the sperm that flies through the air and penetrates all body organs. The mother's injunction that it is dangerous to cough, because the tubercular bacillus could fly through the air, invade the lung of an innocent victim, and kill by tuberculosis, determined the unconscious meaning and fantasies surrounding this patient's perception of the asthmatic attack. The need to hold the air in was an attempt to avoid destroying hated objects by turning the aggression against herself.

These sadomasochistic fantasies, which often took place during masturbation, were analyzed repeatedly. At one point, she commented with some degree of sadness that as she attempted to continually fantasize, "they were no fun anymore." She complained that I had spoiled her fantasies, and now, instead of the tremendous response that she was used to experiencing, they just didn't work. On occasion, because she couldn't enjoy them, she didn't bother to finish them anymore. She even tried to set off asthmatic attacks and at one point said that she tried to breathe deeply in order to induce wheezing. At another, after reading the book, *Candy*, she said: "What a stupid book. At the end, Candy has sex with her father. After I read it, I didn't have sex — I mean asthma — any more." The analysis of the sadomasochistic fantasies, which were repeatedly brought into consciousness and interpreted, deprived them of their earlier impact upon the patient. Characteristically, the satisfactions which accompanied the sadomasochistic fantasies and the asthma attacks were removed, and one sees the patient attempting to recreate these satisfactions in her apparently fruitless attempt to reinduce either the fantasies or the asthmatic attacks. Clinically, one recognizes that these fantasies and psychosomatic symptoms do provide these patients with sources of gratification in spite of the deadly reverberations which could also accompany these illnesses. It is of some relevance that Susan further reconfirmed the impact of the analytic treatment upon her previous conflicts with the comments about *Candy*. She made the slip that she didn't have sex any more with her father and recognized that she meant to say asthma.

Repeated analysis of her oedipal and preoedipal conflicts with the parents and the associative linkages to the asthmatic attacks resulted in an attenuation of the conflict. She could now tolerate whatever residual fantasies were still present without the need to feel overwhelmed by the fantasies or by the asthmatic attacks which they triggered. Just as an erotization of thoughts interfered with her innate abilities, Susan had a great asset: a tremendous sense of humor, which permitted her to reveal the most unpleasant aspects of her life in a jocular manner. As trust in me increased, she was able to work through her defenses against castration anxiety, her penis envy, and her bisexual identification.

The analysis of Susan was not limited to uncovering unconscious fantasies and repressed memories. One had to work through strong resistances, which manifested themselves in several ways. She spent endless hours chattering about her school, constantly complaining about her teachers, classmates, parents, sister, and friends. Whatever interpretation was made at the beginning of treatment, she would express doubt by saying, "maybe," "I think," or "I guess." She rationalized, intellectualized, and dramatized. As the analysis progressed, more overt oedipal fantasies took the place of the previous sadomasochistic ones. She presented me with drawings of Victorian maidens who were seduced and abandoned, or virginal brides or nuns who were led to the altar after endless adventures.

TRANSFERENCE AND COUNTERTRANSFERENCE

It is important to point out that from the start, a therapeutic alliance was established which led to a positive transference. Susan developed strong positive feelings toward me, and as she gave up her symptoms at home, she reenacted them in the transference neurosis that gradually developed.

For example, just before planned short trips away from home and the analysis, she developed sore throats, or minor asthma, which kept her home. It was interpreted to her that leaving home meant growing up and becoming independent from her mother and the analyst. These minor illnesses kept recurring, and she finally understood how she wanted to punish me for leaving her and also how she attempted to keep me with her by being ill, just as she kept close to her mother.

It is interesting to note the countertransference aspects engendered by her asthma attacks and sore throats upon her separation from me. I became aware of my concern that my leaving resulted in her being ill. When I worked this through, she no longer reacted to minor separations with sore throats and/or asthma.

At the beginning of treatment, her clownish behavior and her negativism provoked sadistic reactions from her parents, teachers, and classmates. On one occasion her classmates stamped the word "dog" on her arm. Early in the analysis, she nagged me by asking questions that I in turn interpreted in the context of her wishing to involve me in her sadomasochistic games, so that I would scold her and reject her like the other people in her life.

The negative aspects of the transference appeared in her developing car sickness (only when she was driven to the sessions by her father) and headaches, described previously, related to her oedipal competition. When she was frightened about the intensity of her feelings for her father, a homosexual transference appeared. Fantasies of having an operation to acquire a penis were expressed, as well as rage that I could not give it to her. She finally was able to accept herself as a girl without feeling that she was inferior. The nature of her object relations improved, and she now had good friends of both sexes. Still, this was an aspect of her analysis not totally resolved, owing to her leaving for college.

When she was seen on a follow-up, after four years, she had graduated college cum laude, was a writer, and no longer had asthma. But she had been unable to establish a long-standing relationship to a man.

SUMMARY

This chapter has tried to demonstrate the effect of primal scene shock upon the future psychosexual development of an adolescent girl. It has also focused upon emerging sadomasochistic conflicts arising out of primal-scene trauma and from subsequent later childhood conflict. These sadomasochistic fantasies were repressed by the ego and retrieved as regressed somatized asthmatic attacks.

Genetic, developmental, and dynamic factors were discussed that contributed to the manner in which the ego reacted to a series of traumatic events at the height of Susan's phallic–oedipal stage of libidinal development. In addition, unresolved preoedipal conflicts and fixations were contributory and significant.

To further understand the affect of primal scene on Susan's future development, one has to consider her ego state at the time of the trauma. There was an increased narcissism, heightened by maternal rejection, coupled with overprotection. Identification facilitated the introjection of scenes such as parental intercourse. She conceptualized the sexual act as an attack and identified both with the attacker and the victim through heavy breathing. The birth of her sister and the witnessing of her being nursed by her mother provoked envy and hostility toward her. Later on, the illness of the sister, which followed her mother's miscarriage, reawakened her feelings of rage at her mother for being pregnant, along with murderous feelings toward her sister. By identifying with her parents during parental intercourse, Susan's asthma represented an attempt to deal with her intense jealousy of her mother and with her rage at being excluded during the sexual act. Aggression was regressively discharged somatically. The murderous feelings toward the parents and the hated sibling were internalized, then masochistically acted out in fantasy through the asthmatic attack. When Susan had pneumonia, the lung developed a psychic vulnerability which later predisposed her to the subsequent development of asthma.

Susan's oedipal conflict was intensified by spending her vacation together with her parents in the same bedroom. Her difficulties in breathing coincided with the witnessing of parental intercourse. She identified with her mother in being attacked masochistically as well as identifying sadistically with the attacking father; thus, both sides of her identifications, masculine and feminine, were represented in the asthmatic wheezing.

The secondary gain from her illness resulted in separating her parents and regaining her mother in a regressive infantile relationship where the mother became oversolicitous of her during illness.

Susan's illness helped her establish an object relationship with a nonintruding, nonthreatening, nonhostile analyst. With increasing conscious recognition of an expanding series of sadomasochistic fantasies, she was able to exercise increased conscious control over the fantasies and their effects, so that her ego was able to absorb the recognition of what had been earlier overwhelming impulses. As a consequence, these feelings no longer erupted explosively and regressively in a somatized asthma attack. Objects were no longer dealt with as tormentors or sources of torment, and thoughts were no longer eroticized. This permitted Susan to do well in school, to utilize her creative talents, and establish rewarding friendships.

In a follow-up, the patient has reported no asthmatic symptoms in the past fourteen years. She is gainfully employed in her profession.

REFERENCES

Austen, F., and Lichtenstein, L. (1973). *Asthma, Physiology, Immunopharmacology and Treatment*. New York: Academic Press.

Bacon, C. (1956). The role of aggression in the asthmatic attack. *Psychoanalytic Quarterly* 25:309–324.

Brown, E., and Goitein, L. (1946). The meaning of asthma. *Psychoanalytic Review* 15:544–545.

Faulkner, W. (1941). Influence of suggestion in the size of the bronchial lumen. *Northwest Medicine* 40:367–368.

French, T. (1939). Psychogentic factors in asthma. *American Journal of Psychiatry* 96:87–101.

Freud, S. (1919). A child is being beaten. *Standard Edition* 17:177–204.

_____ (1925). Some psychological consequences of the anatomical distinctions between the sexes. *Standard Edition* 19:248–258.

Knapp, P., Mushatt, C., Nemetz, J., Constantine, H., and Friedman, S. (1970). The content of reported asthma during psychoanalysis. *Psychosomatic Medicine* 32:167–188.

Lamont, T. (1963). Which children outgrow asthma and which do not. In *The Asthmatic Child*, ed. H. Schneer, pp. 58–74. New York: Harper & Row.

Lieberman, M., and Lipton, E. (1963). Asthma in identical twins. In *The Asthmatic Child*, ed. H. Schneer, pp. 58–74. New York. Harper & Row.

Peshkin, M. (1963). Diagnosis of asthma in children, past and present. In *The Asthmatic Child*, ed. H. Schneer, pp. 1–15. New York: Harper & Row.

Siegal, S. (1967). Current trends in bronchial asthma. *New York State Journal of Medicine* 67:921–929.

Sperling, M. (1949). The role of the mother in psychosomatic disorders in children. *Psychosomatic Medicine* 11:377–385.

Trenting, T., and Ripley, H. (1948). Life situations, emotions and bronchial
    asthma. *Journal of Nervous and Medical Disease* 108:380–398.
Wilson, P. (1968). Psychosomatic asthma and acting out. A case of bronchial
    asthma that developed *de novo* in the terminal phase of analysis. *International
    Journal of Psycho-Analysis* 49:300–335.

. 13

PARENTAL OVERSTIMULATION IN ASTHMA

C. Philip Wilson, M.D.

My clinical experience with the analysis of adult asthmatics corroborates and confirms Dr. Karol's hypothesis about the etiologic roles of primal-scene shock and masochism in asthma. The main thrust of my discussion, however, will be to emphasize that primal scene is only one aspect of global patterns of overstimulating parental behavior that in the pregenital maturational phases establish the predisposition to develop asthma and in subsequent developmental phases, particularly the oedipal and adolescent years, play a major role in causing emotional conflict, symptom formation, disturbances in object relations, and asthma. These findings are consonant with those reported by M. Sperling (1963) in her work with children and by me (1968) in my research with adults.

In addition I will review from my clinical material, and that of Dr. Karol, Sperling's hypothesis (1963) that asthma is a manifestation of a pregenital conversion neurosis and that the choice of the respiratory system for symptom development is determined by specific attitudes and fantasies of the mother.

CLINICAL PRESENTATIONS

Case One

A 30-year-old compulsive architect came for analysis of his chronic asthma. He was a nail biter and extremely impatient. He had a childlike sense of humor and was interested in magic, having a magical number of his own that he "discovered" wherever he went. An only child, he was born and raised in Warsaw. At three months he had pertussis, which frightened his mother. During the first year he developed eczema and pruritic rashes in the groin and anus. A bright, verbally precocious child, he was breast-fed until age 2½ and bowel trained with difficulty at the same time he was weaned. His first asthma attack was at age 3, when he was separated from his mother because she had an elective abortion. The mother was an obese, dependent, childish woman who noted on her only child and seldom left the home. The father, a compulsive, narcissistic businessman who dominated the household, took a mistress in the patient's early years. At age 6 the patient was sent under an assumed name to live with a Polish Catholic family to protect him from the Nazis who occupied Poland.

During the two years he lived with this family he was free of asthma, although he experienced many frightening situations when the Germans periodically came searching for Jewish children. The Catholic foster parents were courageous, kindly people. They did, however, make him fend for himself, as they had a large family. At the age of 8, the war was over and he was returned to his parents, whom at first he did not recognize. They did not ask him about his feelings or experiences with the Catholic family, and his asthma recurred.

The father was noisy and exhibitionistic. Nightly after dinner he visited his mistress, returning home late to fall into a deep sleep, "snoring like a horse." The patient, who in his memory was a deep sleeper, shared a room with his mother, his bed right next to hers. He "knew somehow" that his father, who occupied the adjoining room, did come in and have sex with his mother. The patient recalled many times being awakened and fearing his father would choke to death from snoring. Instead of using the communal bathroom shared by the apartment dwellers, the father used to urinate in the kitchen sink, where he also bathed his genitals and buttocks. On a rare occasion the mother weakly argued with father about his behavior, but she was afraid of him and did all she could to please him. The patient was a good boy, never argued with his father, and did all the chores. He did not masturbate and dared have erections only at school. Until adolescence he was overweight and inhibited with girls. He was an excellent student, particularly in mathematics. At age 17 he took off weight, dated girls, and became more assertive, traveling alone in the summer and socializing. He achieved his architect's degree and came to the United States, where, after a number of relationships, he married a successful businesswoman.

Course of Analysis

The analysis paralleled that of a typical compulsive neurotic, except that from the first his asthmatic attacks were kept in focus. The patient reported two fantasies that he said were always in the back of his mind in connection with asthma. In the first he had a great sword with which he was going to cut a person in front of him in two. In the second he had a rifle with telescopic sights aimed at a man's head.

Preoedipal fantasies, dreams, and associations showed that the sword in the first fantasy symbolized the patient's teeth and oral incorporative conflicts, whereas comparable oedipal-phase data revealed the sword to be his phallus. The rifle fantasy had primarily oedipal derivatives. It was the castrating father, projected onto me in the transference neurosis, whom he wanted to shoot. He never argued with or defied his parents or me, and it was a long time in analysis before this attitude changed.

Early memories emerged with the analytic lifting of his amnesia from childhood, which showed that in attempting to resolve his oedipal conflict he identified with sadistic aspects of his father's personality and behavior. Moreover, he had solved the trauma of separation from his parents at age 6 by secretly identifying with the Nazis and in fantasy joined them in torturing and killing Jews who represented his parents. Furthermore, as his Jewish name and identity were covered by a Catholic Polish one when he was placed with the foster parents, he identified with them. He became an expert on Nazi concentration-camp tortures. The sadomasochistic fantasies described below reveal that, in his asthma, he tortured the internalized bad parents, projected onto me in the transference neurosis.

Describing his asthma attacks he said he felt all blown up, that his stomach was like a balloon. He was all trapped with air. He brought this up in the transference neurosis when he was separated from me because he had the flu; what amazed him was that he got no asthma or lung symptoms with the flu. Instead he had a series of sadistic fantasies that he realized were aimed at controlling me as he felt controlled by me and by his parents as a child. In one fantasy, he has a man all harnessed up and puts catheters in his nose, anus, and penis. The one up the penis goes halfway up to make it painful. Then he pours cold water into the catheters and shouts at his victim that he is not to urinate or have bowel movements. He reported a dream in which he tortures people by putting them in a harness around the chest. His associations were to wanting to invent a harness for asthmatics like a parachute jumper's by which he could squeeze or expand a victim's lungs. Another association was that he hoped that I, the analyst, would get flu or asthma. He said that in an asthma attack he could not breathe out dirty foul air; all air was flatus.

During the summer vacation break in the second year of analysis, I received a phone call from the patient, who had been hospitalized for *status asthmaticus*. All I could hear was wheezing on the phone. I told him that he was choking me to death inside himself in rage at my leaving him. His wheezing lessened, and he began to give details of his illness. The hospital physician later called to say the patient was much better, and the next day he was discharged. The rest of the vacation he had no serious asthma, nor did he call me. In analysis in the fall, he said that in his asthma attack he would not cooperate; he fought using the respirator and other treatment; he wanted to die. When he had been able to get me and his internist on the phone, he felt he had control of us, and after my phone interpretation he became aware of a fantasy directed at me. He fantasied he was an Arab terrorist who hijacked an Israeli airplane. In his fantasy, because his demands for money and power were not met, he killed all the families on the plane by blowing it up. These families, he realized, represented me, my wife and children. Following his awareness of these fantasies and their transference meaning, he relaxed and cooperated in the therapy of his *status asthmaticus*. This was his only attack of *status asthmaticus*.

Analysis of the patient's allergies graphically documented their emotional cause (Sperling 1953). He was very allergic to dust, which unconsciously was equated with feces, flatus, and his mother. Whereas his father was very clean, bathing daily, his mother rarely washed. She had a brown spot on her back that they laughingly called her tattoo, which actually was dirt. The patient's sense of smell was acute—as is typical of asthmatics—but he could not smell his mother, which he confirmed when visiting his parents as an adult. When he married, he insisted that his wife always bathe before intercourse so that she would be the opposite of his unclean mother.

He recalled that October, the tenth month, and seven, the seventh day, constituted his magical number, 107, and that the number represented his parents, whom he had left on that date to go to his foster home.

The patient identified with both the mother and father in intercourse, as his catheter fantasies reveal. Oral, anal, and urinary fantasies and conflicts were masked by his asthma.

He confused ejaculation with urination and had fantasies of impregnating women by blowing them up with a urinary ejaculation. His compulsive defenses required long analysis before he was able to let himself experience affects, to cry, or to get angry.

In the terminal phase of analysis, when his wife was pregnant with their second child, more sadomasochistic material emerged. He dreamed he was putting a pipe with compressed air through the first and second floors of his house. It had a plastic nozzle so he could always have air. However, he reflected in the dream that if he ran it through the basement, air would come out moist and smelly because of the humidity.

His associations were that he had tried to explain to his 5-year-old son about birth, telling him that the woman has an opening in her, but he realized the boy would think of the opening as an anus. A pipe reminded him of blowing things up. The first and second floor were like one and two babies and number one (urinating), number two (defecating). His pregnant wife had passed gas the day before and said she now "farted as loud as a weight lifter." She complained that he snored loudly. He recalled that at 12 years of age he had fantasies of a baby being born through his penis, but he feared it would hurt. He saw animal eggs but confused them with feces. His asthma, he thought, was like pipes with air coming out. As a child he used to stick straws in frogs' anuses and blow them full of air. Then he would either float the frogs in water or step on them, bursting them. Later he learned the Nazis had similar tortures for prisoners. In the middle ages a criminal punishment was pulling people apart with horses. The pipes reminded him of penises, with which a man could blow a woman up with air or urine. He recalled that when his mother was pregnant (when he was 3 and his asthma began) he was warned not to punch her swollen stomach. He remembered thinking it would burst like a balloon. In subsequent sessions he had dreams of his wife being dead and of the movie *A Clockwork Orange,* in which some boys kill a woman with a gigantic stone phallus that "bursts her." He also had death wishes toward me. Another memory of his third year returned: of his mother having typhus and his being separated from her for several weeks. He recalled an encopretic episode at nursery school when he was 5. When he was able to experience emotions, his asthma attacks subsided in frequency and intensity. Another shift was from part- to whole-object relations.

Prior to analysis his preferred sexual position was to have his wife on top and his goal was to prolong the act as long as possible. Aspects of his early relations with his parents, particularly his mother, were recapitulated with his wife. Modest and inhibited in public, he tried to be "totally free" at home. He farted frequently and encouraged his wife to do likewise. When he came home from work, he took off all his clothes, even eating dinner nude. When unexpected callers knocked on the door, he had to rush to put on some clothes. He tried to get his wife to be nude with him, but she insisted on wearing a sarong. He purchased a country property with six acres of land, where it was his particular pleasure to urinate and defecate in the woods.

He never wanted to be separated from his wife; they did everything together. He liked to suddenly pinch her: "any round, soft area was suitable"; sometimes she got angry, as he really hurt her. If he reached home before she did, he'd often hide in a closet, enjoying it when he could surprise or frighten her. He bought a house within walking distance of his work and was furious when his company moved its offices to Manhattan. He reacted as if the move were a personal vendetta against him. As he worked through his sexual conflicts and assumed normal sexual relations with his wife, he also became able to separate from her, and he developed healthy sublimations in photography and civic work. These changes resulted from the analysis of his separation conflicts in the transference neurosis. His asthma had developed at the time his mother had an elective abortion when he was separated from her. His murderous rage at his mother and the baby *in utero* was repressed and internalized in his asthma. Also repressed in his symptom was guilt at his pleasure in the baby's death.

Examples of the oral, anal, and urethral fantasies and impulses that emerged in the transference neurosis have been cited. There was preoedipal and oedipal primal scene, which was an aspect of a general atmosphere of overstimulation, including his sleeping in the same room next to his mother where he was exposed to her oral and anal habits and her masochistic subservience to his father. His father's urinary, anal, and phallic exhibitionistic behavior intimidated and castrated the patient. However, both parents were controlling, conscientious people with strict superegos who denied any meaning to their overstimulating behavior. Extreme exhibitionism was coupled with denial. The major symptom that developed in the patient was asthma, which internalized and repressed oral, anal, urinary, and phallic conflicts, drives, and impulses. Except for his asthma he was a "good boy."

Comparison with Dr. Karol's Case

In both this and Dr. Karol's case, we see (1) obsessive-compulsive controlling fathers' and mothers' lacking confidence in themselves who cling to their children — that is, my patient's mother by delaying weaning and bowel training until $2\frac{1}{2}$ years and by sleeping next to the patient until his late adolescence; Karol's mother by giving her daughter a pacifier until she was 7.

(2) Primal-scene and other overstimulating parental behavior that is denied: my patient who slept next to his mother was exposed to parental intercourse from the earliest years. Moreover, the father's snoring after sex with his mistress was a source of sadomasochistic conflict and fantasy. Other overstimulation occurred through his proximity to the body of his "smelly" mother in bed next to him and through the anal, urinary, and genital exhibitionism of his father. In Karol's case we see primal-scene exposure associated with her first asthma attack. However, Karol's patient's parents refused to put a lock on their bedroom door, and letting their daughter sleep with them suggests the strong possibility of preoedipal primal-scene and other overstimulating parental sexual and bathroom behavior, pointing to pregenital conversion as etiologic in her asthma.

(3) Parental organ-system fantasies about the air, breathing, and the lungs were present in both cases. My patient almost died of severe infantile pertussis, which would have made the parents hypersensitive to the fear or wish that he choke to death. Thoughts of death by choking were repeatedly aroused in the mother and son when father snored after sex with his mistress. The mother's unconscious anal and genital exhibitionism, expressed in her uncleanliness, caused a selective repression of the sense of smell in the patient. Another factor augmenting respiratory incorporation was the father's farting and smoking. In my research on the Isakower phenomenon and sand symbolism (1975, 1980),

I emphasized the anal aspects of cigarette smoking, particularly that cigarette smoke can express impulses and fantasies that are masked by flatus. The patient's father was a chain smoker, yet the patient was forbidden smoking and had never done so. He was constantly choked by his father's cigarette smoke, which he hated. This conflict enhanced pregenital conversion and respiratory incorporation. This patient once referred to smoking as "the visual materialization of a fart," and his sadomasochistic fantasies reflect the copraphagic impulses and fantasies that were repressed and internalized in his asthma. Karol's patient's fear of being smothered in intercourse derived from her overhearing the heavy breathing of parental intercourse. Her mother had neurotic ideas about the breath, warning her daughter not to cough in front of people, that a person could kill someone with one's breath. The mother's father had died of lung cancer, and she also had a fear of tubercular infections by the breath.

Case Two

The role of primal scene, overstimulation, and masochism in asthma were highlighted in the case of an adolescent whom I will term the "Gothic boy." Although he was born and brought up in the New York area, he talked, thought, and behaved like someone from a Gothic novel. The patient was a shy, effeminate 15-year-old with an intellectual, old-maidish manner of speech. His asthma developed three months before consultation; at that time, his mother was hospitalized for an unexplained operation. Otherwise healthy in childhood, he was enuretic until age 6.

The mother, an intelligent, rigid, moralistic woman, said that she was not affectionate. She regretted having had her mother, who lived with the family, take care of her children, as she had spoiled them." The father was a religious, self-made, successful businessman who disciplined his children, forbidding them television and movies and demanding top scholastic performance. Fights about discipline were constant. The patient felt his parents were always watching and spying on him.

He had no memory of erections or masturbation but had crushes on certain boys at school. His only friend had been his 11-year-old sister, until in puberty she became contemptuous of him, calling him a "fag." He remembered hitting his sister with a block in early childhood and being severely punished. Since early years he had been overweight, at age 7 weighing a hundred pounds.

When he was 6, his mother bought a stuffed turtle for him. Subsequently, usually to make up for leaving him alone, she bought him other stuffed-animal toys, until he had a large collection. When the family moved to the city just before the onset of his asthma, he was permitted to have half of them; the others were put in storage for him. Into early adolescence the patient invented sadomasochistic games that he and his sister played with these stuffed animals. The animals would behead, strangle, and torture Tinker-Toy figures who represented various humans. Occasionally he made up sexual plays. He was an authority on those beheaded queens, Mary, Queen of Scots and Marie Antoinette, and an expert on female murderers such as Lizzie Borden. Since early childhood he had been preoccupied with death, read the obituary column, and wanted to visit the city morgue.

He preferred cats to people and had four of them as pets. For many years two of the cats slept the first part of the evening in the parental bed next to the mother. Late at night they left mother and came to sleep with the patient. The patient feared and hated his father and blamed him for the infectious death of one of his cats. The parental bedroom door was always open, reflecting the lack of privacy in the home.

In early years the patient had nightmares and was frequently taken into the parental bed. There was no memory of his sister's birth or mother's pregnancy. In latency he played at being the victim of an aggressive boy next door, who used to lock him in closets. He had a strong belief in black magic and tried to kill people he hated by secret voodoo. His one "sin" was secret cigarette smoking. He talked frequently of wanting to be a woman.

In spite of the serious character pathology there was no evidence of psychosis, and the patient had a capacity for insight. Unlike most cases, he had wanted to get asthma to be exempt from athletics, as was the case with an asthmatic classmate. He had one activity in which he excelled, aside from his studies. That was butterfly collecting. His problem was in mounting his specimens, as he could not stand sticking pins in the butterflies.

Course of Analysis

As I have described (1970), the first months of analysis in psychosomatic cases are a crucial period. The analyst has to concentrate upon the masochism and then the repressed aggressive drive components, leaving libidinal material until later. In this case the patient readily brought up his resentment and anger with his mother, father, sister, and teachers — showing, however, considerable resistance to feeling any resentment toward me in the transference until the fifth month of analysis, when he reported the following dream:

> The scene was a room that I could not place. Mrs. W. was there and my sister was in the background. I was shrieking at Mrs. W., saying: "How dare you look through my drawers, you filthy whore!" I continued to scream and yell at her until I woke up. On awakening I felt remorse and also amazement that I'd think of saying something like that to her in the dream, because I'd never say that to her face.

Associations: "Mrs. W. is our cleaning woman. She is basically nice, but in reality she did search my drawers and found a package of cigarettes that I had hidden. She told my mother, who blamed me, and I tried to put it off on my sister, saying they were hers." The patient said that his reputation for moral behavior is very good in the family, whereas his sister's is ruined anyway, so it wouldn't hurt her to be blamed for one more thing. Mrs. W. has been consistently anti-Catholic and has made some hostile remarks about the priests and the Pope. The patient had kept quiet, although he felt like killing her for these remarks, as he has a strong wish to join the Catholic Church. His ideas about morality are the same as the church's.

An interpretation was made to the patient that he was not only screaming at the cleaning woman in the dream but at his mother and at me; that his mother was opposed to the Catholic Church and he knew very well that I, as an analyst, would not agree basically with the doctrines of Catholicism. Likewise, he knew that I was not basically in favor of his smoking, as I had brought it up with him as a problem to analyze. Also I had suggested that he analyze smoking in analytic sessions, which he, with his strict conscience, took as a prohibition. The patient confirmed the interpretion, saying, in a partly questioning voice, "I must have been shrieking worse in my dreams; before I would have gotten asthma. When the dream woke me up, I had some trouble breathing, but it wasn't really asthma and I went back to sleep."

In analysis the patient made considerable progress: formerly obese, he dieted and brought his weight down fifteen pounds. He looked forward for the first time with pleasure and interest to going back to school and planned to take some extra courses in language, which he enjoyed. Whereas in the six months preceding analysis he had missed nineteen days of school because of asthma, since treatment began he had missed one day because of his illness. He began to question why he wanted to be a woman. He saw it now as a very peculiar wish, in that it meant to him to be a hypermoral person like the aspects of his mother that he hates.

The dream described above was a result of a long series of interpretations of defenses against hostile id impulses. The libidinal aspects of the dream did come up in the session, as the patient was puzzled as to why he would call a proper married woman like Mrs. W a whore. His association to whore was that he had first learned the word two years earlier, reading a book in which Ann Boleyn, when she was having an affair with Henry the Eighth, was derided as a whore by the English Catholics.

His asthma cleared as he began to get an understanding of the masochistic meanings of his symptoms and of the defenses he had against aggression.

DISCUSSION

Psychosomatic symptoms, including asthma, frequently appear first in adolescence (M. Sperling 1978), because in this phase the child must develop the capacity to be independent of the parents. The following conflicts appeared to be the crucial precipitants of the Gothic boy's asthma.

1. His mother, who had seldom left him, went to the hospital for a fibroid operation, which frightened him. He was not told what the operation was for and feared his mother had cancer, a disease his grandmother had died of six months before.

2. His sister, five years his junior, no longer would play with him constantly. She now wanted friends of her own outside the family, and she was becoming critical of her brother, calling him a fag.

3. When the family moved to the city, in his fourteenth year, he was deprived of half of his fetishistic animals, which were put in storage. Although he tried to continue his sadistic games with these stuffed toys, he could no longer get his sister to join him, and he had begun to feel ashamed of "these games." They were becoming ego-alien to him.

4. With the increased biological development of adolescence, he was

aware of intense homosexual yearnings for an effeminate classmate; however, his superego forbade him any active homosexual gratification.

5. Frank death wishes came to consciousness toward a crippled classmate whom he envied, and toward certain teachers who ridiculed him for his effeminate mannerisms. No effective sublimations were available for these sadistic fantasies.

6. For many years prior to the development of asthma, he had been fascinated by strangling, beheading, and death. Female murderers particularly interested him.

7. Also prior to the asthma onset, he had wished to get asthma like a classmate. The patient had already feigned illness at camp to get sent home.

8. A powerful preoccupation with black magic had taken hold of him. He had attempted to murder people he hated by stealing a piece of clothing from the hated person, usually a teacher, setting fire to the cloth, and then repeating magic prayers that the person would die by fire. His wishes were never carried out, and he was increasingly guilty for having such feelings.

9. The actual precipitation of asthma was his separation from his mother, which forced death wishes (of an oral incorporative nature) to be powerfully repressed. He was strangled for wanting her to strangle. The asthma also served as a punishment for other sadistic fantasies and his homosexual wishes.

10. The asthma made him sick and dependent on his mother.

11. Perverse fantasies were masked by his asthma. He revealed that behind his wish to be a woman were transsexual fantasies of being castrated and, by surgical operations, being turned into a female with a vagina and breasts. He became angry at the thought that he could not have a uterus, become pregnant, and have children. I cautioned his parents that, in the future, he might try to go through transsexual operations and that his transsexual wishes had serious psychological meaning. They minimized their son's condition, refused the consultation I requested, and withdrew him from therapy, as his asthma had cleared and he was going away to college. A follow-up is not available.

This patient's transsexual wishes and fantasies psychodynamically correlate with and confirm observations of Socarides (1978–1979) in his paper on "Transsexualism and Psychosis." Socarides notes that his patient's wish for sexual transformation defended him against paranoid fears of aggression. The findings in this case fully substantiate Socarides' view that transsexualism is a serious psychological condition and that surgery for it should be considered with the greatest caution, if at all.

Comparison to Dr. Karol's Case

In this case, we see controlling parents who even could force their son, who got excellent marks, to read mathematics at night as a punishment for minor misbehavior. Primal-scene exposure probably occurred because of the lack of privacy, with no locking of doors, as well as the parents' taking the boy into their bed when he had nightmares. Most striking in this case, however, was the unusual relationship of the mother and son. That she unconsciously wanted him to be a female and to infantilize him was clear in that he, rather than his more rebellious sister, was encouraged to do the housework and wash the dishes. Male aggression was legislated against. The mother prevented maturation and promoted the development of fetishism by giving her son the stuffed animals every time she left him. Even more confusing for his development were the cats who slept with the mother and with the patient. The short (one year's) analysis permitted only minimal exploration of the psychodynamic significance of the patient's cats. It did become evident that they represented babies the patient had by the mother. That the warm body of the cat came from mother's bed to the patient's expressed the mother's unresolved incestuous tie to her son.

Specific parental fantasies and preoccupations with air, breathing, or the lungs were not recovered. However, the mother herself said that she was emotionally cold and was inhibited about kissing and hugging. She, as well as the father, was aware of and had done nothing to discourage the patient's and his sister's sadomasochistic beheading and strangling games. We can suspect that such hypermoral compulsive parents might unconsciously share their son's sadomasochistic fantasies. They certainly provided the paraphernalia and opportunity for sadomasochistic play in buying the stuffed animals and Tinker Toys as well as the morbid books on such women as Lizzie Borden. Allergic studies in this case were negative. Sadomasochistic conflicts and fantasies were central in this boy's psychopathology and character structure.

Case Three

In 1968 I reported on a patient who, with no previous history of asthma, developed symptoms of bronchial asthma in the terminal phases of her analysis. The asthmatic attacks, some seventeen in all, responded to analysis; the patient terminated treatment successfully, free of asthma.

The patient, age 25, came to analysis with intense oral conflicts. An alcoholic who drank herself into a stupor every evening after work, she was severely depressed and suicidal. She lost one job after another. Behind a facade of helpless, childlike behavior was overwhelming oral greed. Denial and exhibitionism characterized her neurotic parents' behavior as she grew up. The wealthy neurotic mother was addicted to cigarettes and wine. The father, a very successful real estate executive, insisted that the family was poor, and they lived in a rent-controlled building in an impoverished area. A compulsive man, he did daily exercises in the nude in a ritualistic fashion in front of his wife, son, and daughter. These exercises, which were preceded by a large glass of water and followed by a copious urination, dated from the time of the patient's earliest memory. He also kept binoculars in the living-room window sill so that he could look at certain exhibitionistic women in nearby apartments. A second analysis confirmed my 1968 hypothesis that transference caused by a precipitous superego formation played a significant role in the asthma *de novo*. Also demonstrated clearly was the pathological effect that perverse parental sexual and toilet behavior had upon the patient's psychosexual development.

Follow-up History

Ten years after termination, the female patient returned because of marital conflicts. Sexual intercourse with her husband was infrequent and there were many quarrels. Formerly messy and disorganized, she had become compulsively neat, doing all the housework herself because a cleaning woman might not do the job properly. A long battle for control went on with her husband about choices: what kind of car to buy, where to live, how much money to spend, and where to go on vacation.

She had developed healthy sublimations in music and art that she enjoyed, and she felt pride in her volunteer charity work and her children's development. Gradually, however, she had stopped doing things with her husband, such as playing tennis and bridge with other couples. She had rare asthmatic attacks, which she had been able to control.

Course of Analysis

Analysis centered on her compulsive neurosis, and she reported dreams reflecting anal-phase conflicts. The following example is illustrative. She dreamt that a man was going to make love to her, then she saw a lot of people's anuses with hemorrhoids, some of them very big. She was going to kiss her mother on the mouth and then did not want to. In her associations she thought of baboons having big red bottoms. One of her aunts always talked about manure and had hemorrhoids. In the dream some anuses had hemorrhoids, others didn't. Hemorrhoids reminded her of little penises. She herself had had hemorrhoids, and she wondered if she wanted the hemorrhoidal swellings to be little penises. She remembered so many times seeing Father's penis and his urinating, but he also spent lots of time reading on the toilet with the door partly open. When she first married, she was afraid of smelling and avoided having a bowel movement when her husband was home. She had been reading *The Joy of Sex* and wondered what anal intercourse would be like. It seemed to her that men had more pleasure than women. She hated football games, which her husband was always watching on television.

An interpretation was made that she had confused her vagina with her anus as a child and that she thought both were dirty holes, whereas she envied her father's penis and wanted one herself. Her response was that she remembered seeing her mother's genitals as a girl and was frightened and disgusted. She felt that she must have thought intercourse was like having a bowel movement, because her parents were so cold and matter-of-fact about sex. The kissing made her think of her mother's conflicts and fears about kissing, that you could get infections kissing people, that the mouth, like the anus, is dirty.

She now perceived that her compulsion to look at men's crotches involved the analyst, whom she said she observed coming into sessions. The particular fascination was with whether he had an erection. She realized that when she saw her father's penis, she could be sure it was not erect, that she could not be certain of what was happening if he wore clothes. There had been a reversal of normal female development, in that she was reassured seeing the male genitals nude, and anxious if they were covered.

A major focus of analysis was upon the patient's strict superego and its periodic projection onto the analyst in the transference neurosis. She began to admit to her exhibitionistic behavior. At home she was moralistic and prudish while her husband and children were around; when alone, she wore a bra and panties or a bikini. She went to social gatherings in extremely sexually provocative dresses and was seductive in her behavior. Memories of her father's genital exhibitionism and his voyeurism emerged, coupled with penis envy and transference anger with me. She thought again of her father's daily nude exercises and remembered stepping over his prone body to go to his bureau for her weekly allowance money. She realized that with his binoculars he must have been looking for nude women in nearby apartments and that he was exhibiting to them. She thought that secretly she must want her father or me to see her when she exhibits.

Interpretations were made that she had identified with her exhibitionistic voyeuristic father and was arousing and frustrating men in adult life, just as father had "cock-teased" her in childhood.

In subsequent sessions she began to face her identification with her father's perversions. Like her father, she was proud of her figure and careful of her weight. She wore extremely provocative dresses to social events, dresses that revealed her breasts and nipples, and skirts slit high to her thigh. She wore bikinis both for swimming and in her home, frequently leaving the window shades up. She began to receive anonymous phone calls, which she realized she enjoyed and provoked. Socially she was the target of sexual teasing and was frequently surreptitiously touched or pinched, which she tacitly enjoyed.

She recalled that the night she developed her first asthma she had had an impulse to fellate her lover, who was gratifying her by cunnilingus. She wondered if she had been afraid of biting his penis or being hurt by it. The interpretation was made that she was punished in her asthma for her oral incorporative impulses.

Comparison with Dr. Karol's Case

In this case we see the following parallels to Karol's patient: (1) an obsessive-compulsive controlling father and a weak dependent mother; (2) primal-scene and other overstimulating parental behavior, particularly the father's genital toilet and voyeuristic habits; (3) parental fantasies about the breath, air, and lungs apparent in the patient's mother's inhibition and avoidance of kissing and hugging. The mother was overconcerned with disease transmission by saliva and the breath, and she suffered from chronic bronchitis with its typical cough. (4) As with Karol's case there were sadomasochistic conflicts and fantasies.

DISCUSSION

We are in debt to Dr. Karol for her rich and penetrating asthma paper. By the thorough review of clinical psychoanalytic case material we will arrive at an understanding of the enigma of psychosomatic symptoms. In this we are in the direct tradition of Freud. Over a thirty-year period I have analyzed seven asthmatics as well as treating many more in psychotherapy and supervising the therapy of other cases. My clinical experiences are in agreement with the conclusions that Dr. Karol reaches. Like her, I find that my research correlates with and confirms the work of M. Sperling (1963, 1978).

Different patterns of parental overstimulation were found in each case. Characteristic was the finding that there had been no age-appropriate privacy permitted the child. There were no locks on bathroom or bedroom doors. The parents were typically compulsive, controlling people, unlike the parents of many psychotics, who grossly neglect their children. The asthmatic parent's overstimulation, coupled with its denial, is comparable to the parent–child interactions in nonpsychosomatic patients described by Shengold (1978) in his studies on "Soul Murder."

In Case 1 the boy slept next to his mother until late adolescence, witnessing primal scene and knowing about his father's sex with his mistress as well as being exposed to his father's toilet exhibitionism. In Case 2 the Gothic boy's incestuous and symbiotic tie to his mother was expressed by cats, which slept with the mother and child, by the fetishistic toy animals given to the child, and by the child's being taken into the parental bed, where he probably witnessed a primal scene. In Case 3, the asthma *de novo*, in addition to probable primal-scene viewing because of the characteristically open parental bedroom doors, we can see the pathological results of the father's perverse exhibitionism in the patient's voyeuristic symptoms and body-phallus identification. All three parent pairs show compulsive, controlling fathers and dependent, clinging wives.

Sperling (1978) dissected out various unconscious parental conflicts that she felt predisposed a child to develop psychosomatic symptoms. In

Case 1 we can see a dependent mother who clung to her only son, using him to replace her husband, whom she had lost to his mistress. She unconsciously gratified anal drives and fantasies in her dirtiness, sensitizing her son to olfactory conflict and respiratory incorporation. He could not smell his mother, but on buses he could identify women who were menstruating by his acute sense of smell.

In the Gothic boy, the mother's and probably the father's emasculation of their son was apparent in their intolerance of any aggression and in their strict discipline, in his being assigned female roles, cleaning and dishwashing, that his sister did not share, and by the mother's providing the boy replacements for herself by the fetishistic stuffed animals. In Case 3 the father's perverse exhibitionism to his daughter caused her looking compulsion and body-phallus identification. Her mother was a dependent alcoholic and tried to infantilize her daughter.

The denial in all three families was extreme. In Case 1, except for an infrequent weak protest by the mother, any emotional conflict was denied. It was extraordinary the way the parents had their son return to live with them after an absence of two years without asking him how he felt. Was he afraid? Had he missed them? In Case 2, the parents denied the obvious effeminate development in their son as well as his bizarre sadomasochistic behavior and fetishism. They were interested only in the resolution of his asthma. In Case 3, there was complete denial of the mother's alcoholism and the father's perversions. The denial in Karol's case was highlighted by the parents' refusal to put a lock on their bedroom door, even when asked by their daughter.

These findings are in agreement with Karol's hypothesis about the role of primal scene and masochism in asthma and correlate with and confirm the work of Sperling as well as that of Langs (1974), who noted the sadomasochistic fantasies in his asthmatic case.

For the resolution of Karol's patient's asthma, the analysis of the oedipus complex in the transference neurosis was sufficient, with preoedipal material being secondary. In most of my cases the analysis of preoedipal material was essential for the resolution of their disturbance in object relations and sexual functioning. Whether more preoedipal conflicts will appear when Karol's patient attempts an adult heterosexual relationship remains to be seen.

I do know from my research (1967; see Chapter 7 this volume) on stone symbolism that Karol's patient's Hawaiian hot stone in the genital fantasy might be the little girl's anal-phase idea that intercourse involves one person defecating on or in the other—the vagina and anus being confused, as well as the penis and bowel movement being equated. The hot stone can represent a fecal phallus and the steam flatus.

As concerns primal scene, I have long felt that we should have another term or terms for "preoedipal primal scene." When we use the term *primal scene* we unconsciously think in terms of oedipal or postoedipal primal-scene events. The experiences that our pregenitally fixated psychosomatic patients have been exposed to, however, is very early primal-scene and other exhibitionistic behavior, which provokes reactions that are experienced in the context of preoedipal sensory modalities and fantasies. For example, some patients' preoedipal primal-scene experiences are largely auditory, visual, or olfactory. Their egos record the experience before there has been a well-developed coordination of vision with other sensory and cognitive ego functions.

In the majority of analyzed cases of asthma the primary fixations are at the anal level, which was true of my cases (Sperling 1963). However, as Sperling emphasizes, the fantasies repressed and internalized in asthma attacks are specific for the individual patient but not for asthma in general.

Relevant to preoedipal fixations and fantasies in respiratory symptomatology is Mintz's (1975; see Chapter 10 this volume) important concept of the *internalized air mother*. He notes that the infant swallows air along with mother's milk, and in this process the ambivalently loved mother comes to be symbolized by air. Asthma expresses an internalization of the air mother, precipitated by separation conflicts at later maturational phases. Psychoanalytic research has focused more on bowel training and fantasies about the fecal product. The psychic meanings of intestinal gas have been relatively neglected. In recent papers on sand symbolism, the Isakower phenomenon, and smoking addictions (1975, 1980), I noted the paucity of analytic research on the anal meanings of smoking, and I observed that smoke often symbolizes flatus. The first asthmatic patient whose case I cited was a nonsmoker whose father chain-smoked. He aptly described smoking as the "visual materialization of a fart." Smokers, like asthmatics, repetitiously internalize and externalize objects (the air mother) in their habit.

The analysis of a hyperventilator showed the psychodynamic meanings of the internalized air mother. The patient, a compulsive businessman, came for the treatment of marital conflicts. On his first summervacation separation from me he knocked himself out by hyperventilating and was taken to a physician as an emergency case. Dreams and associations revealed that he was killing me in himself by poisoning himself with air. He resisted strenuously admitting to conscious control of what he was doing. However, analysis revealed that he was an expert on breath holding and air swallowing. Fascinated by air, he had been an expert sky diver (parachute jumper). This man was a "sneaky farter." As president of a company he would let a "quiet one loose," his pleasure being in watching the reactions of his subordinates as they smelled the flatus. He revealed that when very frustrated and angry he would swallow air and save it up for farts. At times, when repressing intense rage, he would swallow such large quantities of air that he was doubled up with cramps — that is, he internalized the object. He was an extremely polite, gentlemanly man whose behavior reflected an identification with his mother, who was a "perfect lady." Analysis revealed that his mother and grandmother, who adored him, were passers of gas, and he identified with them.

In the case of the asthmatic who was enuretic until age 5 (Wilson 1968), when the bedwetting was replaced by asthma, both symptoms served the same purpose. The aim was to keep him tied to his mother, in whose room he slept until age 12. In adolescence his asthmatic attacks decreased in frequency, but he developed another way of using air to terrify and control mother and others. He became an expert underwater swimmer, particularly adept at holding his breath. He would stay under water so long that he frightened people into diving to look for him. He experimented with hyperventilation — that is, the internalized air mother.

Urinary fantasies were prominent in this case. He always used condoms in his sexual affairs. Following intercourse he would always go into the bathroom and urinate into the condom, ostensibly to find out if there were any leaks in the rubber. Unconsciously, urine and ejaculation were equated, and his repressed wish was to kill the woman by blowing her up with urine. The female was represented by the condom, which was blown up like a balloon. This man's asthmatic attacks were a talion punishment for this wish to drown or blow up the mother.

I think it is important to realize that frequently the internalized air mother in an asthmatic attack is composed of flatus. The Warsaw ghetto asthmatic said that in an asthmatic attack he could not breathe out dirty foul air, all air was flatus, *and to breathe was to fart.* That an asthmatic attack can express the displacement up, repression, and internalization of impulses and fantasies about passing gas has not been described in the literature.

It was, of course, an inexact interpretation that aborted the *status asthmaticus* of the Warsaw ghetto patient. Years of experience with psychodynamic intervention in states of psychosomatic suicide, such as *status asthmaticus,* acute ulcerative colitis, or the crisis phase of the emaciated anorectic, show that an interpretation of the masochistic meaning of the symptom in the transference may be lifesaving. In this instance this line of interpretation had been made before, when the patient had severe asthma.

I also agree with Sperling (1963) that the psychosomatic object relationship originates in earliest infancy and that oral fixations and fantasies appear in every analyzed case. A careful psychiatric and psychodynamic evaluation has to be made, and the diagnosis may range from psychotic (Fink and Schneer 1963) to neurotic. In the asthma *de novo* case, psychoticlike material emerged in dreams. For example, she dreamt of me as hamburger meat that she was eating. Primitive acting out occurred in the case of the male asthmatic whose urinary conflicts I detailed (1968). When this patient's asthma cleared, he became more assertive with women and took his girlfriend to a resort. At the end of the weekend he was angry at the poor service. Instead of registering his complaints with the management, he defecated in a glass tumbler and left it on the bureau when he departed. His girlfriend was shocked and told him he was "nuts." Before analysis he would have had asthma in the same situation. This is an illustration of the analyzable acting out of preoedipal impulses and fantasies that replaces psychosomatic symptoms (Sperling 1968, Wilson 1968).

In a significant number of cases urinary fantasies and fixations predominate (Fink and Schneer 1963, Knapp 1963, Sperling 1963, Wilson 1968). In these cases enuresis is replaced by asthma, or the reverse, asthma is replaced by enuresis.

A graphic illustration of the clearing of asthma on separation from the mother, parentectomy (Peshkin 1959), occurred in Case 1 when the patient was sent for two years to live with foster parents and was symptom-free. As regards allergies, Case 1 was allergic to dust and chocolate, which symbolized feces and his mother. The other two cases were not allergic.[1]

---

[1]D. S. Goldman (1986) recently reviewed this area in a chapter: Psychoanalytic, psychoanalytically oriented, and psychotherapeutic treatment of asthma, eczema, and urticaria. In *Psychological Aspects of Allergic Disorders,* ed. S. H. Young, J. M. Rubin, and H. R. Daman, pp. 193–222. New York: Praeger.

In conclusion, asthma, like other psychosomatic symptoms, is a pregenital conversion symptom (Sperling 1973). When it appears in the first years of life, it develops in the context of primal repression and the precursors of the superego. The predisposition to develop asthma is established in the mother–infant relationship. As our cases show, the symptom may occur at any later phase in life when castration and separation anxieties are mobilized. In Karol's case it was the oedipal primal-scene events; in the Gothic boy it occurred in midadolescence, and in the asthma *de novo* case, upon marriage and the termination of analysis.

I have attempted to document further the sadomasochistic fantasies of asthmatic patients as they surface in analysis when the asthma symptoms subside. Our technique of treatment I have detailed elsewhere (1970), as has M. Sperling in her papers. In broad outline it is similar to the technique Boyer (1975) outlines in treating characterological and schizophrenic patients. Volkan (1975) and Kernberg (1975) likewise use parallel approaches, although their terminology differs somewhat. All of us begin with interpreting the masochism, showing the patients their strict superego and its various manifestations, particularly in the transference. Preoedipal material and the defenses against aggressive drive derivatives are interpreted first, with libidinal and oedipal conflicts left until later. The outcome of analysis in my cases was favorable, both in clearing the asthma and in resolving the underlying personality disorder. As Dr. Karol's excellent result shows, analysis is the treatment of choice for psychosomatic asthma.

REFERENCES

Boyer, B. (1975). Treatment of characterological and schizophrenic disorders. In *Tactics and Techniques in Psychsomatic Therapy*, vol. II. *Countertransference*, ed. P. Giovacchini, pp. 361–362. New York: Jason Aronson.

Fink, G., and Schneer, J. (1963). Psychiatric evaluation of adolescent asthmatics. In *The Asthmatic Child: Psychosomatic Approach to Problems and Treatment*, ed. H. Schneer, pp. 205–223. New York: Harper & Row.

Kernberg, O. (1975). *Borderline Conditions and Pathological Narcissism*. New York: Jason Aronson.

Knapp, P. (1963). The asthmatic child and the psychosomatic problem of asthma: toward a general theory. In *The Asthmatic Child: Psychosomatic*

Approach to Problems and Treatment, ed. H. Schneer, pp. 234–255. New York: Harper & Row.

Langs, R. (1974). *The Technique of Psychoanalytic Psychotherapy.* Vol. 1. New York: Jason Aronson.

Mintz, I. (1975). Air symbolism in asthma and related states. Paper given at a meeting of the New Jersey Psychoanalytic Study.

Peshkin, M. (1959). Intractable asthma of childhood, rehabilitation at the institutional level with a follow-up of 150 cases. *International Archives of Allergy* 15:91.

Shengold, L. (1978). The problem of soul murder. *International Review of Psycho-Analysis* 5:457–476.

Socarides, C. (1978–1979). Transsexualism and psychosis. *International Journal of Psychoanalytic Psychotherapy* 7:373–383.

Sperling, M. (1953). Food allergies and conversion hysteria. *Psychoanalytic Quarterly* 22:525–538.

―――― (1963). Psychoanalytic study of bronchial asthma in children. In *The Asthmatic Child: Psychosomatic Approach to Problems and Treatment,* ed. H. Schneer, pp. 138–165. New York: Harper & Row.

―――― (1968). Acting out behavior and psychosomatic symptoms: clinical and theoretical aspects. *International Journal of Psycho-Analysis* 49:250–253.

―――― (1973). Conversion hysteria and conversion symptoms: a revision of classification and concepts. *Journal of the American Psychoanalytic Association* 21:745–771.

―――― (1978). *Psychosomatic Disorders in Childhood.* Ed. O. Sperling. New York: Jason Aronson.

Volkan, V. (1975). *Primitive Internalized Object Relations.* New York: International Universities Press.

Wilson, C. (1967). Stone as a symbol of teeth. *Psychoanalytic Quarterly* 36:418–425.

―――― (1968). Psychosomatic asthma and acting out. *International Journal of Psycho-Analysis* 49:330–333.

―――― (1970). Theoretical and clinical considerations in the early phase of treatment of patients suffering from severe psychosomatic symptoms. *Bulletin of the Philadelphia Association of Psychoanalysis* 20:71–74.

―――― (1975). Sand: the primary symbol of smoking addictions and of the Isakower phenomenon. *Bulletin of the Psychoanalytic Association of New York* 14:4–6.

―――― (1980). Sand: the primary dream symbol of smoking addictions and the Isakower phenomenon. In *Lives, Events, and Other Players,* ed. S. Orgel and B. Fine, pp. 45–56. New York: Jason Aronson.

14

POWER, CONTROL, AND THE THREAT TO DIE IN A CASE OF ASTHMA AND ANOREXIA

Martin A. Silverman, M.D.

Laura, painfully thin, her face pinched and wizened, hunched forward in her chair and spoke laconically and almost inaudibly during her first session. With her delicate features, long blonde hair, sad eyes, and long eyelashes, she was pretty and appealing in a very fragile, plaintive, doll-like manner.

Now 10 years old, she had been asthmatic since age 5, much more so since her older brother had gone off to camp in a flurry of hypochondriacal anxiety two years earlier. She very much wanted to stop wheezing, she said, since it interfered with so many aspects of her life and repeatedly kept her from having fun. Her anorexia troubled her much less, however. She wished her mother would stop worrying that she would starve to death. Her mother, she said, worried about her too much altogether. Paradoxically (though Laura herself saw no inconsistency in it), she enjoyed her grandmother's fussing over her and plying her with all kinds of special foods, in an effort to put meat on her bones.

Laura's asthma had begun in a very dramatic way. She had been a breath holder between $2\frac{1}{2}$ and 5 years of age. When things did not go her way, she would hold her breath, turn dead white, and pass out. Her mother, who always had been very phobic and had been obsessively worried about Laura's health ever since she was born, was terrified every time it happened. Laura's breath holding ended when she reached age 5. To everyone's dismay, however, it was replaced with a relatively mild, but unnerving case of bronchial asthma.

Her father had been very ill with a protracted case of largely antibiotic-resistant staphylococcus pneumonia through the latter part of her mother's pregnancy with her older brother. Afterward, he suffered repeated episodes of pneumonia and other lung disorders. His own childhood had been powerfully influenced by his mother's single-minded devotion to his brother, who had nearly died of staphylococcus pneumonia and had remained in very delicate health thereafter, with repeated respiratory problems that occupied her attention.

The anorexia went back even further, and it was much more subtle in its origin and development. When Laura was born, two years after her brother, her mother was delighted. Not only was Laura a girl, which she had wanted very much, but also, in sharp contrast to her brother, she was quiet, placid, undemanding, and easily contented. Her brother had been a fretful, restless, ever-hungry baby, who never seemed to be getting enough from her. Laura was a small eater, waited patiently for her feedings, and was easily satisfied. The mother had always wanted a daughter and always kept Laura very close to her. Laura's father joked that she couldn't do without Laura and would accompany her on her honeymoon. She fondled and fussed over Laura as a baby and took her with her everywhere she went.

A phobic-obsessive worrier for as long as she could remember, Laura's mother had worried about her daughter's health and welfare from the time she began to walk. She repeatedly worried that something terrible might happen to her, so that she would lose her. Whenever she was even mildly ill, she nursed her with tenderness, lavish attention, special privileges, and little gifts. Laura's thinness frightened her and made her feel hurt and rejected. Laura's refusal to accept the nourishing foods that her mother kept offering her seemed like a rejection of her mother.

Laura's "prudish" mother took care to keep herself well covered at all times, and she could not bring herself to talk with Laura about anything involving the human body. Her father, however, had no compunctions about walking around the house in tight-fitting underwear, despite Laura's frequent objections. Laura had been bathed regularly with her brother, until her mother's own doctor had advised against it when Laura was 2 years old. Her mother had entered psychotherapy because of tension headaches, low self-esteem, and a poor opinion of herself and of women in general. As a child, she had wished that she were a boy. She felt that this had contributed to Laura's own repeated assertion, when she was younger, that she should have been provided with a penis like her brother.

Psychosomatic expression of emotional conflict appeared to be a family tendency. In addition to Laura's anorexia and asthma and her mother's headaches, her father suffered from repeated attacks of various gastrointestinal disorders (including frightening episodes of difficulty breathing and swallowing) and an intermittent bad back, and her brother had undergone psychotherapy for mild asthma and multiple gastrointestinal complaints.

Laura and I worked together in a long course of treatment that lasted until she graduated from high school and went off to college. We had sessions three and then four times a week after the initial evaluative period. Although she had been rather communicative during her first visit, she retreated after that into almost total silence. She appeared to appreciate my extensive efforts to break the impasse and help her to speak by groping for explanations of her protracted silence. My proffered explanations included her difficulty trusting herself and trusting me; discomfort about opening up and exposing her feelings and thoughts to a man; fear of relaxing her guard against her intense rage; feelings of powerlessness and pessimism about achieving success in therapy; depression that sapped her emotional and physical energy; sputtering but helpless outrage over the consulting psychiatrist's telling her she would have to wait for my arrival in the area before she could begin her own treatment, while he took her brother, who had suddenly burst out in a rash of acute psychosomatic symptoms, into weekly treatment with him; fear of giving in to her dependent yearnings, thereby compromising her determined wish to be self-reliant; a need to test my interest, devotion, and willingness to persevere and expend effort on her behalf; a desire to not merely describe to me her feelings of frustration, helplessness, and impotence, but to get me to feel, in all its intensity, what she herself felt; and so forth.

She would hunch over and nod weakly as she labored to force air through her tightly constricted bronchial passages. Her bony ribcage rose and fell, and she struggled to raise her heavy lids to look at me. In response to me, she might even gasp a few words, in a tone of anguished sorrow and pain. For the most part, however, she remained deathly still, except for the rasping of her wheezing inspirations and expirations. When four or five months had elapsed without any essential change either in her behavior during our sessions or in her symptomatology, I found myself growing increasingly concerned (like her mother?) and beginning to wonder whether I was the wrong person to treat her. I gingerly raised this possibility to her. I said that I wanted very much to help her, but that, since she had been almost totally unable to speak to me, perhaps she might find it easier to speak with someone else, maybe with a woman rather than a man. She responded by hunching over even more from the edge of her chair, wheezing a little more laboriously, and pulling her shoulders forward so that she looked even more starved and wraithlike. A large tear rolled down one cheek and dropped to the rug. "If you send me away," she said, "I'll die!"

Things continued pretty much the same over the next three or four months, during which Laura remained all but completely silent while I put into words that she seemed to me to be feeling and shared with her my impressions as to the dynamic conflicts that seemed to underlie her feelings. She showed herself in general agreement with my observations, indicating this by nodding assent, but she did not hesitate to let me know when she disagreed with something I had said.

Finally, eight months after we had begun working together, she suddenly ended her silence and began to talk. The first thing she spoke about was her consultation with the psychiatrist who referred her to me. He had said that her condition was very serious and that she needed several treatment sessions a week. Since his office was quite a distance from her home, he had told her, the best thing for her would be to enter treatment with me, since I soon would be moving, not only to her area, but very close to where she lived. She had been disappointed, she said, but could see the wisdom of his remarks. It would have been all right, she added, if he hadn't taken her brother into treatment. Her brother had come down suddenly with a number of psychophysiological symptoms that had mimicked some of her problems and some of her father's recurrent problems, and the psychiatrist who had turned her away had taken her brother into treatment instead. She could understand his treating her brother, since he knew the family pretty well by then and her brother needed to travel to him only once a week for the relatively quick recovery he made. Still, she said, "It's not fair; it's not fair; I saw him first; why should he take him and not me?" She literally shuddered and shook with rage. The consulting psychiatrist had told her that I would be arriving in a couple of months, but he was wrong. It was eight long months before I arrived. She had had to wait eight months for me, so I had had to wait eight months for her!

At first I was stunned. When I recovered sufficiently to reflect upon what she had said, I found myself impressed not only with the primitivity of Laura's vindictive rage, but also with her obdurate adherence for eight long months to the single-minded goal of wreaking revenge upon the doctors, because they had inflicted upon her the narcissistic injury of being sent away "in favor of" her brother. And she had done this in total disregard of the cost to her in pain, suffering, and deprivation of precisely what she had wanted but which had been withheld from her in the first place. Her masochistic way of dealing with narcissistic mortification was impressive indeed.

During the months that followed, we scrutinized the dramatic beginning of her treatment with me. Not until several years had gone by, however, did we come to understand its full significance. The first topic that emerged, naturally enough, involved her relationship with her brother. She adored, admired, and envied him, but she also was furious at him for what she perceived as his teasing and tormenting of her, his failure to appreciate and respond to her, and his getting favored treatment from her parents.

What occurred with the consulting psychiatrist, she felt, only mirrored what she had experienced within her family over the years. Her love for her brother had always been a source of problems for her. She had been loyal to him, covering up for him to their parents whenever he had needed it and had been prepared to do just about anything for him. She had openly adored him. And what had been his response? He had ignored her overtures of affection; he had repeatedly gone off with his friends and rebuffed her when she had wanted to join in with them; he had turned her in to their parents on multiple occasions.

What especially hurt and incensed her was her brother's practice of teasing and picking on her at the dinner table, until she would lose her temper and begin screaming or throwing things at him. Her father would invariably explode in anger, leap out of his chair, and go after her. As afraid as Laura was of her brother's temper, her father's absolutely terrified her. She would take off at top speed to her room, with her father running after her. Usually, she would barely reach her room ahead of him, just manage to slam and lock the door, and collapse on the floor, her heart pounding, panting for breath. Soon she would be wheezing heavily, far too ill to eat. Seeing him coming after her with his eyes blazing in fury, she pictured him beating her to a pulp "or worse," although she could not remember his actually ever laying a hand on her (Wilson 1980).

Most infuriating of all, according to Laura, was her mother's failure to intervene. She would roll her eyes and groan, but she did nothing either to protect Laura from her brother or to restrain her father. Her mother claimed to be helpless to stop Laura's brother from teasing her or to calm her father down once he got his dander up. Laura was convinced that her mother did not side with her because she favored the males in the family. Her mother counseled her to pay no attention to her brother's barbs. She advised that he couldn't get her goat if she were wise enough not to respond when he goaded her. Laura viewed this as being told to swallow her pride and knuckle under to him. He was always getting favored treatment, Laura felt, going back as far as she could remember. What had happened with the doctors was only another episode in an old story.

Being a girl was a great disadvantage, Laura indicated, especially when it was complicated by the debilitating effects of asthma. At home she was no match for her brother and father. At school she could not compete with the boys athletically or win the interest and devotion she wanted from the other girls, although intellectually she held her own quite well. She was too thin and scrawny and much too quiet and shy to attract the boys' attention. She huffily resented the preference shown by the other girls for involvement with boys. Either they attempted to stir the boys' interest in them or they attached themselves to the boys' athletic activities in the auxiliary capacity of cheerleaders or boosters, rather than concentrating on their own clubs and athletic teams, as Laura would have preferred. (Eventually, Laura grudgingly acceded to the prevailing modes. She tried out for the cheerleaders and came surprisingly close to making the squad, until a bad asthmatic attack prevented her from attending the final tryout—probably, as I noted to her, because her exhibitionistic anxieties had supervened.)

Laura seethed with resentment over her mother's failure to pay her adequate attention (i.e., to make herself totally available to her as her first and foremost priority). She ignored the effort her mother was making, in response to Laura's own request, to stop worrying about her so much and to allow her more independence. She fumed also over her female classmates' tendency to "ignore" her. Nor was I exempted from her wrath.

She put me through a series of severe trials to test my interest, my devotion, my allegiance, my willingness to be available to her, and my readiness to sacrifice myself and my other interests for her, all of which she required to an absolute degree.

How was it, she would complain, that I did not always understand the nuances of what she was feeling? It was my job to understand. If I did not, it had to be that I was not sufficiently interested in her. I was not expending all the effort she had a right to expect from me. And when she was feeling particularly awful, how was it that I did not always know what to say to comfort her and make her feel better? Even her mother used to worry more about her and used to work harder to cheer her up and take care of her and try to make her feel better. Never mind that she used to complain about her mother babying her and worrying so much over her (and still complained when her grandmother did so, even though she obviously loved her grandmother showering attention upon her). And why was her mother paying less attention to her and backing off from trying to get her to gain weight? Was I responsible for that? Was I coming between her and her mother? Was it true that I only listened passively to her mother when she visited me, or was I advising her to pull away from Laura and stop devoting herself to her?

A series of events occurred that literally forced me to demonstrate that I was prepared to go to great lengths to be of help to her. Laura's asthma grew much worse, and her weight began to decline from its already precariously low state. She began more and more to resemble a cachectic concentration-camp victim, racked with pain and suffering, starved and starving, unable to breathe, pursued by the specter of death. Laura began to express the fear that she would die, despite my efforts to save her, or *because* of the inadequacies in my ministrations to her. I had taken away all the anxious and anxiety-provoking, but nevertheless devoted, nursing care her mother had been giving her. I had done so, if not directly, then by strengthening Laura's resolve to grow up and solve her own problems independent of her mommy's care. And I was proving to be a poor substitute for her mother indeed. Instead of helping her, I was killing her!

Not only was I finding myself increasingly anxious about the way things were going in Laura's treatment, but so were her parents and her pediatrician. Her parents began to look into alternative forms of treatment, and her pediatrician began to insist that Laura take the antiasthmatic medications he had been prescribing. She had been using them only sparingly, out of reluctance to depend upon external, chemical means of controlling her wheezing. He started her on chromalin sprays, and he *insisted* that she begin to ingest high-calorie diet supplements, or he would put her into the hospital for tube feedings.

Laura grew more dejected and pessimistic, and she made increasing demands upon me. I was required to shift appointments for her, deferring to the increasing visits to other doctors and to her need to stay after school to make up labs and examinations she had missed because of illness. I had to agree to giving her extra appointments she insisted she needed, at times late at night, on Saturday evening, or on Sunday. She was outraged when I had to be away for a weekend. When I told her once after an extra session early on a Saturday morning that I would be in New York teaching till midafternoon, her eyes flashed and she said, "What do you do that for? Don't you know you're needed *here!*"

"Mixups" in communication between Laura and her parents began to occur, which left her without transportation back home after a session. I found myself faced with the choice of either forcing Laura to walk the mile or so back to her house, wheezing badly and feeling so weak she felt faint, or else driving her there myself. I felt that I had no choice but to drive her on the few occasions when this occurred—just as I felt I had no choice but to accede several times to her request that I come to her house for our session when she felt physically unable to make the trip to my office.

We met in the new den her parents recently had added onto their home, although, as Laura emphasized, she hated that room. It had extended the house so that it now intruded into the flight path of birds that flew down from the woods. Periodically one would fly right into the big picture window and kill itself. What a horrible thing to happen! She felt sick every time she thought about it, and she was very angry at her parents for doing that to the birds. Sometimes, she said, she felt like she didn't have a friend in the world.

"You're talking about yourself," I replied. "You're one of those little birds. You feel little and weak and helpless and unable to deal either with the people around you, who seem so strong and powerful and uncaring about you, or with your own *inner* feelings and needs. And you've decided that the only way you can acquire power is to force people to pay attention to you and do what you want by threatening to kill yourself, by threatening to get terribly sick and die."

Laura burst into tears. Sobbing profusely, she delivered an abusive tirade against all the people, within her family and outside it, against whom she harbored a long list of accumulated grievances for not meeting her wants and needs sufficiently. It was true, too, she said, that she felt helpless not only against them but also against her own self. If she hadn't had desires and wants and needs, the satisfaction of which required the cooperation of people who refused to cooperate the way she wanted them to, she wouldn't need things from them in the first place. She didn't know if she were angrier at them or at herself, and she didn't know if she felt more helpless in dealing with them or in dealing with her own self! And then, to her astonishment (and to mine, too, I have to add), an extremely dramatic thing happened. She stopped wheezing. Also, as she informed me in a telephone call I received as soon as I returned from her home, she was ravenously hungry. She could hardly wait for our next session.

During the following months, nearly four years after we had begun, we worked very hard together at understanding the way in which she had focused her sense of helplessness and powerlessness upon her interaction with me, leading to the need to bully and blackmail me into becoming her dutiful slave by threatening to die unless I did her bidding. We found she had observantly recognized from very early on that she possessed a powerful means of reversing things so that she could obtain control over her parents. She accomplished this reversal by passive-aggressively plucking the strings of their hurt, fear, guilt, and frustrated sense of helplessness when she didn't eat or when she held her breath in a temper tantrum and passed out. After she gave up the breath holding she developed mild, apparently allergic wheezing. This, abetted by the lingering impact of the serious lung problems that had plagued her father and her paternal uncle before him, terrified her parents and provided her with enormous leverage against them. Her family's shared phobic-obsessive fear of aggressive impulses and of murderous fantasies, combined with a tendency to flee from them into substitutive psychosomatic expression, contributed to the crystallization of Laura's use of asthma and anorexia. They were an effective means of acquiring a feeling of power with which to overcome the narcissistic mortification of continual failures and defeats, real and imagined, and to keep her dangerous internal impulses at bay.

As we reconstructed the development of Laura's psychosomatic constellations, preoedipal factors at first predominated extensively. We moved beyond this stage as we scrutinized its transferential expression in Laura's feelings and fantasies about me (e.g., her competition with other female patients of mine or with female acquaintances she came to believe may have been in treatment with me, and her impression periodically that I was more interested in what her mother had to tell me than in what she had to say, or that I was taking her mother's side in conflicts between them). We were then able to address the oedipal conflicts that also underlay her symptomatology. I was able to help her see, behind her rage at and fear of her brother and father, the intense, overwhelming excitement she felt at being picked on, chased, or getting her feelings hurt by them, which had unconscious sexual connotations. Behind her anger and resentment at her mother lay similar excited feelings, which she felt the need to repress, deny, cover over, and transform into opposite feelings.

Laura gradually overcame her anorexia, and by the time she went off to college, seven years after the beginning of her treatment, her asthma had decreased enormously in intensity. I eventually learned, through chance meetings with her mother, that she had a very successful and enjoyable college experience. Afterward she settled in another state, where she now is happily married and is herself a mother. She wheezes slightly on occasion, but her anorexia has not recurred.

DISCUSSION

Child development, as Freud (1905) pointed out a long time ago, is molded by the confluence of three very important factors. First, human infants are born in an extremely immature, in fact premature, state, in which they are utterly helpless and totally dependent upon outside forces for their survival. Second, the road to adulthood is an extremely protracted one. Even after they have acquired sufficient maturity to take a very active part in meeting their own needs, children and adolescents for many years still find themselves highly dependent upon the adult world for sustenance, support, and a vast amount of assistance, emotionally as well as physically, before they are able to take over their own reins and more or less assume independent control over their lives. En route, they are keenly aware of their relative weakness, the incomplete development of their capabilities, and their need to bow to externally imposed rules and expectations. They know very well that they depend upon the adult world to provide for their immediate needs and to train and prepare them for their future adult roles.

Third, the balance between instinctive, automatic stimulus-response patterns and the learning (i.e., cultural transmission) of the methods by which internal and external requirements can be met and life's problems can be resolved is heavily weighted in favor of the latter. Human beings are equipped with very little in the way of built-in, prewired, instinctive mechanisms with which to gain control over the world around them and over the surging impulses emanating from the world within them. Children are forced to slowly and painstakingly acquire the emotional and intellectual skills with which they can obtain mastery over their environment and exercise control over themselves as they respond to their sexual and aggressive urges. Along the way, they are exquisitely (though not necessarily consciously) aware of their relative lack of power vis-à-vis the outside world and of the relative precariousness of their capacity for self-control.

In the best of circumstances, children chafe under the yoke of dependence upon, and domination by, their parents and other adults. They struggle mightily, but with only limited success, against the importunate demands of their internal, instinctual drive derivatives. To assist them in dealing with both sets of issues they use a variety of autoplastic and alloplastic mechanisms. Their own emotional conflicts and their own executive and adaptive styles, which evolve from a complex, spiral interaction between innate tendencies and experiential impact, interweave, in a reciprocally influential interaction, with those of their parents, siblings, and other key persons. Out of this interaction a variety of personal problems can emerge. If their parents' problems impinge directly upon them, this complicates matters even further.

Multiple factors can predispose to an outcome that includes somatic symptoms as an important mode of expression of emotional problems and struggles. Among these factors are an inherent disposition to certain kinds of physical illness, owing to individual physical variations. Different people are subject to different sorts of physical illness. Certain organ systems may be more susceptible to illness than others. Resistance to infection is not the same in everyone, and some individuals are more subject to intense muscular spasm affecting key structures and organs, greater tissue friability in particular body parts, hyper- or hyposecretion of certain body substances, allergic hypersensitivity and reactivity, and so on. Influential family members can encourage or reinforce a tendency to somatic expression of emotional conflict by encouraging certain inclinations and discouraging others and by presenting themselves as models for

psychosomatic identification. Chance, too, can play a part in predisposing a child to an expressive association between intense emotional
conflict and somatic illness. Among others, F. Deutsch (1939), Alexander
(1950), and L. Deutsch (1980) have emphasized the multiplicity of
etiological factors in the generation of psychosomatic disorders.

Although a certain amount of dynamic specificity appears to exist
among the various forms of psychosomatic illness, certain characteristics
appear to be more or less universal. Among these are a tendency to
predominance of pregenital conflicts, with an emphasis on separation
problems, intense mother–child ambivalence conflicts, a strong disposition to narcissistic vulnerability, narcissistic entitlement and narcissistic
rage, and regressive flight from the complexities of triadic interactional
conflict to the seemingly simpler issues involved in preoedipal, dyadic
interaction (Fenichel 1945, Sperling 1978). All of these were quite evident
in Laura.

What was highlighted in Laura's case was the child's use of somatic
illness to gain leverage and power to exert control over her parents instead
of being dominated, controlled, frustrated, disappointed, or pushed
around by them. Laura learned very early in her life that by not eating
she could frustrate, hurt, frighten, and induce painful guilt feelings in her
mother and could manipulate her parents and grandparents into extending themselves on her behalf and devoting themselves to her welfare.
She learned that by holding her breath and passing out she could terrify
and enslave her mother and then that she could accomplish the same ends
by wheezing instead. She discovered that she obtained far more attention
by being sick than by being well and that if she were ill with respiratory
problems, she would be showered with tender, loving care. As time went
on, she made increasing use of her asthma and anorexia to serve
additionally as a substitutive expression of the fantasies of aggressive,
furious attack upon her parents, brother, and friends that frightened her
and made her feel very guilty and of the masochistic rape fantasies that
excited but terrified her. In this way her wheezing attacks and anorexia
came to represent not only the means for gaining a sense of control over
the bigger, more powerful people around her, but also over the sexual and
aggressive impulses within her that dominated and frightened her.
Understanding and analyzing these dimensions as they appeared in the
transference and countertransference enactments taking place in her
treatment enabled them to be accessed and to be traced to their genetic
and dynamic roots within her relationships with her primary objects.

The importance in psychosomatic illness of the wish to control, manipulate, exert power over, and torture one's objects has been noted before (see Hogan 1983, Sperling 1978, 1983). Hogan states: "Masochistic control is a universal, constant preoccupation among anorexic patients. Threats of dying, suicide, etc., always play an important role" (p. 135). Laura succeeded in frightening her parents by threatening to die, and she used her ability to so frighten them in order to blackmail them into submitting to her as their master in important ways. She succeeded in doing so with me as well.

In retrospect, it is clear that this situation had to be dealt with in the treatment in a diphasic manner. At first, Laura *had to* demonstrate to herself that she could control the treatment situation. Only then could she feel safe enough to carry her sadomasochistic, near-suicidal control system over into the treatment situation in its full force. She was then able to verbalize her feelings in such a way that the unconscious, dynamic meaning of what she was doing could be interpreted to her. She was able also to hear what was being called to her attention and to grapple with it *together with me* in a verbal form. This process permitted insight, ego reorganization, and diminution in the feelings of helplessness and powerlessness that had impelled her to employ such drastic, self-destructive means of obtaining a sense of control. She largely gave up her psychosomatic symptomatology in favor of ego growth and developmental progress. The task was not an easy one for either of us, but it certainly was worth the effort.

REFERENCES

Alexander, F. (1950). *Psychosomatic Medicine: Its Principles and Application*. New York: W. W. Norton.

Brenman, M. (1952). On teasing and being teased: and the problem of "moral masochism." *Psychoanalytic Study of the Child* 7:264–285.

Deutsch, F. (1939). The choice of organ in organ neuroses. *International Journal of Psycho-Analysis* 20:252–262.

Deutsch, L. (1980). Psychosomatic medicine from a psychoanalytic viewpoint. *Journal of the American Psychoanalytic Association* 28:653–702.

Fenichel, O. (1945). *The Psychoanalytic Theory of Neurosis*. New York: W. W. Norton.

Freud, S. (1905). Three essays on the theory of sexuality. *Standard Edition* 7:125–245.

Hogan, C. C. (1983). Object relations. In *Fear of Being Fat: The Treatment of Anorexia Nervosa and Bulimia,* rev. ed., ed. C. P. Wilson, C. C. Hogan, and I. L. Mintz, pp. 129–149. Northvale, NJ: Jason Aronson, 1985.

Sours, J. (1969). Anorexia nervosa: nosology, diagnosis, developmental patterns, and power-control dynamics. In *Adolescence: Psychosocial Perspectives,* ed. G. Caplan and S. Lebovici, pp. 185–212. New York: Basic Books.

Sperling, M. (1978). *Psychosomatic Disorders in Childhood.* New York: Jason Aronson.

———— (1983). A reevaluation of classification, concepts, and treatment. In *Fear of Being Fat: The Treatment of Anorexia Nervosa and Bulimia,* rev. ed., ed. C. P. Wilson, C. C. Hogan, and I. L. Mintz, pp. 51–82. Northvale, NJ: Jason Aronson.

Wilson, C. P. (1980). Parental overstimulation in asthma. *International Journal of Psychoanalytic Psychotherapy* 8:601–621.

PART III

THE GASTROINTESTINAL SYSTEM

15

INFLAMMATORY DISEASE OF THE COLON

Charles C. Hogan, M.D., D. Med. Sc.

Weinstock (1962) reviewed the psychoanalytic and psychoanalytic psychotherapeutic treatment of sixty-eight cases of ulcerative colitis and concluded without equivocation that "adequate treatment by psychoanalysis offers a greater possibility for long-term remissions or perhaps cure in the severe unremitting type of ulcerative colitis than any other treatment with the exception of surgery" (p. 248). A review of this paper is of great interest because the author has eliminated the milder and shorter-term cases, leaving only those patients with illness of such severity that they required one or more hospitalizations. These twenty-eight remaining cases had been followed for at least three years after treatment. Twenty-two cases were symptom free three to eighteen years after treatment. The outcome of the other six cases is described in some detail.

When one compares Weinstock's findings about ulcerative colitis to the conclusions presented in the *Fact Book* of the National Foundation for Ileitis and Colitis (Banks, Present, and Steiner 1983), one wonders whether we are discussing the same disease. The *Fact Book* states that "most physicians who treat inflammatory bowel disease no longer feel that stress plays any role in causing this disease" (p. 131) and that colitis patients "have also been labeled with a wide variety of psychiatric diagnoses. Patients and their families have experienced much unnecessary guilt and anxiety because of the myth that Crohn's disease and ulcerative colitis are 'psychosomatic diseases.' " Reading these latter comments, some of us would agree with Jackson (1976) when he muses, "It seems to me remarkable that so much psychopathology can pass unnoticed by experienced physicians" (p. 180).

These two excerpts are excellent illustrations of the disagreements that have arisen in the understanding and treatment of inflammatory bowel disease.

This chapter is organized into four parts, which present (1) the organic pathophysiology of inflammatory bowel disease, differentiating chronic ulcerative colitis from Crohn's disease of the colon, (2) a brief review of some studies of the psychopathology associated with the pathophysiology of the illnesses, (3) a psychoanalytic approach to the understanding and treatment of the psychopathology, and (4) a very brief summary.

I am omitting the multitude of studies based on psychological testing of one sort or another. Perhaps Engel and Salzman's (1973) critical letter to the *New England Journal of Medicine*, complaining about the "objectivity" of one such series, illustrates the difficulties inherent in this approach.

There is a voluminous and interesting body of experimental data on the muscular physiology, the neurophysiology, the biochemistry, and the endocrinology and hormonal mechanics of the colon in disease and health. References to these and other studies are included in excellent reviews and bibliographies by Engel (1954a,b, 1955), Almy and Lewis (1963), Karush and colleagues (1977), and Weiner (1977). I refer the interested reader to these publications.

Like Crohn and Yarnis (1958), Fein (1979) noted that "It is probable that Morgagni as early as 1769 in *De Sedibus et Causis Morborum (The Seats and Causes of Disease)* gave the first clinical description of a case of *intero colitis* with particular involvement of the colon" (Morgagni 1769, p. 1).

Another early investigation of inflammatory bowel disease was intimately connected with Guy's Hospital in London. The first clear description of such inflammation of the colon was included in a series of lectures at Guy's by Samuel Wilks and Walter Moxon, which was published in 1875. They referred to a number of such cases, where death and the pathological findings followed a history of long-standing chronic disease. White (1888) reviewed the pathology in a series of autopsied cases from the same hospital. As one reviews the descriptions, it is clear that ulcerative colitis and Crohn's disease specimens were both present in the series. Ileitis was present in varying degrees in cases 2, 4, 9, 10, and 11.

The history of the early investigations of the psychopathology of ulcerative colitis (and/or Crohn's disease) is fascinating. Such clinicians as Murray (1930a,b), Sullivan and Chandler (1932), Sullivan (1935), Daniels (1941, 1942), and Sperling (1946), as well as many others, will be briefly reviewed and discussed in my general discussion of psychopathology.

WHAT CONSTITUTES INFLAMMATORY DISEASE OF THE LARGE BOWEL?

In this chapter I am dealing with the so-called idiopathic inflammations of the colon. I shall not include those diseases of known bacterial, protozoan, viral, or traumatic etiology.

The early studies listed all idiopathic inflammatory involvements of the colon under the heading of ulcerative colitis. However, Crohn, Ginzburg, and Oppenheimer (1932) described a disease of the terminal ileum in young adults of a granulomatous nature with "a marked tendency toward perforation" (p. 1324). This illness was soon found to involve other portions of the gastrointestinal tract. Atwell and colleagues (1965) noted that "Crohn's disease may affect any part of the alimentary tract from the oesophagus to the anal canal" (p. 970).

It is now evident that we are dealing with two disease entities that seem to be related. There is a large body of medical literature dealing with the similarities and differences found in chronic ulcerative colitis and Crohn's disease. Before proceeding to a description of the two entities, it is worth pointing out that McKegney and colleagues (1970), in a rather extensive study of the patients involved, observed that "There are no significant differences between patients with the two diseases in a large number of demographic, psychosocial, personality, behavioral, psychiatric and physical disease characteristics. In both syndromes, more severe emotional disturbance is associated with more severe demonstrable physical disease" (p. 153).

Ulcerative Colitis as a Physical Entity—Description

The physical characteristics of this illness were tersely but clearly described by Bruno (1979). He begins: "Ulcerative colitis is a confluent, erosive, inflammatory process which is symmetrical and specifically involves the mucosal surfaces of the colon" (p. 6). Bruno elaborates on the distribution of disease patterns, noting that the disease often stops at the midtransverse colon, and there is total involvement of the colon in about 30 percent of the cases. Ulcerative proctitis is the most common form of ulcerative colitis.

Pathologically, this author emphasizes that ulcerative colitis is a process involving one layer of the colon wall, the mucosal. There may be ulcers, complete effacement of the mucosae, ulcers and effacement, with residual mucosal ridges, and/or pseudopolyps with hypertrophy of residual islets of mucosae. The submucosae is occasionally involved, but this is not characteristic of the disease. The disease process is symmetrical and confluent.

This clear definition in most cases of the involvement of only one layer of the colon wall and the confluence of the lesion are important, in that this differentiates ulcerative colitis from Crohn's disease, as we shall see below.

The serious complications of ulcerative colitis may include peritonitis, with or without perforation, toxic megacolon, anal abscess formation, and abscess formation and exsanguination (Goodman and Sparberg 1978). Chronic ulcerative colitis can lead to pseudopolyposis, uncommonly to strictures, perianal abscesses, fistulae, and fissures, and to carcinoma (Crohn and Rosenberg 1925, Goldgraber and Kirsner 1964, Goodman and Sparberg 1978, among others).

Systemic complications may include joint disorders, rheumatoid arthritis, ankylosing spondylitis, sacroileitis, arthritis of inflammatory bowel disease, erythremia nodosum, pyrodermagangrenosum, stomatitis, conjunctivitis, uveitis, iritis, fatty liver, pericholangitis, chronic active hepatitis, cirrhosis, bile duct carcinoma, iatrogenic liver disease, folic acid deficiency vasculitis, pericarditis, myocarditis, goiter, and thyrotoxicosis (Almy 1961a,b, 1975, Engel 1954a,b, 1961, 1973, Goodman and Sparberg 1978, Kern 1975, Roth 1976, among others). Other accompanying symptoms are headache, simple and migraine. I personally have noted the latter to appear for the first time during psychoanalytic treatment of the illness. I have also noted eczematoid rashes that occurred during remissions in two cases.

The initiating symptoms of ulcerative colitis are usually bleeding, diarrhea, bloody diarrhea, and/or abdominal pain and cramps. Less often constipation may be the first complaint.

The prognosis seems to have a mortality rate with a severe attack of 5 to 10 percent; with a moderate attack 1 to 2 percent and virtually 0 percent in mild attacks. There is an annual death rate of 1 percent in patients under 60 and 5 percent in patients over 60. In young adults the twenty-year survival rate is 95 percent of the expected rate. In children the twenty-year survival rate is 60 percent of the expected rate. Goodman and Sparberg (1978) observe, "It seems that ulcerative colitis always relapses eventually" (p. 191).

The operative mortality of total colectomy performed as an emergency procedure is roughly 15 to 30 percent; elective colectomy is 2 percent or less. Between 10 and 20 percent of patients with ulcerative colitis who have been treated with permanent ileostomy will need further surgery.

Clearly, ulcerative colitis is a severe, chronic and often life-threatening disease, which often presents a somewhat gloomy prognosis with conventional treatments.

Crohn's Disease of the Colon as a Physical Entity

Bruno (1979) writes that "Granulomatous colitis or Crohn's disease was originally described as an inflammatory process involving only the terminal ileum" (p. 8) Incidentally, because of this historic definition, it is not uncommon to hear Crohn's disease used as a descriptive term for all cases of ileitis.

As we will note, this illness can involve any segment of the gastrointestinal tract from the mouth to the anus. Iliocolitis is the most common form, but the ileum is not necessarily involved. Anal symptoms may be the presenting problem, and anorectal Crohn's disease is not uncommon.

Bruno writes, "Pathologically, Crohn's disease is an inflammatory process that involves the submucosae, rather than the mucosae" (p. 8). All layers of the small intestine or colon may be involved, which can give rise to the various fistulous tracts mentioned below. In about 50 percent of the cases, granuloma or microgranuloma is present. Eosinophiles and macrophages are found in the crypt abcesses, the transverse fissures, and the lymphoid hyperplasia.

Skip areas of involvement are very common, as well as stricture formation and obstruction. The important and often most devastating complication of Crohn's disease is the tendency toward fistulae formation, which may be iliocolonic, colon-bladder, ilio- or colon-peritoneal, ilio- or colon-abdominal, colon-bladder, rectal-perineal, colon- or iliovaginal, and so on (Korlitz 1979, among others).

There are many similarities between ulcerative colitis and Crohn's. All of the complications described for ulcerative colitis may occur with Crohn's, including the development of massive gastrointestinal hemorrhage or megacolon (Bruno 1979).

The onset of the disease may differ from that of ulcerative colitis. First symptoms may be developmental defects, symptoms of malabsorption syndrome, or other nutritional difficulties. There may be low-grade fever, anorexia, malaise, or persistent nonbloody diarrhea. On the other hand, patients with involvement of the distal colon and/or rectum may produce the typical bleeding or bloody diarrhea as their first symptom.

There has been some controversy over the results and advisability of surgical procedures in Crohn's (Correspondence 1977). From a purely mechanical, physiological point of view, surgery on ulcerative colitis is far more successful than surgery on Crohn's. Korlitz has remarked (1979), "We know also that following any type of surgery for Crohn's disease, there is a recurrence rate of about 15 percent per year" (p. 12).

The annual incidence of Crohn's disease in the United States and northern Europe is three to five per 100,000 population, as opposed to ulcerative colitis for which it is five to ten per 100,000 (Goodman and Sparberg 1978). The incidence of ulcerative colitis has been relatively stable since the 1950s, while that of Crohn's has been "rising by two to three fold between 1958 and 1973" (p. 7).

It bears repeating that McKegney and colleagues (1970) noted that there are no significant differences between patients with the two diseases and that the severity of syndromes correlated with the severity of the emotional disturbances.

PSYCHOPATHOLOGY OF INFLAMMATORY BOWEL DISEASE

As a medical student working in George Draper's department at Columbia Presbyterian Medical Center, C. D. Murray (1930a,b) contributed the first significant psychological studies on ulcerative colitis. He was followed by Sullivan and Chandler (1932) and Sullivan (1935) in New Haven.

During this same period Daniels (1941, 1942) had been working psychologically with ulcerative colitis cases at Columbia Presbyterian Medical Center, following up Murray's early work. Sperling (1946) had begun working with children and reported on the psychoanalytic study of ulcerative colitis in children beginning in 1942.

It was an exciting period of discovery. All approached their patients with a dynamic, generally psychoanalytic approach, and all were impressed by the correlatations of the onset of the disease with preceding emotional conflicts, often involving the loss of a loved object or its symbolic equivalent. All were equally impressed by the discovery of similar emotional disturbances antedating exacerbations of the illness. Starting with Murray, all noted the suppressed anger, which was denied or repressed. Murray, as well as Sullivan, Daniels, and Sperling, was struck by the intense abnormal attachment to the mother or a maternal surrogate. Sullivan noticed the tendency to "helplessness" and "giving up" in such patients.

Daniels (1941), in referring to Alexander's colonic types of personality, made some important observations on the character structures of ulcerative colitis patients. He noted the narcissistic organizations of the personalities of such people, and he felt that the "underlying reaction [is] more a psychotic than a psychoneurotic case" (p. 83). He, along with others, noted that the symptoms often mask a severe depression and he felt that the disease often seemed to be "a type of organic suicide." He, like many others, noted the direct relationship between the severity of the physical illness and the underlying psychiatric disturbance.

Sperling (1946) was also impressed with the aggression and felt that the bloody diarrhea was an outlet for such anger. She, too, noted the ambivalent attachment to the mother and emphasized the relationship of the psychopathology to melancholia. Sperling, more than the others, from an early date was interested in a rather strict psychoanalytic approach and was doubtful about the advantages of supportive psychotherapy.

The most important discovery of these early investigators was how well their patients seemed to do with the often brief and rudimentary use of exploratory psychotherapy. Also, despite a few differences, they were unanimous in their observations on the importance of primitive aggression, the defenses against it, the threatening conflict over the loss of an object, and the role of the mother.

As interesting as this early historical material is, with its abundant clinical illustrations, I shall forego any further detail here. These early years are generally well covered by Engel (1955), Karush and colleagues (1977), and Weiner (1977). These authors also give a rather extensive review of the literature briefly discussed below.

This work was soon followed by that of Groen (1947), who refers back to unpublished work by C. Van der Heide in 1938, who had fully confirmed Murray's findings. He continued his studies on ulcerative colitis and other psychosomatic diseases (Groen 1947, 1951, Groen and Bastiaans 1954, Groen and Birnbaum 1968, Groen and Van der Valk 1956), generally emphasizing supportive therapy. Groen and his co-workers were impressed by the humiliation which accompanied the loss of the object.

Lindemann (1945, 1950) had also begun work in the 1930s that confirmed the findings of Murray and Daniels. He is notable for his initiation of replacement therapy and the anaclitic treatment of ulcerative colitis.

Prugh (1950, 1951) in the early 1950s studied pediatric patients. He noted (1951) "the appearance of spontaneous or experimentally induced angry or aggressive emotions and an immediate activation of a hyper-mobile colonic response" (p. 353).

Daniels and co-workers (1941, 1942, 1944, 1948, 1962) continued their work and reported on two cases who had undergone psychoanalysis (Karush and Daniels 1953). Daniels and his co-workers embarked on what appeared to be a rather comprehensive approach to the evaluation of psychotherapy for ulcerative colitis. The progress of this work was covered in a group of papers (Daniels et al. 1962, Karush and Daniels 1953, Karush et al. 1955, 1968, 1969, O'Connor 1966, O'Connor et al. 1970) authored in general by the group. The culmination of this endeavor was their monograph by Karush and colleagues (1977), in which they summarized their findings. They tried to classify their subjects and to tailor the psychotherapy to the individual patient. With the exception of the two cases reported by Karush and Daniels (1953, 1977) who were treated with psychoanalysis, the other thirty cases were treated with psychotherapy, varying from four months to two-plus years. This study centered on a "team" appproach that included the internist, psychiatrist, and surgeon. Their study certainly demonstrated that at least some of their patients were helped by psychotherapy of various types. Other major contributions of the monograph are the statistical studies of patients treated in the presteroid era; those treated with steroids; and those treated with azulfadine. As shown in most studies, the long-term results do not seem to be very much affected by the use of these drugs.

In even the briefest review of ulcerative colitis, one cannot ignore or treat lightly the contributions of Engel (1952, 1954a,b, 1955, 1956, 1958, 1961, 1967, 1973). He called attention to constipation and bleeding as presenting symptoms. He contributed an excellent review of the literature before 1955, as well as calling attention to the pregenital nature of the defenses, the pathologically dependent relationship on objects, the psychopathology of the mother, and the occurrences of the onset and relapses of the disease with a threatened or fantasied interruption of a key relationship developed with the affect of helplessness, despair, and hopelessness. He first noted that headaches accompanied the disease, occurring more often when the patient was angry and felt in control rather than when the patient felt helpless and hopeless. He was interested in the importance of unconscious aggressive and sadistic impulses. Engel's (1955, 1956, 1958) emphasis was on supportive psychotherapy, and he felt that lifelong treatment was necessary. His discussions of experimental and biological models are too extensive to even approach in this chapter. Although he is an internist and a psychoanalyst, he has seemed to show little interest or faith in the psychoanalytic treatment of these patients.

Another investigator of note is Almy. He and his co-workers (Almy and Tulin 1947, Almy et al. 1949, 1961a,b) were interested in the colon under stress and studied the literature, experimental studies, physiology, pathology, and treatment of ulcerative colitis (Almy and Lewis 1963, Almy and Sherlock 1966, Almy and Tulin 1947). His interest in the physiological and psychological factors involved in ulcerative colitis led him to positions on prognosis and treatment that roughly parallel those of Engel.

Internists and surgeons vary greatly in their view of the role of psychopathology and psychiatric treatment. Many deny any relationship at all and recommend keeping patients away from psychiatrists. The negative position of the National Foundation for Ileitis and Colitis was stated at the beginning of this chapter. It would appear that the majority are in favor of supportive psychotherapy as an ancillary help. Some recommend continuous supportive psychotherapy. Some specifically warn against the use of psychoanalysis or psychoanalytic psychotherapy. Very few recommend psychotherapy as the primary therapeutic approach. It is probably important to note that many surgeons recommend prophylactic colectomy and iliostomy to avoid carcinoma of the colon. Sperling (1969, 1978) refers to some of these data.

An interesting conclusion to this discussion of general psychopathology is provided by a study by Stout and Snyder (1969) of four deceased Simiang gibbons from two different zoos. "According to 'zoo lore' a Simiang gibbon will frequently pine away and die following the loss of a long-time cage mate" (p. 257). Animals who died with chronic debilitation under these conditions in two separate locations were autopsied, and lesions identical to those of human ulcerative colitis were discovered. They were cultured for shigella, salmonella, and pathogenic coliform bacteria, but none were found.

Perhaps it would appear that at least one other species can react to the loss of a love object or its equivalent with a fatal inflammatory disease of the colon.

As one reviews the literature, one finds a multitude of observations linking psychopathology (emotional conflicts) with the pathophysiology of inflammatory bowel disease. Marked disagreements are expressed by a few physicians, who maintain a singular mechanical organic orientation toward physiology and pathology and deny any relevance to psychic conflict.

THE PSYCHOANALYTIC TREATMENT OF INFLAMMATORY BOWEL DISEASE

I have as yet made little mention of traditional psychiatric diagnoses, although most investigators attempt some such classification. Clearly, a small minority of patients are psychotic or give a history of psychotic episodes. Most show obsessional characteristics, but some (note Louis below) also show hysterical features. In my experience, none at the time of consultation, fell into any readily definable, traditional diagnostic category. Only after the masochistic organic self-destruction was relieved did more discernible clinical patterns emerge. In my series they all seemed to be inhibited, impulse-ridden characters who displayed depressive and sometimes phobic symptoms as treatment progressed. They all utilized typical regressed pregenital defense mechanisms and showed the usual personality patterns of people using defenses against primitive impulses and fantasies. I feel that any further attempt at classification would be compulsive and misleading.

Perhaps my note (1983c) and Giovacchini's (1977) comment about his patient may be of some importance here: ". . . a masochistic adjustment that is designed to affect a psychodynamic balance; the defensive constellation of my patient was vital to maintaining a total ego coherence instead of dealing with disruptive impulses" (p. 10). The discrete psychopathology seems to remain hidden in the major life-threatening pathophysiological symptomatology and emerges only as the colitis is relinquished. At that time discrete neurotic constellations are available for analysis. As Giovacchini implied, it is only then that one can clearly discern, understand, and interpret particular defenses and emerging specific impulses.

Even among those investigators who recognize the need for psychotherapy in the treatment of inflammatory bowel disease, there seems to be a remarkable ambivalence. Some specifically caution against the use of psychoanalysis.

This rather cautious distancing is particularly interesting, since the early work on the psychopathology of this disease was so clearly based on psychoanalytic principles (Murray 1930a,b, Sullivan and Chandler 1932, Sullivan 1935, Daniels 1941, 1942, Sperling 1946a,b, among many other later contributors) and so many of the core conflicts were elucidated with unusual unanimity by those early investigators.

It cannot be the result of unreported cases in the literature, Weinstock's (1962) series of psychoanalyzed cases will stand up to any series of medically or surgically treated cases that I have reviewed.

Sperling (1978) reported on her successfully treated cases: "I have follow-up studies from three to twenty-three years on patients whom I have treated for ulcerative colitis. From 1943 to the present I have treated twenty-one patients intensively and eleven for shorter periods of time (p. 348). They were all severe cases of ulcerative colitis before they came for treatment, and none of them developed cancer. I think this is of particular interest in view of the frequency of polyposis and cancer in medically treated cases" (p. 72). She (1964) published a twenty-year follow-up study of a child whom she had treated successfully for severe ulcerative colitis when he was $7\frac{1}{2}$ years old. This series, along with the forty-five patients she had seen in consultation and the nineteen cases she had supervised, compares most favorably to any series of patients treated with other forms of medical, surgical, or supportive therapy.

Also, individual reports of treatment of specific patients are not at all rare (Cushing 1953, Savitt 1977, Sperling 1946a,b, 1955, 1957, 1978, to give but a few).

The incidence of ulcerative colitis is such that, as a public health problem, more abbreviated methods of treatment than psychoanalysis or intensive psychoanalytic psychotherapy might seem to be of medical importance at the moment. Perhaps this concern plays some part in the apparent indifference by such a large body of investigators to a psychoanalytic approach. The time required for psychoanalytic therapy may be seen to be of lesser importance when one observes the lifelong medical supervision and/or surgery that is part and parcel of most other current therapies.

It is also obvious that there are relatively few trained psychoanalysts with interest in, experience with, and techniques for the treatment of psychosomatic diseases. However, we hope that this will soon change. The present scarcity may help explain the relative paucity of active interest in psychoanalytic treatment, but it does not obviate its use or efficacy.

At any rate, we do know that the intensive psychoanalytic study of one case is far more valuable than any statistical study of emotional factors in a number of cases. This is particularly true if the psychoanalytic study of individual cases can be replicated by many analysts and the results compared, as has been done.

My own experience with the psychoanalysis of psychosomatic patients has been facilitated, expanded, and to some extent molded by my participation in the Psychosomatic Study Group of the Psychoanalytic Association of New York, Inc., which is composed of psychoanalytically trained psychiatrists. The group was led by Dr. Melitta Sperling from 1965 until 1973, the year of her death. Since that time the moderator has been Dr. C. P. Wilson. With this long-term research, we have had the opportunity to review and discuss the analyses of numerous cases of inflammatory colitis. My discussion of the psychoanalytic treatment of inflammatory bowel disease calls on this background of mutual help and shared experience.

Psychoanalytic Technique and Modifications

A number of principles, many of them first promulgated by Dr. Sperling, have guided us in our endeavors. I shall spell them out and discuss them with clinical examples.

The first and most important principle is to maintain the primacy of the one-to-one psychoanalytic relationship. We have reason to believe that the team approach complicates the transference relationship, confusing the patient's understanding of transference so that accurate interpretation is impossible. Sperling has discussed this at length (1949, 1955, 1957, 1959b, 1967a, 1969). She further states, "It makes for a division between the somato- and psychopathology and makes it difficult if not impossible to correlate the somatic and psychological factors operating in ulcerative colitis" (1969, p. 346).

It is necessary to have a thorough medical work-up and an internist on call for follow-up examination and consultation. The psychoanalyst, however, must be the "doctor," and all decisions must be made by the psychoanalyst and the patient (after a consultation between the professionals, if necessary).

We realize that this procedure runs counter to admonitions by internists and surgeons, who often feel that psychotherapy should be used as an ancillary help, if at all. Cautionary tales abound in the literature, warning the unwary that the patient should be under the primary and complete control of the internist or surgeon, who is aware of the severity of the disease.

I agree that caution is not only advisable but absolutely necessary, and I feel that patients with inflammatory bowel disease should be treated only by a psychoanalyst who is a physician well trained in handling psychosomatic illness. Naturally, as I have stated, the psychoanalyst should be in consultation with a good internist who is well acquainted with the psychosomatic dimensions of this illness. This is particularly true when it comes to the use or discontinuance of steroids and other medications in the therapy. This is too complicated a question to discuss in detail here, but we frequently find that it is an absolute advantage to discontinue drugs as the patient finds he is able to control his own colon. It has been repeatedly noted that while steroids may help to shorten a severe exacerbation of this illness, they are of little help in reducing the number of exacerbations or ultimately influencing the course of this illness. Obviously one does not immediately cease preexisting medication. When and if it is terminated, it is tapered off with the patient's understanding of the reasons and some agreement on the purpose. The patient must ultimately experience the fact that he controls his own bowel.

One very dramatic example was that of a young man with Crohn's disease of the descending colon and the rectum. This patient had been ill for seven years and was suffering with a severe relapse of six months duration. Surgery had been recommended, and he was brought to my office in a recumbent position. He was on prednisone, valium, and azulfadine at the time.

With modified psychoanalytic treatment he was off all medication in three months, and in six months he was driving himself to my office. I shall return to this case later.

As a second important principle: we do not favor supportive psychotherapy, despite its endorsement by many authors (Almy 1975, Engel 1961, 1973, Karush et al. 1977, Korlitz 1979, to list only a few). While Karush and colleagues found it a valuable adjunct in their series of cases, Weinstock (1962) found in his series that short-term psychotherapy in the hospital was of little value.

We feel that if intensive psychoanalytic psychotherapy is available, it is by far preferable to supportive treatment. The latter is inclined to bring the longings and ambivalence for the mother into an unanalyzed transference situation, at times apparently leading to an exacerbation of the illness. This has been rather thoroughly discussed by Sperling (1967a, 1969, 1978). One clinical example of mine was a middle-aged man with a milder case of recurrent ulcerative colitis of ten years duration. He had previously been seeing a generally supportive psychotherapist while being treated medically by his internist. He had recurrent exacerbations whenever his therapist was away for even a few days. Such exacerbations are not uncommon on separation from a psychoanalyst early in treatment, but usually they do not recur continually after the analysis is in progress. Such transference material has then been analyzed. With this particular patient such exacerbations had been recurring in his previous treatment for five years. He was gratified when he discovered the reasons for the recurrences, but he was also as angry at his previous therapist as he had been toward his mother, who frustrated him with unfilled promises when well but attentively cared for him when he was ill. I shall identify this patient later as William.

Third, we feel that certain modifications of the classic psychoanalytic technique are necessary. In younger patients it is of tremendous importance to place the mother and preferably both parents in treatment. Even the young man with Crohn's disease whom I mentioned above, whom I will call Louis for future identification, was greatly helped by my placing his mother in psychoanalysis with a colleague. Although he was 26, he was totally dependent upon his parents.

In the psychoanalytic psychotherapy of children, Sperling has used concomitant treatment of mother and child. With younger children she usually began treatment of the mother before treating the child.

The modified technique used with other psychosomatic cases is also applicable in the treatment of these patients. Sperling (1946a, 1955, 1957, 1959, 1967a, 1969) Hogan (1983a–e) Wilson, and Mintz (1983) have emphasized the need to handle such patients in a manner similar to that used in handling borderline and narcissistic patients, as described by Boyer (1975, 1980), Giovacchini (1980), Kernberg (1980), and Volkan (1976).

Understanding and handling transference and countertransference in inflammatory bowel disease presents many of the same problems one finds in other psychosomatic conditions. Hogan (1983c) and Sperling (1967a,b, 1969), among others, have gone into this in some detail. Obviously the use of the symptom in the complicated layers of defense must be interpreted in terms of the patient's attempt to control the analyst early in treatment, and this must be related to the control of other objects as well as the primary object.

Patients with inflammatory bowel disease present special problems. If handled poorly, their illness can rapidly prove fatal. It is often incumbent on the psychoanalyst to terminate the acute phase of the illness as soon as possible, and this often requires rather authoritative intervention. It is frequently valuable to interpret the symptom as a substitute for an affect, in much the same manner as dream symbols were interpreted in the early days of psychoanalysis.

Let me return to Louis, the 26-year-old male with Crohn's disease of the descending colon and rectum. He had been severely ill for seven years and had had multiple hospitalizations for cachexia, bleeding, bacteremia, aortic regurgitation, and so on. Various treatments had been instituted at various times. He had been subjected to two courses of hyperalimentation. Steroids had been given for long periods at frequent intervals, including prednisone, hydrocortisone suppositories, and hydrocortisone enemas. Azulfidine and other antibiotics had been given intermittently. Among other medications, Valium, Mylanta, and Gelusil were frequently prescribed. He had been through two courses of supportive psychotherapy and was under constant medical attention. Records of his various hospitalizations and pathological reports are available.

When he came to see me, he was for the most part bedridden, suffering from an acute exacerbation of six months duration. Colectomy and iliostomy had been recommended, despite the generally discouraging results of surgery in Crohn's disease.

I immediately interpreted his need for self-destruction and related his frequent episodes of bloody diarrhea to situations where ordinarily one would expect him to feel hurt, frustrated, and angry. He could see and acknowledge such a relationship. At the end of the first week of treatment, he related his mental state at the time of his current exacerbation six months previously. At that time he had seriously considered murdering a man who had previously humiliated him. He also said he carried a knife with him whenever he could get out of the house.

It became increasingly clear that the immediate, severe exacerbation of six-months duration was a substitution for the intended murder in this fantasy, which he felt he consciously intended to carry out.

As he became increasingly aware of his anger, his acute bowel disturbance cleared, his weight went from about 90 to 130 pounds, and in a few months his general physical health returned to near normal.

Later, as we worked through his identificatory attachment to his mother, his profound narcissistic humiliation accompanying any rejection, his sadism toward his loved objects, and his need for total control of them, he proceeded to obtain work for the first time in five years.

It was evident in this case that immediate interpretative intervention was necessary. Such active participation is obviously more important in acute bowel inflammation than in other conditions; yet this intervention must be thoroughly understood and handled with tact and empathy.

As I have emphasized elsewhere (1983b–d), it is of utmost importance to interpret the masochistic derivatives of aggression and the vicissitudes of these derivatives before approaching the unconscious sadism. (In the case of Louis the sadistic murderous wishes were conscious and volunteered. They were not interpreted.) In inflammatory bowel disease I feel that one sees, to a greater degree than in any other psychosomatic condition, the suicidal qualities of these derivatives. Such a potential imposes the greatest discretion on the analyst. Daniels' (1941) brilliant early observation: "In several cases the disease seemed definitely a type of organic suicide" has been repeatedly confirmed in our observations (p. 183).

We might contrast this patient to Joe, a married 28-year-old chronic ulcerative colitis patient who had started life with eczema, which disappeared after the onset of colitis at age 9. Joe had been in treatment off and on for the past nineteen years, showing by his short stature and mild developmental deficiencies, the results of prolonged colitis and steroid therapy.

When Joe began treatment he was not in acute distress but had frequent episodes of multiple stools, sometimes bloody.

Here again, I interpreted his masochism and his severe punitive conscience early. He readily saw the relationship of his diarrhea to helpless frustration and to what others might have experienced as conscious anger. His need to feel in control of his external perceptions of his spouse and parents was not hard for him to understand, and symptomatic improvement followed.

However, Joe presented a different introductory problem than did the far more seriously ill Louis. He could not free-associate, verbalized few fantasies, dreamed only occasionally, and saw the world in terms of behavior, action, and reaction. His primitive strict superego judged every thought and action as good or bad, better or worse, healthy or unhealthy, and so forth.

Sifneos (1972, 1973) has called this type of patient "alexithymic." An immense volume of literature has evolved around this label, which is applied to patients who seem to have a shallow fantasy life, a paucity of dreams, and a general inability to verbalize emotional responses. These qualities are commonly displayed by patients with inflammatory bowel disease, but not necessarily, as I demonstrated in the case of Louis. Some of the early work on so-called "alexithymia" is summarized in the 1977 volume, Brautigam and Rad (1976) Proceedings of the eleventh European Conference on Psychosomatic Research, Heidelberg.

From a psychoanalytic point of view, such a term for character traits that vary from patient to patient and are the end results of certain defensive processes, seems unnecessary and perhaps misleading.

In Joe's case, the resistance to verbalizing was clear. Although acting-out material and occasional dream material allowed transference interpretations, he would only "allow as how" there might be the possibility of anger, and he refused to work with such psychological presentations. However, at the time of his father's death, as a matter of policy, I charged him for the two psychoanalytic sessions he had missed. The narcissistic hurt and rage were immense. He sought out consultations with other psychiatrists and psychoanalysts, some of whom agreed with him about the unfeeling physician to whom he had subjected himself and recommended immediate change of therapists.

Joe remained, and, more important, he began to verbalize the hostility he had felt toward me over the previous months. Now that he felt justified, and was not subjected to the shame, denial, and resultant splitting occasioned by his primitive superego and the superego precursors he was able to go back and point out what he considered to be my unfeeling personality and my inadequacies. He retraced in anger and detailed each and every slight he had experienced in fact or fantasy over those previous months. As we worked this through in terms of his own intrapsychic conflicts, the "alexithymia" disappeared, free association became possible, and a rich but primitive fantasy life was increasingly available. This case illustrates the overwhelming importance of the use of transference.

Patients with inflammatory bowel disease, like other psychosomatic patients, have severe problems with the fragmented internal representations of their primary objects. The ambivalence toward the perceptions of their loved contemporary objects is of a most primitive sort. The sadism and accompanying shame once directed toward the primary object is now directed toward its projected representation and must be denied. This denial is accomplished with accompanying fragmentation and splitting (Hogan 1983a–c).

In effect, much as the milder psychoneurotic patient is subject to signal anxiety, the psychosomatic patient is subject to signal shame and humiliation from the projected superego fragment that he imposes on the object. He is forced to fantasy control of his object perceptions and his own internalized part representation of the primary object. The unconscious controlling sadistic impulses, with their joyful humiliation and/or destruction of the object, are potential controllers, humiliators, and destroyers of himself as he fantasies unconsciously the projected power in the perceived contemporary object.

William, the middle-aged patient I mentioned earlier, suffered from a milder form of recurrent ulcerative colitis, which had been precipitated ten years earlier by his wife's mastectomy. Although his obsessional aggressive character almost exuded hostility, he would not admit to hostile fantasies. He occasionally acted out but would not admit to anger until he was in the process of attacking someone physically or verbally. Such episodes occurred only when his superego accepted the provocation as right, legitimate, and totally justified. He was unable to acknowledge feeling unless it was accompanied by conscious action and justification.

As in the cases of Louis and Joe, I interpreted his rigid conscience accompanied by his feelings of exquisite shame, and he superficially became aware of the equivalency of his mild attacks of bleeding with one or another frustration. He had few dreams and an absolute dearth of available fantasies. The sessions were full of descriptions of actions of, and reactions to, contemporary characters and events. Such associations inevitably succeed in shutting out the analyst as a person and lead to countertransference reactions of boredom and drowsiness. They are typical of narcissistic characters as well as psychosomatic patients.

As with Joe, a precipitating event allowed William to open himself to analysis of his defenses. One day, while sitting in my waiting room, he heard a loud commotion in my office. I was seeing in consultation an acutely, disturbed paranoid, drugged man, who showed his displeasure with this forced interview by violently and loudly cursing me and his relatives who were present with us.

When William came in to his hour, he smilingly told me how he had been ready to come into my office and save me. On questioning, he admitted to a fantasy of breaking in my door to find me injured on the floor, helpless in the hands of a homicidal maniac. He further fantasied pulling the man away from what he later admitted to picturing as my bleeding body and subduing the attacker with his fists. (William was a large, powerful man, so that such a fantasied confrontation was not totally unreasonable.)

He admitted the possibility of a hostile wish in the feeling that I was being attacked, but there was little affect. However, as he talked lightly about hostile feelings toward "the analyst," I said I felt that he might have had fears of being just such a maniac. He laughed. Then he grew extremely serious and spoke with great concern of his frequent fears of being crazy. He said he was very ashamed of such silly fears and preoccupations. The opportunity arose for me to interpret that in his fantasy he was the attacker. He denied it, but his face paled—a reaction that I called to his attention.

Until this time William's dreams had been very infrequent, but before his next session he had one in which I made affectionate physical gestures, placed my arm on his shoulders, and so on. As he recounted the dream, he felt ashamed and humiliated. The dream was readily and superficially interpreted as a wish for reconciliation and forgiveness, but I placed emphasis on the intense shame he felt over such wishes and impulses.

For the first time he talked of his fears of being a sissy and perhaps a homosexual. He admitted to some youthful homosexual experiences.

As the analysis progressed, the preceding event and this dream became pivotal. He recalled specific fantasies of a homosexual or sadistic nature that shamed him and that he would dismiss as silly and inconsequential. His fears and feelings of humiliation, as well as his wishes to humiliate, became a theme for some months. His fantasy life, which had been present and conscious but had also been disowned and disavowed, became available for analysis. Here again was a case that could be called "alexithymic."

I have presented considerable detail about the opening phases of these three treatment experiences, because I feel that this early conduct of the psychoanalytic psychotherapy of bowel disease is critical. The analyst is usually faced with one or both of these presenting problems: (1) an acute physical problem that may be an immediate threat to the life of the patient, and (2) the resistant need to control the treatment and the analyst, entailing an avoidance of fantasy, feeling, and association.

The first problem must be handled by early interpretation to the patient of his masochism, self-punishment, suicidal impulses, and fear of rage. This interpretation leads to the patient's recognition that he is in emotional control of his gut, and this recognition usually brings some relief and diminution of symptoms.

The second problem must be handled, often coincident with the first, by interpreting the need to control the analyst, the fears of impulses, and the profound shame associated with impulses. This shame is often so profound that patients will consciously acknowledge that they are holding back material because the feeling of humiliation is too much to bear. A fourth case, Sarah, after her "alexithymia" had been analyzed and recognized as a conscious avoidance and denial, would acknowledge her refusal to discuss certain subjects for the first two years of psychoanalytic psychotherapy. When any train of associations would lead to anal material with fantasies, memories, and/or impulses, she would go so far and then refuse. Often, writhing on the couch, she would say, "I won't talk about it. The humiliation is unbearable." Needless to say, her anality was intimately tied to her sexual and aggressive impulses.

The Analytic Content

My material comes from nine cases: (1) Louis. (2) Joe. (3) William. (4) Sarah. (5) A severe case of Crohn's ileocolitis with multiple fistulas who terminated unimproved after six months. (6) A female patient who, although much improved and with her colitis in remission, developed a severe paranoid transference that I was unable to interpret, and she terminated. (7) A female patient with chronic ulcerative colitis who, although much improved, terminated after two years with occasional, mild recurrences. (8) A young male with Crohn's ileocolitis who is currently in psychoanalytic therapy.

Of the four cases already mentioned, William, Joe, and Sarah have been asymptomatic for periods of eight, nine, and seven years.

(1) Louis, who had suffered from a severe Crohn's colitis, was removed from treatment after three years by his parents, ostensibly for financial reasons, even though characterological symptomatology remained and a fistula was still patent. His bowel symptomatology remains in remission after a two-year interruption of therapy. This is the first such remission (four years) in the thirteen-year history of his illness. I anticipate his return to treatment.

In addition to the cases above and those discussed in the Psychosomatic Study Group, I have seen numerous patients in consultation and have supervised other psychoanalysts in the treatment of inflammatory bowel disease.

Patients with inflammatory bowel disease, in addition to their characteristic primitive oral problems involving a lack of separation from the primary object, have particularly severe anal fixations. Louis had recurrent diarrhea during his first year of life. William suffered from constipation throughout his childhood. Joe had colic in the first year of life and was allergic to cow's milk as well as his mother's milk. He was fed with goat's milk. Sarah suffered from recurrent constipation throughout childhood and had been subjected to enemas and suppositories frequently during her early childhood. One of the other patients mentioned had severe infantile diarrhea and had recurrent diarrhea during his latency years.

The mothers of these patients seem to be rather disturbed women. This could be confirmed in detail in the case of Louis, whose mother was in analysis with a colleague. They are controlling, perfectionistic women, who see the child as a part of and an extension of themselves. They are as afraid of losing control of the child as they are of their own impulses. Their unconscious hostility toward the child is the equivalent of their unconscious, destructive, self-punitive fantasies toward themselves. They will often choose one child to play such a role in their intrapsychic life. In my short series of cases, it has always been the oldest child. Two of the mothers had difficulty with recurrent diarrhea and bowel preoccupations themselves. One mother suffered from recurrent constipation. The mother of the Crohn's ileocolitis patient currently in treatment has had ulcerative colitis for thirty years. Louis's father suffered from constipation and diarrhea, spent inordinate time in the bathroom, and was constantly treating himself for hemorrhoids and other anal discomfort. He would fight with Louis over whether the toilet-paper roll should dispense from the top or from the bottom!

The defensive withholding (alexithymia?) was ultimately seen by all of these patients in anal terms. In two, later periods of resistance were accompanied by constipation.

On a purely conscious level, symptomatic periods were accompanied by feelings of helpless resignation, as has been emphasized by Sullivan, Engel, Almy, and others. This seems to be the conscious manifestation of the underlying depression.

The need to control the perceptions of the contemporary object with their symptoms is an aspect of their need to control, humiliate, and destroy the internalized object representation and to manipulate the projection of that internalized object (the contemporary object) by other means. As Sperling has stated many times, "These patients use their objects as fetishes." Just as they experience themselves as an extension of an early object, they experience their objects as extensions of themselves.

The psychological and medical literature offers a great deal of criticism and even some ridicule of the symbolic nature of the colitis, in which there seems to be an attempt to deny it by physiological explanations. Clinically, whether such symbolic expressions are primary or secondary (Reiser 1975), they certainly play an important role in the psychopathology and therapy of patients with bowel disease. In associating to the pathophysiology of an acute attack of bleeding or diarrhea, the patient will frequently volunteer the fantasy of controlling, destroying, or getting rid of a fantasied internal figure. The sadism and aggression associated with the oral and anal phases seem to attach themselves to concrete fantasied internalizations of the object. The equivalency of the attack on the self, as characterized in the pathophysiology of the bleeding and diarrhea, is clearly equated with the sadistic, often bloody attack on the object in dreams and fantasy.

I will elaborate a little on this unconscious fantasy life, which comes to light as the sadistic control of the internalized object is recognized. I do not claim that it is the sole cause of the colitis. I think that even without psychoanalytic knowledge of the association of power and sadism with the anal phase and anal activity, few can deny the repeatedly observed association of vernacular verbal aggression with colonic and anal function. The uses of the terms "shit," "eat shit," "shit on him," "up his ass," "ass hole," and so on, call constant attention to the deprecated, but aggressive, humiliating, and humiliated associations with bowel activity.

Patients will volunteer feelings and fantasies of devouring and "shitting" out particular loved objects along with "bloody" sadistic associations. Such fantasies are probably more sophisticated, concretized elaborations of early vague preverbal fantasies associated with the subjectively experienced, aggressive, powerful anal impulses. In this sense, they are probably amalgams.

In colitis patients, such verbalizations play an important part in the therapeutic experience. The pathophysiology is given verbal expression. To the patient, the experience of holding in and expelling the unwanted representation of the object finally enters verbally accessible consciousness and is associated with the colonic activity. Such associations usually lead to other fantasies of humiliating and humiliation, controlling and being controlled, torture and being tortured, and so forth.

Despite opinions to the contrary, such fantasies are present and therapeutic, whether one conceptualizes them as causative, primary, or secondary. In temporary transference regressions, they may be experienced as "almost real" experiences.

As in other pregenital orientations, the tendency to act out may be extreme. Before developing Crohn's disease, for example, Louis was a very self-destructive child who had an unbelievable number of injuries. To say he was accident prone would be an understatement. Accidents were compulsively frequent—a way of life! As another example, a colleague asked me about a patient with an acting-out character disorder whom he was treating. The patient developed ulcerative colitis for the first time while in analysis after suppressing the acting out—trying to follow the analytic rule of abstinence.

As these patients give up their bowel symptomatology, acting out is common. Joe, who had been a model father, began to lose his temper. He was frequently chagrined and profoundly guilty to find himself out of control and beating his children. Two of my patients threatened suicide during treatment.

Frequently other psychosomatic symptoms appear during treatment. Transient periods of migraine were present in two of my patients.

William developed hives for about six months as an allergic reaction to particular foods. In one case, as I mentioned, eczema was present before the onset of the illness, and it would frequently appear during remissions. In another, eczema was a transient complication.

As we know, these psychosomatic disorders, as well as the major symptoms or impulse equivalents, are clearly more discernible as impulses when the psychosomatic symptom is replaced by acting out. These pregenitally regressed patients retain the unconscious needs of the infant. There is the need for immediate gratification for every wish, and destructive rage arises when gratification is not obtained. To the accompaniment of the mobilized pathophysiology, the wish is denied in a manner that we will try to understand psychoanalytically. How the body utilizes physiology and smooth-muscle discharge in this procedure is not clear, but certainly many investigators are at work on the mechanics of the process. At any rate, the unconsciously denied and repressed impulse has its gratification in the use of the gut as an outlet, a fantasied avenging organ, with the accompanying self-destruction.

When the denial and repression are lifted and the impulse attains some degree of conscious recognition, the derivative of the impulse demands satisfaction. This derivative is indulged with accompanying neurophysiological and striated muscle activity. Another pathophysiological process has replaced the first, but this one is conscious. There is "acting out." Please note that neurophysiological and muscular activity is still present, but on a level of partial consciousness.

As I have indicated in the past, such acting out is frequently accompanied by a mild elation, a continued attempt at denial. It may be followed by resultant punishing injury, remorse, shame, or depression.

In effect there is an ascent of the self-destructive conflict from the unconscious to a partially conscious conflict, and there is a change of the accompanying pathophysiological process from the use of the smooth muscles and physiological responses of the gut to the use of voluntary striated musculature.

The regressive equivalence of inflammatory bowel disease to depression is clearly demonstrable. On a purely observable clinical level, as these patients recognize that they can control their colonic activity, there is inevitably a period of impulse gratification (acting out) followed by a relatively severe depression. Parenthetically, this may be accompanied by phobic symptomatology.

To repeat in other terms: unconsciously, there is a need for reparation in all stages of disease and treatment. In the colitis there is an unconscious discharge of the sadism toward the frustrating internalized object, accompanied by self-destruction, since that fantasied object is, of course, a fantasied part of the patient. As the primitive oral and anal destructive impulses with their accompanying fantasies are acknowledged in consciousness, they are acted out, often with a transient sense of elation and omnipotence that denies the retaliatory superego internalizations. However, since the acting out is commonly self-destructive in itself, or followed by shame and guilt, the superego has its say. Sarah indulged herself in demanding temper tantrums, which temporarily alienated friends and brought ensuing periods of exquisite guilt.

As this usually irrational behavior is understood, a more profound depression makes its intermittent appearance, and libidinal attachments on every level of development can be identified. In William's case, his intense dependence on his wife, which he continually tried to deny, clearly led to memories and early fantasies of his mother, and the effects of his wife's mastectomy became more clearly understandable. Earlier in analysis, his frustration and punitive rage toward the source of this perceived deprivation (and reminder of castration) had been acknowledged. Before working it through, however, he had acted out by indulging in an affair, which he unconsciously, but intentionally, revealed to his wife. The understandable consequences—accusations and temporary emotional abandonment—first precipitated rather profound shame and fear.

As a reconciliation with his wife was slowly effected, William's guilt broadened into a temporary but deep depression where life did not seem to be worth living. He perceived himself as an ungrateful, worthless wretch.

Parenthetically, this depression was relieved as he worked it out in the transference, blaming the analysis for his irrational behavior and repeating the rage at the frustration supposedly imposed by the analyst.

The libidinal organization of colitis patients is perverse in nature, but denied and repressed. Initially male patients seem to engage in sexual performance compulsively, but infrequently and badly, without a great deal of sensual pleasure. This shortfall is often rationalized by a strict moral character structure. Others have had little or no heterosexual or homosexual activity.

Louis had never had intercourse, but had exhibitionistically masturbated through latency. His adolescent and adult masturbation was totally involved with voyeuristic and exhibitionistic fantasies. As analysis progressed, early memories of manually dilating his anus and showing it off to other children came to light. One of his favorite pastimes at the age of 3 and 4 was to run away from home naked, exhibiting himself through the neighborhood. He recalled this material with intense humiliation.

All of my female patients have been vaginally unresponsive at the beginning of treatment, and as in Sarah's case, have revealed a history of poor impulse control of a perverse nature. As a preschool child she enjoyed defecating in public places, where she was not observed but where her products would be discovered. There was no unusual history of nocturnal enuresis, but until adult life there was poor daytime bladder control. Whenever she was excited, she would urinate, and she had experienced some excruciatingly shameful losses of bladder control during adolescent petting with one or another boy friend.

I should note that this historical material, while partially conscious, is not usually available for investigation until psychoanalytic psychotherapy is well under way, and the major symptomatology has either been given up or almost dispensed with.

As oedipal material begins to evolve, both male and female patients reveal rather severe problems in gender identification; and homosexual dreams and fantasies are shamefully admitted. While Louis had indulged in childhood homosexual activity and William in a few adolescent and young adult homosexual experiences, none of my patients indulged in homosexual acting out after the onset of their disease or during treatment.

William, Joe, and Sarah finally worked out rather traditional oedipal solutions in analysis and established reasonably happy heterosexual lives with some reservations. William remained childless, using his wife's physical status as an excuse. Joe had already established a family, despite his ulcerative colitis, and Sarah married and started a family. Louis's future remains undetermined. He is working and his gut is quiet. I trust that he will return to analysis. All remain somewhat obsessional in temperament, but none has obsessional symptomatology.

SUMMARY

This chapter briefly defines, describes, and discusses the physical characteristics, pathology, physical complications, and general prognosis of chronic ulcerative colitis and Crohn's disease of the colon. Differences and similarities are noted. I call attention to the fact that most clinicians offer little hope for full recovery and that the incidence of recurrence, complications, and fatalities is a problem of major proportion.

The history of the discovery and investigation of the psychopathology accompanying and influencing the organic pathophysiology is briefly reviewed and discussed, with some emphasis placed on the minor and profound disagreements between various observers and clinicians.

Both at the beginning and later, the chapter presents the relatively excellent results some physicians have achieved with some patients in the treatment of inflammatory disease of the large bowel with intensive psychoanalytic psychotherapy and psychoanalysis.

Finally, intensive psychoanalytic investigation and treatment of this group of diseases are discussed in some detail, using clinical material from cases that have been treated. Emphasis is placed on the pregenital nature of the psychopathology. Some necessary modifications of traditional psychoanalytic methods are described.

The transitory development of other symptoms is discussed, such as other psychosomatic disorders, acting out, phobias, and depressions. These symptoms commonly complicate treatment but are part and parcel of a successful resolution of the psychopathology. An attempt is made to explain these changes in symptomatology and the part they play in the patient's recovery.

REFERENCES

Almy, T. P. (1961a). Observations on the pathologic physiology of ulcerative colitis. *Gastroenterology* 40:299–306.

―――― (1961b). Ulcerative colitis. *Gastroenterology* 41:391–400.

―――― (1975). Psychiatric aspects of chronic ulcerative colitis and Crohn's colitis. In *Inflammatory Bowel Disease*, ed. J. B. Kirsner and R. C. Shorter, pp. 37–46. Philadelphia: Lea & Febiger.

Almy, T. P., Hinkle, L. E., Jr., Berle, B., and Kern, F. (1949). Alterations in colonic function in man under stress: III. Experimental production of sigmoid spasm in patients with spastic constipation. *Gastroenterology* 12:437–449.

Almy, T. P., Kern, F., and Tulin, M. (1949). Alterations in colonic functioning in man under stress: II. Experimental production of sigmoid spasm in healthy persons. *Gastroenterology* 12:425–436.

Almy, T. P., and Lewis, C. M. (1963). Ulcerative colitis. Report of progress based on recent literature. *Gastroenterology* 45:515–528.

Almy, T. P., and Sherlock, P. (1966). Genetic aspects of ulcerative colitis and regional enteritis. *Gastroenterology* 51:757–761.

Almy, T. P., and Tulin, M. (1947). Alterations in colonic functions in man under stress: I. Experimental production of changes simulating the "irritable colon." *Gastroenterology* 8:616–626.

Atwell, J. D., Duthie, H. D., and Coligher, J. E. (1965). The outcome of Crohn's disease. *British Journal of Surgery* 52:966–972.

Banks, P. A., Present, D. H., and Steiner, P. (1983). *The Crohn's Disease and Ulcerative Colitis Fact Book.* National Foundation for Ileitis and Colitis. New York: Scribner.

Boyer, L. B. (1975). Treatment of characterological and schizophrenic disorders. In *Tactics and Techniques in Psychoanalytic Therapy,* vol. II, ed. P. L. Giovacchini, A. Flarsheim, and L. B. Boyer, pp. 341–373. New York: Jason Aronson.

Boyer, L. B., and Giovacchini, P. L. (1980). *Psychoanalytic Treatment of Borderline and Characterological Disorders.* New York: Jason Aronson.

Brautigam, W., and Rad, M. von, eds. (1976). Toward a theory of psychosomatic disorders. Proceedings of the 11th European Conference on Psychosomatic Research, Heidelberg (1976). Basel: S. Karger.

Bruno, M. J. (1979). An internist's view of inflammatory bowel disease. In *Inflammatory Bowel Disease, Experience and Controversy,* A Teaching Seminar on Inflammatory Bowel Disease by Lenox Hill Hospital (New York) and the American College of Gastroenterology, ed. B. I. Korlitz, pp. 5–8. Boston: John Wright, 1982.

Correspondence (1977). Ulcerative colitis and Crohn's disease of the colon. *Gastroenterology* 72:755–779.

Crohn, B. B., Ginzburg, L., and Oppenheimer, C. D. (1932). Regional entity, *Journal of the American Medical Association* 99(16): 1323–1329.

Crohn, B. B., and Rosenberg, H. (1925). Sigmoidoscopic pictures of chronic ulcerative colitis (nonspecific). *American Journal of Medical Science* 170:220–228.

Crohn, B. B., and Yarnis, H. (1958). *Regional Ileitis.* New York: Grune & Stratton.

Cushing, M. M. (1953). The psychoanalytic treatment of a man suffering from ulcerative colitis. *Journal of the American Psychoanalytic Association* 1:510–518.

Daniels, G. E. (1940). Treatment of a case of ulcerative colitis associated with hysterical depressions. *Psychosomatic Medicine* 2:276–285.

——— (1941). Practical aspects of psychiatric management in psychosomatic problems. *New York State Journal of Medicine* 41:1727–1732.

_____ (1942). Psychiatric aspects of ulcerative colitis. *New England Journal of Medicine* 226:178-194.

_____ (1944). Nonspecific ulcerative colitis as a psychosomatic disease. *Medical Clinics of North America* 28:593-602. *Knowing and the Known.* Boston: Beacon Press, 1949.

_____ (1948). Psychiatric factors in ulcerative colitis. *Gastroenterology* 10:59-62.

Daniels, G. E. , O'Connor, J. F., Karush, A., Muses, L., Flood, C. A., and Lepore, M. (1962). Three decades in the observation and treatment of ulcerative colitis. *Psychometric Medicine* 24:85-93.

Engel, G. L. (1952). Psychological aspects of the management of ulcerative colitis. *New York State Journal of Medicine* 22:2255-2261.

_____ (1954a). Studies of ulcerative colitis: I. Clinical data bearing on the nature of the somatic process. *Psychosomatic Medicine* 16:496-501.

_____ (1954b). Studies of ulcerative colitis: II. The nature of the somatic process and the adequacy of the psychosomatic hypothesis. *American Journal of Medicine* 16:413-416.

_____ (1955). Studies of ulcerative colitis: III. The nature of the psychologic process. *American Journal of Medicine* 19:231-256.

_____ (1956). Studies of ulcerative colitis: IV. The significance of headaches. *Psychosomatic Medicine* 18:334-346.

_____ (1958). Studies of ulcerative colitis: V. Psychological aspects and their implications for treatment. *American Journal of Digestive Diseases* 3:315-337.

_____ (1961). Biologic and psychologic features of the ulcerative colitis patient. *Gastroenterology* 10:313-322.

_____ (1967). The concept of psychosomatic disorder. *Journal of Psychosomatic Medicine* 11:3-9.

_____ (1973). *Ulcerative Colitis and Emotional Factors in Gastrointestinal Illness.* Ed. A. E. Lindner. Amsterdam: *Excerpta Medica.* New York: American Elsevier.

Engel, G. L. and Salzman, L. I. (1973). A double standard for psychosomatic papers? *New England Journal of Medicine* 288:44-46.

Fein, H. D. (1979). History of Crohn's disease. In *Inflammatory Bowel Disease: Experience and Controversy,* A Teaching Seminar on Inflammatory Bowel Disease, sponsored by Lenox Hill Hospital (New York) and the American College of Gastroenterology, ed. B. I. Korlitz, pp. 1-3. Boston: John Wright, 1982.

Giovacchini, P. L. (1977). The psychoanalytic treatment of the alienated patient. In *New Perspectives on the Psychotherapy of the Borderline Adult,* ed. J. Masterson, pp. 1-39. New York: Brunner/Mazel.

Goldgraber, M. B., and Kirsner, J. B. (1964). Carcinoma of the colon in ulcerative colitis. *Cancer* 17:557-665.

Goodman, M. J., and Sparberg, M. (1978). *Ulcerative Colitis.* Clinical Gastroenterology Monograph Series, ed. T. M. Dietsch. New York: Wiley.

Groen, J. (1947). Psychogenesis and psychotherapy of ulcerative colitis. *Psychosomatic Medicine* 9:151–174.

———— (1951). Emotional factors in the etiology of internal disease. *Mt. Sinai
Journal of Medicine* 18:71–89.

Groen, J., and Bastiaans, J. (1954). Studies on ulcerative colitis. In *Modern Trends
in Psychosomatic Medicine,* ed. D. O'Neill, pp. 102–125. New York: Hoeber.

Groen, J., and Birnbaum, D. (1968). Conservative supportive treatment of
severe ulcerative colitis. *Israeli Journal of Medical Science* 4:130–139.

Groen, J., and Van der Valk, J. M. (1956). Psychosomatic aspects of ulcerative
colitis. *Practitioner* 177:572–584.

Hogan, C. C. (1983a). Object relations. In *Fear of Being Fat: The Treatment of
Anorexia Nervosa and Bulimia,* rev. ed., ed. C. P. Wilson, C. C. Hogan, and
I. L. Mintz, pp. 129–149. Northvale, NJ: Jason Aronson, 1985.

———— (1983b). The psychoanalysis of an abstaining anorexic woman. Group
Discussion: Psychoanalytic Treatment of Patients with Psychosomatic
Disorders, C. P. Wilson, Chairman, C. C. Hogan, Co-Chairman.
Meeting of the American Psychoanalytic Association, April 27, 1983.

———— (1983c). Psychodynamics. In *Fear of Being Fat: The Treatment of Anorexia
Nervosa and Bulimia,* rev. ed., ed. C. P. Wilson, C. C. Hogan, and I. L.
Mintz, pp. 115–128. Northvale, NJ: Jason Aronson, 1985.

———— (1983d). Technical problems in psychoanalytic treatment. In *Fear of Being
Fat: The Treatment of Anorexia Nervosa and Bulimia,* rev. ed., ed. C. P. Wilson,
C. C. Hogan, and I. L. Mintz, pp. 197–215, Northvale, NJ: Jason
Aronson, 1985.

———— (1983e). Transference. In *Fear of Being Fat: The Treatment of Anorexia
Nervosa and Bulimia,* rev. ed., C. P. Wilson, C. C. Hogan, and I. L. Mintz,
pp. 153–168. Northvale, NJ: Jason Aronson, 1985.

Jackson, M. (1976). Psychopathology and pseudonormality in ulcerative colitis.
Proceedings of the 11th European Conference on Psychosomatic Research,
Psychotherapy and Psychosomatics 28:179–186. Basle, Switzerland: S. Karger,
1977.

Karush, A., and Daniels, G. E. (1953). Ulcerative colitis: The psychoanalysis of
two cases. *Psychosomatic Medicine* 15:140–167.

Karush, A., Daniels, G. E., O'Connor, J. F., and Stern, L. C. (1968). The
response to psychotherapy in chronic ulcerative colitis: I. Pretreatment
factors. *Psychomatic Medicine* 30:255–276.

———— (1969). The response to treatment in psychotherapy of chronic ulcerative
colitis: II. Factors arising from the therapeutic situation. *Psychosomatic
Medicine* 31:222–226.

Karush, A., Daniels, G. E., Flood, C., and O'Connor, J. F. (1977). *Psychotherapy
in Chronic Ulcerative Colitis.* Philadelphia: W. B. Saunders.

Karush, A., Hiatt, R. B., and Daniels, G. E. (1955). Psychophysiologic correlations in ulcerative colitis. *Psychomatic Medicine* 17:36–56.

Kern, F. (1975). Treatment of extra intestinal complications of chronic ulcerative colitis and Crohn's disease of the colon. In *Inflammatory Bowel Disease,* ed. J. G. Kirsner and R. G. Shorter, pp. 306–308. Philadelphia: Lea & Febiger.

Kernberg, O. F. (1980). *Internal World and External Reality: Object Relations Theory Applied.* New York: Jason Aronson.

Kirsner, J. B., ed. (1980). *Inflammatory Bowel Disease.* Philadelphia: Lea & Febiger.

Korlitz, B. I. (1979). Evidence for Crohn's disease as an extensive process. In *Inflammatory Bowel Disease: Experience and Controversy.* A Teaching Seminar on Inflammatory Bowel Disease, Sponsored by Lenox Hill Hospital (New York) and the American College of Gastroenterology, 1979, pp. 9–14. Boston: John Wright, 1982.

Korlitz, B. I., and Gribitz, D. (1962). The prognosis of ulcerative colitis with onset in childhood: the steroid era. *Annals of Internal Medicine* 57:592–597.

Lindemann, E. (1945). Psychiatric problems in conservative treatment of ulcerative colitis. *Archives of Neurology and Psychiatry* 53:322–324.

_____ (1950). Modifications in the course of ulcerative colitis in relationship to changes in life situations and reaction patterns. *Research in Nervous and Mental Diseases* 29:706–723.

McKegney, F. B., Gordon, R. O., and Levine, S. M. (1970). A psychosomatic comparison of patients with ulcerative colitis and Crohn's disease. *Psychosomatic Medicine* 32:153–166.

Mintz, I. L. (1980–1981). Multideterminism in asthmatic disease. *International Journal of Psychoanalytic Psychotherapy* 8:593–600.

_____ (1983). Psychoanalytic description: the clinical picture of anorexia nervosa and bulimia. In *Fear of Being Fat: The Treatment of Anorexia Nervosa and Bulimia,* rev. ed., ed. C. P. Wilson, C. C. Hogan, and I. L. Mintz, pp. 83–114. Northvale, NJ: Jason Aronson, 1985.

Morgagni (1769). *De Sedibus et Causis Morborum.* London: Miller and Caldwell's. Facsimile of the 1769 edition. New York: Hafner, 1960.

Murray, C. D. (1930a). Psychogenic factors in the etiology of ulcerative colitis and bloody diarrhea. *American Journal of Medical Science* 180:239–248.

_____ (1930b). A brief psychological analysis of a patient with ulcerative colitis. *Journal of Nervous and Mental Diseases* 72:617–627.

Mushatt, C. (1954). Psychological aspects of nonspecific ulcerative colitis. In *Recent Developments in Psychosomatic Medicine,* ed. E. R. Wittkower, and R. A. Cleghorn, pp. 345–363. Philadelphia: Lippincott.

Nemiah, J. C. (1976). Alexithymia: a view of the psychosomatic process. In *Modern Trends in Psychosomatic Medicine,* vol. 3, ed. O. W. Hill, pp. 430–439. New York: Appleton-Century-Crofts.

Nemiah, J. C., and Sifneos, P. E. (1970). Affect and fantasy in patients with psychosomatic disorders. In *Modern Trends in Psychosomatic Medicine,* vol. 2, ed. O. W. Hill, pp. 26–34. New York: Appleton-Century-Crofts.

O'Connor, J. F. (1970). A comprehensive approach to the treatment of ulcerative colitis. In *Modern Trends in Psychosomatic Medicine,* vol. 2, ed. O. W. Hill, pp. 172–188. New York: Appleton-Century-Crofts.

O'Connor, J. F., Daniels, C. E., Flood, C., Karush, A., Muses, L., and Stern, L. C. (1964). An evaluation of the effectiveness of psychotherapy in the treatment of ulcerative colitis. *Annals of Internal Medicine* 60:587–602.

O'Connor, J. F., Daniels, C. E., Karush, A., Flood, C., and Stern, L. C. (1966). Prognostic implications of psychiatric diagnosis in ulcerative colitis. *Psychosomatic Medicine* 28:375–381.

Prugh, D. G. (1950). Variations in attitudes, behavior and feeling states as exhibited in the play of children during modifications in the course of ulcerative colitis. *Research in Nervous and Mental Diseases* 29:692–705.

—— (1951). The influence of emotional factors on the clinical course of ulcerative colitis in children. *Gastroenterology* 18:339–354.

Reiser, M. F. (1975). Changing theoretical concepts in psychosomatic medicine. In *American Handbook of Psychiatry,* vol. 4, ed. M. F. Reiser, pp. 477–500. New York: Basic Books.

Roth, J. L. (1976). Ulcerative colitis. In *Gastroenterology,* vol. 2, 3rd edition, ed. H. L. Bokus et al., pp. 645–649. Philadelphia: W.B. Saunders.

Savitt, R. A. (1977). Conflict and somatization: psychoanalytic treatment of psychophysiological responses in the digestive tract. *Psychoanalytic Quarterly* 46:605–622.

Sifneos, P. E. (1972). *Short Term Psychotherapy and Emotional Crisis.* Cambridge: Harvard University Press.

—— (1973). The prevalence of alexithymic characteristics in psychosomatic patients. In *Psychotherapy in Psychosomatics,* ed. J. Reusch, A. Schmale, and T. Spoerri, pp. 255–262. White Plains, NY: S. Karger.

Sperling, M. (1946a). Psychoanalytic study of ulcerative colitis in children. *Psychoanalytic Quarterly* 15:302–329.

—— (1946b). The role of the mother in psychosomatic disorders of children. *Psychosomatic Medicine* 11:377–385.

—— (1949). Problems in the analysis of children with psychosomatic disorders. *Journal of Child Behavior* 1:12–17.

—— (1955). Psychosis and psychosomatic illness. *International Journal of Psycho-Analysis* 36:320–327.

—— (1957). The psychoanalytic treatment of ulcerative colitis. *International Journal of Psycho-Analysis* 38:341–349.

—— (1959). Psychiatric aspects of ulcerative colitis. *New York State Journal of Medicine* 59:3801–3806.

_____ (1960a). The psychoanalytic treatment of a case of chronic ileitis. *International Journal of Psycho-Analysis* 41:612–618.

_____ (1960b). Symposium on disturbances of the digestive tract: II. Unconscious phantasy life and object-relations in ulcerative colitis. *International Journal of Psycho-Analysis* 41:450–455.

_____ (1964). A case of ophidophilia: a clinical contribution to snake symbolism and a supplement to psychoanalytic study of ulcerative colitis in children. *International Journal of Psycho-Analysis* 45:227–233.

_____ (1967a). Transference neurosis in patients with psychosomatic disorders. *Psychoanalytic Quarterly* 36:342–355.

_____ (1967b). Acting out behavior and psychosomatic symptoms: clinical and theoretical aspects. *International Journal of Psycho-Analysis* 49:250–253.

_____ (1969). Ulcerative colitis in children: current views and therapies. *Journal of the American Academy of Child Psychology* 8:336–352.

_____ (1978). *Psychosomatic Disorders of Childhood.* New York: Jason Aronson, pp. 61–98.

Stout, C., and Snyder, R. L. (1969). Ulcerative colitislike lesion in Simiang gibbons. *Gastroenterology* 57:256–261.

Sullivan, A. J. (1935). Psychogenic factors in ulcerative colitis. *American Journal of Digestive Disease and Nutrition* 2:651–656.

Sullivan, A. J., and Chandler, A. C. (1932). Ulcerative colitis of psychogenic origin: a report of 6 cases. *Yale Journal of Biology and Medicine* 779–796.

Volkan, V. D. (1976). *Primitive Internalized Object Relations. A Clinical Study of Schizophrenic, Borderline and Narcissistic Patients.* New York: International Universities Press.

Weiner, H. (1977). *Psychobiology and Human Disease.* York: Elsevier, pp. 499–574.

Weinstock, H. I. (1962). Successful treatment of ulcerative colitis by psychoanalysis. *British Journal of Psychosomatic Research* 6:243–249.

_____ (1966). Hospital psychotherapy in severe ulcerative colitis. *Archives of General Psychiatry* 4:509–512.

White, W. H. (1888). On simple ulcerative colitis and other rare intestinal ulcers. *Guys Hospital Report* 30:131–162.

Wilks, S. and Moxon, W. (1875). *Lectures on Pathological Anatomy.* Philadelphia: Lindsagand and Blakeston, pp. 408–409.

Wilson, C. P. (1983). Contrasts in the analysis of bulimic and abstaining anorexics. In *Fear of Being Fat: The Treatment of Anorexia Nervosa and Bulimia,* rev. ed., ed. C. P. Wilson, C. C. Hogan, and I. L. Mintz, pp. 169–196. Northvale, NJ: Jason Aronson, 1985.

16

TRANSFERENCE, SOMATIZATION, AND SYMBIOTIC NEED

Robert A. Savitt, M.D.

This chapter describes the course of somatization as illustrated by the reactivation of a duodenal ulcer in the progress of a patient's psychoanalytic treatment. A series of psychoanalytic sessions extending over a period of several months will be described in some detail, giving a microscopic view of the transference neurosis, the concurrent somatization, and symbiotic need. In order to better understand the probable genesis of the original ulcer at age 17, and the subsequent recurrences, pertinent details are presented from the patient's past history as well as from the opening phase of the analysis.

A young married man, age 28, exceedingly bright and an engineer by profession, came to analysis stating that he was bisexual, but that in recent years his homosexual behavior had intensified, so that now his sexual relationships were predominantly homosexual. He thought of dissolving his marriage and living entirely as a homosexual. He felt quite guilty about this, and before making a decision he wished to have psychoanalytic treatment in the hope that it would clarify his position.

Although his primary concern was his sexual behavior, the anamnesis revealed that he had had his first expression of stomach ulcer at 17, manifested by tarry stools and "coffee grounds" vomiting. Subsequently, he had had several similar incidents, each time diagnosed as duodenal ulcer and confirmed by stomach X-rays.

In the past few years, except for occasional heartburn, he had had no significant gastrointestinal symptoms. In fact, three years prior to psychoanalysis, when he was being considered for the military draft, he was X-rayed in a military hospital and the stomach was reported to be normal. However, he was deferred because of his homosexuality. The duodenal ulcer recurred in the early months of his analysis, and the somatization process was reflected in the vicissitudes of the transference relationship.

Rappaport (1959) describes the concept of erotized transference as one in which the patient brings into the analysis a preformed, ready-made set of personal emotional responses and in which an excessive demand to be loved. Glover (1955) writes of "this selective repetition [of symptoms] that distinguishes the transference-neurosis from the spontaneous transference existing at the beginning of analysis. Spontaneous transferences are working transferences. They may, as in the case of character disorders, already have a pathological form. Nevertheless, they represent the potential attachments or aversions which govern the person's current object relations. The transference-neurosis [by contrast] brings to the fore transferences that have a specific connection with processes of symptom-formation" (p. 122).

At the start of the treatment the transference was manifested by an intensely erotized homosexual motif. The night following the second session of the initial interview he dreamed. He reported this at our third meeting (the first on the couch). It was a dream about me, the analyst, in which I appear undisguised (Savitt 1960).

Dream: He and the analyst are on the floor of the analytic consultation room. The analyst has mounted him and is having anal intercourse with him. The patient then gets up, buttons his trousers, smiles, and leaves the office. In the reception room he sees a man and a woman. He feels embarrassed.

Spontaneously, he began to talk about the dream and stated that it portrayed what he actually hoped would happen; namely, that he could seduce the analyst into a homosexual relationship. In this way he would prove that homosexuality was a perfectly acceptable way of life and thereby eliminate any necessity for analysis. Then he could continue homosexuality without the sense of guilt and shame that now troubled him.

In fact, for some months prior to coming to analysis a common fantasy dealt with his smug assurance that he would "clip this guy one," that is, seduce the analyst (whoever he might be) and show him up as a weak, submissive person who could be easily manipulated. "Clip this guy one" was the expression he frequently used in describing his homosexual conquests. The aggressive and sadistic inferences are evident. At this point it is important to know that his preanalytic fantasy pictured the analyst in a submissive, humiliating position in which the analyst performs fellatio upon him. This had always been the pattern of his homosexual relationships, wherein he considered himself as the "feeder" of weak men. In the manifest content of this undisguised first dream, the homosexual procedure is reversed. The analyst penetrates the patient anally; the analyst "feeds" him. It took some months of analysis before it was possible to show him convincingly the latent meaning of the dream; the concepts of penis as breast, anus as mouth, and the bisexual representation of the analyst as well as of himself.

Before the close of the session, I commented that there was more meaning to this dream than was now evident, and that the ensuing analytic work was required to reveal it. In addition, I deemed it necessary at once to call his attention to the resistance to psychoanalytic treatment clearly implied in the dream, namely, his wish to turn the analytic situation into a homosexual seduction.

The continued elucidation of historical details revealed that at age five he had been seduced by a sailor who mounted him anally. Since then he had been aware of what I termed an intense "anal hunger." He readily understood this concept and supplied abundant recollections of anal play and the insertion of phallic objects into his rectum during masturbation. These anal insertions gave him a feeling of strength and filled him up.

Since early adolescence, at the height of his most intense period of loneliness and depression, he had sought homosexual experiences. A frequent masturbation fantasy was that of his father performing anal intercourse upon him. This made his erection feel stronger and larger. Subsequently, after he married a nurse at age 23, following her seduction of him, he required this fantasy while engaged in intercourse with her. For a time in the analysis, and particularly during the reactivation of the stomach ulcer, the analyst replaced the father in this fantasy. Throughout his life he was plagued by a sense of emptiness, which later was only mildly and tentatively alleviated by his homosexual experiences.

In the main he was governed by the need to be on the prowl, hunting for some male with a big penis, to conquer and to humiliate him. Homosexual activity was limited to having his partner perform fellatio upon him. Thus, he became the hostile feeder of men — an expression of his maternal identification. He was aware that he himself had the earnest wish to be fed by sucking on the penises of other men. But he denied himself this gratification, because he knew that if ever he succumbed to the temptation, he would become addicted to this behavior. So long as he himself avoided performing fellatio, he could continue the fiction that he was not a homosexual. This self-deception was essential to the maintenance of his self-esteem.

The analytic working through, as it was reflected in the transference neurosis, gradually showed him that his homosexual experiences represented a search for father's phallus. But with each greedy conquest he failed to find a penis to equal his father's. Always there was "something missing." This was subsequently seen to be the deceased mother's breast. As an unwanted child, he had been openly rejected by his mother. Her death at the height of his oedipal period facilitated the regression to the negative Oedipus complex. His father then became for him a bisexual parent — in the patient's own words, a "two-in-one parent."

The reconstruction of the patient's history confirms that he was conceived at a time of marital disharmony and that throughout his childhood his mother was depressed, although she never required hospitalization. She had wished to abort him, but was dissuaded from doing so. The infant's care was supervised mainly by a variety of relatives and a sister some eight years older. In contrast to his mother's aloofness and coldness, his father was a warm, loving parent who frequently played with and fondled him. As a young boy, he remembered father often placing him upon his lap and kissing his ear and neck.

When he was about six, he became seriously ill with pneumonia and he was taken into the parental bed, replacing father. For the next week mother looked after his needs. This was the first time he felt that she showed an active and genuine concern for him.

Within ten days she developed fulminating pneumonia and died. This was to give rise to the oft-repeated question: "Did she take me into her bed because she loved me or because she had to?"

He recalled the day of mother's funeral; the coffin at home, the tearful relatives, the rainy day. He was not permitted to go to the cemetery, remaining at home with a neighbor. He remembered it as a day in which he felt "very empty" and gorged himself on candy. He then felt full. In recounting this he believed that it was the first time he experienced a subjective sense of bodily swelling, in which he felt that his hands, arms, legs, face, and lips swelled to a gigantic size. With this loss, this total separation from mother, he incorporated her symbolically and denied the separation. This sensation of body swelling was to recur later time and again as a response to object hunger, and in the transference neurosis it became a prominent manifestation of defense against loss and decathexis.

Later that day, when the family returned from the funeral, he observed father's periodic crying. He got on his lap, embraced him and asked, "Why are you crying? You still have me!" Later in the course of treatment, when he reviewed his first experience of stomach bleeding at 17, he associated to the memory of father's weeping and said, "My stomach shed tears."

At 16, during a lengthy period when his stepmother had to be away, he immediately took her place in the marriage bed and figuratively became father's "wife." He cleaned the house, made the bed, marketed, cooked, and looked after father's needs as a wife would. In bed at night he yearned for anal penetration by father, and was disappointed because it did not happen. This was the nearest he came to gratifying the fantasy of being a part of father, to be played with and fondled as he himself did with his penis during masturbation. While in bed with father, he often experienced the sensation of bodily swelling. In such promixity his entire body became phallic.

Here we see the patient as a part object expressing the need to fuse with father in order to become the phallic extension of the parental whole object — that is, to repair by way of anal introjection, the sense of loss, the feeling of "something missing." Later, in the eighty-sixth hour, we will observe in the transference neurosis the other side of the fusion fantasy in which he incorporates the analyst's and father's penis as part objects in order to make himself a "whole person."

When he was 19, after increasing quarrels with his stepmother, he left home. Detached now from his father, his separation anxiety intensi- fied and was manifested by increased perverse activity. The need for phallic reinforcement proved urgent. He embarked on an orgy of homosexuality and for a time became a veritable homosexual Don Juan. No lasting relationships were made. He was insatiable in spite of numerous homosexual affairs.

Margolin (1951) presents us with a rare insight into the correlation between emotional and physiological aspects of stomach activity. In a patient who had a fistulous opening as a result of a gastrostomy, Margolin was able to have almost total visualization of the gastric physiological processes, so that there was an opportunity to correlate physiological stomach response with emotional stimuli on the conscious and unconscious levels. Among other observations he was able to show some of the reciprocal relationships between physiological stomach response and transference manifestations.

This kind of direct observation of the stomach is certainly not possible in a classical psychoanalysis. We must be content with the knowledge afforded us from the unconscious by way of dream symbolism, free association, parapraxes, acting in, acting out, and all other constituents of the analytic situation. It would have been valuable to record before-and-after barium X-ray studies of the stomach, and to have had repeated physiological-chemical analyses of the stomach contents. But this, too, was not feasible.

Now, through the microscopic details of a series of psychoanalytic sessions, it is proposed to show the genesis of the recurrence of the duodenal ulcer as it was reflected in the vicissitudes of the transference relationship.

Thus far we have seen how this patient started his analysis with a spontaneous, ready-made erotized homosexual transference. This revealed his then-current homosexual behavior, in which he played the role of the aggressive, conquering humiliator of men. In the manifest content of the first dream, which appeared so soon after the analysis began, he revealed his need for a nurturing homosexual relationship with the analyst. He hoped to seduce the analyst, and he became submissive and compliant, even to the extent of giving up all overt homosexual activity.

He was angry and frustrated and asked, "Why am I such a good boy, what power do you have over me?" During the seventy-eighth session he stated, "I've been feeling raw in the stomach for the past ten days. I've also been having three mushy bowel movements daily. Last night I vomited, and this is the first time since the analysis began. It felt wonderful to vomit, and I realize that it relates to what we have talked about in the past week. You are now too much with me. During the weekend [no sessions] the image of you was reappearing in front of me."

In the eighty-first hour he remembered recurring masturbatory fantasies during adolescence in which father was pictured as inserting his penis into the patient's anus. (Note the similarity to the theme of the first dream.)

He recalled a primal-scene memory at age 5 when he was still sleeping in the parental bedroom. He felt disturbed about seeing his parents in bed together. He associated to the first homosexual seduction at age 5 by a sailor who mounted him anally. He then said, "I always wanted father to shove his penis into me, to have union with me. I would like you to do this to me. It would show me that you love me."

The need for phallic reinforcement continued as a repetitive theme. He stated that to have the analyst's penis in his anus would make him feel more like a man, like a whole person rather than an empty person. "Mother didn't love me and this deprived me of feeling like a whole person." Here he equates the analyst with the nongiving mother who has castrated him.

In the next few sessions he reiterated the same refrain. The cathexis now shifted to his wife. In the eighty-fifth hour he remarked, "I want to be wholly loved and possessed by my wife. I want her to suck me off to show that she really accepts me even if I'm bad. I now think of sex with my wife day and night. I want to be passive now, just like I wanted Pop to love me sexually. I want her to eat me, I want you to eat me. I want to perform 69."

The patient was now in a state of hypersexuality, and the need to cathect a love object made his choice indiscriminate. It could be male or female, analyst, or wife. But the increased erotism was not primarily on a genital level. His appeal was for a polymorphous perverse experience, in which he would play a passive-receptive role. This he would interpret as a sign of love and acceptance. Hypersexuality was now a façade for expressing his preoedipal and oedipal yearnings. He repeated the question, "Did mother come to bed with me because she loved me or because she had to? I felt guilty about causing her death. Because she didn't love me, I felt unwanted and inferior. She was cold and aloof. You are cold and aloof. She showed very little emotion. She never smiled. I can't recall being kissed or caressed by mother. But father used to kiss me. Even when I was an adolescent he hugged me."

In the eighty-sixth hour:

For the past few days my stomach has been acting up. I have a
tremendous yearning for sex and I need to suck. I want you to play
with me. If I could make you a part of me, then you would condone
homosexuality. What I wanted from father was his penis to function
with. What will I do when the analysis is over? I wanted a sense of
male identification with father so that I could function as a man. I
now feel I've captured father's penis. I'm functioning, mine is as good
as father's, even better.

The next hour was on a Monday, and he had not seen me for two
days. He reported a tremendous sense of emptiness over the weekend;
how much he missed me. He was practically hallucinating my presence.
"Wherever I go I look for you, in the street, in the subway, theater,
restaurants. I miss you, yet I feel you're with me all the time. You've
grown so much a part of me. I can't think of anything else. Yet I'm angry
that I need you, and you don't respond to me."

In the eighty-eighth hour he reported a dream: "My wife is baking
a cake. I felt she would never be able to do it right." Associations:

I always loved cake and ate it until I gorged myself. Mother used to
make this sort of cake. I watched her hungrily, and when she gave me
a piece it was a sign she loved me. . . . I wanted to eat mother and
wanted her to eat me, to take me in, to swallow me, to completely
accept me. . . . I wanted you to do the same, to accept me. I want to
eat you. . . . I didn't want to remember this dream about the cake,
it's too painful. Mother never held me or fondled me, so when she got
into bed with me when I was sick, it meant she loved me. And when
she died, it was a sign of her supreme sacrifice for me. But I think I'm
glad she died. After all, she didn't love me, so there was no loss, and
I didn't need her anyway. I really hate women. I want only to
conquer and hurt them.

(Note the similar attitude expressed toward men in his homosexual
relationships.)

His concern that his wife will not bake the cake right reflected his
belief that his wife did not know how to love him. What he wished from
her was an anclitic relationship in which he would experience gratifica-

tion on a symbiotic basis as well as on the skin-erotic, oral, and anal levels. He wanted another chance. He wished to be her baby — to be taken in, engulfed, and reborn as a whole person. This too was what he desired from me in the transference. The yearning for a nursing situation in terms of Lewin's (1956) oral triad hypothesis were repeatedly rendered with utmost poignancy.

He continued to have "a raw feeling in the stomach." For the first time in the ninety-sixth hour he reported details of his earliest gastric hemorrhage at 17. He had then vomited black material and had some black stools. The doctor told him he had to rest. The patient demanded that the stepmother go away to the country with him alone. They went for a week and occupied the same room. During that week he felt very hungry, ate everything that was fed to him, and gained 15 pounds. To be away with her alone meant that she loved him.

Here we see a redramatization of the serious illness he experienced at age 6 that forced a sign of total acceptance by his mother. At that time he achieved a temporary, precarious positive oedipal victory, but his conquest led to her death. He held himself to blame for this. Her loss facilitated a rapid regression to the negative oedipal relationship with father, with whom he was certain of total acceptance. This set the course for his homosexual orientation.

Thus at 17 the alarming stomach symptoms forced a short period of total acceptance by his stepmother. His rapid recovery, the gorging of food, the weight gain signified the incorporation of an image of a "good" loving mother. This is in contrast to the incorporation of the "bad" mother (as postulated by Garma in 1958) on the day of her funeral. At 17 he had again achieved a temporary oedipal triumph.

In the next few sessions he repeated the cry, "Love me to death. I want to be passive, make no effort. Do with me what you wish. I wanted to be sucked in by my mother just as I now want to be sucked in by my wife." He verbalized a rebirth fantasy, "I'd like to get inside and come out all over again."

There was a repeated wish for fusion with me. He searched for me wherever he went. "I want to be so close to you that there will be no air space between us." At this time the body sensation of swelling was very prominent during analytic sessions as a manifestation of the need to incorporate me. At the same time, as a sign of the wish for mutual incorporation and merging, he described the difficulty of getting up from the couch at the end of sessions. "I feel like in a trance. I feel I'm part of the couch. It's like having to peel myself away from it and come back to full consciousness." Figuratively speaking, he had fused with the couch and, hence, with me.

Another day he stated that he realized his stomach upset of the past few weeks was due to anger and frustration because his wife had not yielded to his unspoken wish for a polymorphous perverse relationship. He wanted her to know this without his asking for it. Also he wanted me to be aware of all his needs and desires without having to verbalize them. Here we see a reflection of the patient's preverbal period in infancy. I can confirm M. Sperling's (1967) observation that somatic symptoms are used by patients as preverbal communications. Later he exclaimed, "I'm so hungry for love now—hungry all the time. I'm at the point where the feeling doesn't leave me. I'm so hungry that my stomach feels sore."

Fenichel (1945) has called attention to this permanent hunger for love as a factor in the causation of stomach ulcer. Thus, a pathological tissue alteration occurs as a consequence of a psychogenic hunger, which makes the person act like a physiologically hungry person does in a sham feeding. The mucosa of the stomach then secretes in anticipation of a feeding—an anticipation that can never be gratified.

He was now in a state of perpetual sexual excitement. While in the bathtub he had a sudden spontaneous erection and ejaculation. He thought to himself that masturbation and homosexuality were easier ways of being gratified. Autoerotic and perverse activities had once acted as pacifiers for his aching stomach, and he was tempted to use these again.

He turned to recollections about the time of his first stomach bleeding at 17. For months preceding this he had been able temporarily to relieve abdominal pain by masturbation and homosexual activity. Also, for about a year prior to the first ulcer, so intense was his need to suck, that he kept chewing and sucking on his buccal mucosa until he developed a mucosal papilloma. He now saw that in response to his oral needs he had created a breast-nipple equivalent, upon which he could suck at will. Continued biting and sucking enlarged and macerated the papilloma to the point where it became precancerous and required surgical removal. This antedated the development of the stomach ulcer, and its removal may have acted as an added trauma, which soon led to stomach ulceration.

In conjunction with this memory he remarked, "Truthfully, what would make me feel better would be to suck on your penis, to have a perpetual 69 with you." The wish for a permanent nursing and clinging relationship continued as a theme of the transference neurosis.

Currently he also focused on a more recent example of somatization, of which he had been aware for several weeks. He had developed anal verrucae. He wished me to look at his anus, touch it, penetrate it. It was clear that in response to his "anal hunger" and the wish for penetration by me, he had erotized the anal mucocutaneous junction. I interpreted this as a parallel to the erotization of the buccal mucosa at 16, in response to the intense oral need in that period of his life.

On several occasions I had informed him that he was clearly on the way to a recurrence of his duodenal ulcer and suggested that he report to his physician for examination and treatment. He interpreted this as my caring for him and loving him. His somatic symptoms would abate for a day or two following my suggestions.

It was my hope that frequent interpretation and the correlation of the past and the present as reflected in the transference might prevent the recurrence of the ulcer. But he kept testing me, and it became evident that he was seeking an answer to the question: Would his analyst finally love him if he became dangerously ill?

During the 115th session he mentioned a significant dream: "I was eating all night. I went to the bathroom and the stool was dark. I thought, this may be the beginning of the bleeding." Associations: "When I went to bed I was hungry for a little loving, but my wife was reading. I was angry. She hasn't been paying much attention to me lately. I felt my stomach and it was as if my hand was in a hollow."

He now wondered, if he became sick enough would his wife give him more loving, just as his mother had finally given him some "loving" at 6 when she took him into her bed during his serious illness? He added, "Who can wait so long? It's as if I'm going to be fed next week, but I'm hungry now."

This material reflected his insatiability, his inability to delay gratification, and his recently increasing, excessive demands for a polymorphous sexual response from his wife. This was his way of testing her complete, unconditional acceptance of him. He complained bitterly of stomach pain and informed her that he wanted to have a gastrectomy. He watched slyly for her reaction and felt pleased when she expressed deep concern. He also wondered what would be my reaction if he became very sick.

The next day he reported that he had passed several tarry stools. A few days later stomach X-rays confirmed the recurrence of an active duodenal ulcer. This was no surprise to either of us. He had been under his internist's management for several weeks, and he continued with the Sippy diet.

Again, I interpreted the secondary gain involved in the recurrence of his ulcer. In his need to test the question, "If I get sick enough, will she do anything I want her to do"? he was figuratively asking his wife to die for him, as a way of proving that she loved him. His mother had in fact died as a consequence of having cared for him during his critical childhood illness, but this had not proven to his satisfaction that she had loved him. Indeed, now he might himself die from stomach bleeding in a vain attempt to force a love and acceptance that in reality was clearly evident from his wife.

I reemphasized his masochistic need to develop a critical illness with which to punish himself, and his sadistic use of somatization to punish his wife and his analyst. I pointed to the hidden guilt he had experienced for having "killed" his mother, and that although he had boasted that he had never mourned this loss, he had indeed "swallowed" her on the day of the funeral when he gorged himself with candy and experienced the distorted perception of body swelling. The vicissitudes of his life thereafter were a way of showing his mourning reaction.

As for conquering the analyst by striving to compel a homosexual response from him, this too was his manner of restaging the futile childhood struggle with his rejecting mother.

Time and again he complained of his frustration with me, of my coldness, my aloofness. But continued interpretation slowly convinced him that within the framework of the analytic situation he was being given an adequate amount of attention and acceptance; that his sense of emptiness was in direct proportion to his insatiable demands based on his earlier infantile deprivation; that in his unconscious I was his "bad" nongiving mother and that his wife was similarly regarded.

He told me that he hated me, that insight from the analysis had robbed him of the conviction that he could seduce me. This provided the chance to work through his sadomasochistic needs and passive oral and anal strivings. He spoke of his hatred for and dependence on his father, who also had not totally accepted him (that is, by way of an actual homosexual union). His father had died several years prior to his entry into analysis. He recalled that at this critical time he had felt so completely empty that he doubted that he could exist without him. Shortly after his death there was a recurrence of tarry stools and stomach pain. At the same time his homosexual activity assumed a desperate urgency. Frantically, he went from one affair to another in his search for a man with a big phallus. But this gave him only temporary relief from his "hunger." He also reported recurrent dreams in which father appeared, asking him to join him in death.

He wished that I would die so that he could prove that he could do without me, but within the same hour he said, "I feel I've been playing with you. I need to suck on you, to suck on your penis, to drain you, to drain you dry." This offered the opportunity to consolidate his awareness of the penis-breast equation, and to make a start on splitting the bisexual concept of his analyst and of his father as a "two-in-one parent."

We recall that in the patient's infancy and childhood his father had effected a maternal relationship to him. At that time this parent supplied the mothering, need-fulfilling role and in essence became the phallic mother. In his early adolescence he was keenly aware of his father's masculinity, the bulge of his muscles, the bigness of his hands and fingers, the size of his penis. During this time he first developed fantasies of anal incorporation of his father's phallus as a prominent part of his masturbatory behavior. This represented his attempt at masculine identification. But this identification was only partially successful, because it became evident that anus was primarily equated with mouth and the penis from the "motherly" father was really an oral feeding to replace the breast of his nongiving mother.

At this particular point of his analysis, when he was reporting the development of anal verrucae, he also focused upon the symptoms of vomiting and diarrhea. He was now expelling three to four "mushy" bowel movements daily. He described the diarrhea "like gagging rectally," as if the lower bowel were acting in the same way as his mouth did when he vomited. Vomiting and diarrhea had been prominent symptoms during emotional upheavals in the past, although he had vomited only once since starting analysis. He associated to fellatio wishes and equated "mouth vomiting" with "rectal vomiting."

The alimentary tract is the passage through which receptive and expulsive needs are played out. The mouth is primarily an organ of reception by which the individual takes in what is "good" and pleasurable. But at times it also functions as an organ of expulsion, as seen in instances of vomiting and the spitting out of that which is "bad" and unpleasurable.

The anus functions essentially as an organ of expulsion for that which is undesirable. But as we have seen in this patient, it may perversely serve the incorporative role as manifested by his "anal hunger." Here, too, anus was equated with vagina as an expression of his feminine identification.

Stomach and intestines are in between the mouth and anus and serve as areas in which there occurs the metabolic processing of what is acceptable and nonacceptable. This then is integrated into the whole physiological economy. Psychologically, the gastrointestinal tract is one of the main body areas through which the vicissitudes of the symbiotic needs are also processed in the interests of the psychic economy.

He could now understand that the anal penetration by the analyst that he portrayed in the first dream communicated his wish for a "feeding" from his maternalized father. Mother and father were one, and his self-representation was similarly bisexual. He spoke of adolescent pregnancy fantasies, of the wish to have his own male children, and of treating them like the "best mother in the world." These disclosures were accompanied by an increase in the frequency of the sensation of body swelling.

His comprehension of the bisexual representation of the analyst and his ability to split me into maternal and paternal components now also facilitated the analysis of his relationship to his wife. He had married her about a year after his father's death. She had seduced him into a heterosexual relationship, but it became evident that he had regarded this as a seduction by a male. His conception of her was that of a phallic woman. She was narrow-hipped and small-breasted and boyish in appearance. He often complained of the smallness of her breast and of his hunger for larger ones.

In this connection it is worth noting that his concept of his wife's body during intercourse was that of an amorphous headless body, consisting of a torso and extremities, but without genitalia. In the course of treatment the refinement of his castrated body image went through the following stages of development: a headless body with a vagina; headless body with a penis; female body with a male head; a male body with a male head, and finally a female body with a female head. With the clarification of what was masculine and what was feminine, he could now accept his own masculinity and his wife's femininity. Until then she had represented the phallic woman. By attaching a head to these respective fantasied body images he succeeded in endowing the former amorphous body with genitality. He was on his way to genital primacy and he could now turn from *coitus a tergo* to the face-to-face position in intercourse.

As his relationship to his wife matured, so did the self and object representations ripen. Insatiable preoedipal demands diminished and were replaced by secondary process thinking and behavior. His stomach ulcer healed, and there has been no recurrence in a follow-up of many years. As a manifestation of the therapeutic alliance, overt homosexual activity was given up early in the analysis and has not again been resumed.

DISCUSSION

In the study of psychosomatic disorders the role of possible constitutional factors merits consideration. In an elegant and well-documented paper on the etiology of duodenal ulcers, Mirsky (1958) discusses the predisposing and precipitating factors.[1] Each in itself is essential but is not the sole determinant. When they exist during inauspicious combinations, ulceration may occur.

Mirsky cites evidence pointing to a correlation between the occurrence of duodenal ulcers and the greater number of parietal cells in the stomachs of such predisposed individuals.[2] This leads to gastric hypersecretion with a concomitant greater concentration of plasma pepsinogen than is found in persons without any gastrointestinal disturbances. He supports the probability that this is genetically determined, but this innate given, although essential, is not the only deciding factor. What is additionally necessary, but also not in itself a sole determinant, is psychic conflict, usually relating to ungratified passive-dependent and oral wishes.

Thus, a patient who is burdened with the genetic component of gastric hypersecretion, when exposed to a life situation that provokes

---

[1] I am indebted to Dr. Max Schur for calling my attention to Mirsky's manuscript.

[2] The presence of a larger number of parietal cells in stomachs of individuals predisposed to ulcer is a constitutional histological given. This raises a question: do patients who develop ileitis and ulcerative colitis also have a specific intestinal tissue structure that serves as a predisposing factor, which, when allied with a psychic conflict, precipitates the appropriate lesions?

a noxious psychic conflict, may develop an ulcer. Both factors are necessary.

No physiologic studies were performed on my patient, but on the basis of his subjective gastric complaints during that period of his analysis in which the ulcer was reactivated, there is presumptive evidence that he was a gastric hypersecretor. A noxious psychic conflict, to which Mirsky refers as an essential precipitating ulcergenic factor, is of course elaborately delineated in the preceding material of this manuscript.

Mirsky (1958) summarizes his basic thesis by stating:

Although the presence of gastric hypersecretion indicates that a subject can develop an ulcer, it does not mean that he *will* do so. The only conclusion that can be derived from our data is that a typical psychodynamic pattern and gastric hypersecretion are frequent concomitants irrespective of the presence or absence of a duodenal lesion. The hypersecretion is a physiological predisposing factor while some significant social experience serves as the precipitating factor in that it induces the psychological reactions specific to the individual. [p. 297f]

Jacobson (1964) states:

In a patient's associations, imagery and memory material referring to oral deprivations may express deprivations during infancy, which were not merely oral in the narrow sense of the term but may have been experienced in the entire realm of the complex mother–infant interrelationship. Frequently, psychosomatic manifestations associated with such "oral" memory material give us special clues to the early infantile past. [p. 36]

Indeed, the somatic features of this clinical presentation, as they developed within the framework of the transference neurosis, offer us a reasonably valid reconstruction of the original mother–infant relationship.

Because of her emotional illness, the mother was not available as a physically or psychologically nurturing object. She had rejected the newborn infant from the start, and it will be recalled that she had wished to abort the fetus. The normal course of symbiosis was therefore impoverished, with its consequent distortion of the separation–individuation phase, disturbed sense of identity, and impaired body image (Mahler and Gosliner 1955).

Until it was resolved during psychoanalytic treatment, he acted out his ungratified symbiotic needs through part-object and object hunger. Always there was a wish for and a readiness to fuse.

There had been no object constancy, but the early care given him by various female relatives and an older sister provided a fragmented symbiotic process that ensured his physiological survival. The one figure who gave him some continued sense of object relationship was the "mothering," tender, and loving father. This may have been the main factor in obviating the development of a psychosis.

The repetitive need to fuse is evidenced from the beginning of his analysis and throughout most of its course, as well as by numerous phenomena in the movement of his life situation. The first dream so soon after the initial interview revealed the ever-present wish to merge with the object by way of homosexual union. It was an example of the preformed, erotized transference readiness with which he came into treatment.

He displayed a keen voyeuristic hunger. He frequented areas where he viewed the bulging muscles and well-defined crotch of males. He devoured this with his eyes and felt temporarily filled up. Thus he adored the muscular strength and large hands of longshoremen when he watched them at the waterfront; or he loitered in gymnasia and their dressing rooms hoping to see what he could of naked male bodies and genitalia. He was an ardent balletomane and worshiped the male dancers from afar.

Early in adolescence he manifested this "anal hunger" by repeated anal insertions of phallic objects, in order to make his erection stronger during masturbation. To these anal manipulations was later added the fantasy of his father mounting him anally as a way of achieving phallic reinforcement. When he married he had to invoke this fantasy in order to achieve satisfactory intercourse. During the analysis the analyst replaced the father in this fantasy. As we have seen, these anal insertions in actuality and in fantasy were a symbolic fusion and feeding process in which the phallic insertion was the breast and the anus the mouth.

The development of anal verrucae in the early months of analysis was another sign of his wish to be fed anally, and revealed the erotization of the anus as an orifice for penetration. He compared it to a puckering of the mouth in anticipation of receiving food, and he hoped that I would examine it, finger and probe it homosexually.

The altered state of consciousness manifested by the distorted

perception of body swelling and the sensation of fusing with the couch
during sessions reflected the periodic loss of ego boundaries and the
symbiotic need for merging with the analyst. It indicated a temporary
regression to what Mahler (1967) called the "state of undifferentiation, of
fusion with mother in which the 'I' is not yet differentiated from the
'not-I' " (p. 742). At 17, when he acted in his wish to be father's "wife,"
the swelling sensation represented an engulfment of father in which the
patient's entire body became phallic and he became father's phallic
extension. This, too, is related to the nurturing fantasy of father
mounting him anally.

The almost visual hallucinatory invocation of my person during
weekend intervals, when he looked for me wherever he went, was an
example of the separation anxiety he experienced. On these occasions he
felt extremely frustrated and depressed. He wished to absorb me totally
and said, "I want to be so close to you so that there will be no air space
between us."

Under the impact of the analytic process he attempted to establish
symbiotic union with his wife. He yearned for an anaclitic relationship in
which he would be perpetually passive, loved, fed, absorbed, and reborn.
"I'd like to crawl inside and come out all over again."

When his excessive demands, first upon his analyst and then his wife
were not gratified, he responded with anxiety, rage, and a resomatization
of his vulnerable organ, the stomach, through which he nonverbally
communicated his elemental hunger and yearning for closeness. Hunger
and sucking were frequent free-association themes with special reference
to the prolonged thumb sucking extending into adolescence. The development of the buccal papilloma at 16 was recalled with poignancy. This
breast-nipple equivalent located in the forepart of his alimentary tract was
evidence of fusion with a maternal part object over which he had
omnipotent control, and upon which he could suck at will. It was part of
the process of incorporating the bad, malignant, nongiving mother, and
like his mother, it provided no gratifying nourishment. It activated a
continuous sham feeding which kept the stomach in a nonhomeostatic
state of physiological imbalance. It was like having mother's breast on
demand, to chew, macerate, suck, devour, and destroy. It was a part
object for his aggression and oral sadism.

He approached each relationship with the expectation of being
emotionally nurtured. Just as the self-created breast-nipple in his mouth

gave no physiological nourishment, neither did any human relationship provide satisfactory emotional nourishment. So great were his needs, so insatiable his demands, that expectations could not be fulfilled. In a sense each relationship was also a psychological sham feeding, following which he would say, "This isn't it, there's something missing." During the analysis this was clearly seen in the transference neurosis and with great clarity in his erotomania and hypersexual demands made upon his wife. Even when she was most giving, he could not feel gratified.

With the psychic regression witnessed in the transference neurosis there occurred a concomitant "partial retransformation of ideational and emotional into somatic, physiological expressions" (Jacobson 1964, p. 12). We may presume that in the preverbal period of infancy the patient had an unusual need to express his discontent and disharmony through physiological organ language.

Schur (1955) cites instances of "regression carried to a preverbal, pre-ego stage of development where reaction to stimuli is in the closest sense psychosomatic" (p. 127). He speaks of this as resomatization and hypothesizes that this phenomenon occurs when there is a prevalence of primary process thinking and inability to use neutralized energy, as seen in instances where the individual is overwhelmed by anxiety and aggression.

Sperling (1967) appropriately states that the psychosomatic patient needs a somatic channel for immediate discharge in situations in which he feels helpless and threatened with loss of control. The use of somatization to manipulate and control the analyst has been clearly seen here in the transference situation.

There was a marked deficiency in self-representation. He had a distorted sense of identity and body image. He considered himself not a "whole person" and continually defended against castration anxiety by the aforementioned anal insertion of phallic objects; by fantasies of father's or the analyst's penis penetrating his anus; by searching for men with large penises for homosexual union. There was a constant need for phallic reinforcement.

His fragmented symbiotic relationship in infancy militated against his developing an adequate sense of body image and self-representation; not having had a gratifying mother, he could not conjure up an image of a feminine nurturing object. He could only accept a relationship with a phallic person because his father had been the benign, loving, need-fulfilling object, and remained so in his fantasy even after his father's death. His self-representation and identification were bisexual, just as his father, as an object, was bisexual—that is, "a two-in-one parent."

He imagined himself as a female in the role of the best courtesan in the world, who could drive men into frenzied erotic ecstasy; or that he would give birth to many male children to whom he could be the best mother in the world. His feminine self-representation was also seen when he wished to serve as father's "wife" when the stepmother was absent. Like his father he was maternal in his relationship to people.

Just as he regarded himself to be "not a whole person," his object representations were similarly fragmented. Rather, people were part objects. In his homosexual encounters he was primarily responsive to those males who were very muscular and who possessed "big penises." Nothing else about the person mattered.

We have noted that during intercourse the concept of his wife's body was also that of a part object, perceived as an amorphous headless body consisting of a torso and extremities but without genitalia. He dared not endow it with a female head and a vagina. Going to bed with a woman unconsciously meant that he would destroy her, just as he had "killed" his mother when she took him into her bed during his childhood illness.

The analysis of his self and object representations facilitated the acceptance of himself as a male with a phallus and of his wife as a female with a vagina. This then inevitably led to a culmination of his long-delayed separation–individuation phase, which was achieved some months before termination of his analysis. In the course of resolving the transference neurosis he was able to give up certain of his father's personal belongings, which for him had a phallic and fetishistic quality. These he had kept in his bedroom following his father's death, even after he married. They were symbolic of father's presence in the bedroom, which nourished him emotionally and sustained his genital prowess during intercourse.

It is important to acknowledge that this patient had several prior peptic ulcer recurrences. These apparently healed temporarily when he resorted to the pacification provided through the perversion of homosexuality and the acts of anal masturbation. The former was a "feeding" by incorporating someone else's phallus as a part object; the latter was a "self-feeding," at will and on demand, by inserting phallic objects into his rectum.

As was noted in his associations, masturbation and homosexuality were easier ways of being gratified. Autoerotic and perverse activities had once functioned as pacifiers for his aching stomach, and in the course of his analysis he had tempting thoughts of regressing to these again. Thus, by way of a psychopathological process he had been temporarily able to remedy his defective body image and, with it, to heal the stomach ulcer. But with object or part-object loss there was always the danger of resomatization. This was clearly portrayed when, following the death of his father, he resomatized his ulcer and regressed immediately into homosexual erotomania and became a veritable homosexual Don Juan.

In the process of his therapeutic analysis, body-image repair had also occurred with a concurrent healing of the peptic ulcer. But now the healing seemed to be a consequence of a matured ego structure, and on the basis of the psychological interaction of a masculine (himself) relationship with a recognized female object (his wife). He could now permit her to serve as a gratifying, emotionally nourishing whole object.

One does not know if life's vicissitudes may again facilitate a regression with a consequent resomatization. But it is postulated that psychoanalysis has armed him with an ego structure that may be capable of forestalling or minimizing the chances for such a regression. A follow-up of many years reveals no recurrence of stomach ulcer.

SUMMARY

A 28-year-old married male with bisexual behavior developed a recurrence of a duodenal ulcer in the course of psychoanalytic treatment. Under the impact of the transference neurosis resomatization took place and brought into sharp focus a recapitulation of his inadequate, infantile symbiotic relationship with his mother. This had facilitated the development and maintenance of a negative oedipal involvement with a maternal father.

By way of homosexuality he expressed his ever-present need to merge with the "mothering" father, and through him with the mother. Homosexuality provided temporary emotionally nurturing objects and part objects. The repetitive pleas for love, the insatiable desire to suck and be sucked, the wish to eat and be eaten, the pseudohallucinatory invocation of the analyst's presence wherever the patient went in the intervals of separation between analytic sessions, the sensation of fusion with the analytic couch, the distorted anatomical subjective perception of bodily swelling during analytic sessions — all these eloquently attested to the infantile primal hunger that could not be allayed. It is postulated that psychologic and environmental factors pertinent to his life situation as outlined in this paper, in conjunction with a presumed genetic physiological predisposition, combined to cause the original duodenal ulcer in his adolescence and were also responsible for later recrudescences of this lesion.

This patient, his life history, his symptomatology, his therapeutic and working alliance in the psychoanalytic procedure, have served as a contribution to the further understanding of the psychosomatic process and its resolution, particularly as it may refer to the subject of duodenal ulcers.

REFERENCES

Fenichel, O. (1945). *The Psychoanaltic Theory of Neurosis.* New York: W. W. Norton.

Garma, A. (1958). *Peptic Ulcer and Psychoanalysis.* Baltimore: Williams & Wilkins.

Glover, E. (1955). *The Technique of Psychoanalysis.* New York: International Universities Press.

Jacobson, E. (1964). *The Self and the Object World.* New York: International Universities Press.

Lewin, B. D. (1956). *The Psychoanalysis of Elation.* New York: W. W. Norton.

Mahler, M. S. (1967). On human symbiosis and the vicissitudes of individuation. *Journal of the American Psychoanalytic Association* 15:740–763.

Mahler, M. S., and Gosliner, B. J. (1955). On symbiotic child psychosis: genetic, dynamic, and restitutive aspects. *Psychoanalytic Study of the Child* 10:195–212.

Margolin, S. G. (1951). The behavior of the stomach during psychoanalysis. *Psychoanalytic Quarterly* 20:349–373.

Mirsky, I. A. (1958). Physiologic, psychologic, and social determinants in the etiology of duodenal ulcer. *American Journal of Digestive Diseases* 3:285–314.

Rappaport, E. A. (1959). The first dream in an erotized transference. *International Journal of Psycho-Analysis* 40:240–245.

Savitt, R. A. (1960). On the undisguised dream about the analyst. Presented before the American Psychoanalytic Association, Midwinter Meeting.

Schur, M. (1955). Comments on the metapsychology of somatization. *Psychoanalytic Study of the Child* 10:119–164.

Sperling, M. (1967). Transference neurosis in patients with psychosomatic disorders. *Psychoanalytic Quarterly* 36:342–355.

_____ (1975). The psycho-analytic treatment of ulcerative colitis. *International Journal of Psycho-Analysis* 38:341–349.

EPILOGUE: PSYCHOTHERAPEUTIC TECHNIQUES

C. Philip Wilson, M.D.

The "Golden Years" of psychoanalysis lie before us in the application of new psychodynamic therapeutic approaches to patients with severe preoedipal psychopathology. Therapeutic techniques must be adapted to the varying defenses of the ego. There are, of course, many varieties of ego structure in psychosomatic patients. Technique varies with different patients and with the degree of regression encountered. It varies also according to the individual style and experience of the therapist. I tend to see patients face-to-face in the first dyadic phase of treatment. Some, however, can be analyzed along more classical lines, with the couch being used from the beginning.

The masochistic meanings of the patient's psychosomatic symptoms are interpreted first in the context of current conflict and the transference. The analyst focuses on the psychosomatic symptoms and interprets the defenses against bringing up symptoms and the associated conflicts in sessions (Wilson, Chapter 4, this volume). Techniques range from direct confrontation with the suicidal meanings of symptoms in life-threatening psychosomatic crises to the interpretation of subtle defenses against the understanding of the masochistic meanings of less severe symptoms.

Triadic oedipal material is usually interpreted in the later phases of treatment.

The technique of interpretation is determined by multiple factors, such as the transference and the quality of object relationships. A crucial consideration is the split in the ego and the extent to which this split is comprehended by the self-observing functions of the patient's ego. The first phase of therapy involves making the healthier part of the patient's ego aware of the split-off, primitive, impulse-dominated part of the ego and its modes of functioning.

Typical defenses and character qualities are: (1) denial and splitting; (2) belief in magic; (3) feelings of omnipotence; (4) the demand for perfectionism in people and things — the alternative is worthlessness; (5) the need to control; (6) displacement and projection of conflict; (7) ambivalence; (8) masochistic perfectionism as a defense against conflicts, particularly those of aggression; (9) a pathological ego ideal of beautiful peace and love; (10) a fantasied perfect, conflict-free mother–child symbiosis.

Although psychosomatic symptoms themselves are manifestations of projections and projective identifications, these patients project unacceptable aspects of the personality — impulses, self-images, superego introjects — onto other people, particularly the therapist, with a resulting identification based on these projected self-elements. The extreme psychoticlike denial of conflict is caused by primitive projective identification onto others of archaic destructive superego introjects. Because these patients in their projective identifications can pick up almost imperceptible nuances in the tone of voice, facial expression, movements, and even feelings of the analyst, they provoke intense countertransference reactions.

In the first phase of treatment, these patients usually do not free-associate, as also happens in the analysis of children and of patients with character disorders (Boyer and Giovacchini 1980). The therapist takes an active stance, frequently using construction and reconstruction. Behavioral responses can be interpreted. Dreams have to be used in the context of the patient's psychodynamics. First the therapist interprets the masochism of these patients — their archaic superego and the guilt they experience in admitting to any conflict. Next, the therapist interprets defenses against facing masochistic behavior; then, when the ego is healthier, defenses against aggressive impulses. Such interpretations are inexact and frequently are not confirmed by the patient's associations. For these patients who have an archaic, punitive superego and a relatively weak ego, the analyst provides auxiliary ego strength and a rational superego. Interpretations should be made in a firm, consistent manner; with such patients the analyst needs to have authority.

There is a special technique in the analysis of psychosomatic patients. Early in treatment the analyst must demonstrate to the patient the need for immediate gratification (the impulse disorder, that is, the primary narcissism).

It is important that the psychiatrist be in charge of the treatment process. A split transference with the medical specialist can vitiate treatment. Hospitalization should be reserved for true emergencies.

When psychosomatic symptoms subside, acting out increases. Patience is essential in the analysis of these patients, whose symptoms, at their most primitive level, mask preverbal conflicts and traumas. Psychosomatic patients, all of whom have preoedipal conflicts, have the means to communicate the impact and effects of their early preverbal traumas.

With the majority of cases, in the technique of analysis or analytic psychotherapy, the first phase of treatment, the transference, is handled along the principles set forward by Kernberg (1975) and summarized by Boyer (1979) in regard to borderline cases:

1. The predominantly negative transference is sytematically elaborated only in the present, without initial efforts directed toward full genetic interpretations.

2. The patient's typical defensive constellations are interpreted as they enter the transference.

3. Limits are set in order to block acting out in the transference, as this is necessary to protect the neutrality of the therapist (The patients' reactions to these limit-setting parameters will have to be analyzed at a later stage of treatment.)

4. The less primitively determined aspects of the positive transference are not interpreted early, since their presence enhances the development of the therapeutic and working alliance (only if we look at these alliances as part of the positive transference), although the primitive idealizations that reflect the splitting of "all good" from "all bad" object relations are systematically interpreted as part of the effort to work through those primitive defenses. (Related to this effort is the importance of interpreting all-or nothing-ego functioning in every aspect of the behavior of these patients, not just object relations.)

5. Interpretations are formulated so that the patient's distortions of the therapist's interventions and of present reality, especially the patient's perceptions during the hour, can be systematically clarified.

6. The highly distorted transference, at times psychotic in nature and reflecting fantastic internal object relations pertaining to early ego disturbances, is worked through first in order to reach the transferences related to actual childhood experiences.

The early interpretation of the masochism correlates with the therapeutic technique used in the therapy of schizophrenic, borderline, and character disorders by Boyer and Giovacchini (1980), Kernberg (1975), and Volkan (1976).

ANALYSIS OR ANALYTIC PSYCHOTHERAPY?

Substantively similar psychodynamics and techniques of treatment are utilized in analytic psychotherapy as in analysis with modifications determined by the frequency of sessions. The technique of interpretation used by Mushatt (Chapter 8) in once-a-week psychotherapy is closely related to Mintz's detailed psychoanalytic treatment (Chapter 10). The remarkable results described in Mushatt's analytic psychotherapy have been replicated in many other cases by the contributors to this volume and other members of our psychosomatic research groups. Welsh's (1983) discussion of his successful treatment of a male bulimic anorexic (Martin) succinctly illustrates the effectiveness and limitations of analytic psychotherapy.

Most therapists interested in symptomatic or behavioral change would have considered Welsh's patient "cured." However, his therapist had hoped for a deeper resolution of his conflicts and for more ego growth. Nonetheless, there was some ego development that came from the insight and working through in the treatment. He understood enough about his feelings and conflicts so that he no longer feared an absolute loss of control, and his impulses were not so frightening and potentially overwhelming. Martin was left with a greater sense of mastery that came from self-knowledge, rather than a false and pathological mastery of his eating and weight. With insight into his homosexual conflicts, rage, self-punitiveness, and need for omnipotent control, his masochism became less severe and he was able to keep his job without provoking his boss into firing him. However, he was too afraid to venture further in treatment, which would have upset his schizoid, but stable, existence.

CURRENT AND FUTURE RESEARCH

The recent almost epidemic increase in eating disorders, particularly restrictor and bulimic anorexia nervosa, has resulted in expanding an effective application of analysis in the treatment of these diseases. Recent publications detail the techniques of treatment, the transference-, countertransference, object relations, and family psychopathology in what for psychoanalysts are large numbers of patients (Goldman 1986, Reiser 1988, Risen 1988, Wilson et al. 1983). In addition, since eating-disorder symptoms may be replaced by psychogenic equivalents, including other psychosomatic symptoms, such as asthma, there has been a renewed focus on the use of analysis in psychosomatic patients. In our textbook on the analytic treatment of anorexia nervosa and bulimia (Wilson et al. 1983), we report on the analytic treatment of forty-four patients. The analytic treatment of a large number of eating disorder patients is detailed in two new books: *Bulimia: Psychoanalytic Treatment and Theory,* H. J. Schwartz, M.D., editor; International Universities Press, 1988; and *Eating to Live or Living to Eat,* C. P. Wilson, C. C. Hogan, and I. L. Mintz, editors, Jason Aronson, Northvale, New Jersey, in press.

Tapes of two recent panels of the American Psychoanalytic Association are available: Panel on "Compulsive Eating: Obesity and Related Phenomena," Pietro Castelnuovo-Tedesco, Chairman, Winter Meeting of the American Psychoanalytic Association, December 11, 1985, New York, N. Y. Tapes are obtainable from Teach Em, Inc., Pluribus Press, 160 East Illinois Street, Chicago, Illinois 60611. Panel on "Anorexia Nervosa and Bulimia," Pietro Castelnuovo-Tedesco, Chairman, Spring Meeting of the American Psychoanalytic Association, Denver, Colorado, May 1985. Tapes are obtainable from Teach Em, Inc., Pluribus Press, Inc., 160 East Illinois Street, Chicago, Illinois 60611.

Printed summary reports of these panels have been published in the *Journal of the American Psychoanalytic Association* (L. W. Reiser 1988, S. E. Risen 1988).

Successful analytic results occur in a large number of patients suffering from psychosomatic symptoms. Many patients, however, are not amenable to analysis or stop analysis prematurely without symptom or personality-disorder resolution.

Some factors that vitiate analytic treatment are: (1) weak motivation and limited capacity for insight in patients; (2) the resistance of significant others (with children and adolescents, the parents) to cooperate in the treatment process and if necessary to do conjoint therapy themselves; (3) failures in the technique of the analytic therapist; (4) countertransference conflicts of the therapist; (5) split transference with other medical specialists; (6) the acting out of psychosomatic patients, which frequently is manifested by terminating abruptly and prematurely; (7) chronic, long-term borderline or psychotic symptomatology.

Some cautionary notes on the analytic treatment of psychosomatic patients are:

1. For thorough analytic results it is crucial to uncover and work through the patient's defenses against his most primitive, pregenital sadomasochistic impulses and fantasies.

2. If the psychosomatic patient is faced with a sudden unexpected trauma, such as the death of an important object, or the illness of the analyst or of the patient himself, he can react by severe symptom exacerbation (potential psychosomatic suicide). Parameters of technique are important in such situations. The patient's reactions to these parameters will have to be analyzed later in therapy.

3. Since most patients, when referred for treatment, have experienced many previous medical and psychotherapeutic therapies with no lasting results, it is crucial for the analyst to uncover their repressed anger and mistrust of the previous therapists and of the analyst himself. This is particularly important because these patients tend to magically idealize the new therapist and split off and repress their negative feelings.

Deutsch (1980, 1987, 1988a,b) has demonstrated the urgent need for psychoanalytic questioning of assumptions and the sharing and integrating of data in multidisciplinary psychosomatic research (genetic, physiologic, neuroendocrinal, sociologic, etc.). Pollock (1977) postulated a "combinatorial" specificity, a biopsychosocial configuration that would be unique for each psychosomatic disease, and Knapp and colleagues (1970) detailed a psychodynamic methodolgy for the *prediction* of psychosomatic symptoms (asthma) in patients who were in therapy. While M. Sperling (1978) and my colleagues and I (1983) subscribe to the concepts of pregenital converison, primary symbolization, and etiologic parental psychopathology, Reiser (1975) and others maintain that the fantasies of these patients are *post hoc,* thus constituting secondary symbolization. Deutsch (1980) has emphasized that analysis can resolve psychosomatic symptoms whether they are primary or secondary. Most psychoanalysts do not routinely follow up their analyzed patients because it can seriously interfere with the patients' working through their separation-individuation conflicts, which often are unresolved at the time of termination. This remains a controversial issue. No one is more skeptical of results than the experienced psychoanalyst. In spite of long-term follow-ups we are aware that, given the vicissitudes of life, symptoms may recur.

Deutsch (1987) reported on a twenty-year follow-up of an asthmatic he analyzed, who for many years has been free of asthma and who evidenced healthy functioning compared with the identical twin, who was also asthmatic. This twin was treated for a time with psychotherapy. The unanalyzed twin evidenced much lower levels of ego functioning and a history of continuing asthma. Wilson (1988b) reported on a twenty-year follow-up of a case of severe regressive, restrictor anorexia nervosa. She had been successfully analyzed with a complete resolution of her psychoticlike fear-of-being-fat, obsession-with-being-thin, body-image pathology. She married, had two children, a boy and a girl, and evidenced healthy interpersonal and career functioning.

Sperling (1978) reports a twenty-five-year follow-up of the analysis of an eleven-year-old girl, Olga, whose symptoms of *petit mal* and epilepsy (she had one *grand mal* seizure at 11 years of age) stopped after six months of analysis, long before the underlying fantasies and conflicts were resolved. Relative to basic fantasies in psychosomatic disease, Sperling noted that Olga's recurrent basic fantasy was of an insane person who in cold blood cut up people and cut off their limbs. Many years later, when the patient had completed analysis and was married and had children, her doodlings still dealt with this theme of mutilation. I (1982) have a fifteen-year follow-up of one case of ulcerative colitis.

My observations on prognosis and results with bulimic anorexics (Wilson et al. 1985) apply to psychosomatic patients in general. In discussing four analyzed bulimic cases I noted that one adolescent who alternately abstained, gorged, and vomited resolved her conflicts in a year's analysis. She was neither amenorrheic nor dangerously underweight. The treatment prevented the development of phobic fear of being fat (anorexia nervosa). Both the second and third cases abstained, gorged, and vomited, but they did not use laxatives. Neither brought her weight down to dangerously low levels. Diagnostically they suffered from mixed neuroses with severe preoedipal conflicts. Both patients, unlike the abstaining anorexic, had an abundant psychosexual fantasy life and had masturbated in childhood.

Experienced analysts have expressed doubts to me about the possibility of analyzing any bulimic. Cases I have analyzed and supervised have experienced a full resolution of their fear-of-being-fat body image and their obsession with being thin. In my experience, if the bulimic anorexic process can be analyzed *in statu nascendi,* as my first case was, the prognosis is excellent. However, a longer and more complicated treatment is required for chronic adult bulimics, as I documented in my fourth case. Of course, the prognosis depends also on the psychodynamic diagnosis of the individual case and on the presenting situation. If the addicted bulimic is seen when acutely alcoholic and/or under the influence of drugs, these problems complicate the management and treatment of the case.

We need further research on the results of analytic treatment of psychosomatic illness. Hogan has a book in press (International Universities Press) on the psychoanalytic treatment of ulcerative colitis.

If psychosomatic disease can be treated analytically *in statu nascendi* in childhood or adolescence, the prognosis may be favorable, even without prolonged therapy. Furthermore, some children and adolescents may have enough psychic health to outgrow a psychosomatic disease with no therapy at all. However, the clinician must keep in mind that short-term symptom resolution may be a transference cure and that spontaneous clearing of symptoms may have been caused by developmental shifts in psychic functioning, particularly changes in object relations.

NEW OBJECT VERSUS TRANSFERENCE OBJECT

As with other patients with preoedipal psychopathology, in psychosomatic patients the analyst, in addition to being a transference object, is a new and different object who promotes healthy maturation (Wilson 1971). The following clinical material illustrates a patient's growing insight into the transference. Processes of internalization were involved in the appearance of the asthma, which is described elsewhere.

Six months into the third year of analysis, a bulimic anorexic patient evidenced a "flight into health." Her episodes of bulimia stopped, she curtailed her use of Ducolax to one or two a day. She reported improvements in her sexual relations with her boyfriend. On her job she received a promotion and was assigned to work on an important case with a senior lawyer; her salary was doubled. She began an exercise program. Most significant of all, her periods returned, albeit they were irregular. To the patient and external world, these healthy changes seemed remarkable. However, she began to develop increasingly severe epidoses of bronchial asthma. She had had minimal asthma in early adolescence; tests showed her to be allergic to dust and molds.

The following material documents the replacement of bulimic symptoms by asthma.

The patient began a session reporting that she awoke with asthmatic wheezing after the following dream:

Dream. I made a serious factual mistake in a letter to a client. There was a bulimic woman who went out of control and began ravenously eating a box of chocolates. My mother and a policewoman came into the room and began screaming at the woman to stop gorging. Then I was walking down a deserted waterfront area, crying and feeling lonely. Next I was talking to a priest about how lonely I am. The priest was confused with my analyst.

Associations. "When I first began to gorge and vomit, my mother once caught me doing it and yelled at me. The bulimic woman in the dream must be part of me that would like to gorge and vomit again, the way I used to do when anyone left me or anything bothered me. Last night I felt depressed and cried. I have been crying on and off in recent days and have not told you about it. Last night I was angry at the time analysis takes and the money I pay you. When I used to go to confession, the priest would absolve me of guilt if I confessed; you don't do that. You confront me with my problems and my conflicts in asserting myself. I guess I saw mother, and sometimes must see you, like a policewoman. I know you aren't, and you tell me about my strict perfectionistic conscience. I guess that may be the policewoman inside me. Sometimes I can't believe the things that analysis uncovers; that it is healthy to assert myself. The mistake in the letter to the client is my obsession with being perfect; I have to endlessly check and recheck my work. The senior partner the other day told me I worry too much, that people make mistakes and we are only human. It is not that I just recheck my work, I have a law clerk working for me and I do her work for her. I even make her reprints of law opinions she should look up for herself. She has not learned to use our law library yet because I baby her so much. She teases me and calls me 'Mamma X,' always taking care of her."

My interpretation to the patient was to remind her that I had told her I was not going to see her for sessions the following week and that she had not mentioned her feelings about separation; that she wished I was a priest (mother), who would always be there for her; that I'd have no one else to love except her; and that I'd have no self-interest, not cancel sessions, and not charge her. The patient confirmed the interpretation, saying, "It is funny, I forgot about the canceled sessions. I must be angry with you and want to go on vacation myself. I am sick and tired working the way I do."

This patient's developing insight into her archaic punitive superego is expressed in the appearance of the policewoman in the dream and the confusion of the image of the priest with the analyst. These conflicts were lines of interpretation that had been made repeatedly. This clinical material also shows the projective identification that can occur with such patients. Many times she did react to me as if I were a priest, even distorting the content of interpretations to conform to a projected hypermoral criticism. She focused on slight changes in my voice to prove I was angry with her. Again, projective identification occurred when the patient focused on my facial expression to prove anger and hostility. Thus the patient would say, "Why don't you smile or respond to me? You look cold today."

EGO-SYNTONIC, SADISTIC, AND MASOCHISTIC IMPULSES, CONFLICTS, AND FANTASIES

In the analysis of all patients, but particularly psychosomatic cases, it is important that the patient develop capacities to face, tolerate, and sublimate sadistic and masochistic impulses, conflicts, and fantasies. For example, the successfully analyzed woman who dreamt of scooping out the contents of my skull slept well the night that she had the dream. She accurately interpreted her dream and was aware of her anger with me. Such dreams had occurred in her analysis, but they were nightmares from which she woke up terrified. For therapeutic results the analysis of her punitive archaic superego was crucial.

The patient's defenses against facing masochistic behavior are interpreted first. In our clinical material we underemphasize the sadism. To give an example: In the ulcerative colitis case described in Chapter 6, the patient, in describing the anal perversions of her lover *laughed* when associating to the (perverse) gastroenterologist who used glass dilators to "cure her tight anal sphincter." This laugh masked her identification with the gastroenterologist, which expressed sadomasochistic childhood fantasies. Among the repressed, sadistic fantasies causing her bleeding were those of being a male with a tremendous fecal phallus with which she could anally enter and torture females. The anal obsessions of the mother and grandmother, which included frequent painful enemas, aroused fantasies (identification with the aggressor) of being a sadistic phallic female who tortures helpless victims. There is a strong resistance to the uncovering of such sadistic material.

Taylor (1986),[1] like other self psychologists, does not utilize our therapeutic approach and does not agree with the wish-fulfillment function of fantasies and dreams. Furthermore, he supports unquestioningly the concept of alexithymia. However, his hypotheses on object relations correlate with and confirm our research. He states that these patients tend unconsciously to select partners with whom they can repeat the pathological object relations of childhood.

Relative to my hypotheses about psychosomatic disease are Hughes's (1984) confirmatory observations that anorexics have used projective identification all their lives to deny their hatred and to prevent themselves from seeing their objects as separate from themselves. She emphasizes that as these patients develop, they fear that they are actually becoming the mother (and/or father) of their internal world whose attributes they have so admired, envied, and jealously hated. They attribute great power to the mother of their inner world and try to control her, not realizing that the power that they attribute to her is a consequence of their projections of hate and anger. They experience it rather, as if "taken over by

---

[1]We would agree with Taylor's hypothesis that psychosomatic diseases are disorders of psychobiological regulation.

another," or as one patient of hers put it, "They live in the body of another."

Hughes agrees that the sense of fusion with the mother can be fueled by the pathology of the actual mother, as she uses, in some instances, the child for expressing a pathological part of herself. The child who is selected to play this role colludes with the mother's projections, so that the *folie à deux* relationship is difficult to break.[2]

AN ANALYTIC APPROACH TO HOSPITAL AND NURSING CARE

The following recommendations by Mintz (1983) for hospital treatment of anorexia nervosa and bulimia apply (with the modifications that would be required by the particular psychosomatic syndrome) to other diseases, such as asthma or colitis. The increasing clinical incidence of anorexia nervosa has been noted by many investigators and has manifested in the emergence of self-help anorexia nervosa societies, the development of anorexia nervosa treatment centers, and hospital care units. Inpatient hospital care can be a crucial treatment requirement, either on an emergency basis or for more prolonged care.

Whom to Hospitalize

Further scrutiny of differing approaches is therefore warranted. Some therapists and hospital treatment centers feel that a three-month hospitalization in the beginning phase of treatment is necessary for all anorexic patients. The view here is that hospitalization should be reserved for acute, severe regressive behavior, where either medical or psychological reasons indicate that the patient is in danger of dying or becoming severely ill from marked emaciation, convulsions from electrolyte imbalance, cardiac arrhythmias, or severe depression with suicidal impulses or psychosis. Selvini Palazzoli (1978) emphasized the importance of treating the patient out of the hospital whenever possible and in spite of marked weight loss. She pointed out that therapists might contemplate hospital-

---

[2]J. McDougall recently presented a paper, "One Body For Two: A Psychoanalytic Approach to Psychosomatic Phenomena," to the Boston Psychoanalytic Society, March 30, 1988.

izing patients for their own peace of mind. Mild to moderate anorexia nervosa, however, can be successfully treated in outpatient clinical services or in office practice.

The Purpose of Hospitalization

The period of hospitalization should be as short as possible. The goal is to provide massive hospital support systems to carry the patient through the severe regression and to restore a reasonable modicum of health so that the patient is able to function safely outside the hospital. This would include correcting any electrolyte imbalance or other blood chemistries, resolving severe depression, suicidal danger, and psychosis, and improving body weight to a level that is no longer dangerous. This general approach also applies to the treatment of psychosomatic diseases, such as asthma and ulcerative colitis. This attitude is beneficial to the patient and cuts down on hospital costs. It also tends to emphasize to the patient that the primary goal of the treatment is not weight gain, but resolution of the conflicts that have resulted in the development of anorexic symptoms.

Patients' Attitude Toward the Hospital and Staff

An essential feature of the psychoanalytic treatment and hospital management of anorexic patients is the recognition of these patients' unconscious conflicts. This permits therapist and hospital staff to understand patients' feelings and problems thoroughly and to act rationally and incisively in helping patients to resolve them. The more clearly therapist and staff understand patients, the more help they can give them.

   In reviewing the medical regimes at different hospitals, Bruch (1973) emphasized the difficulty in making effective comparisons among the different facilities, but did emphasize that good results in the hospital seemed to be correlated with the skills of the staff personnel. She also pointed out that hospital staff members often feel overwhelmed with anger, frustration, and anxiety in response to these patients' difficult behaviors. Bettelheim (1975) described in detail the important effect of the staff's conscious and unconscious reactions to patients on the progress of treatment.

   Cohler (1975) described a residential treatment for anorexia nervosa and emphasized the complex feelings of the treating therapist. He stated that because anorexic patients are so difficult to treat, "the therapist's feelings of anger and hopelessness . . . [are] a genuine and intrinsic part of the treatment process and not, as is often believed, an element of countertransference" (p. 387). He felt that the therapist's ability to tolerate these feelings helped patients to change.

It is true that not every reaction of the therapist is a countertransference. Some reactions may stem from not understanding the patient's problem. It is rarely therapeutic for a therapist to feel helpless, hopeless, frustrated, and angry in dealing with patients, and anorexic patients are no exception. If anything, such feelings are counterproductive, providing patients with a sense of increased sadistic gratification from their hostile antagonistic behavior, increased doubt about the therapist's capacity to understand and treat them, and intensified feelings of being overwhelmed by and guilty about impulses. It is crucial to be able to absorb and try to understand any feelings that patients express without a sense of frustration or anger and without rejection or abandonment.

Silverman (1974) reported on the hospital treatment regime in a pediatric ward and emphasized a firm approach in correcting severe medical abnormalities with concomitant four-times-a-week intensive psychotherapy. He felt that hospitalization was required for a period of three months. He also emphasized the importance of a careful evaluation of the patient's metabolic status.

Sours (1980) reported on the hospital care of anorexic patients in an acute stage; he emphasized the importance of focusing on the needs of the individual patient and using experienced staff. He commented on the important role of the nursing staff and the danger of nurses identifying with, or coercing, anorexic patients.

Anorexic patients constantly test the therapist and try to induce intimidation, anxiety, and rejection. They expect the therapist to worry about them when they are sick, just as the mother did.

Anorexic patients who are hospitalized for severe, life-threatening symptoms are considerably regressed psychologically. As in most regressed states, ideas, attitudes, behavior, expectations, goals, frustration tolerance, and object relationships are all affected. Previously thoughtful, realistic and considerate behavior fades away and is replaced by infantile, hostile, provocative, demanding, and petulant attitudes. Independent, goal-oriented behavior is replaced by coercive, manipulative, and unrealistic demands. In a general way, patients behave toward therapist and staff as they behave toward their authoritarian parents.

Anorexic patients, who have a major and overwhelming fear of being controlled, unconsciously resort to controlling food because they cannot control their own lives or other people. They learn they can control people by frightening and coercing them with the threat of becoming sicker. This unconscious attitude may not be clearly perceived by hospital staff, who can be subtly manipulated and coerced by these patients.

PATIENTS' BEHAVIOR

Regressed Goals

Anorexic patients attempt to achieve regressed, infantile, dependent, and sadistic goals. The need is to be helpless and dependent on the one hand, and manipulative and sadistic on the other, with the guilt from the latter behavior assuaged by immediate punishment in the form of starving and depression. There is the wish to be treated as someone special, to get extra attention and concern, to be catered to, worried over, and indulged. These attitudes and conflicts have been present for years and are intensified during the anorexic syndrome.

This behavior is not premeditated but, rather, arises out of deeply felt needs and requirements associated with feelings of marked weakness and, often, feelings of total inability to cope with the world. These feelings are completely out of keeping with patients' true abilities and capacities. The regression accentuates the state of helplessness, which subsides considerably as the regression recedes and patients improve. Anorexic patients often have difficulty making the simplest decisions, organizing daily activities, and exercising even a modicum of independence or assertiveness.

Displacement of Major Issues

These patients attempt to engage therapist and nursing staff in endless discussions about food, eating, dieting, and thinness. Patients may admit that they think about nothing else during their waking hours. To the degree that patients are able to engage the staff in food preoccupations, patients' displacements from major issues onto food are reinforced and progress is impeded. The more these topics are discussed, the less the possibility of getting to the real sources of concern.

Struggles with Control

The problem of who controls whom is a major source of concern. These patients feel that they have been told what to do all their lives, that they have been overcontrolled and have behaved like obedient little robots or, as one patient put it, like little puppets with someone else pulling the strings. They are both terrified and desirous of being controlled. Being controlled is equated with being cared for, but on an infantile level. This ambivalence takes the form of alternating, opposing behavior and attitudes (i.e., withdrawn, defiant, and sadistic behavior at one moment, followed by activity that serves to encourage sympathy, help, and concern at the next).

A teenage boy acknowledged that he had to obtain perfect grades, because knowledge is power and he could control events with it. It was, therefore, not surprising to hear him state that he would never reveal certain personal information, because he felt that the more the therapist knew about him and his vulnerabilities, the more control the therapist would have over him. A seventeen-year-old girl offered all kinds of rationalizations as to why she did not wish to continue treatment. A more thorough discussion of her fears revealed that she was growing fond of the therapist, and this frightened her into wishing to stop. She reasoned that the more that she liked him, the more she would wish to please him, and by wanting to please him, she would then fall under his control. She added that she recognized that the therapist might not try to control her at all, but that she would still be victim of being controlled.

Although patients may be primarily obedient and "controllable," the seeds of inner unrest are evident in early obsessive-compulsive character traits that serve the purpose of control. The exacting, perfectionistic quality of their work illustrates the need to control their academic performance. Frequent, compulsive rituals also reveal this controlling propensity. Here, too, lie the seeds of the defensive displacement from large issues to small ones that is so characteristic of compulsive behavior. Long before their anorexia, many patients have learned to shift what they could not accomplish in one area of life to controlling how their books are arranged on the shelf. The anorexic syndrome follows the same pattern, displaced now onto food. When patients cannot deal with an important event in life, they control how the food is arranged on the plate, or what they eat. Patients' behavior in the realm of control is of far-reaching psychic relevance and importance and should not be trifled with casually.

Punitive Conscience

Anorexic patients have a very strict punitive conscience that contributes to a rigid, critical attitude toward their own and others' behavior. Therefore, they are very sensitive to criticism, feel guilty very easily, and expect to be criticized frequently—perhaps as harshly as they criticize themselves. Just as they are the recipients of severe feelings of guilt, they are experts at evoking guilt in others by their appearance, behavior, and comments. People tend to feel badly about how patients look, what they do, and what they say. Usually they tend to compensate for these feelings by babying them and catering to their whims and needs.

Feelings of Aggression

Finally, these patients have a tremendous problem with their feelings of aggression. During most of their lives they have been obedient and compliant. They have been unable to be firm or assertive, to stand up for their rights, or to be unruly, difficult, uncooperative, irritable, or angry at times. They have feared that any expression of aggression would be uncontrollable and would be met with punishment and disapproval. There is little outward evidence of aggression, until the treatment begins to shift the aggression from self-destructive anorexic behavior or depression to an externalized form, such as irritable, sullen, or uncooperative behavior.

ATTITUDE OF STAFF TOWARD PATIENTS

Medical care by the internist or pediatrician should be directed toward correcting the emergency situation that prompted patients' hospitalization. Toward that end, accurate weekly weighings, some awareness on the part of the nursing staff about how patients eat, and intravenous supplementary feedings and fluids may be indicated. These procedures can be accomplished, however, without attempts to coerce patients to eat or to put on weight. Any sense of desperate concern and worry over patients' condition is ill-advised and counterproductive. Patients unconsciously view such concern as the consequence of their ability to control the staff through illness. Thus, their urge to stay sick or to get worse will increase, since control over the staff is unconsciously more important than getting better.

A hard-hearted, indifferent, cold, or rejecting attitude toward patients is *not* advocated: all patients have the right to medical care by a thoughtful, considerate, and sensitive hospital staff. However, patients must recognize that the doctors and nurses are quite capable of dealing calmly with the situation, without conveying any sense of undue apprehension or panic. As most of the hospital care is performed by members of the nursing staff, their attitudes, behavior, and actual nursing care are of great importance in facilitating patients' recovery.

DEALING WITH PATIENTS' DEPENDENCY

The nursing staff should deal with patients' dependent, helpless, waiflike appeal for attention, affection, love, and special consideration. Understanding the patient's dependency problem helps one decide how to deal with it. Patients who are sick physically and regressed psychologically require the help of a very thoughtful, sensitive, and caring person, but someone who can help without over-indulging, who can be sensitive without being seductive, and who can be considerate without being fearful. These patients require thoughtfulness with encouragement, responsiveness with realism, and calmness with strength.

It is helpful to recognize the disparity between the helpless, waiflike attitude that patients present and their true underlying capacity. These patients have intellectual ability and many areas of ego strength that they neither recognize nor utilize. The tenacity that is evident in the stubborn need to starve can be channeled into the dogged pursuit of getting well. The intellectual capacity that is manifested in consistently obtaining excellent grades can be used toward the thoughtful resolution of life's problems. These patients are not without resources. They just do not use them in a healthy fashion. It is helpful and important for the staff to recognize these abilities and not be seduced into undue sympathy by patients' woeful appearance. Rather, staff members should encourage patients' assertiveness and ability to make decisions, to tolerate frustration, to work hard to get well, to face and discuss difficult problems, and to see their own strengths. Despondency and helplessness can be countered by indicating to patients that they can get well if they work at it. Furthermore, patients are more encouraged by the display of a quiet, consistent, and firm recognition that they have the necessary ability to get well than through any vociferous pep talks.

Most anorexic patients are aware of many problems that they consciously refrain from discussing. They become pessimistic and complain about not improving, without acknowledging that improvement in great part, is a result of problem solving and working in treatment. Unrealistically and in infantile fashion, patients expect to get better just by being in the hospital. Their complaints of lack of progress arise out of regressed thinking and behavior. These complaints can serve to evoke sympathy and indulgence from the staff, along with guilt that they aren't doing more to "make" patients better. The staff's guilty response can be displaced onto the therapist, accompanied by feelings of resentment toward the therapist for not "curing" patients. This curious staff attitude can take place even when the nurses recognize that a patient is not being cooperative, talking effectively, or working in treatment. The patient has subtly evoked enough guilt so that the staff cannot clearly perceive that there is little reason for improvement. Guilt can obscure staff's objectivity as much as undue sympathy.

It should be helpful and reassuring to the hospital staff to recognize that, under almost all circumstances, they should be able to help patients medically and prevent death. This is especially true if they are objective about medical findings and are not manipulated by patients into permitting them to enter a dangerous medical phase that then remains untreated. The internist and pediatrician can remain watchful and relatively unintrusive, as long as patients do not present a critical medical problem. They can be quite thin without being perilously ill or close to death. By being unobtrusive yet firm, staff members offer patients reassurance that they are not attempting to control them. When their condition deteriorates dangerously, however, the physician and nursing staff must be firm and consistent in doing whatever is medically essential to save patients' lives.

If the staff enter into discussions about food with patients—and patients will attempt to promote this—then the staff unwittingly help patients avoid the confrontations necessary for them to get better. In addition, patients and staff have divergent goals; patients talk about food so as to avoid eating it, while nurses talk about food in the hope of encouraging patients to eat. Patients will never comply; in fact, they unconsciously use the discussions about food to sadistically toy with, provoke, and antagonize the staff. Ultimately, as the discussions about food proceed endlessly, the staff become aware that nothing positive will be achieved, and the frustration and impotence of the staff members to be helpful to patients lead them to feel pessimistic, discouraged, and resentful. One cannot forbid patients to talk about food and diets, since they have the right to talk about whatever they choose. But one does not have to become the unwitting victim of a ploy that is antitherapeutic and frustrating. It is possible to listen politely, and with interest, yet with the recognition that to encourage this type of discussion will lead nowhere.

DEALING WITH PATIENTS' SELF-STARVATION

Forcibly coercing patients to eat serves a short-term goal of weight gain and produces a long-term liability of weight loss and increased defiance. Patients angrily comply with the authoritarian requirement that they eat in the hospital; as soon as they leave, they revert to starving. To force patients to eat as a therapeutic modality flies in the face of their entire life experience. They already feel that they can't control their lives—that they never have been in control. As one patient succinctly put it, "Not eating is all I've got." Sperling (1978) has warned that force-feeding without consideration for personality change can result in decompensation and psychosis.

The hospital staff should take a very specific position on this issue. Patients should be permitted to eat whatever they choose; no attempt should be made to influence them. They should be told that they will in no way be forced to eat. However, they must also recognize that starving is the somatic equivalent of suicide and that it is the duty of staff members to attempt to prevent them from dying. If their weight reaches a point of acute danger, then the staff members will provide them with supplementary nutrition. Patients may wish to know that weight loss is necessary for such nutritional supplements, so that they may feel free self-destructively, to lose further weight, or sadistically, to attempt to get just above or below the specified weight to see what the internist will do. Spelling out these details is unwarranted, and one who does so only falls into the trap of focusing on weight loss instead of on problem solving. The reply should be left vague; for example, the weight will be determined by a series of medical and hematological circumstances.

DEALING WITH PATIENTS' CONFLICT OVER CONTROL

It is imperative that patients realize that the staff is available to help them, rather than to control them. A great deal of the life experience of these patients has left them feeling quite the opposite: that people are out to control them. In the hospital among a group of strangers, they feel even more helpless and vulnerable to the demands of others. The staff should recognize and be aware of patients' fear of being controlled and avoid doing or saying anything to increase it.

Patients will fear and complain about being controlled even when no attempt has been made to control them. It can be pointed out that the hospital staff are available to be helpful, not to order them about or make all their decisions. In individual conversations with patients and in group meetings, the staff members should encourage patients to express their own ideas and to consider various alternative solutions; they should not fall into the attitude of "helpfully" providing solutions for patients. Patients often approach a staff member and ask what they should do. The staff member should be adroit enough to encourage patients to figure it out without making them feel rejected or antagonized. Infantile needs to be helpless, to be told what to do, and to be controlled take over and tend to preclude independent reasoning. The hospital staff should not unwittingly reinforce these regressed behavior patterns.

DEALING WITH PATIENTS' PUNITIVE CONSCIENCE

It is certainly important not to be critical of these patients' attitudes or behavior, no matter how frustrating they seem to be. The most inoffensive comments about patients' attitudes or behavior can be silently perceived and responded to as a critical remark. If such an interchange comes to the attention of the nurse, it is helpful to indicate that the remark was not meant to be critical and that perhaps the reaction reflects a sensitivity on the patient's part.

If one recognizes that a strict punishing conscience sets in force a series of self-punishing reactions, then one should be prepared to look for and recognize the various manifestations of self-destructive behavior. In anorexic patients, the primary self-destructive behavior is the starving.

These patients truly enjoy food and wish to eat, but they deprive themselves of the enjoyment and satisfaction of eating. Most anorexics are able to tolerate the starving because the feelings of hunger are repressed and not experienced. When the repression fails, the hungry feelings return and patients binge. The gorging is then followed by feelings of extreme guilt, which often set off vomiting.

Self-destruction takes many forms, however, including psychosomatic diseases such as asthma, which can be associated with subclinical anorexia. Other forms of self-destructive behavior can take place within the hospital setting and should be recognized as such. For example, patients may get moody or depressed. This indicates a shift in the self-destructive trajectory from self-punitive behavior (suffering through starvation) to self-destructive behavior (suffering through self-recrimination). The different clinical forms of the self-destructive drive and the underlying ego structure and defenses have been described in more detail elsewhere (Mintz 1980). This depression should not be viewed with alarm, particularly if it is associated with a tendency to eat more. It suggests that the conflict is shifting from food preoccupations to psychological manifestations and therefore should be welcomed as a sign of progress. It is easier to treat a patient suffering from unhappy feelings and ideas than one who has no complaints other than a fear of being fat.

In a few patients, the self-destructive attitudes are so strong that anorexic starving, depression, and suicidal feelings are all present at the same time. Here the presence of the depression signals a self-destructiveness so intense that is is not absorbed by the self-destructive starving alone; the punitive conscience requires additional penance in the form of severe depression. These patients are usually more ill and more difficult to treat.

Another manifestation of this self-destructiveness takes the form of uncooperative, provocative, and antagonistic behavior. To provoke and frustrate the very people whose job it is to provide help when one is sick, hospitalized, and separated from friends and family, and realistically subject to the rules of the hospital staff, is truly a self-destructive act. If staff members are not well trained and alert to the possibility of this type of behavior, they may respond consciously or unconsciously with retaliatory actions. Or, equally inadvisable, they may feel unduly frustrated and give up trying to help patients at a crucial time. The provocative, antagonistic behavior may reflect the beginning of an intrapsychic shift from the anorexia to difficult behavior patterns; if so, it should be recognized and accepted as such and considered in a potentially positive light, rather than with despair.

DEALING WITH PATIENTS' AGGRESSIVE, HOSTILE BEHAVIOR

There is overwhelming clinical evidence that self-destructive behavior is an alternative to externalized aggressive behavior and represents the other side of the same coin. While staff should never attempt to provoke hostile reactions in patients, increasing manifestations of anger can indicate an intrapsychic change and herald an evolving improvement. More specifically, expressing anger toward the staff is more beneficial than acting self-destructively provocative with the staff.

Characteristically, these patients have always had difficulty in being reasonably and firmly assertive, in standing up for their rights, and in tolerating other people's anger and criticism. The aggressive drive can take the form of unruly, uncooperative, surly, and procrastinating behavior. This behavior is in marked contrast to previous behavior, which characteristically was cooperative, obedient, and submissive. In addition to recognizing that this type of change can be positive and that these "difficult" patients are beginning to deal with their conflicts over aggression, the staff need to be able to tolerate and absorb patients' aggression without feeling threatened or defensive, without attempting to minimize the seriousness of their feelings, and without retaliating. It is of tremendous help to patients to realize that they can express feelings of anger without being punished, ignored, or abandoned. It increases their self-esteem, improves the quality of their relations with people, accentuates the value of verbal communication, improves mastery, and aids sublimation.

It is not enough for patients to externalize various aspects of their aggressive drives. To be able to act unruly, obnoxious, and provocative may be a necessary intermediate phase in treatment, but it should not be viewed as the end point. Otherwise, one can end up with permanently obnoxious individuals. It is hoped that the accompanying treatment will provide patients with sufficient insights into their problems over aggression to enable them to channel the aggression into more socially acceptable behavior.

THE PREVENTION OF PSYCHOSOMATIC DISEASE

The psychological profile of psychosomatic families is present in such a large proportion of cases that education of parents, particularly mothers, in the attitudes summarized in the family psychological profile seems advisable.

Presentations to our psychosomatic research groups of the analysis of five mothers and two fathers of psychosomatic patients who were in analysis with colleagues (Wilson, four mothers and one father; Hogan, one mother; Mintz, one father) fully and graphically confirmed Sperling's hypotheses about the etiologic role of parental psychopathology in psychosomatic disease. These parents themselves had psychosomatic symptoms: four had spastic colitis, one was a subclinical anorexic, and one had psoriasis of the scalp. Parental identification played a significant role in the etiology of the child's symptoms. As these children in analysis separated from the parents, the latter evidenced severe conflict, particularly depression and depressive equivalents.

Galenson (1987) recently noted that psychodynamic treatment of the mothers of four anorexic infants resulted in a cure of the baby's eating disorder which is confirmatory of Sperling's (1978) experience in the analysis of a two-year-old anorexic child and her mother.

Many aspects of the psychodynamics that are masked by psychosomatic symptoms should be investigated. The role of unconscious conflict in the etiology of cancer, pathological body image in disturbances of object relations, and family psychodynamics merit further exploration.

REFERENCES

Bettelheim, B. (1975). The love that is enough: countertransference and the ego processes of staff members in a therapeutic milieu. In *Tactics and Techniques in Psychoanalytic Therapy*, vol. 2, ed. P. J. Giovacchini, A. Flarsheim, and L. B. Boyer, pp. 251–278. New York: Jason Aronson.
Boyer, L. B. (1979). Countertransference with severely regressed patients. In *Countertransference: The Therapist's Contribution to the Therapeutic Situation*, ed. L. Epstein and A. H. Feiner, pp. 347–374. New York: Jason Aronson.

Boyer, L. B., and Giovacchini, P. L. (1967). *Psychoanalytic Treatment of Schizophrenic, Borderline, and Characterological Disorders.* New York: Jason Aronson.

———— (1980). *Psychoanalytic Treatment of Schizophrenic, Borderline, and Characterological Disorders.* 2d rev. ed. New York: Jason Aronson.

Bruch, H. (1973). *Eating Disorders: Obesity, Anorexia Nervosa, and the Person Within.* New York: Basic Books.

Cohler, B. J. (1975). The residential treatment of anorexia nervosa. In *Tactics and Techniques in Psychoanalytic Therapy,* vol. 2, ed. P. L. Giovacchini, A. Flarsheim, and L. B. Boyer, pp. 385–412. New York: Jason Aronson.

Corbin, E. (1972). Rectal itching and anal incorporation. *Bulletin of the Philadelphia Association for Psychoanalysis* 22:81–82.

Deutsch, L. (1980). Psychosomatic medicine from a psychoanalytic viewpoint. *Journal of the American Psychoanalytic Association* 28(3):653–703.

———— (1987). Reflections on the psychoanalytic treatment of a patient with bronchial asthma. *The Psychoanalytic Study of the Child* 42:239–261.

———— (1988a). Further reflections on the psychoanalytic treatment of patients with bronchial asthma. The Melitta Sperling Memorial Lecture, April 18, 1988, as yet unpublished.

———— (1988b). Overstimulation by a father: an alternate view of Charles Ives. In *Fathers and Their Families.* Hillsdale, NJ: The Analytic Press.

Galenson, E. (1987). Personal communication, November 16, 1987.

Goldman, D. S. (1986). Psychoanalytic, psychoanalytically oriented, and psychotherapeutic treatment of asthma, eczema, and urticaria. In *Psychological Aspects of Allergic Disorders,* ed. S. H. Young, J. M. Rubin, and H. R. Daman, pp. 193–222. New York: Praeger.

Hughes, A. (1984). Book review of *Fear of Being Fat,* ed. C. P. Wilson, C. C. Hogan, and I. L. Mintz. *International Journal of Psycho-Analysis* 65:498–499.

Jackel, M. M. (1968). The common cold and depression. *Journal of the Hillside Hospital* 17:165–177.

———— (1969). The common cold and depression. Abstract by E. Halpert. *Psychoanalytic Quarterly* 38:347–348.

Kernberg, O. F. (1975). *Borderline Conditions and Pathological Narcissism.* New York: Jason Aronson.

———— (1976). *Object-Relations Theory and Clinical Psychoanalysis.* New York: Jason Aronson.

Knapp, P. H., Constantine, H., and Friedman, S. (1970). The context of reported asthma during psychoanalysis. *Psychosomatic Medicine* 32:167–188.

Mintz, I. L.(1980). Multideterminism in asthmatic disease. *International Journal of Psychoanalytic Psychotherapy* 8:593–600.

———— (1983). An analytic approach to hospital and nursing care. In *Fear of Being Fat: The Treatment of Anorexia Nervosa and Bulimia,* rev. ed., ed. C. P. Wilson,

C. C. Hogan, and I. L. Mintz, pp. 315–324. Northvale, NJ: Jason Aronson, 1985.

Pollock, G. H. (1977). The ghost that will not go away: specificity theory today. *Journal of the American Academy of Psychoanalysis* 5:421–430.

Rand, C. S. W., and Stunkard, A. J. (1983). Obesity and psychoanalysis: treatment and four-year follow-up. *American Journal of Psychiatry* 140(9): 1140–1144.

Reiser, L. W. (1988). Panel report: Compulsive eating, obesity, and related phenomena. *Journal of the American Psychoanalytic Association* 1:63–171.

Reiser, M. F. (1975). Changing theoretical concepts in psychosomatic medicine. In *American Handbook of Psychiatry*, vol. 4, ed. M. F. Reiser, pp. 477–500. New York: Basic Books.

Risen, S. E. (1988). Panel report: Anorexia Nervosa: theory and therapy, a new look at an old problem. *Journal of the American Psychoanalytic Association* 1:153–162.

Ruddick, B. (1963). Colds and respiratory introjection. *International Journal of Psycho-Analysis* 44:178–190.

Selvini Palazzoli, M. (1961). Emaciation as magic means for the removal of anguish in anorexia mentalis. *Acta Psychotherapica* 9:37–45.

——— (1978). *Self-Starvation: From Individual to Family Therapy in the Treatment of Anorexia Nervosa*. New York: Jason Aronson.

Silverman, J. (1974). Anorexia nervosa: clinical observations in a successful treatment plan. *Journal of Pediatrics* 8(1):68–73.

Sours, J. A. (1980). *Starving to Death in a Sea of Objects: The Anorexia Nervosa Syndrome*. New York: Jason Aronson.

Sperling, M. (1978). *Psychosomatic Disorders in Childhood*. New York: Jason Aronson.

Taylor, G. J. (1986). Psychosomatic medicine and contemporary psychoanalysis. In *Stress and Health Series, Monograph 3*, ed. J. Goldberger, pp. 1–391. New York: International Universities Press.

Volkan, V. D. (1976). *Primitive Internalized Object Relations: A Clinical Study of Schizophrenic, Borderline, and Narcissistic Patients*. New York: International Universities Press.

Welsh, H. (1983). Psychoanalytic therapy: the case of Martin. In *Fear of Being Fat: The Treatment of Anorexia Nervosa and Bulimia*, rev. ed., ed. C. P. Wilson, C. C. Hogan, and I. L. Mintz, pp. 305–314. Northvale, NJ: Jason Aronson, 1985.

Wilson, C. P. (1967). Stone as a symbol of teeth. *Psychoanalytic Quarterly* 36:418–425.

——— (1971). On the limits of the effectiveness of psychoanalysis: early ego and somatic disturbances. *Journal of the American Psychoanalytic Association* 19:552–564.

_____ (1978). The analysis of the mother of a restrictor anorexic adolescent. Case presentation to the Psychosomatic Discussion Group of the Psychoanalytic Association of New York, February 17, 1148 Fifth Avenue, New York.

_____ (1981). Sand symbolism: the primary dream representation of the Isakower phenomenon and of smoking addictions. In *Clinical Psychoanalysis,* ed. S. Orgel and B. D. Fine, pp. 45–55. New York: Jason Aronson.

_____ (1982). Fifteen-year follow-up of a case of ulcerative colitis. Case presentation to the Psychosomatic Discussion Group of the Psychoanalytic Association of New York, February 14, 1148 Fifth Avenue, New York.

_____ (1984). The analysis of a young man with ulcerative colitis. Case presentation to the Psychosomatic Discussion Group of the Psychoanalytic Association of New York, May 16, 1148 Fifth Avenue, New York.

_____ (1986). The psychoanalytic psychotherapy of bulimic anorexia nervosa. In *Adolescent Psychiatry,* pp. 274–314. Chicago: University of Chicago Press.

_____ (1988a). Bulimic equivalents. In *Bulimia, Psychoanalytic Treatment and Theory,* ed. H. J. Schwartz. New York: International Universities Press.

_____ (1988b). Long-term follow-up of a case of restrictor anorexia nervosa. Case presentation to the Psychosomatic Discussion Group of the Psychoanalytic Association of New York, January 20, 1148 Fifth Avenue, New York.

_____ (1988c). Psychoanalytic treatment of anorexia nervosa and bulimia. In *The Eating Disorders,* ed. B. J. Blinder, B. F. Chaitin, and R. Goldstein, pp. 433–446. Jamaica, NY: S. P. Medical and Scientific Books.

Wilson, C. P., Hogan, C. C., and Mintz, I. L. (1983). *Fear of Being Fat: The Treatment of Anorexia Nervosa and Bulimia.* Rev. ed. Northvale, NJ: Jason Aronson, 1985.

Wilson, C. P., and Mintz, I. L. (1982). Abstaining and bulimic anorexics: two sides of the same coin. *Primary Care* 9:459–472.

INDEX